The Nazi Voter

The Nazi Voter

The Social Foundations of

Fascism in Germany, 1919–1933

Thomas Childers

The University of North Carolina Press

Chapel Hill and London

© 1983 The University of North Carolina Press
All rights reserved
Manufactured in the United States of America

98 97 96 95 94   9 8 7 6 5

Library of Congress Cataloging in Publication Data

Childers, Thomas, 1946–
The Nazi voter.

Bibliography: p.
Includes index.
1. Elections—Germany—History. 2. Germany—
Politics and government—1918–1933. 3. Social
classes—Germany—Political activity—History.
4. National socialism—History. I. Title.
JN 3838.C44 1983 324.943'085 83-5924

ISBN 0-8078-1570-5
ISBN 0-8078-4147-1 (pbk.)

To *my parents*

Contents

Tables

Abbreviations

Parties and Organizations

aA	agrarpolitischer Apparat (National Socialist agricultural organization)
ADB	Allgemeiner Deutscher Beamtenbund (Socialist-oriented civil-servants league)
ADGB	Allgemeiner Deutscher Gewerkschaftsbund (Socialist federation of trade unions)
AfA	Allgemeiner freier Angestelltenbund (socialist white-collar union)
BdL	Bund der Landwirte (conservative agricultural organization)
BVP	Bayerische Volkspartei (Bavarian People's party)
CNBL	Christlich-Nationale Bauern- und Landvolkpartei (Christian National Peasants' and Rural People's party)
DDP/DSP	Deutsche Demokratische Partei (German Democratic party); after 1930 Deutsche Staatspartei (German State party)
DBB	Deutscher Beamtenbund (German Civil Servants' League, politically unaligned)
DBb	Deutscher Bauernbund (German Peasants' League)
DHV	Deutschnationaler Handlungsgehilfenverband (conservative white-collar union)
DKP	Deutschkonservative Partei (German Conservative party, before 1918)
DNVP	Deutschnationale Volkspartei (German Nationalist People's party)

DVFP	Deutschvölkische Freiheitspartei (German völkisch Freedom party)
DVP	Deutsche Volkspartei (German People's party)
Gedag	Gewerkschaftsbund deutscher Angestelltenverbände (conservative association of white-collar unions)
GdA	Gewerkschaftsbund der Angestellten (liberal white-collar union)
GDB	Gesamtverband Deutscher Beamtengewerkschaften (conservative civil-service union)
KPD	Kommunistische Partei Deutschlands (German Communist party)
KVP	Konservative Volkspartei (conservative splinter party)
MSPD	Mehrheits-Sozialdemokratische Partei Deutschlands (Majority Social Democratic party)
NSBO	Nationalsozialistische Betriebszellenorganisation (National Socialist Shop-Cell Organization)
NSDAP	Nationalsozialistische Deutsche Arbeiter Partei (National Socialist German Workers' party)
NS-F	Nationalsozialistische-Frauenschaft (National Socialist Women's organization)
NSFB	Nationalsozialistische Freiheitsbewegung (National Socialist Freedom Movement, 1924)
OHL	Oberste Heeresleitung (Supreme Army Command)
RDA	Reichsbund Deutscher Angestellten-Berufsverbände (Reich Association of German White-Collar Organizations—conservative association of white-collar unions)
RLB	Reichslandbund (Reich Agrarian League)
RPL	Reichspropagandaleitung (Propaganda Directorate of the NSDAP)
RVdI	Reichsverband der deutschen Industrie (Reich Association of German Industry)

SPD   Sozialdemokratische Partei Deutschlands (Social
        Democratic Party of Germany)

USPD   Unabhängige Sozialdemokratische Partei Deutschlands
        (Independent Social Democratic Party of Germany)

VRP   Reichspartei für Volksrecht und Aufwertung
        (Volksrechtspartei), (Reich Party for People's Justice and
        Revalorization)

ZdA   Zentralverband der Angestellten (socialist association of
        white-collar unions)

Publications

DA   *Der Angriff*

DAZ   *Deutsche Allgemeine Zeitung*

NSB   *Nationalsozialistische Bibliothek*

NSMH   *Nationalsozialistische Monatshefte*

VB   *Völkischer Beobachter*

Archives

BA   Bundesarchiv Koblenz

BHStA   Bayerisches Hauptstaatsarchiv Munich

GStA   Geheime Staatsarchiv Preussischer Kulturbesitz Berlin

HA   NSDAP Hauptarchiv

ZStA   Zentrales Staatsarchiv Potsdam

Acknowledgments

Many years have elapsed since this project was begun as a dissertation at Harvard, and many people have contributed to its completion. I owe particular debts of gratitude to Franklin L. Ford, who directed the dissertation and whose continued support made numerous research trips to Germany possible; to Mary Nolan, who read the manuscript in its earliest form and offered valuable criticism; and to Gerald D. Feldman and Charles S. Maier, whose careful reading of the work in its later stages provided me with sound advice and direction for additional revision. Along the way Hans Mommsen, Hans-Ulrich Wehler, Larry E. Jones, Carl-Ludwig Holtfrerich, Frank Trommler, and Jane Caplan have shared their considerable knowledge of German politics and society with me and have contributed directly or indirectly to this undertaking. I have also been fortunate to participate in the ongoing international project "Inflation und Wiederaufbau in Deutschland und Europa 1914–1924" sponsored by the Stiftung Volkswagenwerk and directed by Gerald Feldman, Carl-Ludwig Holtfrerich, Peter-Christian Witt, and Gerhard A. Ritter. In sessions in both Berlin and Berkeley I have benefited greatly from the expertise of its members, but especially from my contact with Robert Moeller and Andreas Kunz.

Special thanks are also due to Thomas Trumpp of the Bundesarchiv, who has been helpful above and beyond the call of duty, and to Mary Hyde of the Harvard/M.I.T. Computer Center, whose aid in creating the statistical program used in this study was invaluable. Neither the archival nor statistical work undertaken for this study would have been possible without the generous financial support of a number of institutions. The Alexander-von-Humboldt-Stiftung, the Stiftung Volkswagenwerk, the American Council of Learned Societies, and the Center for European Studies at Harvard all provided critical funding at different stages of the project, and to them I would like to express my gratitude.

There are others to whom I am indebted for more general but certainly no less important contributions to this work. Arthur G. Haas introduced me to the study of German history, offering encouragement, support, and inspiration at a critical moment in my career. Walter A. McDougall, S.

Robert Lichter, and David E. Kaiser have given their friendship and knowledge over the years, gifts for which I am deeply grateful. I am also beholden to Lewis Bateman, my editor at Chapel Hill, who has believed in this book and encouraged me at almost every stage of its preparation. This work, however, could never have been completed without the understanding and loyalty of my wife, Barbara, who has stood with me through many ups and downs, or my parents, who have never waivered in their support for as long as I can remember. Finally, I would like to offer a special word of thanks to Charlotte Mildenberg and Gisela Bloch, who suffered and survived the horrors of National Socialism and who have shown me the meaning of human dignity and courage. This book is theirs too.

The Nazi Voter

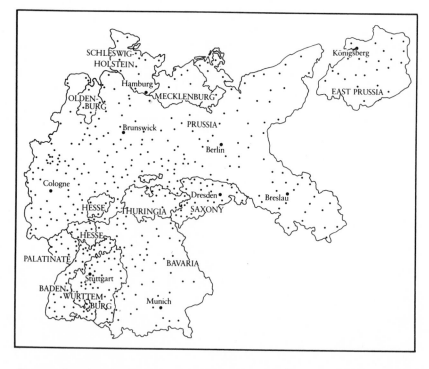

Geographic distribution of electoral units used in this study.

Introduction

On the morning of 15 September 1930, early editions of newspapers across Germany brought the first reports that Adolf Hitler's National Socialist German Workers' party (NSDAP) had scored a stunning electoral triumph. Only two years before, the party had languished in obscurity, unable to attract even 3 percent of the vote. Yet when the polls closed on the evening of 14 September 1930, ending the first national campaign of the depression era, the NSDAP had become the second largest party in the Weimar Republic. That dramatic breakthrough was a portentous milestone in German political history, marking the first of a series of impressive electoral performances that within two years would transform the NSDAP into the most popular and powerful party in Germany. In the immediate aftermath of the 1930 elections, political commentators in Germany and abroad posed the obvious questions: Where had this Nazi constituency come from? How had the Nazis done it? They are questions that have shaped the study of German electoral politics ever since.

In spite of periodic controversies about these questions, the imposing mass of popular and scholarly literature generated by the NSDAP's rise to power has produced a widely accepted body of common knowledge concerning the social composition of the Nazi constituency. German fascism, the traditional interpretation contends, was a middle-class movement supported at the polls by elements of the downwardly mobile *Kleinbürgertum* desperately afraid of proletarianization. Catalyzed by acute economic distress, particularly after the onset of the depression, these elements of the profoundly troubled *Mittelstand* deserted the parties of the bourgeois center and right for the radical NSDAP. Although the National Socialists claimed to be a socially heterogeneous people's movement, "its basic source of recruitment . . . ," Karl Dietrich Bracher concludes, "was in the petty bourgeois middle class and small landowning groups that had been hardest hit by the outcome of the war, economic crises, and the structural changes of modern society."[1] The appeal of fascism was, therefore, based on "the psychological reaction of this lower middle class" to both the recurrent traumas of the postwar era and the gradual deterioration of its socioeconomic status and political influence.[2]

In the sizable literature devoted to the rise of National Socialism, only those studies that eschew class-based interpretations and attribute the success of the NSDAP to a breakdown of the traditional class system and the emergence of "mass society" fail to identify the lower middle class as the social nucleus of the National Socialist electorate. Stressing instead the strains of "uprootedness," "anomie," and "displacement" associated with the disintegration of the traditional class structure, exponents of the "mass society" hypothesis contend that the "unattached and alienated of all classes are more attracted to extremist symbols and leaders than are their class-rooted counterparts."[3] Followers of "totalitarian movements," Hannah Arendt maintains, were not members of particular social classes or confessional groups but "atomized, isolated individuals."[4]

Although the psychological and mass-society schools have enjoyed periods of scholarly vogue, analyses of party membership and electoral constituency have consistently indicated that the National Socialist following possessed a clearly defined class and confessional identity. Methodological and conceptual approaches have varied, but most studies have located the bulk of Nazi support among the young, the lower middle class, the Protestant, and the rural or small-town segments of German society. Summarizing these findings, Seymour Martin Lipset, in a classic essay on the subject, concludes that "the ideal-type Nazi voter in 1932 was a middle-class self-employed Protestant who lived either on a farm or in a small community" and was "strongly opposed to the power of big business and big labor."[5]

For well over a decade, however, this traditional view has been under revision, challenged by a steady stream of dissertations, journal articles, and, most recently, a book. Whether dealing with party members or Nazi voters, these works have raised serious doubts about the lower-middle-class emphasis of the established literature. A variety of methods, ranging from simple visual comparisons to sophisticated statistical techniques, have been employed to analyze the elections of 1930 and 1932 in a variety of electoral districts, some urban, some rural, some Protestant, some Catholic. Although focus and emphasis have varied somewhat, these works have generally concluded that the social sources of Nazi support were far more diverse than suggested by the conventional wisdom. Indeed, they are in broad agreement that the NSDAP drew significant support not only from the Protestant *Kleinbürgertum* in town and countryside, but from other middle-class groups, some workers, and even Catholics.[6]

Yet, having mounted a sustained assault on the traditional interpretation, these revisionist works have raised as many questions as they have answered. If the social bases of Nazi electoral support were more varied than traditionally assumed, drawing votes from the wider bourgeoisie, the working class, and the Catholic population, then one must proceed to the next stage of inquiry and pose the obvious questions: *Which* elements of the socially and occupationally diverse *Mittlestand* voted Nazi? *Which* workers? *Which* Catholics? Was their support equal in depth and duration or were there shifts, trends, and variations that can be isolated? Under what economic conditions and political pressures were these different groups inclined towards National Socialism and in response to what sorts of appeals? How did the NSDAP structure its approach to these different elements of society? What were its campaign appeals, promises, and electoral strategies? How did they change over time, and how did they differ in style and content from their bourgeois and Marxist rivals? These questions, though often raised, have not been systematically addressed in either the traditional or more recent literature. They represent, therefore, the points of departure for this inquiry.

To deal effectively with this complex set of issues, an analysis of National Socialist voting must transcend the remarkably narrow geographic and chronological parameters of both the traditional and more recent literature. Not a single study exists that is not either confined to a small, often regional sample or restricted to the last elections of the Weimar era, those of 1930 and 1932. This severely limited focus has had significant implications for an understanding of the socioelectoral dynamics of German fascism. The Nazi constituency was not socially static. It changed substantially, as we shall see, over time and in response to changing political and economic conditions. Analyses of the party's electoral constituency have, however, been confined almost exclusively to the depression years, with little interest in the evolution of the party's composition and appeal through the consecutive shocks of hyperinflation (1922–23), harsh stabilization, (1924–28), and finally depression (1929–33).[7]

Though certainly understandable, this traditional emphasis on the depression period seriously distorts the process of electoral change within the Weimar party system. The dramatic growth of Nazi electoral popularity after 1928 is inconceivable without the fundamental breakdown of traditional partisan loyalties, especially within the middle-class electorate, that had been underway since the early twenties. The elections of 1924, the first in which the Nazis participated, were held in the aftermath of the hyperinflation and in the midst of an extensive and controversial program of economic stabilization, and they marked the onset of a profound, if subtle, realignment of electoral sympathies. The sudden emergence and surprisingly strong performance of the Nazis and a number of special interest parties in 1924 provided the first glimpse of what within the next four years would become a fundamental breakdown of voter identification with the established parties of both the bourgeois center *and* right. Even the return of political stability and relative economic recovery between 1924 and 1928 did not impede that breakdown. Instead, the disintegration of traditional bourgeois electoral loyalties continued, seriously undermining the sociopolitical foundation of the Weimar party system well before the effects of the Great Depression were felt in Germany.[8]

The importance of the inflation has, of course, been readily acknowledged in most studies of electoral politics in Weimar Germany. Contemporary analysts were quick to point out the profound economic, social, and psychological dislocations associated with the inflation, and subsequent treatments have concluded that the inflation contributed to the radicalization of important elements of the middle-class electorate.[9] Yet, perhaps because the Nazi vote virtually evaporated after the "inflation election" of May 1924, the critical electoral realignments of the pre-depression period have not been subjected to serious analysis. This lacuna in the literature is particularly significant since the fragmentation of traditional middle-class electoral sympathies actually accelerated in the ensuing period of stabilization. Indeed, the harsh stabilization of the mid-twenties proved as destabilizing to traditional bourgeois voting patterns as did the inflation that preceded it. Thus, if the collapse of the Weimar party system and the evolution of the National Socialist constituency are to be examined effectively, they must be analyzed together, and that analysis must begin, not with the severe economic contractions of the Great Depression, but with the economic and political turmoil of the early twenties.

In addition to extending the chronological parameters of the traditional literature, a fruitful investigation of National Socialist electoral support must also expand the geographical boundaries of the existing scholarship.[10] A growing number of sophisticated and valuable case studies of towns, cities, counties, and regions are available for the Weimar period,[11] and more are desperately needed. Yet, although case studies can provide an examination of electoral behavior in a tangible context of local personalities, organizations, and traditions, this advantage must be weighed against the difficulty of generalizing from local observations.[12] Regional variations, particularly in the rural electorate, were commonplace in German political life, even in the highly centralized Weimar Republic, but national patterns of socioelectoral behavior *can* be isolated, and it is precisely the degree of conformity or deviation from these national patterns that give local trends their proper context and larger significance. Indeed, without an empirically determined model of national voting patterns with which local observations can be compared and contrasted, the findings of case studies remain illuminating but fragmentary. By providing an analysis of partisan electoral strategy and voting behavior in Germany from the entrance of the Nazis onto the electoral scene in 1924 to the final tumultuous campaigns of the Weimar era in 1932, this study hopes to provide that national framework.

The first requirement of such an undertaking is the use of a large national sample, and the following analysis is, therefore, based on a sample of approximately five hundred cities, towns, and rural counties from every area of the Reich. (See map.) Since the Gemeinde, or community, forms the smallest electoral district for which comparable social, economic, and political data are available, it has been selected as the basic unit of analysis. Two hundred such towns and cities, ranging in size from roughly fifteen thousand to more than one million inhabitants, form the urban sample from which all inferences are made. Specifically, every city of over twenty thousand inhabitants in Germany is included in the urban sample, as well as a number of smaller towns for which the relevant data are available. Only those communities that underwent significant changes in population due to redistricting or incorporations have been deleted. Analysis of the vote in the countryside, on the other hand, is based on a sample of approximately three hundred rural counties. This rural sample consists of all counties in which no village exceeded ten thousand in population. Indeed, almost half of these rural Kreise contained no village of over five thousand inhabitants. Again, only those counties that experienced significant redistricting have been eliminated from the sample.

Using the 1925 census, which classified the postwar German population according to economic sector, occupational status, religious affiliation, age, and sex, the demographic characteristics of each of the five hundred communities and rural counties of the sample have been coded and serve as the major social variables of the following analysis. Data on income and education, potentially key factors in determining social position, were not collected in 1925 but may be derived in fragmentary form from other sources. Figures on unemployment, bankruptcies, and other variables of economic change are available for a large number of the sample's districts and have been incorporated in the analysis. The central focus here, however, is concentrated on the structural variables of economic activity and social/occupational standing.

The Reich Statistical Bureau employed six major categories to define economic activity or sector in 1925: (1) agriculture and forestry, (2) industry and handicrafts, (3) commerce and transportation, (4) administrative and professional services, (5) health services, and (6) domestic services.[13] Within each of these *Wirtschaftsabteilungen*, the population was classified according to occupational standing (*Stellung im Beruf*). These occupational classifications were: (1) independents, 95 percent of whom were self-employed proprietors of the so-called old middle class; (2) civil servants and white-collar employees, a group that corresponds closely to the much-discussed new middle class; and (3) workers. Domestics and "assisting family members," a group of little significance outside the agricultural sector, were also counted, as were pensioners, rentiers, and others living on accumulated assets, investments, and rents.[14]

These census classifications do not, of course, provide a mirror image of social reality in the Weimar Republic. Census classifications are rarely defined as precisely as historians or sociologists would prefer, and a number of the 1925 economic categories in particular contain some disparate elements. However, the 1925 census does offer distinct advantages over the 1933 *Berufszählung* on which the overwhelming majority of Weimar electoral studies are based. Most important, use of the 1925 figures allows one to cross-reference occupational standing and economic sector. This means that one can determine, for example, whether a worker was employed on a farm or in a steel factory, a distinction of obvious importance in electoral sociology. Moreover, the 1925 census provided figures for each of the twenty-three economic branches (*Wirtschaftsgruppen*) that made up the larger economic sectors (*Wirtschaftsabteilungen*). As a result, it is possible, though it has never been undertaken in any of the electoral analyses of National Socialism, to disaggregate and restructure the broad economic and occupational categories of the census, creating new variables that more accurately reflect the social and economic complexities of the period. This restructuring of the census data is explained in detail in appendix 1, on methodology, but briefly it is accomplished by ignoring the six rather amorphous economic categories described above and creating new classifications based on the smaller and more homogeneous economic branches. Using these transformed categories, it is, for example, possible to differentiate between handicrafts and industry, between mining and small-scale manufacturing, between transportation and commerce, and occupationally between white-collar employees and civil servants. Use of these reconstructed economic and occupational categories in the electoral analysis described below permits far more differentiated findings than those yielded in the existing literature. One can not only discover a significant relationship between National Socialist voting and the blue-collar population but ascertain in which economic sectors that relationship was strongest.

Having restructured the census data for the five hundred cities, towns, and rural counties of the sample, the election results for each of the Reichstag campaigns of the Weimar period are analyzed by multivariate regression analysis. The most vexing problem confronting the student of electoral politics in the age before polling became common is the lack of survey data. Election results were reported by town, county, or, in some large cities, by district,[15] and the electoral behavior of individuals or groups such as shopkeepers or white-collar employees can, therefore, be approached only indirectly. Inferring individual behavior from aggregate figures, however, constitutes the so-called "ecological fallacy" about which so much has been written in the methodological literature on voting.[16] Yet, aggregate figures are the only ones available for the study of elections in the prepolling era, and every analysis of such elections is, of necessity, ecological in nature. Nor does ecological analysis necessarily imply a "fallacy." Indeed, if certain safeguards, or controls, are used and if the statistical analysis is buttressed by other modes of research, the potential pitfalls of ecological techniques can be avoided. Although one must be aware of its limitations (these are explained fully in the Methodological Appendix), multivariate regression analysis still offers the most effective means of isolating and measuring the impact of a large number of social, economic, and religious factors on past voting behavior. Aside from providing a much needed test for existing hypotheses, the judicious use of regression analysis can identify relationships or potential relationships that often go undetected when employing traditional methods of electoral geography or other "optical comparisons." Forms of regression analysis have, therefore, been selected as the primary statistical procedures in the analysis that follows.

The use of a broad national sample, revised census data, and multivariate regression techniques can certainly define more precisely relationships between party voting and important socio-occupational groups, but it reveals little about the motivational factors behind those relationships. To deal with this complex question, one must go beyond the familiar but rarely useful "upper and lower middle class" terminology so common in the literature. Social position in Germany, as elsewhere, was a complex amalgam of occupation, income, education, and family background. Without survey data, however, it is impossible to determine perhaps the critical social factor in electoral behavior—voter self-image. Income is an obvious candidate for determining a voter's sense of social identity, but contemporary social observers repeatedly noted the wild discrepancies between income and political orientation. Civil servants living on indisputably proletarian incomes, for example, simply did not behave politically like coal miners.[17] Similarly, family background in Germany was officially measured by father's occupation, not income.[18] In a society where profession was listed in telephone directories along with family name, occupational status loomed very large indeed. So pervasive was this emphasis on *Beruf* in German social life that even during economic dislocations of the hyperinflation, status, as Robert Michels observed, tended to be determined not by changing economic situation but stability of occupation.[19]

Not surprisingly, this deeply engrained sensitivity to occupational status was prominently displayed in German political culture. For the parties of the Weimar Republic, occupation was clearly the critical determinant of voter self-image, and their campaign literature vividly reflected that conviction. From the Nazis to the Communists, the Weimar parties relentlessly directed their campaign appeals to highly defined occupational groups and dealt with occupation-specific issues. Campaign literature was addressed explicitly to artisans, farmers, white-collar employees, civil servants, pensioners, and so on, groups that conform closely to the revised census categories used in the following statistical analysis. (For illustrations of this campaign literature, see the different party leaflets in appendix III.) These were not abstract sociological classifications but terms enjoying widespread public currency and conveying immediate social content to voters.[20] Indeed, the parties of the bourgeois center and right at times even emphasized the lingering corporatist aspects of occupational status, addressing campaign literature to "the peasant estate" (*Bauernstand*), "the civil service estate" (*Beamtenstand*), and, in a tortured but typical extension of that mentality, to the "white-collar estate" (*Angestelltenstand*). The Marxist parties, while certainly rejecting this corporatist terminology, were no less occupationally oriented. Their campaign appeals were also aimed at specific *Berufsgruppen*, usually urging them to close ranks with other "working people" in the march toward socialism. These occupationally formulated appeals of the Weimar parties were supplemented by campaign literature addressed to Protestants, Catholics, women, and youth—the major confessional and demographic groups of German society—but the social vocabulary of German electoral politics in the Weimar Republic was clearly dominated by occupation.

Without survey data, one obviously cannot determine the motivational impulses behind a vote, but the occupation-specific nature of Weimar campaign literature certainly offers some suggestive clues. If one cannot ask Weimar voters how they felt about a particular issue or party, one can, by systematically analyzing these partisan campaign appeals, at least ascertain which issues the parties thought important to each of the major socio-occupational, confessional, and demographic groups in German society and determine how these issues were presented to the different elements of the electorate. When this day-to-day electoral literature is examined, important differences in partisan political orientation, social focus, and desired constituency are thrown into vivid relief, as are important shifts of sociopolitical emphasis within each party from campaign to campaign.

Such an analysis is greatly facilitated by two highly salient features of German campaign practice in this period. First, elections in the Weimar Republic were dominated by the print media. Use of the radio came quite late and was never a significant factor in electoral campaigning before 1933. Instead, the parties relied on the distribution of leaflets, pamphlets, and posters to saturate the electorate, while their rallies and other public events were given prime coverage in the partisan press. Since the archives of the German Federal and Democratic Republics possess extensive collections of this campaign literature, it is possible not only to re-create the campaigns of the era but to determine the public image the parties endeavored to project.[21]

Remarkably, the existing studies of Weimar electoral politics have paid scant attention to this substantial body of campaign literature. Although several studies offer general discriptions of Weimar campaigns and others investigate appeals to a particular segment of the population, no systematic analysis of this valuable electoral material has been undertaken.[22] Indeed, no thorough examination of National Socialist electoral strategy and propaganda before 1933 exists.[23] That omission is particularly significant in studies of the social bases of Nazi electoral support, since the party clearly targeted specific groups within the electorate for particular attention at different junctures. The NSDAP's appeals to specific demographic and occupational groups, therefore, represent perhaps the best source for charting the shifting social focus of Nazi electoral strategy before 1933. Moreover, the broad ideological positions of the party, which have received extensive scholarly attention, were greatly reinforced on a day-to-day basis by precisely this occupation-specific approach to the electorate, and Nazi appeals to a number of important groups—civil servants and white-collar employees, for example—are not what one would expect from the easy generalizations found in much of the existing literature. Thus, in the following chapters the campaigns of the NSDAP will be examined in depth, focusing on the party's campaign organization, strategy, propaganda techniques, and appeals. To be effective, however, an examination of National Socialist electoral organization and strategy must not be undertaken in a vacuum. As a result, the NSDAP's occupational appeals, its views on foreign and domestic affairs, and its targeted social constituencies will be compared and contrasted with those of its rivals for each of the Reichstag elections of the Weimar era.

In addition to campaign literature, another source of great potential value for the study of National Socialism's social appeal exists in the massive body of material collected by Theodor Abel and subsequently analyzed by a number of scholars.[24] This material consists of almost six hundred essays written in 1934 by members of the NSDAP who had joined the party during the Weimar years. They were written in response to an appeal in the Nazi press calling on these early Nazis to explain why they had turned to National Socialism. Largely biographical in nature, the essays describe in varying degrees of detail familial background, occupational status, age, sex, previous political affiliations, and other aspects of the respondents' personal histories. For obvious reasons, the essays do not constitute a representative sample of the membership or the electorate of the NSDAP. They do, however, offer important insights— the best we are likely to get—into the social and psychological attractions of National Socialism. When considered in conjunction with the other approaches outlined above, the Abel Collection represents an extremely valuable source in determining the social foundations of fascism in Germany and that material has, therefore, been integrated into the analysis that follows.

To complement the statistical analysis of the Weimar elections and the examination of partisan campaign literature and strategy, the interaction between the parties and organizations representing social and occupational groups will also be treated. Solicitation of interest-group support was a major element of partisan electoral strategy and the various *Interessenverbände* had been important actors on the political stage in Germany since at least the last decade of the nineteenth century. Perhaps no other facet of German political life has received such extensive scholarly attention, and the rich literature devoted to the various organizations, particularly those representing middle-class interests,[25] will be drawn upon in the following analysis. In addition, the publications of these organizations will also be examined to gauge the response of their client groups to political and economic developments during the NSDAP's rise to power.

Finally, the expanding literature on the membership of the NSDAP must also be considered. Recent studies have made significant strides in refining the rather amorphous membership statistics compiled by the party and contain useful guides for tracing the NSDAP's shifting social appeal.[26] Distinctions between the party's members and voters must, however, be kept in mind. The Nazi rank and file and electoral constituency certainly overlapped, but they were not identical. Numbering approximately eight hundred thousand in 1932, the National Socialist membership did not represent a sociological microcosm of the party's roughly fourteen million voters. Membership in the party required formal enrollment and the payment of dues, implying a greater degree of commitment and public support for the party than merely casting a vote. Consequently, certain demographic and occupational groups acquired either a greater or lesser salience in the NSDAP's rank and file than in its broader electoral constituency. Youth, and young men in particular, tended to stand out more in the membership and in the various Nazi street organizations, for example, than in the party's electorate. Conversely, the Weimar authorities frowned on civil service affiliation with the NSDAP, and after 1929 officials in the massive Prussian administration were actually forbidden to join the party. Not surprisingly, civil servants were "underrepresented" in the rank and file, and yet played an important role in Nazi electoral strategy and in the party's constituency. Moreover, statistics on the NSDAP's membership, no matter how refined the social and occupational categories, lack an essential comparative dimension. No comparable membership figures are available for the other Weimar parties, and as a result comparisons must be made with the general population. When white-collar employees are reported to be "overrepresented" in the party's membership, it is, therefore, impossible to determine whether this reflects a particular white-collar affinity with National Socialism or whether white-collar employees might also be "overrepresented" in the membership of all the major bourgeois parties. The social composition of the NSDAP's membership does, nevertheless, provide another valuable indicator of the party's sociopolitical appeal and will, therefore, be taken into account in the following chapters.

When these sources are used together with the methods described above, a new and multidimensional perspective of the National Socialist constituency emerges. That constituency was neither as static nor as narrow as the existing literature suggests. Nor can the social dynamics of the movement be adequately described as a "revolt of the lower middle class." The sources of National Socialist strength at the polls were sociologically fluid, spreading far beyond the lower middle class to elements of the affluent *Grossbürgertum*, the socially prominent civil service, and to sectors of the blue-collar working class. Moreover, the social composition of the Nazi electorate evolved and changed during the successive periods of inflation, stabilization, and depression, as did the focus of its electoral strategy. The economic shocks of the Weimar period affected the diverse elements of the German electorate in different ways, and support for the NSDAP varied from group to group and from period to period. For some, a vote for National Socialism was a crisis-related act of protest, whereas for others it represented an expression of longstanding social and political affinities. Only when the shifting composition of this support is isolated and examined in relation to changing economic and political conditions can the complex of social factors that lay at the root of fascism's success be adequately explained. This study is, therefore, not intended as a treatment of high party politics or as a history of the NSDAP. It is instead an examination of the Nazi constituency—how it was formed, from which social groups, under what conditions, and with what promises. Above all, it is an attempt to explain the social appeal of fascism in Germany, to understand who voted for Hitler's NSDAP and why.

I

The Sociology of German
Electoral Politics, 1871–1924

From its foundation during the revolution of 1918 until its demise with the Nazi assumption of power in 1933, the Weimar Republic was burdened by a series of overlapping political, economic, and social problems that gradually undermined its viability. Forced to assume the responsibility for the lost war and the hated Treaty of Versailles, the republican government was born with a profound crisis of political legitimacy that escalated steadily during the political and economic turmoil of the immediate postwar period (1919–23). Political murders, attempted coups from both the radical right and left, a tense international situation, and an inflation of utterly terrifying proportions created a protracted period of crisis that produced cabinet instability and the recurrent use of emergency decrees to maintain the integrity and functioning of the state. In the period of recovery that followed (1924–28), the return of political stability temporarily masked the corrosive impact of a harsh economic stabilization that by 1928 had dangerously eroded support for the parties of both the traditional center and right. The era of economic depression that ensued (1929–33) revealed the full extent of that decay, when failing businesses and rising unemployment radicalized voters and dealt the Weimar Republic a death blow. These interrelated economic and political traumas were, of course, reflected in dramatic electoral shifts in each of these periods, and the interaction between them will be examined in the following chapters.

Yet, on a more fundamental level, electoral politics in the Weimar Republic continued to be structured by a well-defined set of social, confessional, and regional cleavages that had shaped the contours of the German party system since its inception in the last half of the nineteenth century. These deeply engrained divisions had complex, often intertwined historical roots, evolving from centuries of dynastic conflict, the bitter religious strife of the Reformation, and the ongoing transformation of German society as industrial development gathered momentum after 1850. In spite of convulsive changes in the political and economic environment, the parties of the Bismarckian, Wilhelmine, and Weimar eras remained firmly entrenched along these lines of social, religious, and regional cleavage.[1]

The most salient of these cleavages reflected the shifting fronts of social conflict. Between the foundation of the Reich and the reemergence of the Social Democratic movement in the 1890s, the electoral scene was dominated by a struggle between traditionally powerful agrarian interests, centered in East Elbian Germany, and the emerging commercial and industrial sectors of the urban economy. Both the conservative and liberal movements had experienced serious internal schisms before 1871, but those divisions did not alter the essentially unchanging social composition of their respective clienteles. While the left-liberal Progressives and their National Liberal rivals represented different sets of commercial and industrial interests and differed on numerous economic and political issues, their electoral support was drawn from similar social sources: the entrepreneurial *Bürgertum* of the rapidly expanding towns and cities, with an admixture of civil servants, professionals, and independent peasants, particularly in north-central and southwest Germany. Similarly, the conservatives, despite a split into German Conservative and Free Conservative parties, tended to share an overwhelmingly rural constituency, augmented by strong support from the civil service and military establishments, and, in the case of the Free Conservatives, representatives of heavy industry as well.[2] Despite fluctuations in the popularity of these parties individually, together they commanded a clear majority of the German electorate in each of the seven elections of the Bismarckian era. Between 1871 and 1890 the liberals averaged approximately 37 percent of the vote, the conservatives 23 percent. (See Table 1.1.)

Although at times the campaigns of the period assumed the aura of a classic ideological struggle, the essence of Bismarckian domestic policy was to forge an alliance of "state preserving and productive forces" on the basis of shared economic interest. This strategy of *Sammlung*, with its "marriage of rye and iron" and its shifting liberal-conservative combinations, was pursued with varying degrees of success by Bismarck and his successors and carried profound implications for the party system and for German political culture. It not only eroded the ideological integrity of both liberalism and conservatism in Germany but in the long run tended to reduce the parties spawned by these movements to the status of glorified interest groups with dwindling bases of popular support.[3]

The degenerative condition of the traditional liberal and conservative

Table 1.1. The Elections of the Bismarckian Era (percentage of vote)

Year	Lib.	Cons.	Lib.+ Cons.	Conf.	Soc.	Other
1871	46.5	23.0	69.5	18.6	3.2	9.2
1874	39.9	14.1	54.0	27.8	6.8	11.8
1877	39.2	17.7	56.9	24.8	9.1	10.0
1878	33.6	26.6	60.2	23.1	7.5	10.3
1881	38.7	23.7	64.4	23.2	6.1	10.3
1884	36.9	22.0	58.9	22.6	9.7	10.5
1887	36.4	25.0	61.4	22.1	7.1	10.6

parties was greatly magnified during the 1890s, when a revival of the tariff issue under Caprivi provoked another protracted conflict between industry and agriculture. This struggle, which ebbed and flowed for over a decade, prompted the formation of a number of special interest groups determined to influence both liberal and conservative parties. These *Interessenverbände*, especially the powerful Bund der Landwirte (BdL, 1893), the Bund deutscher Industrieller (BdI, 1895), and the older Zentralverband deutscher Industrieller (ZdI, 1876) were well organized and well financed. They were, therefore, able to exert tremendous pressure on the established parties, which, without exception, had retained their character as *Honoratiorenparteien*, parties of notables, with only very rudimentary grassroots organizations. Moreover, the rise of these and other well-organized lobbies tended to accentuate the often conflicting economic interests within the existing parties, greatly complicating liberal and conservative efforts to contain the increasingly self-conscious components of their traditional constituencies.[4]

Among these *Interessenverbände*, the BdL was by far the most active in its efforts to mobilize a middle-class constituency that would transcend the existing parties. Originally formed to represent large-scale grain producers, the Bund was determined to develop a mass-based organization capable of exerting decisive pressure on the major bourgeois parties. As a consequence, the BdL presented itself to the farm population of Germany as the most vigorous and influential defender of *all* agrarian interests in an era when the position of agriculture seemed to be increasingly threatened by the rise of powerful industrial and commercial interests. Real or potential conflicts of interest between East Elbian estate owners and small farming peasants in the south and west were, therefore, consistently minimized as the Bund sought to forge a solid agrarian front against those urban forces. Its program of agricultural protectionism was, therefore, couched in inflammatory rhetoric directed against what the BdL considered the excessive Marxist, left-liberal, and Jewish influence in German economic and political life.[5]

In addition to its efforts to recruit small farmers, the BdL also appealed to elements of the entrepreneurial *Mittelstand* that felt threatened by the rapid expansion of cartelized big business and organized labor in the 1880s and 1890s. Anxiety over the decline of the small artisan producer and shopkeeper had been voiced by a number of handicrafts and commercial organizations in the 1880s, but it was in the following decade that the concerns of what became known as the "old middle class" crystallized into a set of social and economic demands with considerable political potential.[6]

Organizations representing handicrafts and commercial small business were numerous and remained badly fragmented throughout the imperial period, but during the 1890s a number of small regional parties making explicit appeals to disgruntled artisans, shopkeepers, and independent peasants enjoyed a surprising degree of success at the polls. In addition to repeating the usual demands for a return to a corporatist economic order (a *Ständestaat*), a restoration of official legal status to the guilds (a measure actually adopted by the imperial government in 1897), and the abolition of the increasingly popular consumer cooperatives and newly established department stores, these parties were rabidly anti-Semitic, identifying Jews with both liberal capitalism and Marxist socialism.[7] These views were quickly echoed by the BdL and the German Conservative party (Deutschkonservative Partei—DKP), which became the first major party to adopt anti-Semitism as a formal plank in its platform in 1892. Yet, not even the antiliberal, antisocialist, and anti-Semitic DKP could overcome its popular association with the East Elbian aristocracy, the high civil service, and big agriculture and, therefore, proved unable to integrate the small business movement effectively into its constituency.[8] In this regard, the plight of the DKP was typical of the dilemma confronting all the traditional middle-class parties in the Wilhelmine period. Because of their highly salient interest structure and their character as *Honoratorienparteien*, the established liberal *and* conservative parties found it increasingly difficult to mediate between the fractious elements of the *Mittelstand* and to integrate their often conflicting interests into a cohesive electoral platform.

The continuing fragmentation of the *Mittelstand* into competitive, occupationally defined interest groups and the concomitant difficulty encountered by the traditional bourgeois parties in finding an effective formula for *Sammlung* was accelerated after 1890 by far-reaching structural changes in the social and occupational composition of the German middle class. The rapid proliferation of the large industrial and commercial enterprises so detested by the proprietors of the old middle class, both urban and rural, had produced a dramatic surge in the tertiary sector of the labor force. Between 1881 and 1907 the number of civil servants and white-collar employees soared from roughly 500,000 to over 2 million. While the number of self-employed proprietors grew by only 8 percent in this period, the members of what was now described as "the new middle class" virtually quadrupled. Moreover, when the first postwar census was conducted in 1925, it revealed that civil servants and white-collar employees, now numbering over 5 million, comprised almost 17 percent of the Weimar work force, a percentage only slightly lower than that of self-employed proprietors.[9]

Within the new middle class, the *Berufsbeamtentum*, or professional civil service, was firmly established as an elevated social stratum. Regardless of rank, civil servants appeared to contemporaries as a remarkably homogeneous group, sharing the traditional prestige afforded to representatives of the state in Germany and enjoying a host of special benefits, both legal and social, that sharply distinguished them from other groups. Although civil-service salaries were not high, they were certainly competitive with much of the private sector and after 1907 included additional supplements for dependents. Civil servants could also claim a secure pension for themselves and their families, guaranteed paid vacations, sick pay, and other special privileges of office (*Amtsrechte*). Most important, however, was the fact that civil servants enjoyed permanent lifetime job tenure, a legal and professional privilege that made them the envy of the white-collar world. This privileged position, a product of the *Beamtentum*'s prominent identification with the state, fostered a powerful homogenizing ethos that was both socially and politically conservative. It tended to minimize conflicts of interest between the different ranks and to promote a strong sense of social solidarity and elitism that survived both war and revolution.[10] "Civil servants," Theodor Geiger wrote in 1932, "are not a class or even an estate; in our bureaucratically burdened German world they are almost a caste."[11]

In contrast, the social and political orientation of white-collar employees, the *Angestelltenschaft*, was a matter of considerable debate. Springing from a wide variety of social backgrounds,[12] these clerks, secretaries, stenographers, administrative and sales personnel, largely in the private sector, did not command the legal, professional, or social benefits of civil-service status, nor were they either self-employed proprietors or manual laborers. Marxist social theorists were, therefore, quick to argue that since these employees were economically dependent, they composed a special segment of the proletariat and were natural allies of the blue-collar working class—a view vehemently rejected by both liberals and conservatives within the white-collar population.[13]

Given their ambiguous position between labor and management, it was hardly surprising that when white-collar employees began to organize into professional associations in the 1890s, differences of political and social vision would emerge. Though hardly the first of the disputes that arose between the white-collar associations before the war, the debate over occupational insurance in 1911 was certainly the most serious and the most revealing. All the white-collar *Verbände* of the Wilhelmine era had long endorsed some form of insurance package for white-collar labor and had joined forces in a Central Committee to lobby for such a plan. However, while the nonsocialist majority in the Committee insisted on a plan clearly separate from that of blue-collar labor, a minority pressed for a unified plan to cover all employees, both blue- and white-collar (all *Arbeitnehmer*). The majority position prevailed and was formally enacted into law later in the year, but the white-collar movement had suffered what would become a permanent schism. The socialist-oriented associations withdrew from the Central Committee to form their own organization, which became the forerunner of the socialist white-collar union of the Weimar era, the Allgemeiner freier Angestelltenbund (AfA-Bund). The liberal and conservative *Verbände*, on the other hand, retained some formal organizational ties until the collapse of the Empire, but troublesome differences continued to separate them. While, for example, the most important of the conservative associations, the Deutschnationaler Handlungsgehilfenverband (DHV), assumed a strongly anti-Semitic and antifeminist position, refusing membership to both Jews and women, the liberal associations staunchly rejected this stance.[14] Moreover, while the nonsocialist *Verbände* were united in their determination to differentiate white- from blue-collar labor and their opposition to Marxism, their interests were certainly not identical with those of management or of the small shopkeepers and artisans of the old middle class, a realization that would be greatly intensified by the economic and social strains of the war.

In addition to the fragmentation of middle-class interests, rapid industrial and commercial expansion after 1871 produced other far-reaching demographic changes that fundamentally altered the lines of social cleavage within the German party system. Between 1871 and 1910 the population of the Reich rose by no less than 50 percent, soaring from just over 41 million to almost 65 million. Moreover, that growth was centered primarily in urban and increasingly industrial areas. In 1871 when Bismarck extended universal manhood suffrage to the electorate of the new Reich, 63 percent of the population lived on the land and approximately 45 percent of the labor force was engaged in some form of agriculture. By 1907, when the last prewar census was conducted, the rural, agricultural population had been surpassed by urban, largely industrial gains. On the eve of World War I, 60 percent of the German population lived in towns or cities and 40 percent of the labor force was employed in industry and handicrafts, 34 percent in agriculture. Moreover, the number of persons employed in industry and handicrafts, the majority of whom were blue-collar workers, had nearly doubled, jumping from 6.9 million in 1871 to 11.3 million in 1907.[15]

These demographic trends, which became increasingly pronounced after 1890, were intimately linked with the most significant electoral development of the Wilhelmine era, the seemingly inexorable rise of Social Democracy. The German Social Democratic party (Sozialdemokratische Partei Deutschland—SPD) had been founded in 1875, the product of a merger between Ferdinand Lassalle's progressive workers' party and another proletarian organization with a stronger Marxist orientation under the leadership of Wilhelm Liebknecht and August Bebel. The new workers' party developed ties to the fledgling "free" labor unions, and, with its advocacy of a "free people's state" and a "socialist society," was quickly branded as an "enemy of the Reich." Between 1878 and 1890, Bismarck subjected the party to a series of harsh repressive measures, while simultaneously seeking to woo its working-class supporters with a package of progressive labor insurance laws. Yet, in spite of Bismarck's efforts to undermine the party, the Social Democratic vote continued to climb slowly throughout the 1880s, and when Wilhelm II permitted the antisocialist legislation to lapse in 1890, the SPD immediately emerged as the largest single party in Germany.[16]

The end of the antisocialist legislation allowed the SPD, which in 1891 formally adopted Marxism as its party doctrine, to intensify its efforts to organize the rapidly expanding working class. In 1890 a General Commission was established to serve as an umbrella organization for the free trade unions which, in the following years, became closely associated with the SPD. Although membership in the unions fluctuated, the socialist-oriented free trade unions, as distinct from the smaller Christian and liberal Hirsch-Duncker unions, counted over 2 million members in 1910. Equally important to Social Democratic efforts to recruit and mobilize working-class support, the years of underground activity during the Bismarckian repression had provided the socialist movement with an extensive and cohesive network of local organizations.[17]

Skillfully using this expanding organizational apparatus, the SPD rolled to a succession of electoral triumphs that stretched virtually unbroken to the eve of World War I. Despite continued government harassment and demographically antiquated electoral districts that afforded vast overrepresentation to the rural, small-town population, the SPD's vote climbed steadily from 19.7 percent in 1890 to 34.8 percent in the last prewar election. With their doctrine of class conflict and a constituency drawn primarily, though not exclusively, from the new industrial working class, the Social Democrats not only posed a serious challenge to the dominance of the liberal and conservative parties but seemed to represent a growing threat to the entire social and political fabric of the Wilhelmine Reich.

In an effort to meet this challenge and to find a political formula capable of transcending the divergent economic interests of the middle-class electorate, the liberal and conservative parties of the Wilhelmine era returned to Bismarck's antisocialist strategy. While industry and agriculture were ultimately able to find a rough compromise solution to their bitter dispute of the early 1890s—industry's acceptance of agricultural tariffs in exchange for agriculture's support for a massive naval construction program[18]—the liberal and conservative parties sought to rally the disparate elements of the urban and rural *Bürgertum* against the specter of red revolution.[19] The revival of this strategy, coupled with the promise of an aggressive imperial policy, did not completely resolve the differences between industry and agriculture, nor did it prove an adequate mechanism for integrating the fractious *Mittelstandsbewegung* into the traditional party system. Political mobilization by the BdL, the Pan-German League, the Colonial League or the other nationalist, antisocialist organizations did not necessarily result in electoral gains by the liberal or conservative parties. Indeed, efforts to establish a new national party of the German *Mittelstand* continued into the war. The nationalist, antisocialist strategy did, however, perform an essential ideological function, providing the liberal and conservative parties with a tenuous sociopolitical legitimacy as protectors of the German *Bürgertum* and the German national state against the dangers of Marxist collectivism and international decline.[20]

Thus, in the years between the expiration of the antisocialist law and the outbreak of World War I, the basic social cleavage of German electoral politics underwent a profound transformation. After 1890 the conflict between liberalism and conservatism, which had dominated the elections of the Bismarckian era, was gradually transmuted into a struggle between those deeply divided movements and the socialist party of the German working class. Whereas the liberal and conservative parties had represented 60 percent of the electorate in 1887, their combined constituencies accounted for only 38 percent of the votes cast in 1912. In absolute terms the liberal-conservative electorate actually expanded slightly in this period, growing from about 4 million in 1890 to 4.5 million in 1912. It did not, however, keep pace with the steady growth of the voting population, which swelled from 10 million to 14 million during the Wilhelmine era. The National Liberals, for example, actually attracted five hundred thousand more votes in 1912 than in 1890, but their percentage of the vote fell from 16.3 percent to 13.7 percent. The liberal/conservative vote still exceeded the socialist totals in 1912, but the gap was rapidly closing. Moreover, the antisocialist strategy was given different emphasis by each of the liberal and conservative parties and in no way implied a united front. Indeed, the Progressives, who possessed few ties with the major industrial or agricultural interests and had suffered a series of debilitating schisms since 1890, actually formed a regional electoral alliance with the SPD in 1912 in an effort to revive their dwindling political appeal. This limited cooperation, roundly condemned as it was by the other nonsocialist parties, did not, however, signal a shift in the party's overwhelmingly middle-class electoral base or in its vehement rejection of Marxism.[21] It was, instead, a circumscribed and tentative effort to bridge what had become the most well-defined cleavage of German electoral politics, a cleavage around which almost three quarters of the German electorate was organized by the close of the imperial period. War and revolution would reshape the liberal and conservative parties and would permanently divide the working-class movement, but the deep social cleavage dividing the constituencies of these parties would survive both disruptions to dominate the electoral politics of the new republic.

The second major division around which the German party system developed was religious in nature. The unification of the German states under Prussian auspices had brought a sizable Catholic minority into a predominately Protestant Reich, and in 1870 the Catholic Center party (Zentrum) was founded to represent the interests of that confessional minority. Thus, unlike the liberal, conservative, and socialist parties, the Zentrum defined its constituency not by social and economic interests but by religious affiliation. The social composition of the Zentrum's electorate was, therefore, far more diverse than those of the class-based parties, and its position on social and political issues reflected that diversity. While the party championed confessional schools and opposed the

Table 1.2. The Elections of the Wilhelmine Era (percentage of vote)

Year	Lib.	Cons.	Lib.+ Cons.	Conf.	Soc.	Other
1890	34.3	19.1	53.4	18.6	19.7	8.3
1893	25.3	19.2	44.5	19.0	23.3	13.2
1898	23.6	15.4	39.0	18.9	27.2	14.9
1903	23.2	13.4	36.6	19.7	31.7	12.0
1907	25.4	13.6	39.1	19.4	29.0	12.6
1912	26.0	12.2	38.2	16.4	34.8	10.6

secular educational policies of the liberals, a position the Zentrum shared with the conservatives, it also supported genuine parliamentary government and progressive constitutional reform traditionally associated with the liberal parties. Similarly, while the party tended to favor government protection of handicrafts and small business interests, it maintained close ties with the Christian trade unions and possessed a long tradition of support for progressive labor reform.[22]

Above all, the Zentrum was determined to protect the Church, its institutions, and its flock. Since the greatest concentrations of Catholics were found in the southern and western states, the party sought to guarantee the independent position of the Church by vigorously endorsing a federal rather than centralized structure for the new Reich. The Zentrum had not been founded as an opposition party, but because of its strong stand on states' rights, it quickly became a rallying point for anti-Prussian sentiment, attracting the collaboration of disaffected minorities and particularists such as the Hannoverian Guelfs, the Poles, the Bavarians, and a party representing the newly annexed provinces of Alsace and Lorraine.[23]

Bismarck, from the very beginning, harbored serious reservations about the existence of a large Catholic party in the new German state, particularly since the Reich was flanked by two hostile Catholic powers, France and Austria. Those misgivings were greatly exacerbated when the Zentrum emerged from the first Reichstag elections as the third largest party, a position bolstered by its regional and particularist allies. Fearing that the Zentrum, supplemented by the institutions and organizations of the Church, would become "a state within the state" opposed to the existing order, and fearful of a potential liberal-Zentrum combination in the Reichstag, the chancellor launched an official policy of persecution against German Catholicism in 1873. During the following five years a series of laws were passed in Prussia that, among other things, banned the Society of Jesus, gave the state veto power over ecclesiastical appointments, and placed the education of the clergy under the supervision of the state. When the German bishops, with support from the Vatican, refused to recognize these statutes, the government responded by arresting and/or deporting hundreds of Catholic clerics. By 1877 over one-quarter of all parishes in Prussia were without a priest, and the Church had been declared an "enemy of the Reich."[24]

In the short term, the *Kulturkampf*, as the struggle was dubbed in 1873, yielded mixed results for Bismarck. A liberal-Zentrum combination had certainly been foreclosed, but at a high price. Both the Progressives and National Liberals were vehement in their anticlericalism and particularly outspoken in their contempt for Pope Pius IX, whom they considered the very embodiment of social and political reaction. They, therefore, became enthusiastic supporters of the *Kulturkampf* and rallied to the chancellor. Yet, while Bismarck's campaign succeeded in winning widespread public support in Protestant Germany, it fundamentally alienated the sizable Catholic electorate and cemented its allegiance to the embattled Zentrum. Indeed, the party's vote doubled in 1874 as Catholics registered their defiance of the Reich government and its persecution of the Church. With almost 28 percent of the vote, the Zentrum, rather than weakening under the chancellor's attacks, emerged from the campaign as the second largest party in the Reich.[25]

Bismarck gradually abandoned the *Kulturkampf* after 1878, and a cautious reconciliation between the Reich and the Church was effected in the early 1880s. The integration of the Catholic electorate into the mainstream of German politics had, however, suffered a severe setback. Although the Zentrum's share of the national vote slipped gradually as the *Kulturkampf* faded, it rarely fell below a solid 19 percent. With this bedrock of electoral support—support drawn almost exclusively from the Catholic population of the Reich—the Zentrum remained the largest nonsocialist party in the Reichstag. The remarkable resilience of the Zentrum's vote in the face of shifting economic and political tides between 1874 and 1912 was a vivid reflection of the persistence of the traditional division between Protestant and Catholic in Germany, a division that remained the most durable in both the imperial and Weimar party systems. Not only did Bismarck's anti-Catholic campaign deepen that cleavage, his strategy, used first against the Zentrum and then the SPD, of rallying a majority by isolating a politically vulnerable "out group" and branding it as an "enemy of the Reich," did much to establish a style of political behavior that remained a prominent and ultimately tragic element of German political culture.[26]

Though hardly of the same magnitude as the social and confessional divisions of the prewar party system, regional and ethnic cleavages also played a significant role in German electoral politics. These divisions, often overlapping the religious lines of cleavage, were produced by both centuries of dynastic rivalry among the German princes and by Prussia's absorption of several national minorities in its steady expansion after 1640. Thus, along with the class-based and confessional parties, the Danes, Poles, Alsace-Lorrainers, and Hannoverians entered the political fray in 1871 with their own partisan organizations. Although some, such as the Bavarian Peasants' party, also targeted a particular social constituency, most of these parties were self-consciously regional or ethnic in their appeal. For the Poles and Danes this meant an emphasis on their minority status in the new Reich, while the Hannoverians, still unreconciled to Prussian annexation in 1866, stressed their particularist dynastic past. Although separated by geography and history, virtually all shared a deep mistrust of Berlin, and this, in turn, made them useful allies of the Zentrum. Individually insignificant, together these parties accounted for approximately 10 percent of the votes cast in the elections of the Bismarckian era. Although unable to keep pace with the dramatic growth of the population and increasingly challenged by the proliferation of special interest and radical agitational parties after 1890, the regional vote hovered at about 6 percent of the national electorate in the last campaigns of the imperial period, a lingering reminder of Germany's divided past.[27]

Political and Social Conflict during the War

The outbreak of war and the kaiser's dramatic call for a political truce, a *Bürgfrieden*, until the conflict had been brought to a victorious conclusion resulted in an almost total cessation of partisan politics during the first years of the war. Although the question of Germany's war aims constantly threatened to rupture this truce, that issue was successfully stifled until the summer of 1917 when the Reichstag Peace Resolution revived open partisan debate. Until then the parties of the Empire, from the Conservatives to the Social Democrats, focused their attention on the war effort, indefinitely postponing thorny questions of domestic politics.[28]

In the meantime, the kaiser and the civilian authorities gradually slipped from view, virtually abdicating political and economic power to the military Supreme Command (Oberste Heeresleitung—OHL). The eclipse of the political parties and the concentration of decision-making authority in the OHL in turn greatly enhanced the position of the highly organized forces of industry. Desperately needed for the production and distribution of war materials, heavy industry, in particular, exerted tremendous influence on the military authorities. As the war progressed, representatives of industry working with the military, the civil bureaucracy, and, finally, organized labor, increasingly determined the allocation of capital, labor, and raw materials throughout the economy. Not only did industry profit from this arrangement, the great industrial enterprises reaped enormous benefits from the government's inflationary fiscal policy, which sought to fund the war effort without raising taxes. The tremendous expenditures demanded by the war were covered by issuing unbacked currency from the Reichsbank, creating an inflationary spiral that allowed big business to expand plants and invest with an eye to the postwar future, while raising prices and drawing substantial profits. Industry's exploitation of this situation became so blatant that even the military authorities finally protested, albeit not until the spring of 1918.[29]

Contributing to industry's strong position during the war was management's self-conscious drive for vertical expansion in key sectors of the economy. The great iron and steel concerns, for example, sought to guarantee access to badly needed raw materials by buying up the mines, while in other branches, such as the chemical industry, companies organized *Interessengemeinschaften* to pool resources. Moreover, the major industrial associations, the BdI and the ZdI, cooperated during the war to present an imposing united front to both the military authorities and organized labor. When in early 1918 the two joined forces in the German Industrial Council, this move represented one more step on the road to a formal union, a union consummated in the following year with the formation of the powerful Reich Association of German Industry (Reichsverband der deutschen Industrie—RVdI). Thus, the concentration and cartelization of economic power, already far advanced before 1914, was greatly accelerated by the war. Conflicts between the different branches of industry certainly persisted, but while the collapse of the monarchy and the establishment of a republic substantially reduced the political clout of the traditional agrarian elites in Germany, the corporate giants of industry and commerce entered the Weimar Republic stronger and better organized than at any time during the Empire.[30]

For the artisans and shopkeepers of the old middle class, the unchecked ascension of big business during the war greatly aggravated long-standing fears about the social and economic deterioration of their *Stand*. In the early stages of the war the imperial authorities had no intention of abandoning small proprietors and producers, but the enormous production and distribution requirements of the war effort gradually resulted in a pronounced government preference for big, well-organized industrial concerns. This preference was particularly evident in the allocation of badly needed raw materials and in the extension of credit. As the war dragged on, small business interests attempted to organize nationally to win a greater share of government contracts and other economic considerations, but they were no match for the giants of industry and commerce, particularly after the adoption of the Hindenburg Program in late 1916. Under the direction of the OHL, this economic program called for a vast increase in armaments production on a fixed schedule and led to an even greater official reliance on heavy industry. Not only were raw materials and credit increasingly funneled to the large industrial concerns, the OHL was authorized to close undermanned and inefficient businesses in order to make maximum effective use of available labor. In practice, this meant the forced closing of many small artisan shops and the relocation of their proprietors and employees in plants designated by the military authorities. It is estimated that by 1917 one-third of all handicrafts shops had been closed, either because the proprietor had been drafted or because of forced shutdowns.[31]

Pressed by big business and its powerful associations on the one hand, shopkeepers and independent artisans were also confronted by the increasingly influential forces of organized labor. The small business movement had always been hostile to Social Democracy and the unions associated with it, but as the war lengthened, the military authorities seemed to place a much higher premium on maintaining a smooth production schedule than on protecting traditional entrepreneurial rights. Thus, union demands for recognition of collective bargaining, for higher wages, a reduced work week, and a greater role in the training and certification of apprentices seemed particularly threatening to the divided and poorly organized representatives of small business. No longer able to count on government intervention for protection, the artisans and shopkeepers of the old middle class felt increasingly isolated, convinced that their once securely sheltered position in society was being steadily eroded by the conflicting, yet powerful, currents of big business and big labor.[32]

A similar mood of resentment and alienation also surfaced in the farm population during the war, greatly intensifying long-standing tensions between town and country. The decades following the agricultural depression of 1875 and 1898 had been years of mounting prosperity and productivity for German agriculture. In that period prices for livestock and dairy products as well as grain had climbed steadily, spurred by the rising demand of an expanding urban population and sheltered by a system of protective tariffs on agricultural imports. Although the grain-producing estate owners of East Elbia drew the most extensive and direct benefits from this system, the peasant proprietors of small and medium-sized farms in central, western, and southern Germany also shared in the general recovery of the last prewar decades.[33]

The war brought that period of prosperity to an abrupt end. Despite improvements in production after 1898, the Reich was by no means agriculturally self-sufficient. In 1914 Germany still imported approximately 20 percent of its food, and it was apparent that if the war were to drag on, German farmers simply could not meet the nation's food needs.[34] Thus, as the war machine bogged down in the fall of 1914 and the Allied blockade tightened around Central Europe, the government faced the distressing prospect of severe food shortages. Anxious to avoid social unrest, especially in the urban areas where war production was concentrated, the regime introduced—in piecemeal fashion—a series of compulsory regulations designed to bring agricultural production and distribution under government control. Under this compulsory system (the *Zwangswirtschaft*), controls on crop and livestock production as well as price ceilings on all agricultural goods were introduced, and an extensive network of rural inspectors was established to assure compliance with the new regulations.[35]

From the very outset these government measures provoked a mood of sullen resentment in the countryside, where farmers found themselves periodically subjected to unannounced audits, midnight inspections, and government seizures. Moreover, while the large estates could adjust their production to cope effectively with the government's pricing and rationing policies, the smaller farms—like the small businesses of the towns and cities—had far less flexibility. By 1915 small farmers were already bitterly complaining about the very real shortages of feed, fertilizer, fuel, equipment, manpower, credit, and draft animals, and the escalating attempts of both civilian and military authorities to regulate agricultural production greatly intensified their sense of frustration. Indeed, farmers were increasingly convinced that the authorities had sided with powerful industrial producers and urban consumers—meaning above all the blue-collar working class—against the *Landwirtschaft*. Prices for industrial goods (farm equipment) they pointed out, were maintained at high levels and credit was more readily available to industrial concerns, while the regime's "fear of the street," the BdL charged, kept prices for agricultural products at the lowest possible ebb.[36]

Efforts to circumvent government regulation, especially on the black market, were extensive and, from the regime's point of view, maddeningly successful. However, as farmers turned increasingly to the black market in 1915–16, they provoked not only redoubled government attempts at control but acrimonious Social Democratic charges of hoarding and price gouging. This mutual resentment between town and countryside reached crisis proportions during the bitter "turnip winter" of 1916–17, when severe food shortages led to widespread hunger riots in cities across the Reich. While the Social Democrats spoke of "crimes against the working class" by avaricious farmers, and peasants complained of "state socialism," the government's response was to tighten controls on the agricultural sector and crack down on black-market activities. These policies merely deepened the already prevailing mood of bitterness and isolation in the countryside. By the end of the war, German farmers, especially the proprietors of modest family farms, were convinced that they had borne a disproportionately heavy burden in the government's wartime controlled economy and that their pleas for understanding and support had been ignored.[37]

The war also brought economic hardship to the civil servants and white-collar employees of the new middle class. For the *Angestellten-schaft*, in particular, economic developments during the war threw into vivid relief the social and economic divide that separated it from the entrepreneurial *Mittelstand*, while reducing the gap that had set it apart from the blue-collar working class. Indeed, just as the war intensified entrepreneurial mistrust of organized labor, it greatly facilitated the transition of the white-collar movement from a collection of loose professional associations to a set of politically and socially self-conscious unions determined to use the traditional weapons of organized labor to deal with management. Before the war, such tactics were widely considered "improper for the *Stand*" (*Nicht standesgemäss*), but by 1918 even the most conservative, antisocialist white-collar unions had embraced collective bargaining and the strike.[38]

White-collar labor felt that it had been driven to adopt such methods because of its steadily deteriorating economic position during the war. Between 1914 and 1917 the cost of living rose by approximately 185 percent, but, as one union survey disclosed, white-collar salaries had climbed only 18 percent. In addition to this decline in real income, white-collar salaries had fallen in relation to blue-collar pay across the economy. In contrast to the small nominal gains registered by white-collar employees, blue-collar wages had jumped by 100 percent in the war-related industries and by 40 percent in other sectors. On the average, white-collar salaries still exceeded blue-collar wages, but the gap was rapidly closing.[39]

Contributing to this situation, white-collar leaders felt, was the understandably great demand for blue-collar labor and a substantial influx of women into the white-collar job market. The number of women holding white-collar positions had risen steadily in the prewar years, but the enormous military demands for manpower after 1914 greatly accelerated that trend. Drawing on a virtually limitless pool of cheap female labor, white-collar leaders feared, would allow management not only to depress salaries further but to replace recalcitrant male employees at whim.[40]

These growing concerns did not, however, produce any lasting unity within the white-collar movement. By 1917 the socialist-oriented unions had established their own Arbeitsgemeinschaft freier Angestelltenverbände (AfA) which drew white-collar employees from all sectors of the economy into one large organization. Their pleas for collaboration with the representatives of the blue-collar working class were, however, rebuffed by the nonsocialist Verbände, which maintained a loose alliance until the end of the war. That cooperative relationship, in turn, did not survive the revolution and the founding of the republic. In early 1919 the liberal, prorepublican unions withdrew to form their own Gewerkschaftsbund der Angestellten (GdA), leaving the conservative associations together in the Gewerkschaftsbund deutscher Angestelltenverbände (Gedag). Thus, at the very outset of the republic, the white-collar labor movement was divided among three major unions, each with a definite political orientation.[41]

The Berufsbeamtentum also suffered a serious economic decline during the war, but despite ominous rumblings of discontent, especially from the middle and lower ranks, the civil servants did not follow the organizational course pursued by their white-collar counterparts in the private sector. Perhaps more than any other occupational group, civil servants, living on fixed incomes, struggled under the impact of the wartime inflation. Salary scales for public officials had not been particularly high before the war, but between 1914 and 1917 real income for civil servants sank dramatically, falling by 57 percent in the higher grades, 51 percent in the middle echelons, and 46 percent in the lower ranks. Although civil servants certainly continued to enjoy job security and considerable social prestige, this drastic loss of purchasing power put enormous strains on their traditional style of life, reducing many to an absolutely proletarian level of existence. Reports from the regional military commands on the morale in the local population increasingly stressed the sagging economic position of public officials, noting, as one not uncommon assessment did in 1916, that "the mounting inflation is making it impossible for many civil servants to provide adequate food and clothing for themselves and their families."[42]

The deteriorating economic position of the *Berufsbeamtentum* did produce efforts to organize civil servants, leading in 1916 to the establishment of the Interessengemeinschaft deutscher Reichs- und Staatsbeamtenverbände. This organization ultimately became the German Civil Servants' League in 1918, but even this potentially powerful association found it difficult to assume the overtly political character of the white-collar unions or to display the wide range of political views found in those *Angestelltenverbände*.[43] Although civil servants from the various ranks hardly constituted a homogeneous, undifferentiated monolith, the traditions of government service, which united the local postman with the *Staatsekretär* in Berlin, provided a powerful integrative ethos that was not to be found within the deeply divided *Angestelltenschaft* or among the entrepreneurs of the old middle class. The war strained this unity and the revolution, with its promise to "democratize the civil service," jolted the castelike status of the *Berufsbeamtentum*, but neither was capable of dissolving the fundamentally antidemocratic, authoritarian, and elitist core of that ethos which survived to plague the new republic.[44]

Across the great social divide, the war imposed severe economic burdens on the blue-collar working class while bringing substantial gains to organized labor. Although blue-collar wages certainly rose in relation to white-collar and civil-service salaries, these gains, beginning from a relatively modest prewar base, hardly kept pace with the wartime rate of inflation. Indeed, the spectacular increase in nominal wages, especially in war-related industries, did not prevent a steady decline in the standard of living for most blue-collar families. Food shortages, chronic after 1916, were exacerbated by shortages in coal, clothing, and housing, especially acute in the great industrial centers, while low pay and long hours generated a rising tide of working-class discontent. During the severe turnip winter of 1916–17, the first great wave of strikes washed over the Reich, and sporadic storms of labor unrest continued into the revolutionary uprisings in the fall of 1918.[45]

Yet, even as conditions steadily worsened for blue-collar workers, the war greatly enhanced the position of organized labor. The exigencies of war production early convinced the ruling military authorities of the necessity of finding some accommodation with the representatives of both industry and labor. The Hindenburg Program, therefore, resulted in an uneasy collaboration between army, industry, and labor from which industry drew tremendous economic benefits and through which organized labor ultimately won a number of long sought-after concessions. Anxious to avoid labor strife that might hamper production, the military worked closely with the unions, and in the process extended to them de facto recognition as the legitimate representatives of labor. The army also encouraged management to deal in a cooperative way with the unions, whose reform-oriented leaders hardly seemed a threat to the existing order. Management, however, was hardly willing to accept the standard union demands for recognition, for collective bargaining, for parity between management and labor in contract negotiations, or for the eight-hour day. Only when the socialist revolution loomed on the near horizon in the fall of 1918 did management reluctantly turn to the union leadership, offering to accept some of these demands and to establish a "social partnership" to steer the economy through the perilous revolutionary shoals just ahead. For its part, the union leadership had long preferred the attainment of immediate economic benefits to the official revolutionary stance of the SPD and was particularly concerned that political and economic chaos would destroy their organizations and negate labor's hard-won gains. Thus, in an extraordinary agreement, reached in November 1918, management acceded, with some significant qualifications, to the major union demands, while the unions promised to work for the "maintenance of the economy," meaning essentially that they would act to restrain labor radicals and to prevent the long-promised socialization of industry. By entering this compact with the representatives of management, the union leadership acknowledged its desire for the continuation of the existing economic structure at the very moment when the leaders of the SPD were declaring the long-awaited socialist revolution.[46]

The willingness of the unions to join forces with management against the threat of socialist revolution was, in fact, symptomatic of the widening rifts within working-class politics. Despite the dramatic rise of the SPD after 1890, the party had been increasingly plagued by internal dissension concerning both its ideological posture and its political strategy. The Social Democrats had adopted a Marxist program at Erfurt in 1891, formally committing the party to the destruction of capitalism and the creation of a socialist economy, but in the following years both the party and the unions became actively engaged in securing immediate reforms of the current system that would benefit their working-class clientele. The political corollary to this revisionist economic orientation was the party's growing faith in electoral politics and the inevitability of a Social Democratic majority. Although revisionism was never formally incorporated into the party's platform, Social Democratic strategy throughout the Wilhelmine era was dominated by a policy of democratic reformism cloaked in orthodox Marxist rhetoric.[47]

The unity of the party, already strained by this ambivalent posture, did not survive the war. The factions of the SPD's left wing, disappointed in the leadership's enthusiastic endorsement of the war effort and its acceptance of *Bürgfrieden*, broke with the party in 1916, refusing to vote financial credits for the war. While the "Majority Socialists" (MSPD) had evolved into a reformist, democratic party desiring gradual political, social, and economic reform, the "Independent SPD" (Unabhängige Sozialdemokratische Partei Deutschlands—USPD) and the "Spartacus League," as the two rebellious factions were labeled, viewed the war as the last great crisis of capitalism and espoused a more traditional view of Marxist revolution.[48]

Electoral Change in the Early Weimar Republic

The differences within the socialist movement quickly came to a head when the kaiser abdicated in November 1918 and power was vested in a cabinet headed by the Majority Socialists. Shortly thereafter the MSPD reluctantly declared the establishment of a republic, accepted the armistice terms demanded by the Allies, and created a Council of People's Representatives, composed of Majority and Independent Socialists, to preside over the new provisional government. Within the Council, disagreement over the shape and substance of the future German state quickly emerged. Under the leadership of Friedrich Ebert, the MSPD vigorously advocated the formation of a democratic republic that would, despite some economic and social reforms, maintain the existing economic system. To realize this goal, the party pressed for immediate elections to a national assembly, which would then draft a constitution for this new German republic. The USPD, however, was opposed to this course of action, preferring instead to see power reside in the revolutionary councils (*Räte*) that had sprung up across the Reich, at least until the power bases of the traditional conservative elites, especially in the army and civil service, had been purged and the seeds of a new socialist economic order had been sown.[49]

Confrontation between these uneasy coalition partners was at last occasioned by the dramatic Spartacist uprising in early January. When the Spartacus League staged massive riots in Berlin to prevent the planned elections, the MSPD, fearing a descent into anarchy, a Bolshevist revolution, and a possible Allied invasion, turned to the army and the newly formed paramilitary organizations, the Free Corps (*Freikorps*), to suppress the coup and restore order. Outraged that Ebert had employed the hated military and the right-wing *Freikorps* against rioting workers, the USPD broke with the government, and hopes for the restoration of proletarian unity in the new republic dissolved.[50]

The extent of the divisions within the socialist camp were amply displayed in the campaign for the constituent assembly in January 1919. For the first time voters could choose between two socialist parties, the MSPD and USPD, or boycott the election in protest, as the German Communist party (Kommunistische Partei Deutschlands—KPD), founded on New Year's Day by the Spartacists, suggested. On the far left, the KPD demanded the replacement of all political organs and authorities of the previous regime by representatives of the Workers' and Soldiers' Councils, who, in turn, would secure "the confiscation of all dynastic assets and incomes, . . . the expropriation of all middle-sized and large-scale farms, and the nationalization of the banks, mines, and all large concerns in industry and commerce."[51] While sharing the radical left's impatience with the ruling Majority Socialists, the USPD offered a more moderate socialist alternative. The Independents railed against the MSPD's wartime collaboration, labeling it a "capitulation to imperialism," and attacked the party for its failure to proceed with the long-promised socialization of the economy. These policies, the USPD charged, constituted a failure to "fulfill the duties demanded by the class interests of the proletariat." In contrast to the stalling of the MSPD, the Independent Socialists therefore demanded "the immediate initiation of socialization so that the conditions of capitalist domination can be broken." Goading their former coalition partners, they called for "the quickest possible transformation of the capitalist class state into a socialist society."[52] The MSPD, however, refused to be budged from its commitment to parliamentary democracy and evolutionary economic change. The party agreed with its socialist rivals that "conditions of economic dependence, as they have been created by modern *Grosskapitalismus*, vitiate the essence of democracy," conceding that "political equality remains a dead letter so long as crass economic inequity exists." Thus, the MSPD joined the calls for "the transformation of the private capitalist economy into a socialist one." At the same time, however, the party warned that the gains of the revolution were endangered by "the terrorism of a small minority." Spartacist radicalism would only revive the forces of reaction and result in "chaos and anarchy." In the same vein, the party condemned "wild experiments" that, "given the current weakened state of our economy, would completely exhaust the economic organism," reducing Germany to "a rubble heap." The economic and political demands of the radical left would not bring the working class closer to its goal, the MSPD maintained. They would, instead, "not only destroy democracy but the possibility of socialism."[53]

Yet, in spite of this internecine strife, the socialist parties scored impressive gains in 1919. With almost 38 percent of the vote, the MSPD alone had surpassed Social Democracy's best prewar performance, and together with the USPD's 7 percent, the two working-class parties had taken a major step toward attaining a socialist majority. Moreover, the MSPD, backed by the Zentrum and the Deutsche Demokratische Partei (DDP), was able to form a majority coalition and begin the task of drafting a constitution for the new republic.

The gap between the socialist parties, however, did not diminish in the aftermath of the elections. Fresh from its greatest electoral triumph, Social Democracy was confronted by the grim realities of the postwar world. Severe shortages of food, coal, and housing persisted, despite the termination of hostilities, and were greatly aggravated by the dislocation of demobilization. In this grim situation, the MSPD was caught between the conservative union leadership, determined to insure economic stability and therefore strongly inclined to continue its collaboration with management, and the demands of the party's rank and file for genuine revolutionary change. Specifically, the leaders of the Allgemeiner Deutscher Gewerkschaftsbund (ADGB) saw the revolutionary workers' councils as a radical challenge to their position as the legitimate representatives of labor and feared that plans for nationalization of industry advanced by the USPD and supported by the Räte would lead to economic ruin. These views were widely shared within the MSPD leadership, which, having committed itself to parliamentary democracy, had to consider the position of its Democratic and Zentrum coalition partners, neither of whom was prepared to follow a radical political or economic course.[54]

As it became increasingly apparent in 1919 that the MSPD had little intention of proceeding with the nationalization of industry or expanding the council system, the government was challenged by a series of violent general strikes in Berlin, in the Ruhr, and in Saxony. Determined to maintain order and prevent a slide into "Bolshevist conditions," the Majority Socialists repeatedly turned to the military to suppress labor unrest. It was, therefore, symptomatic of the MSPD's predicament that it could cooperate with the unions and the rank and file to foil the right-wing Kapp Putsch in March 1920 and yet immediately squander that nascent sense of solidarity by unleashing the army once again on striking Communist workers in the Ruhr.[55]

By 1920, worker disaffection with the MSPD was widespread, and the party's belated agreement to a vastly diluted form of workers' councils in industry hardly disguised the fact that the revolution, with the Majority Socialists at the helm, had run aground far short of the socialist promised land. The extent of working-class disappointment with the party was reflected in the Reichstag election held in June. While the MSPD suffered a major setback, its vote plummeting from 37.9 percent to 21.6 percent, the left greatly expanded its constituency. The USPD, which only a year earlier had attracted just over 7 percent of the vote, collected 18 percent, while the Communists (Kommunistische Partei Deutschlands—KPD), participating in their first campaign, added another 2 percent. (See Table 1.3.)

A substantial realignment of forces had occurred within the socialist camp, leaving working-class electoral sympathies sharply divided. Yet, in spite of that fragmentation, the working-class parties still maintained a solid constituency, representing approximately 40 percent of the electorate. Like the liberal and conservative movements before it, Social Democracy had experienced a deep and bitter schism, but war and revolution had not diminished the most fundamental cleavage of German electoral politics. The Marxist parties, despite some desultory efforts by the MSPD to attract a middle-class constituency, remained overwhelmingly parties of the blue-collar working class. Their campaign literature and their efforts at membership recruitment remained directed at the various elements of the *Arbeiterklasse* in the cities and the countryside, and the sociopolitical chasm that separated them from the parties of the bourgeois center and right remained the most prominent in the shifting topography of the German party system.

Equally important for the shape of Weimar politics, the sociopolitical dislocations of the war and its aftermath, while greatly increasing tensions within both liberal and conservative camps, failed to alter the class-based nature of their electoral orientation. Thus, although the liberals entered the campaign for the National Assembly as divided as before, they continued to compete for an essentially urban middle-class vote. During the war, the National Liberals had repeatedly voiced their enthusiastic support for annexationist war aims, while the Progressives, along with the Social Democrats and Zentrum, had persistently advocated a more moderate course. In an adumbration of what in 1919 became "the Weimar Coalition," these three parties provided the principal support for

Table 1.3. The Elections of the Early Weimar Era (percentage of vote)

Year	Lib.	Cons.	Lib.+ Cons.	Conf.	Soc.*	Other
1919	23.0	10.3	33.3	19.7	45.5	1.5
1920	22.2	14.9	37.1	18.0	41.6	3.3

* Includes USPD, KPD, MSPD.

the ill-fated Reichstag peace resolution of 1917 and had steadily inten-sified pressure on the regime to abolish the archaic three-class suffrage system in Prussia. By November 1918, the enmity between the two liberal parties had grown so intense that even the threat of a Bolshevist Germany could not produce a merger between the two. Consequently, after per-functory attempts to find a formula for cooperation, most National Lib-erals entered the campaign for the National Assembly under the banner of the newly formed German People's party (Deutsche Volkspartei—DVP), while the Progressives, joined by some members of the National Liberal left, founded the German Democratic party (Deutsche Demo-kratische Partei—DDP). The latter immediately proclaimed its allegiance to the new republic, but the DVP publicly favored the establishment of a constitutional monarchy. In addition, the DDP laid considerable stress on the necessity of social reconciliation between the classes, possessed rela-tively few ties to organized industrial and commercial interests, and con-tinued the 1912 Progressive strategy of limited cooperation with the So-cial Democrats. The DVP, on the other hand, retained the close National Liberal association with big business and emphasized its commitment to private enterprise.[56]

Yet, while the two liberal parties followed divergent political paths, their electoral appeals, as in the Empire, were still directed almost exclu-sively at a middle-class constituency. The DVP's platform, published in November 1918, left little doubt about the social locus of its targeted constituency. Labeling itself "the party of the *Mittelstand*," the DVP pledged its unswerving support for the "preservation and strengthening of a broad middle class in industry, commerce, and handicrafts." It also expressed its desire for the "strengthening and multiplication of the free peasantry" and the "safeguarding of civil servants, officers, and teach-ers."[57] Perhaps because of its cooperation with the Social Democrats, the DDP also sought to assure the nervous middle-class electorate of its commitment to "the maintenance of private property." The party, as its program of December 1918 was at pains to emphasize, "condemns the transfer of all means of production to public hands, as demanded by Social Democracy." Moreover, the Democrats stressed that "in contrast to the Social Democratic program, we are convinced of the value and necessity of handicrafts and small retail trade."[58]

The elections of 1919 were held in the immediate aftermath of the revolution and the Spartacist uprising, and left liberalism, with its promise of social reconciliation and its espousal of moderate social and political reform, found considerable resonance in a middle-class electorate fearful of Social Democracy and Marxist economic experiments. In this tense and politically fluid situation, the DDP appeared as the most responsible restraining influence on the powerful Social Democratic rulers of the provisional government and emerged from the January campaign with almost 19 percent of the vote. The DVP, reluctant to accept the new republican government, claimed only 4 percent.[59]

If support for the DDP had been surprisingly broad in 1919, it also proved to be remarkably shallow. When voters were called to the polls eighteen months later in the first Reichstag campaign, the danger of Marxist revolution had faded, while the problems confronting the republican government had multiplied. The inflation, inherited from the imperial regime, continued, exacerbated by the demobilization of millions of troops, mounting social obligations, and Allied reparations demands. Political violence was widespread as bands of paramilitary organizations roamed the streets and the wave of political assassinations that had begun to rise in 1919 was rapidly approaching its crest. In addition, the government had reluctantly accepted the universally hated *Diktat* of Versailles in June 1919, calling down on the Weimar Coalition the wrath of every opposition party from the Communist left to the newly constituted conservative right. Thus, after almost a year and a half of cabinet responsibility, the DDP, like its MSPD partner, suffered a jarring setback in June 1920. The Democratic electoral edifice, so imposing a year earlier, simply collapsed, the DDP vote crumbling from 18.6 percent to 8.3 percent. These Democratic losses were, however, almost entirely matched by DVP gains. The DVP, under the leadership of Gustav Stresemann, had maintained an ambivalent attitude toward the republic, blasted the Treaty of Versailles, and was not saddled with government responsibility. It, therefore, emerged in 1920 as a credible alternative for dissatisfied liberal voters. With almost 14 percent of the vote, the DVP had registered impressive gains over its 1919 (4.4 percent) performance. Thus, despite the precipitous decline in Democratic popularity, the liberal share of the vote remained relatively stable. Though still sharply divided between a nationalist, business-oriented right and a republican, progressive left, liberal voters in 1920 still constituted approximately 22 percent of the German electorate.[60]

Unlike the liberals, the conservatives emerged from the ruins of the Hohenzollern monarchy shaken but united for the first time in decades. In November 1918 the DKP and a number of other small conservative parties merged to form the antirepublican, monarchist German Nationalist People's party (Deutschnationale Volkspartei—DNVP). Yet, having joined forces, the conservatives still faced the same electoral dilemma that had puzzled them throughout the Wilhelmine era. While providing the new party with adequate funding and influential supporters, the traditional conservative interest structure of agrarians, civil servants, military personnel, and some representatives of heavy industry offered little potential for an expansion of the DNVP's electoral constituency. In fact, the conservative share of the vote had dwindled steadily during the Wilhelmine era, declining from 25 percent in 1887 to a mere 12 percent in the last prewar election. Efforts to broaden the party's appeal by embracing the anti-Semitism that flourished in the 1890s and by courting the anticapitalist, antisocialist *Mittelstandsbewegung* had not paid significant electoral dividends.[61]

In the postwar political environment, the conservatives were determined to expand beyond the traditional core of their constituency. Consequently, the newly formed DNVP not only renewed the conservative commitment to agriculture and the civil service/military establishments, it intensified the conservative campaign to become the spearhead of middle-class protest. Its electoral platform in 1918–19 contained the obligatory defense of private property "against Bolshevist intrigues" but went on to assail "the abuses of internationally oriented big capitalism" as well. In addition, the Nationalists insisted that "the *Mittelstand*, so seriously weakened by the war," required "state support for its recovery," while civil servants, teachers, and others in "intellectual professions" were "to be protected from the danger of proletarianization."[62]

In 1919 this strategy failed to halt the seemingly ineluctable erosion of conservatism's electoral appeal. With only 10 percent of the vote, the Nationalists had clearly been unable to transcend the traditional conservative constituency of *Bauern und Beamten*. The political and economic disappointments of the following months, however, proved extremely beneficial to the DNVP. In this period of mounting public disaffection with the new regime, the party skillfully maneuvered to become the most prominent spokesman of the antirepublican right. On the domestic front, the Nationalists blasted the republic's continued regulation of the agricultural sector (*Zwangswirtschaft*) and its unceremonious termination of the Empire's special protective legislation for the handicrafts and small retail trade. To guarantee the restoration of small business and farm influence, the party called for the establishment of a corporatist "economic parliament based on occupation."[63] At the same time, the DNVP firmly established its nationalist credentials by leading the assault on the *Diktat* of Versailles. Assiduously cultivating the "stab-in-the-back" legend, the Nationalists brutally attacked the government parties for their "betrayal of the German people." The responsibility for this "treaty of shame," indeed, for the loss of the war, was attributed exclusively to the parties of the Weimar Coalition, the Marxist Social Democrats, the Jewish left-Liberals, and the Catholic Zentrum.[64]

Finally, the DNVP sought to win votes from the numerous *völkisch* and anti-Semitic groups that had resurfaced in 1919. Although the adoption of an anti-Semitic plank in the conservative platform of 1892 had not produced the desired electoral surge its framers had anticipated, the party had never renounced anti-Semitism, and after 1918 it assumed a prominent place in conservative political literature. Calling for a return to "Christian values and German family life," the DNVP, especially in its appeals to farmers, warned voters in 1920 about the "ominous Jewish predominance in the government and public life that has increased steadily since the revolution."[65]

In the confusing vortex of military defeat and socialist insurrection in 1918–19, this amalgam of antirepublican, nationalist, monarchist, and anti-Semitic rhetoric had failed to attract the attention of the voting public. In the altered circumstances of 1920, however, it struck a highly responsive chord. With just over 15 percent of the vote, the DNVP halted a thirty-five-year conservative decline and scored an unexpected electoral triumph. Though still widely associated with the elites of the old Empire, especially in the civil service and big, grain-producing agriculture, the DNVP had succeeded in presenting itself as a *bürgerliche Partei*. Indeed, in 1920, the DNVP surpassed both the DDP and DVP to become the largest party of the bourgeois center and right.

Just as the basic social cleavage of German electoral politics had survived war and revolution, the confessional divisions of the Empire also remained intact. The Catholic Zentrum entered the republican era with its organizational and electoral orientation virtually unchanged. Although the party's liberal wing, led by Matthias Erzberger, had assumed leadership of the Zentrum during the war, the party's appeal remained solidly based on religious affiliation. As a bow to the new age of mass politics, the party did alter its official name, becoming, in addition to the Center, the Christian People's party, but its policy of political moderation, social conciliation, and religious toleration did not change.[66] The party had cooperated with the SPD during the war, pressing for electoral reform in Prussia and a nonannexationist peace, but the Zentrum remained firm in its rejection of socialism. Its platform of 1918 spurned the idea of a socialist state and demanded instead the establishment of a "democratic republic" that would guarantee "the preservation and strengthening of the Christian cultural and educational ideal in the life of the people."[67]

Although the territorial losses dictated by the Treaty of Versailles meant a decline of the Catholic population, the Zentrum's constituency remained both strong and stable. Even after the defection of the party's Bavarian wing in 1920, the Zentrum could still count on a solid 13 percent of the vote. Contributing greatly to this stability was the entry of women into the electorate as mandated by the Weimar constitution. As the elections of 1919 and 1920 quickly demonstrated, women tended to cast their ballots in disproportionate numbers for parties with a strong religious orientation. This was particularly true of Catholic women, who during the Weimar Republic became the backbone of the Zentrum's constituency.[68] With its confessionally based and remarkably stable electorate, the Zentrum became an indispensable participant in Weimar coalition politics, taking part, regardless of shifting economic and political conditions, in every cabinet until the fall of the Brüning government in the summer of 1932.

Another electoral reform introduced by the Weimar constitution had a direct, if somewhat delayed, impact on the third traditional cleavage of the German party system. Under the Empire's system of single-member districts, regional parties had accounted for between 5 and 10 percent of the national vote. The new republican constitution, however, introduced a system of proportional representation that guaranteed a party one parliamentary mandate for every sixty thousand votes within a given district, while any additional votes were credited to the party's national slate. Under this system, small splinter parties were under little compulsion to compromise with their larger rivals before or during the campaign. In many cases, a party with less than 1 percent of the national vote could count on representation in the Reichstag. Given this arrangement, the number of seats in that body fluctuated from election to election, depending on the extent of voter turnout. Thus, in the campaign for the National Assembly, twenty-nine parties vied for a legislative mandate, including the German-Hannoverian party, the Brunswick Electoral League, the Mecklenburg Village League, the Schleswig-Holstein Peasants' and Agricultural Workers' Democracy, the Bavarian Peasants' League, and other regional parties.[69]

In addition to these explicitly regional parties, proportional representation also encouraged the proliferation of the special interest parties that had first attained prominence in the 1890s. These parties, while usually possessing a circumscribed regional base, sought their constituencies by appealing to shared economic or occupational interests. While claiming to be nonideological (often even unpolitical!), most of these parties, such as the German Civil Servants' White Collar Employees' and Middle Class party, or the Democratic Middle Class party, appealed almost exclusively to elements of the German *Mittelstand*, were rabidly opposed to socialism, and tended to be strongly nationalistic in orientation.[70]

These parties were also joined by a third set of small splinter groups striking a highly ideological posture. Like most of the regional and special interest parties, they were overwhelmingly middle class in composition, though a number of them advanced doctrines of social integration that would, they maintained, end class conflict. Some, like the Christian-Social People's party, were religious in orientation, while others, like the German Socialist party and later the German Racialist (*Völkisch*) Freedom party (Deutschvölkische Freiheitspartei—DVFP), espoused a radical anti-Semitic, anti-Marxist, nationalist people's community (*Volksgemeinschaft*).[71]

In the ideologically polarized atmosphere of 1919 and 1920, these regional, special interest, and radical fringe parties had little impact on national electoral politics. In the elections to the National Assembly they collectively won approximately 130,000 votes, or 2 percent of the national vote. In the following year, their totals increased by 100,000 votes, but their share of the electorate, at 3 percent, remained quite small. Despite some significant shifts of electoral sentiment, the major liberal, conservative, socialist, and confessional blocs had maintained an apparently firm grip on their constituencies through the shocks of war, defeat, and revolution. Yet, it was from this as yet insignificant fringe of the party system that Anton Drexler's German Workers' party, founded in 1919 and transformed in the following year into the National Socialist German Workers' party (Nationalsozialistische Deutsche Arbeiter Partei—NSDAP), would begin its dramatic assault on the Weimar Republic.

The NSDAP in the Weimar Party System, 1919–1923

The early history of the NSDAP is by now a familiar story to students of German history. Founded as the German Workers' party (Deutsche Arbeiterpartei—DAP) in Munich during January 1919, it was

merely one of a number of *völkisch* parties that clustered along the periph-
ery of German politics in the immediate postwar period. At the outset
hardly more than a debating society, the party would undoubtedly have
languished in obscurity had it not been for the extraordinary organizational and propagandistic talents of Adolf Hitler, who joined the party,
as member number thirty, in September 1919. Yet, although it was Hitler's remarkable energy, political acumen, and oratorical magnetism that
thrust the party first into the local Munich limelight and ultimately cata-
pulted the movement into national prominence in 1923, the ideological
foundations of National Socialism were already laid when the Führer arrived on the scene as a political investigator from the Reichswehr.[72]

From its very inception, National Socialism refused to accept the basic
cleavages of German politics. Like other *völkisch* parties, the DAP was
bellicosely nationalistic, opposed to Jewish influence in the state and society, and vehemently anti-Marxist. Yet, unlike the others, the DAP was
determined to win working-class support for these causes. Thus, in its
earliest programmatic statements in January 1919, the party emphasized
its commitment to the "enoblement of the German worker," describing
itself as "a socialistic organization of all people's comrades (*Volksgenossen*) engaged in mental and physical work." The German Workers'
party, however, rejected Marxist socialism, claiming that the socialization of private property would "signal the collapse of the German economy." Instead, the DAP advanced a "form of profit sharing" and the creation of "labor cooperatives in the cities . . . and the countryside." There
would be "no dictatorship of the proletariat," the party's basic principles
explained, and "no rule by bayonets." There would, instead, be "equal
justice for all," and everyone would "feel himself to be a free German."[73]

While the party claimed to be advancing the cause of the German
worker, it also pledged to fight "against all those who create no values,
who make high profits without any mental or physical work." These, the
party maintained, "are mostly Jews. They live the good life, reaping
where they have not sown. They control and rule us with their money."
The Jews were a foreign element in Germany, the DAP charged, governing the country "in their own interests." Germans, the party declared,
should "be governed only by Germans."[74]

When the party's platform was rewritten in the following year and the
famous Twenty-five Points were drafted, these promises to the working
class were retained and even slightly expanded. Not only did the party
renew its pledge to "profit sharing in big business" and "the confiscation
of all war profits," it demanded the nationalization of all (previously) incorporated companies (trusts). In addition, the party also proposed to

"break interest slavery" by abolishing "income unearned by labor or effort."[75]

While these demands, often couched in a vocabulary borrowed from the Marxist parties, lent the DAP a vaguely leftist patina, the Twenty-five Points offered a distinct shift in emphasis from the 1919 program. That program had clearly isolated the worker as its primary audience. The Twenty-five Points, however, reflected the party's desire to broaden the social spectrum of its support. In particular, the party, which in 1920 officially changed its name to the National Socialist German Workers' party, began its cultivation of a middle-class constituency. Calling for the "creation and maintenance of a sound *Mittelstand*," the NSDAP demanded "the immediate communalization of the big department stores and their leasing to small shopkeepers at low rents." Aware of the great dissatisfaction of small business during the war, the party also promised "the most favorable consideration to small businessmen in all government purchases and contracts, whether on the national, state, or local level." Finally, in a bow to an oft-stated desire of the *Mittelstandsbewegung*, the party advocated the establishment of corporatist "chambers, based on occupation and profession" to execute Reich policy in the states.[76]

While attempting to broaden its social base, the party also stepped up its nationalistic and anti-Semitic campaigns. The NSDAP, of course, denounced Versailles, calling for the abrogation of the treaty. Invoking the right of self-determination, the party demanded "the union of all Germans . . . in a Greater Germany" and went on to demand additional territory "for the nourishment of our people and for the settlement of our excess population." At the same time the Nazis advocated the termination of all non-German immigration to the Reich and the expulsion of those non-Germans who had arrived after 2 August 1914. Moreover, German citizenship, the Nazis made abundantly clear, was a matter of blood. According to the National Socialist formula, only people "of German blood" could become "people's comrades," and only people's comrades could become citizens of the Reich. As Point Four of the program concluded: "No Jew, therefore, can become a *Volksgenosse*." Jews and other "non-Germans" were thus to be excluded from the rights of citizenship and expelled from all public offices at every level of government.[77]

These ideas, drawn from the pens of Alfred Rosenberg, Dietrich Eckart, Gottfried Feder, Hitler, and other leading figures of the young National Socialist movement, were neither particularly new nor the private political property of the NSDAP. A number of nineteenth-century political theorists and organizers had advocated a synthesis of nationalism and socialism and some had given their conceptions an anti-Semitic *völkisch* twist. Moreover, several parties, particularly the German Völkisch Freedom party (DVFP), had advanced similar themes, though with significant differences in emphasis, after 1919.[78] What did distinguish the NSDAP from the others was the skill and the tenacity with which the party's views were packaged and presented to the public, and this was in large part the work of Adolf Hitler.

From the very moment of his entry into the tiny DAP, Hitler was determined to transform the party into a mass political organization. Although he encountered tenacious resistance from members of the party's executive committee, whose organizational practices he relentlessly criticized, his own tireless activity (he was unemployed) and his surprising success as a political orator quickly made him indispensable to the party. By the end of the year, Hitler had become both propaganda chief and a member of the party's executive committee.[79]

During 1920 Hitler's reputation as a fiery and effective speaker continued to grow, attracting increasingly larger audiences to his carefully orchestrated and often tumultuous public appearances. Hitler was, of course, aware of his mounting importance to the NSDAP and skillfully used his position to expand his influence within the party. Not only did he develop a considerable following within the local NSDAP, he multiplied his contacts with party leaders outside Munich, many of whom were just founding their own organizations and needed speakers for their meetings and rallies. Moreover, when the party acquired its own official newspaper, the *Völkischer Beobachter* (*VB*), it came under Hitler's direction, offering him another opportunity for public exposure.[80]

By 1921, when the NSDAP held its first national congress, the National Socialists, largely as a consequence of Hitler's activities, had become familiar figures on the *völkisch* right of Bavarian politics. Although the NSDAP was still largely confined to Bavaria and southern Germany, its membership had climbed to over three thousand, and the *VB*'s circulation in January 1921 reached eleven thousand. The rapid growth of the NSDAP, of course, pleased the old party leadership, but the concomitant rise of Hitler's popularity within the party was a source of considerable misgiving. In an attempt to curb Hitler's mounting influence, the executive committee in July 1921 announced its intention to merge the NSDAP with another *völkisch* party and to relocate the organization's headquarters in Berlin. Sensing an opportunity for a confrontation with the foot-dragging old guard, Hitler resigned in protest. Suddenly faced with the loss of the party's strongest attraction, the executive committee immediately crumbled, hastily accepting Hitler's conditions for his return to the party. According to a letter addressed to the executive committee, a special National Socialist congress was to be convened to elect Hitler party chairman and to vest in him dictatorial power over all party affairs. This special party congress, held in late July, overwhelmingly endorsed Hitler's plan, breaking the power of the old leadership and formalizing Hitler's control over the party's organization. Within weeks his followers had assumed the major administrative posts in the party, and the core of a permanent party bureaucracy had been formed.[81]

Having solidified his grip on the party apparatus in Munich, Hitler moved to extend his control over the National Socialist locals throughout Bavaria. During the following months, local leaders were coaxed, cajoled, and threatened, and at the party's second national congress in January 1922 Hitler succeeded in winning formal recognition of the NSDAP's new leadership. Thereafter, political propaganda would emanate from party headquarters in Munich, and local leaders were forbidden to form alliances with other *völkisch* parties. Despite periodic clashes with recalcitrant local leaders, Hitler, by the end of the year, had firmly institutionalized his role as leader of the party and had begun to craft a centralized bureaucratic structure to organize and control the expanding activities of the NSDAP.[82]

During this period of internal consolidation, Hitler had steadfastly refused cooperation with other *völkisch* organizations, fearing that any alliance or merger would merely dillute the NSDAP's influence and weaken his own control over the movement. By early 1923, however, Hitler was in firm command of the party and ready to test the broader political waters. Having ruled out participation in electoral politics, Hitler was convinced that the republic must be toppled by revolution, and in early 1923, the Weimar government seemed particularly vulnerable.[83]

Since the elections in 1920, the parties of the Weimar Coalition had been unable to form a majority government, and six short-lived minority cabinets had followed in rapid succession. The political fragility of the government, vividly reflected in the lingering plague of political assassination and threats of insurrection from both the left and the right, was greatly exacerbated by economic developments. With its legitimacy already called into question by its acceptance of the armistice and the Treaty of Versailles, the weak republican government was determined to avoid a postwar recession and mass unemployment among the millions of demobilized veterans. To prevent this and to meet the enormous social costs of the lost war—pensions to millions of disabled veterans, widows, and other surviving dependents of the war dead—the Weimar governments continued the inflationary policy inherited from the imperial regime.[84] The result was a dramatic deterioration of the mark's value. In January 1919 a dollar brought 8.20 RM; by December 1922, 7,589.27 RM. While this policy did, indeed, permit a revival of industrial production between 1919 and 1923,[85] it also had a severe impact on large sections of the German population and contributed directly to a major international confrontation with the victorious states. After accepting, with great protest, the principle of reparations embodied in the Versailles settlement, the Weimar governments repeatedly refused to accept specific Allied plans to fulfill Germany's obligations. The Allies, on the other hand, were equally adamant in their refusal to permit payment offered in devalued German currency. Negotiations reached an impasse in 1922 and in January of the following year, French and Belgian troops occupied the Ruhr.[86] A broad political and economic crisis rapidly developed in Germany, with rampant inflation, separatist uprisings in the Rhineland, a Communist coup in Hamburg, and a mobilization of rightist forces centered in Bavaria.

It was in this atmosphere of political and economic crisis that Hitler enlisted the NSDAP in a conspiratorial alliance with a number of other völkisch and right-wing groups to overthrow first the Bavarian and ultimately the Reich governments. Having established connections with rightist leaders throughout the Reich, Hitler was selected as the political leader of this Kampfbund in the spring of 1923 and threw himself into preparations for the Putsch. Absorbed by these plans in the following months, Hitler paid less and less attention to his own party, even permitting the NSDAP's military street organization, the Sturmabteilung (SA), to be merged with Free Corps units not under his own command. Hitler was clearly the driving force behind the coup, despite the participation of men of far greater national reputation such as General Erich Ludendorff, but having committed himself to an alliance, Hitler was forced to rely on persons over whom he had no real control. This proved particularly critical, since differences on tactics and timing developed between the conspirators, and when at last the Putsch was launched from the Bürgerbräu beer hall on November 9, 1923, it was a fiasco. The conspiracy was immediately crushed, Hitler was arrested, and the NSDAP was banned throughout the Reich.[87]

The NSDAP, however, did not disappear as so many splinter parties had done. With the revolutionary path to power now apparently blocked, the remnants of the party quickly regrouped and, with Hitler's grudging approval, began preparations for an entry onto the stage of Weimar electoral politics. But what position would the NSDAP assume in the German party system? Where would National Socialism establish itself along the well-defined lines of social, confessional, and regional cleavage? From what groups would the party draw the support that within less than ten years would make it the largest political party in Germany? The answers to these questions are to be found in the National Socialist electoral campaigns of the Weimar period, and the first of those came less than six months after the humiliation of the Beer Hall Putsch.

11
Inflation and Stabilization: The Elections of 1924

In January 1923, French and Belgian troops marched into the Ruhr in retaliation for alleged German failure to fulfill its reparations obligations. Although German domestic politics had been in a state of considerable turmoil since the establishment of the republic, the invasion of the Ruhr precipitated a series of interrelated political and economic crises which, in large part, shaped the contours of German electoral developments in the following year. The minority cabinet, headed by Wilhelm Cuno, responded to the invasion by halting reparations payments and adopting a policy of passive resistance in the occupied areas. In order to support inactive workers, the government was compelled to initiate a massive subsidy program for the Ruhr. This project, however, greatly exacerbated inflationary pressures on the mark, which had been steadily mounting since the beginning of the World War. As government demands for currency rose, the Reichsbank allowed the presses to roll. In January 1923, a dollar brought 17,972 RM on the Berlin market; by August, shortly before passive resistance was halted, the exchange rate had reached an astronomical 109,996.15 RM to the dollar.[1]

Although the value of the mark had deteriorated drastically since the last quarter of 1922, economic life in Germany during the autumn of 1923 acquired an almost surrealistic quality.[2] In August, a streetcar ticket in Berlin sold for 100,000 RM. One month later the same ticket cost 4,500,000 RM and by November 150 million RM. A Berlin Hausfrau could purchase a kilo of potatoes for 20 RM in January. By October she needed 90 billion RM. Bread was even more than five times as expensive as potatoes (467 billion RM per kilo in early December), and the price of beef, at 4 trillion RM per kilo, simply defied imagination. Between June and November the price of fifty kilos of heating coal soared from 1,865 RM to 1,370 billion RM, an increase of 134,508,445 times.[3] Nor was Berlin an exceptional case. The cost of living and the rate of inflation were even higher in many other German towns and cities.[4] "Life," one

German glumly declared, "was madness, nightmare, desperation, and chaos."[5]

At the height of the crisis in August, as a wave of strikes swept over the country, Gustav Stresemann persuaded the Social Democrats to join the DVP, DDP, and Zentrum in Weimar's first Great Coalition. Shortly after its formation, the Stresemann government formally terminated the policy of passive resistance and quickly sought means of arresting the continuing deterioration of the mark. Under the circumstances, drastic measures seemed necessary. Despite serious differences between the DVP and SPD over several major issues, the tenuous coalition managed to acquire parliamentary sanction to issue emergency decrees for the stabilization of the currency. Armed with this authority, the government moved to establish fiscal responsibility.[6] A temporary currency, pegged to the price of gold and backed by the mortgage value of all national assets, private as well as public, was introduced and a new bank was established to issue it. On 15 November, one week after the unsuccessful Beer Hall Putsch, the so-called *Rentenmark* was placed in circulation, and public response to the new currency was encouraging.[7]

Yet, before the effects of these fiscal reforms could be felt, the Great Coalition was shaken by a series of political tremors that threatened to destroy the fragile foundations of the republic. The end of passive resistance in the Ruhr was seized upon by separatist elements in the Rhineland as a propitious moment to sever ties with Berlin and establish an independent Rhenish state. Separatist demonstrations erupted in Bonn, Düsseldorf, and other Rhenish cities, and in late October, independent Rhenish republics were proclaimed in Aachen and Koblenz. Although enjoying only marginal indigenous support, the Rhenish separatist movement remained a grave threat to the unity of the German state and contributed significantly to the atmosphere of crisis pervading the embattled republic throughout the last turbulent months of 1923.[8]

Nor was the Rhineland the only region to pose a threat to the political integrity of the republic. The inclusion of the Social Democrats in the Stresemann cabinet and the government's termination of passive resistance had precipitated a storm of protest from rightist forces, especially in Bavaria. In Munich, where radical rightist organizations flourished, the reactionary government responded by refusing to implement directives from Berlin and by implicitly encouraging Bavarian separatist forces. Even the declaration of a state of emergency by the Reich government in September failed to silence the inflammatory rhetoric of the Bavarian authorities or to curb the conspiratorial activities of the radical *Wehrverbände* clustered within Bavaria's frontiers.[9]

Meanwhile, members of the KPD were taken into Social Democratic governments in Saxony and Thuringia, and rumors of an imminent Communist coup supported by the party's secret paramilitary organizations were widely circulated.[10] The Munich government thereupon severed relations with Saxony and Thuringia, an action in itself symptomatic of the growing centrifugal tendencies astir in 1923, and rightist formations throughout Bavaria were reported ready to march not only on Dresden and Erfurt, but on "red Berlin" as well.

At last provoked by an abortive Communist uprising in Hamburg in late October and fearful of mass violence in the South, Reich military authorities acted swiftly to purge the Saxon and Thuringian governments of their Communist members.[11] Yet, to the dismay of the Social Democrats, the provocative actions of the rightist Bavarian cabinet were treated with considerable forbearance. Increasingly disenchanted with the economic and social initiatives of its DVP coalition partners, the SPD withdrew from the national cabinet on 2 November, citing the government's eagerness to act against the left in contrast to its leniency toward right-wing extremism. The Reichstag's anticipated vote of no confidence, however, was delayed when the Hitler Putsch of 9 November forced postponement of the crucial parliamentary session. Although the coup in Munich was quickly stifled by local military authorities, the Stresemann cabinet did not survive until the new year. Having borne the fury of the Rhenish, Saxon, and Bavarian tempests, the government finally collapsed in late November, toppled by Social Democratic and Nationalist votes.[12]

With the suppression of the Munich Putsch, a year of political and economic trauma for the republic drew to an uneasy close. By the turn of the new year, the currency reform of the Great Coalition showed tangible signs of halting the deterioration of the mark, and the emergency decrees of Stresemann's successor promised to bring a measure of stability to the ravaged economy. The parliamentary system, too, had survived, but only by recourse to temporary rule by emergency decree. Shortly after the fall of the Stresemann government, a new minority cabinet under Zentrum leader Wilhelm Marx was formed, and the Reichstag once again enacted legislation enabling the government to execute emergency measures without parliamentary approval until 15 February 1924.

Utilizing this authority, the Marx government introduced a series of stringent deflationary measures that contributed to the immediate stabilization of the economy. They also entailed the de facto suspension of the eight-hour workday, a massive and unprecedented dismissal of civil servants and public employees, a severe restriction of credit, and a startling rise in unemployment. In addition, the government's Third Emergency Tax Decree, which revalued debts and mortgages at only 15 percent of their original value, ignited a fire storm of protest from creditor circles. The inflation crisis of 1923 was quickly giving way to the stabilization crisis of early 1924.[13]

Under these circumstances, the Marx government survived the termination of the Enabling Act in mid-February by less than a month. With vociferous opposition to the government's austerity program voiced by both the right and the left, establishment of a viable parliamentary coalition proved just as elusive as it had four months earlier. Thus, before the government's Third Emergency Tax Decree could be formally reviewed by the Reichstag, Reich President Ebert was persuaded to dissolve the chamber and call for new elections on 4 May.[14]

The Reichstag campaign in the spring of 1924 was the first in which the National Socialists participated. Although the failure of the Munich Putsch had hurled the already fractious *völkisch* movement into disarray, a modicum of order had been restored in the first months of the following year. Shortly after the abortive coup, Hitler had entrusted the leadership of the party to Alfred Rosenberg, a man with little organizational experience and little personal authority in the party—qualifications that may have highly recommended him to Hitler. With its leader arrested and its organization banned throughout Germany, the NSDAP floundered. During the months preceding the Putsch, Hitler had given little thought to organizational matters or contingency plans should the plot miscarry. As a result, the party waivered on the brink of disintegration in the aftermath of the coup.[15]

Sensing an opportunity to assume the leadership of the *völkisch* movement, Alfred von Graefe, leader of the DVFP, began negotiations with Rosenberg and other Nazi leaders for an amalgamation of the two organizations. Cooperation between the DVFP and NSDAP was strenuously endorsed by the Nazi leadership in northern Germany, where Gregor Strasser hoped to exploit the DVFP connection to strengthen National Socialist influence. At a meeting with von Graefe in Salzburg, Rosenberg steadfastly refused to accept a merger of the two parties but agreed to the formation of an electoral alliance. The country would be divided on a proportional basis and policy would be determined by consultation between the leadership of the two parties.[16] Although tensions remained, not only between the DVFP and the NSDAP but within the Nazi regional organizations as well, the *völkisch* coalition approached the Reichstag elections of May 1924 with a surprising degree of outward unity.

This show of solidarity, however, masked sizable rifts within the movement. Many National Socialists not only objected to collaboration with the DVFP but also opposed on principle any participation in parliamentary elections. During the early spring this opposition was frequently expressed in party gatherings throughout Germany, prompting numerous explanations of National Socialist electoral strategy. In Hessen, for example, the local branch of the Nazi-*völkisch* coalition, the Völkisch-Soziale Block (VSB), exhorted those "who stand behind Ludendorff, Hitler, and Graefe" to prepare for the upcoming elections. National Socialists all over Germany were "fighting shoulder to shoulder beside the *Völkischen* against the parliamentary system." The party press left its readers in little doubt about the coalition's ultimate objective: "The VSB enters the parliament as the deadly foe of the parliamentary system, not to build up the November republic but to destroy it." [17]

The Nazi-*völkisch* coalition had hoped to approach the campaign by focusing on the highly unpopular stabilization policies of the Marx government. That strategy, however, was quickly linked to the sharply divisive debate on German reparations policy that reemerged in the spring of 1924. The reparations question—how much and in what form Germany was to pay—had not been settled at Versailles or at subsequent international conferences, and the debate was revived in early 1924 when an international committee of economic experts, appointed by the Reparations Commission and chaired by Charles Dawes of the United States, formulated a new scheme of payment to be presented to the German government. This committee had been working since January to establish Germany's capacity to meet its reparations obligations, and in early April, with the German campaign in full swing, the committee presented its recommendations to the commission. These recommendations, quickly dubbed the Dawes Plan, called for a graduated schedule of payments, beginning with approximately one billion marks in 1925–26 and increasing to a normal annual payment of 2.5 billion by 1928–29. It did not, however, define total German liability. Taxes and duties levied by the Reich government, as well as payment of dividends issued by a number of industrial corporations and the Reichsbahn—now to be organized as a private company—were to be sources of needed revenue. Since a stable currency and a balanced budget were viewed as prerequisites for German recovery, the functions of the Reichsbank were to be supervised by an internationally composed general council, and the transfer of payments, to be made in German currency, was to be effected by a reparations agent stationed in Berlin. Although not formally a part of the plan, evacuation of the Ruhr within one year was anticipated in exchange for German acceptance of the report. [18]

Despite the restrictions on German sovereignty implicit in these proposals, the Marx government was convinced that acceptance of the plan offered the best guarantee for the continued recovery of the economy, and on 16 April, the cabinet announced its intention to comply. Since implementation of the agreement required legislative approval by a two-thirds majority, the composition of the soon-to-be-elected Reichstag assumed an even greater significance. Acceptance of the plan rapidly emerged as the central controversy of the campaign, inextricably linking domestic and foreign policy issues.

The experts' report was immediately denounced by the DNVP and the *völkisch* coalition as a "second Versailles" and by the Communists as "a plan for the colonization of Germany."[19] Yet, having absorbed months of abuse from both extremes for the unpopular deflationary policies introduced by emergency decree, the government parties were determined to stand their ground on foreign policy issues. While conceding that the position of the middle parties on domestic questions was "uncommonly difficult," one Zentrum deputy stated frankly that foreign affairs offered the most promising terrain for a credible "self-defense" against the onslaught from the extremes. After all, he reasoned, Germany's domestic problems were largely determined by international developments, and a campaign strategy that treated the Reich's economic and social situation as the unavoidable product of the lost war might substantially reduce the "odium of responsibility" ascribed to the embattled coalition parties. Such a strategy would shed a more positive light on the difficult role of the middle parties and at last allow "the attacked to become the attacker and accuser."[20]

As the spring campaign developed, the government parties therefore attempted a shift from the troubled defense of domestic policy to an assault on extremist, especially Nationalist and *völkisch*, opposition to the Dawes Plan. Indeed, the "primacy of foreign policy" became a leitmotiv of their electoral literature during both campaigns of 1924. Attempts by the right, especially the more established DNVP, to undermine the government's position in negotiations concerning the experts' report were roundly condemned as obstructionist and provocative. Such efforts, the Democratic *Berliner Tageblatt* charged, not only encouraged the nationalist elements in France but "prove how frightfully concerned the DNVP is that the Reich government could achieve success . . . by its policy of liberation through sacrifice and how determined it is to place partisan goals above every foreign policy achievement."[21] Continued economic recovery and the final evacuation of the Ruhr depended on Germany's acceptance of the experts' report, the governing coalition maintained. A victory for the right would only end in financial ruin and war.

Anton Erkelenz of the DDP spoke for all the government parties when he declared that the election had become "a referendum on Germany's foreign policy." May fourth would be a day of decision, he argued. "It is either mobilize with [the DNVP's Helfferich] for a new war or with Stresemann for payment. A middle course, a compromise, a gray area between them does not exist."[22]

In response, the DNVP acknowledged that foreign policy would play a major role in the campaign, and strident opposition to the unconditional acceptance of the experts' report became a touchstone of the right's electoral strategy. While the coalition parties, supported on this issue by the SPD, emphasized the dangers of a Nationalist victory, citing the unfavorable reaction to be expected in Western capitals,[23] the right responded by accusing the government parties, including the Social Democrats, of complicity in a Western attempt to enslave the Reich. "The Western powers," one conservative paper maintained, "support the government parties because a Marx-Stresemann victory would be a confession of German weakness . . . and would insure the inability of Germany to pursue a policy of strength. It would guarantee the continuation of that futile policy of reconciliation [*Verständigungspolitik*], which has driven Germany deeper and deeper into slavish dependence on France and more and more under the oppression of the Treaty of Versailles."[24]

Yet because the right also hoped to convert the widespread unpopularity of the government's deflationary program into electoral capital, the DNVP and the *völkisch* coalition assailed the government parties for their efforts to reduce the election to a referendum on the Dawes Plan. "It is absurd," the conservative *Der Tag* asserted, "to maintain that 'whoever is for the experts' report must support the old cabinet and whoever is against it must vote for the right.' On the contrary, the report is . . . in its entirety burdensome, oppressive, and repugnant to us. However, if we allow the weak parties of the left to take the helm, if we allow them to implement the experts' report, we will slide ever deeper into the mesh of the enemy net."[25]

While the government parties argued that domestic economic progress could be achieved only by acceptance of the report, the right viewed this as a ploy to dilute voter dissatisfaction with the government's own emergency economic program. One rightist publication typically charged that the coalition parties hoped to convince middle-class voters "that acceptance of the report is an absolute necessity . . . if they don't want to starve." The DDP and SPD, in particular, were accused of leading the German people into such misery and despair that a desperate *Volk* might indeed acquiesce in the "slavery" offered by the experts in exchange for the bare minimum of existence. The continued decline of the German economy could be expected if these parties were permitted to influence the formulation of policy.[26]

While the reparations and stabilization controversies dominated the political literature of the parties, the spring campaign was launched under the lingering impact of the tumultuous political developments of the previous winter. The smoldering separatist movement in the Rhineland was not extinguished until February, and sporadic flashes of violence continued into the early spring. Moreover, the Reichstag campaign had just begun when the Hitler-Ludendorff trial swept the NSDAP to the forefront of national political consciousness. The trial began in Munich in late February, and for a full month the dramatic courtroom proceedings dominated the front pages of the national press. Ingloriously defeated in his efforts to unseat the republic by violent means, Hitler turned the trial into a major triumph of National Socialist propaganda. In his closing statement on 27 March, Hitler sounded the themes that would dominate Nazi electoral literature in the campaigns of 1924. Asserting flatly that he was "resolved to be the destroyer of Marxism," Hitler went on to explain that in the November Putsch the National Socialists had

> wanted to create in Germany the precondition that alone will make it possible for the iron grip of our enemies to be removed from us. We wanted to create order in the state, throw out the drones, take up the fight against international stock exchange slavery, against our whole economy being cornered by trusts, against the politicizing of the trade unions, and above all, for the highest honorable duty which we, as Germans, know should be once more introduced—the duty of bearing arms, military service. And now I ask you: Is what we wanted high treason?[27]

With these unsettling tremors of the previous year still reverberating across the political landscape, German voters went to the polls on 4 May 1924, and the extent of public disaffection with the political and economic dislocations of the postwar years was clearly reflected in the startling surge of the radical, antirepublican parties. Together the KPD, DVFP, and DNVP polled an ominous 38.6 percent of the vote and controlled 42 percent of the seats in the newly constituted Reichstag. Most impressive were the gains of the DNVP, which became the second most powerful party in Germany. In 1920 the party had attracted 14.9 percent of the national electorate; in May 1924, 19.5 percent. Since the elections to the constituent assembly in January 1919, the Nationalists had attracted over two million new voters. (See Table 2.1.)

Table 2.1. The Election of 4 May 1924 (percentage of vote)

Völkisch (NSDAP)	DNVP	DVP	Zentrum	DDP	SPD	KPD	Other
6.5	19.5	9.5	16.6	5.7	21.6	12.6	8.3

The success of the DNVP had been anticipated by political observers, but the strong showing of the *völkisch* coalition produced something of a mild surprise. Despite organizational difficulties and internecine disputes, the National Socialists and their allies collected almost two million votes. With 6.5 percent of the national total, the Nazis not only surpassed each of the small special interest and regional parties but the well-established DDP as well. Moreover, while Nazi support was centered in southern Germany, particularly in Bavaria, the *völkisch* coalition's ability to win votes in the north served notice that the appeal of National Socialism was hardly a regional phenomenon.[28]

Equally portentous, though often ignored, the small special interest and regional parties such as the Business party, the Tenants' party, and the Bavarian Peasants' and Middle-Class party, made substantial gains. Such parties, whose appeal was directed almost exclusively at different elements of the middle-class electorate, had been active on the electoral scene since the early days of the German party system in the late nineteenth century but had played only a marginal role in the first two national campaigns of the Weimar era. Together they had failed to win even 4 percent of the national vote in the elections of both 1919 and 1920. In May 1924, however, these parties emerged with a surprisingly strong 10 percent of the vote. Along with the impressive performance of the *völkisch* coalition, the showing of the special interest and regional parties provided a clear signal that an increasing number of voters, and particularly middle-class voters, had begun to seek alternatives to their traditional political options. Indeed, in the wake of the inflation and stabilization crises, those parties associated with government responsibility suffered potentially damaging setbacks. The DVP, DDP, and Zentrum together lost over 2 million votes, while the SPD also stumbled. Voter dissatisfaction, however, seemed particularly pronounced with the liberal parties. The DVP, which in 1920 had won almost 14 percent of the vote, lost over a million votes and claimed just over 9 percent of the electorate, while the DDP constituency fell from 8.3 percent to 5.6 percent in the same period. Liberal crossovers may have found their way into one of the special interest parties or selected a more radical alternative, but regardless of their ultimate destination, the liberal middle had suffered a serious loss.

Because of the surprising thrust of the radical parties and the persistence of divisions between the republican forces, especially the DVP and SPD, efforts to form a viable government were again confronted with all but insurmountable obstacles. Repetition of the government instability of the previous year seemed inevitable. Attempts by Stresemann to entice the DNVP into a coalition with the DVP, DDP, and Zentrum failed in August when the Nationalists demanded that Count Westarp, their party chairman, be named chancellor and the DNVP be admitted into the Prussian cabinet. The Nationalists also attempted to link a conditional acceptance of the Dawes legislation with their entry into the coalition, but this strategy also misfired. In fact, during the crucial Reichstag debate in August, the party divided, with just enough Nationalist deputies voting for acceptance of the Dawes Plan to ensure its passage. Following the vote, Stresemann once again pressed for Nationalist participation in a Reich cabinet, and the DNVP, now anxious to enter the government, dropped its earlier demands. The Zentrum, however, made its support for the Nationalist entry into the government contingent on the DDP's agreement, and the Democrats, after considerable equivocation, finally balked. An impasse having been reached, the Reichstag was dissolved in late October and new elections were called for December.[29]

These partisan negotiations had been given prominent coverage in the press, and efforts to form an antisocialist coalition government provided the central focus for the year's second national campaign. The DNVP and DVP were determined to establish a Reich government that would not only reduce Social Democratic influence but would exclude the DDP as well. Although the formation of this *Bürgerblock* was acrimoniously debated throughout the fall, the sense of impending crisis that had dominated the spring campaign was noticeably absent. Indeed, the political and economic environment had undergone a considerable transformation in the eight months since the May election. Although the establishment of a stable majority government remained problematic, the threats of Rhenish and Bavarian separatism as well as armed insurrections by the political extremes had greatly diminished. On the international scene tensions had subsided, and negotiations for French withdrawal from the Ruhr appeared to encourage cautious optimism. Moreover, if the inchoate signs of economic revival had only been partially discernible in the spring, declining unemployment and rising real wages throughout the summer and fall signaled the unequivocal improvement of the economic situation. A massive influx of foreign capital, especially from the United States, had begun following German acceptance of the Dawes Plan, and these funds acted as a catalyst to economic revival. The effects of these positive trends were unevenly distributed across the economy, and the re-vitalization of some sectors lagged behind the general pace of recovery. However, the desperate pall of economic crisis that had lingered through-out the spring had clearly begun to lift before the fall campaign was launched.[30]

The domestic political situation had also undergone substantial change since the spring. While prospects for Nationalist participation in a center-right cabinet had increased during summer and fall, the threat from the *völkisch* right had clearly subsided. Following their surprisingly effec-tive cooperation during the spring campaign, the National Socialists and *Völkischen* soon proved unable to bridge the steadily widening rifts in their coalition. Although an amalgamation of the NSDAP and DVFP was, in fact, accomplished in late August, this show of *völkisch* unity was short-lived. Strasser and Rosenberg, who joined Ludendorff and Graefe in founding the new National Socialist Freedom Movement (Nation-sozialistische Freiheitsbewegung—NSFB), were unable to assert their leadership over the various Nazi factions, and almost immediately wide-spread and highly prominent defections from the new party began. In Bavaria, for example, Julius Streicher and Hermann Esser bolted the new national party, establishing their own rival organization. The *völkisch* movement, it seemed, was neither anti-Semitic nor radical enough to suit Streicher's tastes. The NSFB was roundly condemned as bourgeois and Bavarian National Socialists were publicly urged to boycott the ap-proaching elections.[32]

The delicate fabric of *völkisch* unity had begun to unravel in northern Germany as well. Many Nazi leaders there shared Streicher's aversion to electoral participation and particularly disliked formal association with Graefe's party. Disturbed by the bourgeois character of the *völkisch* cam-paign literature and the upper-middle-class background of its leadership, Adalbert Volck and Ludolf Haase formed a North German Directorate to preserve the "revolutionary" principles of National Socialism. The Di-rectorate openly advocated total abstention from the new campaign and even encouraged those Nazis who did vote to cast Nationalist ballots.[33]

The NSFB, therefore, entered the fall campaign in disarray. Lacking a cohesive national platform, a national organization, or adequate financial support, the *völkisch* movement lost over half its constituency in the De-cember election. With a bare 3 percent of the vote, the radical *völkisch* right had assumed a position on the fringes of German electoral politics,

Table 2.2. The Election of 7 December 1924 (percentage of vote)

Völkisch (NSDAP)	DNVP	DVP	Zentrum	DDP	SPD	KPD	Other
3.0	20.5	10.1	17.3	6.3	26.0	9.0	7.8

which it would occupy until the onset of the Great Depression in 1929. (See Table 2.2.)

While the liberals continued to flounder and the special interest parties slipped as well, the DNVP consolidated its grip on the dissatisfied electorate that it claimed in May. Undoubtedly benefiting from crossovers from the disintegrating *völkisch* constituency, the Nationalists added over a half million votes to their earlier total, giving the party 20.5 percent of the national electorate. Although some Nationalist deputies, under extreme pressure from agrarian and industrial interests close to the party, had aided in passing the controversial Dawes legislation, the DNVP nonetheless continued its condemnation of the plan in the subsequent campaign. Despite this equivocation, the appeal of the party may have been significantly enhanced by its apparent readiness to participate at last in a strong *Bürgerblock* government.

The DNVP's rising popularity, despite the obvious inconsistencies of its approach to the Dawes Plan, was indicative of the nature of German electoral politics. The specifics of particular issues, no matter how vehemently debated on the Reichstag floor, assumed a secondary position in the campaign strategies of the Weimar parties, each of which was determined above all else to establish its position on the traditional lines of class and/or confessional cleavage. Thus, even the hotly debated Dawes legislation was framed in the traditional ideological language of class politics. The underlying conflict, as one Nationalist editorial explained, "isn't a matter of political issues of the day, nor is it merely a question of whether the Dawes Plan can be implemented or whether the German Nationalists enter the cabinet. It is a matter of the fundamental nature of the state." The choice confronting the electorate in December, the DNVP argued, was "*Bürgerblock* or socialism," and the Nationalist goal was to achieve "the concentration of all bourgeois elements against Social Democracy."[34]

In spite of the DNVP's espousal of a classless *Volksgemeinschaft* and an occasional nod to the German worker,[35] the party's call for the coalescence of all bourgeois forces in a united antisocialist *Bürgerblock* represented an unequivocal appeal for class voting. Indeed, one Nationalist spokesman commented that nothing was more characteristic of "the domestic condition of the German people" than its division into "two camps," one socialist and one rightist. Those parties that sought to bridge the gap between these two camps, the DDP and the Zentrum, were, therefore, vilified as saboteurs of bourgeois unity. DNVP campaign literature charged that the Democrats, in particular, had "divided the *Bürgertum*" and "proven themselves the representatives of Social Democratic interests." Voters were, therefore, urged to desert the DDP and in doing so, "show the DVP . . . and Zentrum the way to the right, isolating the Social Democrats."[36] Polarization of the German electorate along class lines was the essence of the Nationalist campaign strategy in both elections of 1924.

While avoiding the inflammatory rhetoric of the DNVP, the campaigns of the German People's party were no less sharply focused on an exclusively middle-calss constituency. Social Democracy, therefore, served as the main target of DVP campaign strategy. The party repeatedly condemned the SPD as a signatory to the Treaty of Versailles and as a threat to the revitalization of the German economy. "The foundations that we have laid [for recovery] will be destroyed again," the DVP warned, "if radicalism and socialism rise to power. The left bloc will turn back the wheel of progress and once again drive the *Volk* into class conflict. . . . The German People's party decisively opposes these moves and, by its rejection of all attempts at socialization, will fight for a continuation of its policy of construction and recovery."[37]

The DVP certainly reproached the Nationalists for their obstructionist tactics in foreign affairs, but Stresemann's party clearly preferred an extension of the government toward the right over a return to cooperation with the SPD. Reflecting this rightward reorientation, the DVP enthusiastically championed the cause of bourgeois unity during the fall campaign. Concerned about the appeal of middle-class special interest parties, the DVP repeatedly assailed single-issue politics for "bringing confusion into the bourgeois camp."[38] A vote for special interest or regional parties, the DVP warned, "merely strengthens Social Democracy and weakens the national cause."[39] The consolidation of Germany's foreign and domestic position, the DVP contended, could be attained "only by a true victory of the bourgeois parties, with the exclusion of the Democrats, whose recent behavior can no longer be considered *bürgerlich*."[40] Thus, while urging moderation in foreign affairs and condemning the Marxist concept of class conflict on the domestic scene, the campaigns of the DVP in 1924 were not designed to minimize existing sociopolitical divisions within the Weimar state but to extract maximum electoral value from them.

No less dependent on an essentially middle-class constituency than the DNVP and DVP, the German Democratic party nevertheless refused to adopt the socially divisive electoral strategy employed by its bourgeois rivals. "The raison d'être of our party," one prominent Democrat explained, "is to prevent the disintegration of our people into two great groups. We feel it our responsibility to build bridges between segments of the people that otherwise threaten to split apart."[41] Although the DDP unequivocally rejected socialism and directed its campaign almost exclusively at elements of the middle-class electorate, it objected vehemently to the "*Bürgerblock* or socialism" dichotomy propounded by the DNVP and DVP.[42] "Nothing can be more ruinous," Hans Delbrück wrote in a campaign letter addressed to independent voters, "than the schism of the *Volk* into *Bürgerblock* and proletariat." In order to develop Germany's great potential, he concluded, "parties are demanded that strive to mediate between natural social conflicts."[43]

In response to the charges of sabotaging bourgeois unity, the Democrats countered that "by splitting the *Volk* into two camps," the DNVP and DVP "want to mobilize the bourgeoisie against the other strata of society."[44] This *Bürgerblock*, the DDP contended, did not even represent the legitimate interests of the middle class but instead advanced the demands of a "supercapitalism" dominated by big business and big agriculture. "The *Bürgerblock*," the Democratic *Berliner Tageblatt* maintained, "is ultimately nothing more than an attempt to stabilize this egotistical supercapitalism by parliamentary means. It is the bloc for protective tariffs, the bloc against the eight-hour workday, the bloc for shifting the burdens of reparations payments onto the masses, the bloc to prepare for the restoration, the reaction, and the old system."[45]

The DDP thus rejected the divisive vocabulary of class conflict, but, like its DNVP and DVP rivals, the German Democratic party was well aware of the social sources of its electoral support. Its campaigns were, therefore, addressed almost exclusively to self-employed proprietors, white-collar employees, and civil servants. Yet whereas the DNVP and DVP sought to emphasize social divisions, the campaigns of the DDP in 1924 aimed at educating its middle-class constituents in the ways of social conciliation and cooperation.

The *Mittelstand* to which these appeals were addressed was not, of course, a socioeconomic monolith. The strains and conflicts within that variegated class were perceived quite clearly by the parties of the bourgeois center and right, which competed vigorously for the vote of its various elements. Although emphasis varied predictably along ideological lines, these parties sought to address the specific interests and concerns of the *Mittelstand*'s major social and occupational groups. Campaign appeals were, therefore, directed specifically at the shopkeepers and craftsmen of the old middle class and the white-collar employees and civil servants of the new. While each party stressed issues of common middle-class concern, especially the fear of social and economic leveling popularly associated with the policies of the left, social differentiation according to occupational status characterized the campaigns of the bourgeois parties throughout the Weimar period. Correlations between party vote and occupational categories based on these contemporary distinctions are, therefore, crucial if the important variants of middle-class voting behavior are to be isolated.

The Old Middle Class

The vote of the old middle class can be most effectively analyzed by examining the three economic sectors in which self-employed proprietors were most heavily represented: handicrafts, commerce, and agriculture.[46] Having lost the benefits of the Empire's protective legislation, which had attempted to cushion the shocks of rapid industrialization by preserving the small shop and even the archaic guild system, handicrafts and commercial organizations viewed the Weimar system with antipathy almost from its inception. Small business interests were particularly outraged at what they considered to be systematic government discrimination against the small merchant and artisan both during and after the war. The republic's continuation of regulatory measures to curb prices and prevent profiteering, they maintained, had been applied almost exclusively to the small businessman whose swollen prices merely reflected his own spiraling overhead. Because of the rapidly rising cost of supplies, shopkeepers could never be sure of replenishing their stocks, regardless of the retail prices they charged. Factories were reluctant to sell to the domestic market for paper marks, and foreign goods could rarely be obtained. Under these circumstances, an extension of credit to customers, a common practice of small retailers before the war, was hardly feasible. "Shopkeepers," one consumer noted, "treated their customers almost as enemies—they deprived them of stock that could not be replaced."[47] Continuation of the wartime *Zwangswirtschaft*, merchants therefore complained, left the small shopkeeper exposed to government harassment and consumer hostility while big business and big labor received preferential treatment.

This grim litany of *Mittelstand* grievances was repeated with mounting shrillness as the postwar inflation escalated into hyperinflation in 1922–23. The savings of the small merchant and artisan had been lost and retirement funds depleted, handicrafts publications contended, while operating costs rose and sources of credit dwindled drastically. Moreover, while the republican regime ignored the plight of the small shopkeeper, large department stores and consumer cooperatives were claiming an ever-increasing share of the retail market. As a result, small shops, one typical artisan journal lamented, were being forced "to close and their proprietors compelled to seek work as day laborers in factories."[48]

The stabilization of the economy in late 1923 did not bring the relief demanded by artisan and retail interests. In fact, the onset of stabilization greatly exacerbated the already precarious position of small business. On 7 April 1924, the Reichsbank announced a policy of restricted credit, and its effects were almost immediately apparent. The number of bankruptcy petitions soared, rising by 160 percent from the final quarter of 1923 through the first quarter of 1924, and the trend continued unabated into the following year. Indeed, more bankruptcies were filed in 1924 than in the five previous years combined, and more than half of these reflected failures of small businesses or private persons, primarily in the commercial sector. During 1923 fewer than two hundred bankruptcies had been recorded in commerce, whereas in 1924 the total reached almost four thousand.[49] "Countless craftsmen have lost their independence," the State Commission of Saxon Handicrafts glumly reported, "and many more are on the verge of collapse. If this trend is not halted, the commercial middle class will vanish in the foreseeable future as a stratum of conciliation in the life of our people and state."[50]

The resentment of these small shopkeepers and craftsmen was perhaps best expressed by the owner of a small organ-making shop, who in his disaffection with the Weimar government turned to National Socialism:

> With a great deal of work I succeeded in getting a few contracts, but all my hopes were in vain. The inflation put an abrupt end to all my efforts. I could no longer pay my people and my assets dissolved. Hunger and deprivation moved in with us. I cursed a regime that permitted such misery, for I had the feeling that an inflation of these dimensions was not necessary. . . . But the objective was attained. The *Mittelstand* that was still modestly prosperous was wiped out—that middle class that was still the enemy

of Marxism, even though it hadn't the faintest chance of fighting successfully.[51]

This hostility toward the Weimar system was loudly amplified by handicrafts and commercial organizations representing small business. Although their antipathy was clearly inspired by immediate and very real economic hardship, it found its most programmatic political expression in an anticapitalist, antisocialist, corporatist critique that not only condemned prevailing economic conditions but assaulted the very foundations of the republic's economic and political order. Formulated in a traditional corporatist vocabulary that tirelessly emphasized the role of the corporate estate (*Stand*) and called for political representation on an occupational basis, this critique of the Weimar system pervaded the literature of the major artisan and small business organizations throughout the Weimar era. While staunchly opposed to the socialist influences in the modern economy and in the new state, these groups were also outspoken in their condemnation of Weimar's supercapitalism. Many viewed the reorganization of the political and economic system along corporatist lines as the only effective means of reasserting the rights of small merchants while reducing the exorbitant influence of both big business and big labor.[52] The goal, as one prominent spokesman for the handicrafts movement put it, was "to establish . . . a liberated and ordered economic system in place of the brutal, egotistical free economy and in place of class struggle."[53]

More than any other party, the National Socialists forcefully articulated these middle-class resentments during the campaigns of 1924. Their electoral appeals, stated in a variety of forms, consistently stressed the necessity of protecting the interests of the small shopkeeper and self-employed artisan against the perils of both Marxist socialism and finance capitalism. Like the traditional parties of the bourgeois center and right, the DVFP/NSFB prominently condemned Social Democracy and demanded Germany's "emancipation from Marxism and bolshevism with their un-German class hatred."[54] Yet unlike the liberal and conservative parties, the Nazis directed their main assault not against the Marxist left but on the "pernicious threat" posed by the influence of "finance capital." The rapidly deteriorating condition of the old middle class was, in fact, seen by the *völkisch* coalition as a symptom of a greater malaise infecting German society. The German people, the Nazis contended, were being divided into hostile camps by the machinations of international finance capital. The proletarianization of the *Mittelstand* and the resultant class antagonisms were the direct result of the "domination of international Jewry and stock-market capital" over postwar Germany. "The social question," Nazi propaganda argued, had "reached its present divisive and disastrous sharpness primarily through the work of international *Grosskapital*."[55]

In this deplorable situation, the other parties were unable to help small business because the parties to which the *Mittelstand* had traditionally turned were "capitalist-oriented" and therefore did "not even think of going after the trouble at its root."[56] The artisan and merchant could be "liberated from big capital" only by "breaking interest slavery." But, the Nazis complained, "all the so-called bourgeois parties—the Democrats, the DVP, the DNVP—refuse to abolish capitalism. . . . They are all supporters of big capitalism and their leaders are inextricably tied to this system." As a result, these traditional parties could "never solve the social problem and eradicate class hatred." The end of class conflict would arrive only with the establishment of a true *Volksgemeinschaft* in which social divisions would dissolve and all Germans, regardless of their former class, would "feel bound to the fate of the *Volk*."[57] However, this people's community, the Nazis warned, would necessitate the implementation of "fundamental, earthshaking economic reforms." Ultimately, the principle of *Gemeinnutz vor Eigennutz* ("the common good before the individual good") would prevail in the *völkisch* state and "the profit economy" would be replaced by "an economy based on need" (*Bedarfswirtschaft*).[58]

Perhaps to allay the fears provoked by this vague radical rhetoric, the *völkisch* coalition prominently endorsed the principle of private property, praising it as the "foundation of culture." Yet even this pledge of support was qualified. "Cartels, syndicates, and trusts," the DVFP's electoral platform declared, "will be fought as unsocial."[59] Similarly, Nazi propaganda sought to distinguish between "creative" and "parasitic" capital, the former being the product of "honest labor" and hence German, whereas the latter was the fruit of unproductive interest and therefore Jewish. While parasitic capital would be fought ruthlessly, capital "that generates values," the Nazis rather opaquely explained, would be protected in the future *völkisch* state. To break the deadly hold of international Jewish finance capital, the DVFP platform demanded the abolition of all income derived without work, the closing of all stock exchanges, an end to speculation, and the nationalization of the banks.[60]

Yet while maintaining this unrelenting assault on the capitalist system of the new republic, the thrust of Nazi propaganda was usually directed quite carefully at the influence of "Jewish," "international," or "interest" capital. Indeed, economic anti-Semitism was perhaps the most salient feature of National Socialist anticapitalism in 1924. In Nazi appeals to artisans and merchants, Jews were identified with those aspects of modern capitalism most repugnant to the old middle class—big business, the banks, and of course, the department stores. "Today," the Nazis charged, "the greatest economic power resides in the hands of the Jews who possess a strong worldwide network. Since the war all Jews have become rich."[61] According to *völkisch* campaign literature, the German *Mittelstand*, in particular, had suffered as a result of this Jewish conspiracy. "The Jews are the beneficiaries of our misery," one typical National Socialist pamphlet declared. "They stuff their pockets with gigantic profits from swindles in paper currency. With the aid of their banks they exploit us shamelessly through the most contemptible interest usury of all times. They destroy industry, commerce, and agriculture, create horrible unemployment, confiscate apartments and houses, and laugh at the stupidity of the Germans who repeatedly allow themselves to be divided politically into different parties."[62] Moreover, the other parties were merely fronts for this conspiracy, the Nazis charged, since "from the German Nationalists to the most radical leftists" the political parties of the Weimar Republic were either "led by Jews" or were "dependent on international Jewish finance capital."[63]

The *völkisch* coalition, on the other hand, was committed to combating this alleged threat, and as a result, the Nazis asserted, it had already attracted the support of "masses of artisans and merchants." This outpouring of middle-class support for National Socialism, the party maintained, was not only because of "the feeling that the *völkisch* movement . . . is fighting with all its might against the proletarianization of the *Mittelstand* but also because of the practical objectives that it has articulated for the recovery of these strata."[64]

What were these practical objectives? First, and most prominently, the party attacked the department stores and the presumed threat they posed to traditional small businesses. "Department stores," the Nazis declared, had "already robbed many honest merchants of their livelihood," and should be dissolved without delay.[65] In addition, the *völkisch* coalition demanded that government be compelled to diversify its spending, assuring small business of a larger share of public contracts. The party's platform also called for the revocation of the government's "unsocial" profiteering ordinances which, the Nazis charged, "always hit the small shop but leave big business untouched." The party also condemned the existing tax structure, especially the sales and profits taxes which, they maintained, "strangle handicrafts and commerce." Government tax policy represented nothing short of "tax bolshevism," leading to the systematic impoverishment of the German *Mittelstand*. Finally, the DVFP promised to abolish the existing structure of parliamentary representation, "which has no interest in small business," and to replace it with a corporative system based on representation by occupation. Under this new *völkisch* system, the Nazis insisted, "the once-flourishing . . . guilds and traditional corporations" would be reestablished in "a healthy environment" and would "flourish once again."[66]

In their appeals to the old middle class, the major bourgeois parties sounded similar themes, though predictably in less radical terms. The Nationalists, for example, employed a rhetorical vocabulary similar to that of the Nazis, claiming that by voting DNVP, "German craftsmen can be certain they will not be led between the crushing millstones of international *Grosskapital* or Jewish socialism."[67] Similarly, the DDP condemned "the excesses of the cartels and syndicates," while the DVP denounced the eight-hour day, called for an end to emergency profiteering ordinances, and advocated a program to revive activity in the construction trades.[68] Yet in spite of these appeals, the *völkisch* coalition made significant inroads into the middle-class constituencies of the liberal and conservative parties.

When multivariate regression techniques are used to examine the 1920–24 elections in the urban communities of the sample,[69] a strong, positive relationship clearly emerges between liberal voting and the old middle class. The figures of both the DVP and DDP are even stronger when the old middle class in handicrafts and retail trade is isolated. Though lower than the liberal figures, the DNVP-handicrafts/retail coefficients are also strong for the 1920 election, reflecting a significant liberal-conservative cleavage in the first Reichstag campaign of the republic. Between 1920 and 1924, however, the relationship between both liberal and conservative voting and the old middle class in handicrafts and retail trade deteriorates sharply, while the National Socialist coefficients for the May election are quite high. Indeed, of the various socio-occupational variables considered in the urban sample, the old middle class in handicrafts and retail trade proves to be the most powerful predictor of the Nazi vote in 1924. As the figures of Table 2.3 reveal, that relationship weakens for the December election, but while the liberal figures rebound strongly, the conservative coefficients significantly do not. Indeed, in this urban sample, the liberal-conservative cleavage of 1920 had been replaced by a liberal-*völkisch* division in 1924.

Integrating these statistical indicators with the other evidence considered above, it seems that both the DVP and DDP possessed a relatively solid base of support within the urban old middle class in 1920. In the

Table 2.3. Party Vote and the Old Middle Class (OMC), 1920–1924

	Protestant (N=152)			Catholic (N=64)		
	1920	1924a	1924b	1920	1924a	1924b
NSDAP	NA	.421	−.569*	NA	−.723	−.351
DNVP	.210	−.612	−.319	−1.09	−1.41	−1.64
DVP	.386	.281	.392	.838	.725	.853
DDP	.417	.315	.236	1.01	.540	.627
Z	.106*	.112*	.066*	−.290*	.775	.209
SPD	−.165	.212*	−.639	−.435	−.266	−.427
KPD	−.255	−.455	−.346	−.908	−.357	−.261
Other	−.119*	−.128	−.240	−.754	.117	−.269

OMC in Handicrafts[a]

	Protestant (N=152)			Catholic (N=64)		
	1920	1924a	1924b	1920	1924a	1924b
NSDAP	NA	.927	.368	NA	−1.15	−.389
DNVP	.554	−.591	−.616	−2.16	−2.26	−2.80
DVP	.292	.247	.459	−.102*	.967	1.22
DDP	.589	.472	.424	1.89	1.03	1.52
Z	.218*	.234*	.190*	−.491*	1.79	.753
SPD	−1.35	−.577	−.469	−.425	−1.26	−.682
KPD	−.515	−.451	−.199	−1.29	−2.53	−1.85
Other	−.899	−.400*	.310*	−1.01	.117*	−.277

OMC in Commerce[a]

	Protestant (N=152)			Catholic (N=64)		
	1920	1924a	1924b	1920	1924a	1924b
NSDAP	NA	1.66	.204	NA	.454	2.44
DNVP	−1.21	−1.24	−.557	−2.33	−2.96	−1.85
DVP	.206	−.154*	.129*	.441	−.922	−.261
DDP	−.634	−.762	−.267	.503	−.624	−.755
Z	−.232*	−.286*	−.359	−1.49	−2.14	−3.56
SPD	−3.84	−2.80	−2.25	−.261	−.158	−.206*
KPD	−.674	−1.71	−1.81	−1.15	−.781	−.885
Other	.310*	−.507*	.807	−1.01	−.453	−.759

Table 2.3. (continued)

| | OMC in Agriculture[a,b] | | | | | |
| | Protestant (N=121) | | | Catholic (N=125) | | |
	1920	1924a	1924b	1920	1924a	1924b
NSDAP	NA	.519	.136	NA	.811	.362
DNVP	.417	.861	.372	−.976	−.222	−.111
DVP	.388	−.125	.106*	.166	.600	.468
DDP	.386	.164	.220	.168	.929	.656
Z	.112*	.151*	.141*	1.43	1.85	.907
SPD	−.292	−.359	−.825	−.469	−.230	−.537
KPD	−.278	−.193	−.216	−.106*	−.454	−.191
Other	.382	.346	.289	−1.66*	.146*	.201*

NOTE: The figures are unstandardized regression coefficients (b), controlling for new middle class, *Rentnermittelstand*, blue-collar workers, religion, and urbanization (population size).
a. Presents coefficients for the OMC by economic sector, controlling for the OMC in all other economic sectors in addition to those variables listed above.
b. Size of farm has also been controlled.

* These coefficients are not significant at the .05 level.

turbulent wake of the inflation and stabilization crises, the liberal parties, compromised by their participation in the unpopular governments of the period, suffered some crisis-related defections. The primary victim of Nazi success within the urban old middle class, however, appears to have been the conservative DNVP. In 1920, the Nationalists, like the DVP, had benefited from small business discontent with the socialist-left-liberal government and from more general antirepublican sentiments within elements of the old middle class. The DNVP, however, was still prominently associated with agricultural interests, and hence high food prices for urban dwellers. Thus, as the economic situation deteriorated in 1922–23 and competition from the National Socialists mounted, the DNVP was unable to solidify its role as a rallying point for antirepublican protest within the urban old middle class. Based on the figures in Table 2.3, it therefore appears that during this period of acute economic distress, protest voters from the troubled liberal electorate augmented the traditionally conservative, antirepublican irreconcilables within the old middle class to form the core of National Socialist electoral support in 1924. A significant variation of this pattern emerges, however, when one turns from the city to the countryside. Like the artisans and shopkeepers of the urban old middle class, farmers had been wary of the new republic from the very outset. Although peasant councils had been established in some areas during the revolution, farmers had played a relatively passive role in the events of 1918–19.[70] Traditionally hostile to Social Democracy, peasant attitudes toward the new government were also shaped by very pragmatic issues, by the republic's handling of the postwar economy and especially the decision to continue the hated wartime controls on agriculture. Small-holding peasants and estate owners, who already felt that their interests had been sacrificed in order to feed the urban consumer during the war, were united in their contempt for the *Zwangswirtschaft* and were outraged by the republic's insistence on maintaining it. Although the first postwar Social Democratic governments were keenly aware of this sentiment, the continuation of the Allied blockade until mid-1919, the loss of approximately 15 percent of Germany's agricultural land in the Versailles settlement, and the disappointing harvests of 1918–19 meant that the end of hostilities had by no means brought an end to Germany's food problems. To the SPD-dominated cabinets of 1919–20, continued regulation seemed the only viable solution. Thus, the audits, inspections, price ceilings, and seizures were perpetuated under the new regime, poisoning relations between the Weimar authorities—especially the SPD—and much of the rural population.[71]

Yet, while Germany's farmers chafed under government regulation until mid-1920 and were faced with continued levies on grain until 1923, the inflationary policies of the new regime had beneficial effects on the agricultural sector. In the first years of the inflation, those farmers with any business acumen used the depreciation of the currency to pay off mortgages in highly inflated paper marks and to liquidate other long-standing debts. With easy credit and abundant cash on hand, many proprietors undertook the modernization of their farms, purchasing machinery, introducing electrical power, and generally upgrading the physical condition of their holdings. These practical endeavors were often accompanied by extraordinary splurges on luxury items such as pianos, as some farmers sought to improve their standard of living and to hedge against inflation through a "flight into possessions."[72]

Still, the economic picture for German farmers was at best mixed as the inflation gathered momentum during 1922. Prices for agricultural goods failed to keep pace with those of commercial and industrial products, and while some farmers had invested wisely, many, especially small farmers, had engaged in unprofitable stock-market speculation or simply hoarded increasingly worthless paper marks. Moreover, while industry and much of the commercial sector had begun converting all transactions to gold values by early 1923, most agricultural business, especially on small and medium-sized farms, was still done with paper marks. Many farmers were, therefore, not only losing ground during the hyperinflation, they were to be among the first serious victims of stabilization in late 1923 and early 1924.[73]

The first step toward stabilization of the currency was taken in the summer of 1923 when the Reich government announced that henceforth all income-tax payments were to be made according to gold values. Farmers, still accepting paper marks for their goods, were, therefore, caught short. Those who had already sold part of their harvests for inflated paper currency before stabilization were now forced to dump their remaining goods at cut-rate prices in order to buy seed, fertilizer, and other necessities for the coming year. Losses from such sales in paper marks were estimated at 40 percent for the 1923 harvest.[74] This, however, was only the first blow that stabilization would inflict. To generate additional government revenue, the cabinet also altered the established method of assessing real property, immediately raising the tax liability of all landowners. In addition, a special financial charge on land was introduced to back the government's new stabilized currency, the *Rentenmark*. This measure amounted to a forced remortgaging of land in short-term, high-interest *Rentenmark* credits and was greatly resented by farmers who felt that once again they were being singled out to bear a disproportionately heavy burden in the government's search for economic and social stability. Nor was this dissatisfaction without foundation. When the final tax legislation of the stabilization period had been enacted—under emergency decree—in early 1924, it was estimated that the tax burden carried by the agricultural sector had tripled since 1913.[75]

As operating costs and tax obligations mounted for German farmers, agricultural prices began to fall. Stabilization brought to an end the artificial protection of the domestic farm market that inflationary conditions had created. As a result, agricultural imports rose sharply, leading to a collapse of farm prices between November 1923 and the summer of 1924. At the same time, the government's restriction of credit merely exacerbated the mounting economic woes of the farm proprietor. Although the Reichsbank did act to make special credits available to agriculture in 1924, these credits were inadequate to meet the pressing short-term needs of German farmers. Inflation had eliminated the reserves of the agricultural credit cooperatives, the traditional source of loans to small farmers before 1914, and with stabilization these organizations were forced to turn to the central banks for funds. Given the risks inherent in agricultural production, interest rates for short-term loans lurched suddenly upward, soaring to four times their prewar level. Nor did farmers feel that these loans could be used to make capital improvements on the land. Instead, they were needed to meet daily production costs, to pay taxes, and to make interest payments on the loans themselves.[76] In this rapidly deteriorating situation, some agricultural spokesmen were already warning of "a new agricultural crisis" when the Reichstag campaign got underway in the spring.[77]

As the battle for the farm vote unfolded in 1924, it became quickly apparent that little of real significance separated the major nonsocialist parties in their approach to the problems confronting the agricultural sector. Between 1919 and 1924 all had pledged their commitment to a "strong and healthy German peasantry"; had lambasted socialism in all its forms; praised private enterprise; endorsed, without enthusiasm, vague schemes for land reform and resettlement; deeply regretted the continuation of the *Zwangswirtschaft*; promised relief from the crushing burdens of taxation; and hoped to provide new credit to financially strapped peasantry. Each sought ties with agricultural interest groups, and each hoped to expand its constituency by systematically appealing to the rural voter.[78]

Yet, in this struggle, the DNVP enjoyed very real advantages. As heirs to the agrarian, conservative heritage of the imperial era, the Nationalists could point to a long tradition of pro-farm activity and could count on the support of the most important of the postwar agricultural interest organizations, the Reich Agrarian League (Reichslandbund—RLB). It possessed a strong territorial base east of the Elba and, because of its close association with the Lutheran Church, found additional support in the countryside all across Protestant northern Germany. Perhaps most important, however, the DNVP was not a "system party." It had not participated in any of the postwar governments that had extended agricultural controls, and it had remained the most vocal advocate of tariff protection for German farm products.[79]

Despite these advantages, the DNVP encountered a number of obstacles on the path to the rural vote. The heritage of the old conservatives was, after all, hardly an unmixed blessing. Although the party was determined to broaden its rural—and urban—base, the DNVP discovered that it was hard to shake its inherited image as the party of big, grain-producing agriculture. Moreover, the party could not count on the nationwide grass-roots organizational work of the BdL, whose greatly diminished stature with the new republican authorities was apparent to all. In the altered circumstances of republican Germany, the Bund, traditionally the most powerful advocate of agricultural interests, simply could not match the influence of either industry or labor, and in early 1921, it merged with a number of regional farm organizations to form the RLB.[80] Although the leadership of this new organization remained close to the DNVP and to east Elbian grain interests, its structure was highly decentralized. Forced to compete with regional organizations such as the Schleswig-Holstein Bauernverein and the Hessische Volksbund, the Catholic Bauernvereine in the south and west, and the liberally oriented German Peasants' League (Deutscher Bauernbund—DBb), the RLB did not prove to be the effective instrument of peasant mobilization that the BdL had been before 1914.[81]

This rivalry between the various rural *Interessenverbände* closely paralleled the DNVP's mounting difficulties with regional peasant parties between 1919 and 1924. Some, such as the Bavarian Peasants' party, had roots in the Empire; others, such as the Mecklenburg Village League, had been founded after the war. Regardless of origin, all emerged with considerable vigor under the republic's system of proportional representation, greatly complicating Nationalist rural strategy. It was in the countryside that regional parties enjoyed their greatest success, even those without an explicitly agricultural orientation. Indeed, among no other group in the electorate was regionalism a more potent political force than among the peasantry.[82]

If these regional parties were obstacles to the antidemocratic DNVP, they were hardly solid props of the Weimar system. Despite some differences in emphasis, all were fanatically antisocialist, associating the new parliamentary system with domination by the SPD and urban consumer interests. Many were anti-Semitic, identifying Jews with the banks and the nefarious "forces of international finance" that were presumably behind the ruinous taxation and the mounting threat of foreclosure. Although all had clamored for an end to the *Zwangswirtschaft* and a return to "free enterprise," virtually all endorsed some form of corporatist economic order that would revive the influence of agriculture in national economic life and restore the traditionally honored position of the *Bauernstand* in German society. These views were even shared to some degree by the generally more moderate Catholic Bauernvereine, whose staunch opposition to Marxism, reservations about parliamentary democracy, and interest in some form of corporatist economic order caused serious tensions within the Zentrum.[83] A vote for a regional party was, therefore, more than an endorsement of federalism or a political expression of *Heimatliebe*. By 1924 it represented a clear rejection of big labor, big business, and the centralized state that secured the preeminence of both.

Given these sentiments and the regional divisions of interest within the peasantry, it was hardly surprising that the DNVP chose to downplay specific economic proposals and focus on precisely these "threats to the German *Bauernstand*" in its rural campaigns of 1924. The party, of course, continued to demand tariff protection and tax reforms for farmers, but the central thrust of its *Wahlpropaganda* was directed *against* the Socialists, the banks, the Jews, and the urban liberals who cooperated with all of them. "Whether estate owner or small peasant, both are threatened by the antiagrarian policies of the black–red–yellow parties," the DNVP charged in a typical appeal to farmers in 1924. "If you don't give your vote to the Nationalists, then you can't be surprised if the Jewish, consumer viewpoint wins the upper hand and leads to the ruin of agriculture."[84]

The two liberal parties, of course, could not indulge in this sort of inflammatory rhetoric. Both voiced their commitment to some form of tax relief, to nebulous resettlement plans, and laid the blame for the hated *Zwangswirtschaft* squarely on the SPD.[85] By 1924, however, both parties had been coalition partners of the Social Democrats and both shared some responsibility for the unpopular legislation of the inflation and early stabilization periods. The DDP, in particular, suffered from its close association with the Social Democrats, both in the Reich government and in Prussia. Even the DVP warned rural voters that the Democrats had "for ages viewed agriculture with distance and hostility," and in a thinly veiled reference to the DDP's prominent connections to the Jewish community, reminded farmers of the "commercial standpoint" and "cosmopolitan character" of the pro-Democratic press . . . the *Berliner Tageblatt* and the *Frankfurter Zeitung*.[86] In 1920 less than 5 percent of the DDP's vote had come from towns with fewer than two thousand inhabitants,[87] and the party was acutely aware of its marginal appeal in the countryside. Moreover, the DDP's alliance with the moderate German Farmers' League (DBb), an organization representing small and medium-sized farming in the west-northwest, had broken down by 1924, a casualty of precisely these urban-rural tensions within the party's interest structure. The DDP, in short, was far too closely identified with urban interests to sustain a major constituency in the countryside.[88]

While the DVP shared some of these same handicaps, the party nonetheless hoped to offer an alternative to those moderate rural voters for whom the Democrats were too progressive and the Nationalists too reactionary. It maintained ties to the DBb and to a number of regional affiliates of the RLB, primarily in north-central Germany.[89] In its appeals to farmers in 1924, the party cited its support for the termination of the *Zwangswirtschaft* in 1920, its opposition to Social Democratic efforts at socialization, and, ironically, its role in securing the Dawes Plan. While the DNVP, the Nazis, and the various peasant parties attacked the plan, seeing in its acceptance the specter of even greater taxation, the DVP presented it to rural voters as a solution to the agricultural credit crisis. Since German industry absorbed so much domestic credit, squeezing agriculture out of that market, foreign sources were needed. By providing foreign capital to German industry, the Dawes Plan would ease pressure on domestic credit sources, freeing much-needed funds for agriculture.[90] This line of argumentation, of course, only drew greater attention to the DVP's close association with industry, and the party felt it had to warn farm voters against the dangers of narrow interest voting: "Agriculture can only flourish in peaceful cooperation with other occupational estates [*Berufsstände*]. Compromise is in the best interests of agriculture, which needs *the parliamentary support of other groups*. A further escalation of interest conflict within the *Volk* only raises the danger of a civil war, in which the countryside would be particularly vulnerable."[91]

A somewhat similar image problem also haunted the National Socialists in their campaign for the rural electorate. The Nazis had long embraced the *völkisch* view of the peasantry, idealizing its simple folk virtues, its organic relationship with the soil, its faith in the *Volk*, and its loyalty to the fatherland, but aside from a call for colonization in the east, the party's official program was remarkably silent about agriculture.[92] Moreover, in the years between 1919 and 1924, the party had repeatedly found it necessary to reassure peasants about its views on socialism and private property. Farmers should not be concerned about the "socialism" of the party, the NSDAP had typically explained in 1922. "You are thinking of the false Jewish socialism (Marxism) of the Sozis and Communists. National Socialism expressly recognizes private property but demands that every producer subordinate his private interests to the interests of the German *Volksgemeinschaft*. For you, dear farmer, that means the following: As long as you manage your holdings as a responsible [*pflichttreue Wirt*] farmer, your holdings will remain untouched and in good standing. But if you allow your farm to fall into waste and rot, then a better German should take your place."[93] To farmers who already felt harassed by the Marxist left, the banks, and the government, this sort of rhetoric could hardly have been reassuring.

If the *völkisch* coalition had little to offer in practical terms, it did address iteslf to the very real and pressing problems confronting agriculture in 1924. In particular, the Nazis emphasized the harsh impact of stabilization, especially the heavy tax burden imposed on farmers. The peasantry had been duped by the bourgeois parties responsible for stabilization, the Nazis argued. While the inflation had been bad, a criminal device "used by Jews on the Berlin stock market to plunder all honest and hardworking *Stände*," stabilization had been even worse. The very same bourgeois parties that had promised relief from economic turmoil and had "made so many fine speeches about a free peasant corporate estate [*Bauernstand*]" were now ruining farmers with their policy of stabilization and high taxes. "Last year everyone was clamoring for the stabilization of the currency and even you, farmer, rejoiced when the *Rentenmark* brought a temporary end to inflation. But at what price? . . . Gradually, you are sensing that times have not gotten better. Instead, you feel the prosperity you had attained over the past few years has suddenly vanished." Just ask yourself, the Nazis prodded their peasant audience, "are you better off today than you were then?" [94]

Playing on the deep peasant resentment over the increased taxes and dwindling sources of credit for agriculture, the Nazis predicted dire consequences if farm indebtedness was allowed to climb. "It is obvious that you can't carry these burdens for long," the Nazis commiserated with farmers. "You receive much less for your products than the prewar prices but have to pay double the earlier gold price for industrial goods. This is unbearable, especially in conjunction with the tax burdens you have to shoulder." [95] Given the increased taxation and forced mortgages to support the *Rentenbank*, the specter of bankruptcy, foreclosure, and expropriation loomed on the horizon. "When at some point in the future you can no longer get enough for livestock and grain to make a living and you can't pay your taxes," the Nazis warned, "the mortgage Jews" will "come . . . and take your farm for the bank." [96]

Behind this systematic impoverishment of the *Bauernstand*, the Nazis declared, were the forces of international Jewish capitalism and their puppets in the German party system. Together they had swindled the German people on a colossal scale during the inflation and in the ongoing process of stabilization, but with the Dawes Plan, the Nazis charged, "international Jewish capital is preparing to burden the German economy with forced mortgages so immense that our present tax obligations will seem like child's play in comparison. What will remain of the farmer when three fourths of his property belongs to international Jewry? Agriculture already stands in the midst of a monstrous crisis. If it collapses, we will have a hunger revolution in which no farm is safe because the reds recognize no law." [97]

The urban-rural tension, so obvious in the campaigns of the liberal parties, was attributed in National Socialist propaganda to the Jews and their representatives in the "Dawes parties." According to the Nazis,

"They are the same men and parties who stand behind Jewish whole-salers and protect them." These Jewish middlemen "don't pay the peasant anything [for his products] but take money out of the pockets of the citydweller, turning each against the other."[98] In National Socialist propaganda anti-Semitism was, therefore, intended to bridge the yawning urban-rural cleavage that plagued the other parties, allowing the NSDAP to extend its constituency on both sides of that divide.

The figures of Table 2.3, however, strongly suggest that this Nazi effort to woo disgruntled peasants had only marginal success. The Nazi/old-middle-class coefficients are far lower in the rural counties than in the urban sample, even for the May election. The conservative figures, on the other hand, are predictably high in the countryside, registering substantial gains over their 1920 levels. The DNVP/old-middle-class relationship is, as suspected, far stronger in the rural Protestant sample than in the cities. The liberal coefficients, however, drop in 1924, especially in May, and remain low in December as well. *Völkisch* gains in the countryside may have resulted from the defection of disenchanted liberal voters or former conservatives radicalized by the economic jolts of late 1923–24. With the current state of statistical methodology, measuring crossovers in a complex multiparty system is a hazardous proposition at best. However, given the pronounced slippage of the liberal/old-middle-class figures, the gains of the DNVP, and even the modest National Socialist showing, it seems clear that the rural base of liberal support had seriously eroded by 1924, as peasants moved to either the traditional right, a special interest party, or the *völkisch* fringes.

The elections of 1924, therefore, represent an important transitional stage in the evolution of voting preferences in the old middle class. For destabilization of electoral patterns within that group, traditionally associated with the period from 1928 to 1933, had clearly begun well before the severe economic contraction of the depression years. Although it would be an oversimplification to suggest that artisans, retailers, and peasants had been irrevocably radicalized by the dislocations of inflation and stabilization, their identification with the traditional representatives of bourgeois politics had been profoundly shaken. A comparison of the May and December coefficients indicates that a shift from the *völkisch* movement toward its more moderate rivals was already underway before the close of 1924, but voting patterns within the old middle class did not revert to the traditional liberal-conservative cleavage so evident in 1920. Galvanized by the crises of 1923–24, disaffected elements of the old middle class turned from the traditional parties of bourgeois center and right toward new alternatives. The numerous splinter parties obviously attracted many of these discontented voters, but the fractious *völkisch* coalition was by far the most successful among them. Although the popularity of National Socialism sank as the year progressed, that dwindling appeal did not redound to the benefit of the traditional representatives of the *Mittelstand*, even in the ensuing period of economic recovery. As the elections of 1928 would confirm, the disaffection with both liberal and conservative options that surfaced within the old middle class in May 1924 was not merely the product of transient economic distress, but the result of congenital dissatisfaction with the long-term structural trends in the German economy.

The *Rentnermittelstand*

A similar breakdown of the 1920 socioelectoral pattern occured among the pensioners, widows, disabled veterans, small investors, and others who depended on fixed incomes for their livelihood. Together these groups formed what was commonly referred to as the *Rentnermittelstand*, a segment of the German middle class traditionally considered to be the most salient victim of the inflation and stabilization crises. While some propertyowners undoubtedly benefited from the nullification of debts and some high-income entrepreneurs also profited from inflation speculation, the dramatic depreciation of the currency reduced many creditors, holders of fixed-interest securities, and recipients of insurance payments from private companies to virtual poverty. As savings evaporated, retirement funds dwindled, and government bonds were drained of value, a groundswell of discontent mounted among the small investors, the disabled, the elderly, and other pensioners suddenly deprived of their economic security.[99]

Among those most drastically affected by the inflation were millions of small investors and savers who had regularly set aside a significant portion of their income in private savings, government and municipal bonds, or other capital assets. With the disintegration of the currency in 1922–23, these investments, often representing the assiduous saving of a lifetime, were reduced to a mere fraction of their anticipated value. The enduring bitterness engendered by this situation was expressed by one angry man—a convert to National Socialism—as he described how his parents lost everything during the inflation: "Their savings at the bank, all their money dissolved into nothing. In addition, their home of many years went to strangers—sold for the price of a pound of butter—and they were simply thrown out onto the street. The realization that they had lost everything my father had worked for in his whole life put my parents in an early grave. It was absolutely inconceivable to the old people that the bundles of bills in their hands were simply worthless."[100]

As the situation deteriorated, a number of pressure groups were organized to prevent complete financial ruin and to bring pressure on government to protect the interests of creditors, savers, and investors. By the close of 1922 these regionally organized groups had formed a national organization, the Association of Mortagees and Savers, to prevent continued repayment of loans and mortgages in devalued currency and to achieve a revalorization of those debts already liquidated in worthless paper marks.[101]

The Reich government, however, continued to insist that "a mark equals a mark," denying any distinction between the gold mark of prewar transactions and the inflated paper mark employed to liquidate current financial obligations. In November 1923, the German Supreme Court rejected this interpretation, arguing that the government's policy was in conflict with the principles of "Trust and Good Faith" found in the German Civil Code. This decision forced the government's hand. Hoping to avoid massive legal proceedings that would have delayed economic recovery, the Marx government began consideration of a law to effect a revaluation settlement. The bill that emerged from these deliberations limited revaluation of private paper mark debts to 15 percent of their original gold mark value and exempted all government obligations from any revaluation until after the reparations issue had been resolved. Under this legislation, those debts that had already been settled were not affected, and settlement of outstanding obligations was postponed until January 1932. Realizing that this scheme would encounter considerable opposition, the Marx government presented the bill to the public in the Third Emergency Tax Decree of 24 February 1924. By incorporating it in this emergency decree, the Reich government insured that the revalorization settlement went into effect under the Enabling Act of 8 December 1923, which allowed its implementation without approval by the Reichstag.[102]

Predictably, the Third Emergency Tax Decree outraged the pensioner and small-investor interests that had been organizing for over a year. During the spring campaign, leaders of the various regional organizations persistently courted the major bourgeois parties, seeking support for a revocation of the decree. When, however, the newly elected Reichstag failed to rescind the measure, the revalorization movement hatched two fledgling political parties to campaign for creditor and saver interests in the fall. While the influential Association of Mortgagees and

Savers continued to function as a pressure group, hoping to work within the existing party system, these new special interest parties were prepared to challenge their established rivals on the battlefield of electoral politics.[103] The bourgeois parties, they contended, had become the pawns of big business and big agriculture, promising much and delivering little. Only a party unfettered by obligations to these entrenched interests could represent the pensioners, savers, small investors, and other creditors devastated by the inflation and stabilization crises.[104]

Although these new parties alluded to the "betrayal of the inflation," both actually concentrated their electoral propaganda on the effects of stabilization. Indeed, the targeted constituency of both parties consisted of those creditors dissatisfied with the rate of revalorization specified in the Third Emergency Tax Decree. This orientation was made vividly explicit in the names adopted by the two: the Revalorization and Construction party and the Revalorization and Reconstruction party. In both cases, revocation of the decree served as the focal point of the campaign platform. Calling on the Reich government to honor the Supreme Court's decision, which seemed to imply full revalorization, the creditor parties blasted the Third Emergency Tax Decree as a "swindle without parallel in world history." With this irresponsible measure, the government had "driven the great mass of the people into distress, misery, and even despair." According to both parties, the decree was to blame for the severe contraction of capital and credit in 1924 and had ultimately destroyed "the will to save" within the German people. It not only represented a grave injustice but had contributed mightily to the deepening erosion of public confidence in government. The battle to abolish the decree, the revalorization parties solemnly declared, was therefore "a moral struggle for the reestablishment of morality and justice" in Germany.[105]

During the fall campaign neither party adopted an explicitly ideological posture, but both assailed the Weimar party system for its "divisiveness" and "incompetence." They also condemned heavy government spending, class struggle, and "all Bolshevist experiments," while castigating the bourgeois parties for accepting "the modern half-capitalist, half-communist economic system." The liberals and conservatives, the revalorization parties charged, were willing to tolerate this state of affairs "as long as things went well for a few big industrialists and big landowners." The government's claim that no funds were available for a full revalorization was simply a ruse to protect these interests. "There is money there," one revalorization party claimed. "Big industry, the big banks, and big agriculture are still available." While the government tarried, the assets of thousands of honest, hard-working Germans had "disappeared into the pockets . . . and accounts of big business." "Like wolves in the night, the agrarian and industrial magnates have fallen on the savings of the people," the party charged, "and many an immoral man has shamelessly enriched himself." [106]

The revalorization parties were poorly organized and poorly financed and their immediate impact on national politics in 1924 was minimal. However, the widespread creditor resentment they hoped to mobilize did play a significant role in the campaigns of 1924, as more established parties clamored to exploit that dissatisfaction. The *völkisch* coalition, in particular, mounted a major campaign offensive to attract a constituency among these disaffected pensioners and savers. Though remaining characteristically vague on specifics, the DVFP demanded "a just revalorization of medium and small savings accounts" as well as the immediate revocation of the government's decree. This "shameful law," the coalition bitterly asserted, had "robbed the entire middle class, workers, and civil servants of all their savings," while bringing "indescribable misery to millions of aging people." The Third Emergency Tax Decree, the Nazis claimed, had delivered the elderly to "hunger, despair, and death." The inflation had been a form of "finance bolshevism," amounting to "the most shamelessly and ruthlessly executed expropriation of all times," and the government's revalorization policy had given this crime "the official stamp of approval." It meant the "breach of public promises" and "annulled private obligations to creditors," thus "unjustly dumping billions upon billions into the lap of debtors." [107]

Nazi opposition to the government's revalorization program also overlapped with the party's assault on the republic's treatment of the elderly, disabled veterans, and the surviving dependents of those lost in the war. Indeed, the first two demands of the party's social platform called for "a generous extension of government assistance for the elderly" and, secondly, pledged that "the highest duty of the *völkisch* state would be to provide for the "security of the war's victims (welfare for disabled veterans and surviving dependents of the war dead)." [108] Disabled veterans, the party claimed, belonged to "the poorest of the poor," and had been abused by the republican government. "What has happened to us disabled veterans?" one widely distributed *völkisch* pamphlet asked. "Instead of support and understanding," the disabled veteran received nothing but "scorn and ridicule." The Nazis conceded that pensions had been provided for in the Reich Welfare Law of May 1920, but maintained that when payments at last started to flow, they came in worthless inflated currency. "Anyone not wishing to starve had to go begging. To the disgrace and dishonor of revolutionary Germany, disabled veterans had to sit on the street and display their mutilated limbs like billboards in order to get a few beggar's pennies tossed at them by the parasites of the revolution."[109]

Other pensioners had suffered greatly under the impact of the inflation, and the Reich government's emergency legislation had only exacerbated the situation, the Nazis asserted. The Great Coalition had reduced the pensions and benefits of public employees and civil servants, while others living on fixed incomes, the Nazis scornfully noted, were receiving "only a fraction" of their expected benefits.[110]

To the pensioners, veterans, and small investors wounded by inflation and enraged by the government's stabilization measures, the Nazis consistently maintained that the *völkisch* coalition alone had been steadfast and forceful in representing their interests. The DVP, DDP, and Zentrum were "notorious government parties incapable of offering serious opposition" to the revalorization policy they had helped formulate. Equally suspect in Nazi estimation was the DNVP, especially during the summer and fall of 1924 as the Nationalists maneuvered to establish a *Bürgerblock* government. "Can you dare to give your vote to a party that is so unreliable on the important issues [a clear reference to the DNVP's split vote on the Dawes Plan] and that is ready to form a coalition with the drafters of the Third Emergency Tax Decree? Never!" The *völkisch* movement, on the other hand, was pictured as "entering the campaign in inner agreement with the program of the Association of Mortgagees and Savers" and had, as Nazi pamphlet literature pointed out, named an influential member of that organization as a special adviser to its Reichstag delegation and placed his name on a secure place in the party's national electoral list.[111]

Like the National Socialists, the DNVP also focused much of its campaign propaganda on the plight of the pensioner and saver, and, like the *völkisch* coalition, it placed prominent leaders of the revalorization movement on its national ticket. Though never committing itself to a definite figure, the DNVP vigorously championed a higher rate of revaluation. Hergt, the party's national chairman, was even reported to have promised that "within twenty-four hours after their entry into the cabinet, the Nationalists will bring about a revaluation of 100 percent."[112] The DNVP repeatedly charged that the Reich government had failed to recognize the material and psychological needs of the inflation's middle-class victims. The ruling coalition, Hergt declared, "has irresponsibly neglected the moral obligations owed to owners of gilt-edged securities, supposedly guaranteed by the state, to holders of war bonds . . . the truest of the true in the hardest of times . . . to all those who sacrificed body and health in the war, and to the middle class, so severely weakened by economic developments." The DNVP, therefore, demanded that the government eliminate this alleged inequitable treatment and ensure that "the *Mittelstand* alone" was not forced to "bear the costs of war."[113]

Although the Nationalists directed most of their rhetorical salvos at the government parties in 1924, they occasionally trained their sights on the *völkisch* coalition, especially during the fall campaign. Nationalist electoral literature repeatedly stressed Nazi refusal to close ranks in the antisocialist *Bürgerblock*, and Nazi unwillingness to consider participation in a Reich government may have diminished the movement's attractiveness between May and December. "A vote for the National Socialists will not lead to the right," one conservative article explained, "since they repeatedly declare that they do not want to participate in a cabinet. Votes cast for them are, therefore, lost to the objective of the campaign: the creation of a nationally oriented government . . . which will bring the era of revolution to a close."[114] Similarly, the DNVP urged pensioners and savers to ignore the new special interest parties, warning that a vote for "such splinter parties pushes the Social Democrats into the saddle."[115] As the DNVP forcefully pressed for the formation of a center-right coalition to deal with the problems confronting the victims of the inflation and stabilization, the Nationalists may have appeared as a more practical choice at the polls than either the renegade National Socialists or the newly formed revalorization parties.

Regardless of motivational factors, the disintegration of the liberal-conservative cleavage, so prominent in 1920, had also begun in this important element of the electorate. The principal casualty, however, was not the conservative DNVP but the liberal center. Forced on the defensive by the relentless rightist assault and handicapped by their prominent role in the cabinets of 1922–24, the two liberal parties were unable to establish a credible public position in the highly charged atmosphere of 1924. The DVP strongly condemned Nazi and Nationalist promises to pensioners and small investors as "vague" and "irresponsible" and, in the summer of 1924, even endorsed an increase of the rate of revaluation, indicating that 25 percent might be acceptable. Still, Stresemann, speaking for his party and the government, bitterly complained that the DVP "cannot satisfy utopian hopes."[116]

The DDP also pointed out that the Third Emgergency Tax Decree need not be the last word on the revalorization issue. Yet at the same time the party appealed to the pensioners and small investors to keep the revalorization problem in perspective. "It is fundamentally wrong for an impoverished *Rentner* to orient his voting behavior according to whether the [party] list contains men whose mouths are crammed with promises of revaluation. . . . The decisive consideration," the party plaintively stressed, "must be the position on the great questions of domestic and foreign policy and not on a single issue, no matter how painfully it touches one's personal life. You must decide if the listed candidates are for the republic and peaceful development or for monarchy and new disorder, if they are for accommodation with the outside world or for a new war. After all," it concluded, "the fate of revalorization depends on all these things."[117]

These arguments, however, failed to impress the leaders of the revaluation movement and the constituencies that they represented. The tension between the liberal parties and the revalorization forces heightened during the fall when representatives of the Association of Mortgagees and Savers approached the leadership of the non-Marxist parties in an effort to secure support of their demands for higher revalorization. While the DNVP, NSFB, and Zentrum accepted the association's recommendations, the liberals balked. As a result, the association pointedly refused to endorse either the DVP or DDP in the December election.[118] The failure of these parties to attract significant support from the circles represented by the association is strongly suggested by the figures of Table 2.4. While the liberal vote in 1920 is correlated with the *Rentner* variable, that relationship disappears in 1924. The conservative figures, on the other hand, surge in the May election and continue to hold strong in December. Given the demographic composition of the *Rentnermittelstand* and the aggressive Nationalist manipulation of the revalorization issue, it is perhaps not surprising that the DNVP's coefficients remain high for both elections in 1924. Certainly more remarkable are the Nazi figures, which rank a surprisingly strong second, especially in May. For a "party of youth," the Nazis had spent a surprising amount of time and energy courting voters from the *Rentnermittelstand*, and the figures of Table 2.4 show that their effort was not without effect. Although the *völkisch* coefficients slump in December, there is no corresponding resurgence for the liberals. Neither the DVP nor the DDP attain even their modest levels of 1920. Indeed, the figures indicate that the liberal-conservative cleavage of that initial Reichstag election had been replaced by a conservative-*völkisch* split.

Measured by objective economic standards, the inflation may not have had the long-term catastrophic effects on the *Mittelstand* so often attributed to it. Evidence in recent studies indicates that many of the inflation's middle-class victims had managed to recoup their losses by 1928 at

Table 2.4. Party Vote and the Rentnermittelstand, *1920–1924*

	Protestant (N=152)			Catholic (N=64)		
	1920	1924a	1924b	1920	1924a	1924b
NSDAP	NA	.485	.191	NA	1.23	.406
DNVP	.598	.749	.876	1.18	.611	.817
DVP	.421	−.371	−.128	.201*	−.492	−.318
DDP	.152	−.138	−.177*	−.343	−.171*	−.173*
Z	.317*	.389	.236	−.205	−.984	.168
SPD	−.582	−.170	−.396	−.449	−.525	−.712
KPD	−.268	−.557	−.388	.207*	.252*	.189*
Other	−.203	−.925	.106*	.425	.352	.340

NOTE: The figures are unstandardized regression coefficients (b), controlling for old middle class, new middle class, blue-collar workers, religion, and urbanization (population size).

*These coefficients are not significant at the .05 level.

the latest. However, the traumas of hyperinflation followed by the harsh realities of stabilization must not be minimized.[119] The pronounced rightward shift of electoral sympathies within that sector of the middle class dominated by small investors, pensioners, creditors, and others most susceptible to the pressures of inflation and dissatisfied with the government's revalorization policy clearly dates from the "inflation election" of May 1924. Thereafter, despite stable economic conditions, this politically salient segment of the voting public refused to return from rightwing or special interest fringes of German electoral politics, and was essentially lost to the prorepublican parties of the liberal center.

The New Middle Class

Along with artisans, shopkeepers, pensioners, and small investors, the salaried employees of the new middle class were also hard hit by the economic crises of 1923–24 and thus represented a potential reservoir of antirepublican sentiment. Unemployment among white-collar employees was widespread in late 1923 and remained high throughout the spring of the following year. For clerical and sales personnel the situation was particularly grim. In January 1924, the ratio of applicants to jobs available in sales stood at approximately eighteen to one. By early May, this gap had diminished but still remained at fifteen to one, a ratio exceeded only by that of clerical employees. As joblessness in other occupations declined significantly during the summer and fall, unemployment among white-collar personnel persisted at dismally high levels. As the December elections approached, approximately fourteen applicants continued to be recorded for every available sales and clerical post.[120]

White-collar salaries were also depressed in 1924, lagging far below prewar standards. Working a fifty-four-hour week, a high-level bank official in Berlin received only about one-half the value of his 1913 salary. Although low-ranking employees fared somewhat better, as salary differentials between high- and low-level positions contracted throughout the economy, the threat of layoffs loomed more threateningly for the lower echelons. Moreover, while the wages of the average unskilled worker rose by 20 percent between April and December 1924, white-collar salaries registered only modest gains. A clerk employed in a Berlin retail establishment who earned 143 RM per month in April saw his salary rise to 154 RM by December, an increase of only 8 percent. The income of white-collar personnel still exceeded that of most unskilled workers, but in 1924 the gap between white- and blue-collar pay seemed to be rapidly diminishing.[121]

Dissatisfaction with these trends was consistently expressed by the major white-collar unions, though with significant differences in emphasis. The *völkisch*, Christian-national DHV, for example, voiced its deep concern over the plight of those public employees laid off at various levels of government, noting that most did not possess adequate pensions or severance pay. "A great many, including sales personnel with valid contracts, stand before a great void," the union lamented, "and in these circles misery and bitterness are understandably great."[122] The DHV also complained that the loss of savings resulting from the inflation, coupled with the dwindling business opportunities produced by stabilization, meant that white-collar aspirations for economic independence had been crushed. The only hope for white-collar personnel, the DHV militantly contended, was to be found in union representation, which alone could frustrate the designs of "antisocial management."[123]

The liberal Gewerkschaftsbund der Angestellten (GdA) expressed similar concerns, worrying that the Reich government, in its desire to revive the economy, would give free reign to management. The GdA warned that powerful interests wished to reverse "the democratization of the economy" in order to restore the "economic freedom" of management. The GdA, therefore, demanded that the parties of the new Reichstag recognize "the equality between management and labor in the state and the economy as guaranteed by the constitution." Indeed, the parties, the GdA argued, should pledge to "protect the Weimar constitution" which assured white-collar employees "equality and upward mobility." [124]

The socialist Zentralverband der Angestellten (ZdA) concurred with this endorsement of the republic but naturally offered a more aggressive critique of existing economic conditions. "Under the hypocritical mask of a 'Volksgemeinschaft' and a so-called 'Bürgerblock,'" the capitalist forces of big agriculture were attempting to "establish a regime of the propertied classes," the ZdA charged. "Capitalism wants to make you a slave again," the union warned white-collar employees, and all that could prevent this was "a strong, united, and self-conscious Angestelltenschaft" working shoulder to shoulder with its working-class brothers. [125]

While the white-collar unions were in rough agreement on the need for vigilance against the forces of management, their attitudes toward blue-collar labor were sharply divided. Both the DHV and GdA were determined to maintain the social and economic distinctions between white- and blue-collar status. Consequently, both endorsed the preservation of separate social agencies for Germany's white-collar employees. These organizations, such as the white-collar insurance and health administrations, perpetuated the gap between manual and nonmanual labor and were intended to do just that. In DHV literature the white-collar population was portrayed as an "estate" (Stand), a distinct social order with its own unique spiritual and economic role to play in politics and society. As such, it required its own social services and political organizations. While the liberal GdA also supported the separation of white-collar from working-class institutions, the socialist ZdA did not. It alone espoused the view that white-collar employees were members of the working class, and it alone urged a united social and political front with blue-collar labor against management. [126]

Given the high level of white-collar discontent in 1924, the Angestelltenschaft would seem to have offered a natural target for National Socialist electoral recruitment. The membership of the DHV seemed particularly receptive to National Socialist ideas. This völkisch union was blatantly anti-Semitic and antifeminist, refusing membership to both Jews and women; was antipacifist; endorsed an expansionist foreign policy, including the recovery of Germany's colonial possessions; and was vehemently anti-Marxist. It condemned the "socialist parties and unions which seek class domination by the industrial workers" as well as "all those who want to reestablish the state of the propertied classes." Both these alternatives were "outspokenly materialistic and Marxist, completely oriented toward material interests" without an appreciation of ideals or *völkisch* questions. Between the two fronts of big capitalism and Marxist socialism, the DHV argued, a great mass of people were waiting for new political solutions.[127]

Although these attitudes obviously suggest strong affinities with the *völkisch* movement, the Nationalists, much more than the Nazis, sought to transform them into tangible electoral gains. The DHV was not officially linked to any party, but it had established intimate ties with the DNVP. Although differences remained between the two on a number of economic and political issues,[128] a fundamental harmony had developed in the early years of the republic and extended into 1924. During both campaigns of that year the Nationalists dwelt on the theme that only persistent vigilance by the DNVP had thwarted Social Democratic efforts at the "systematic destruction of all white-collar social institutions."[129] Nationalist campaign literature complained that the SPD had relentlessly "demanded . . . the abolition of separate white-collar insurance and health funds as well as the distinct job referral agency for white-collar personnel."[130] Nationalist legislative initiatives to ease the plight of the unemployed and underpaid white-collar employees were constantly emphasized, noting that politically conscious white-collar employees should support the DNVP for "the protection of the middle class, for the continued education of his children, and against the proletarianization of his estate [*Stand*]."[131]

The DVP's white-collar campaign also vigorously supported separate social agencies for salaried employees. The party endorsed the separate job referral agency and health insurance plans for white-collar employees, while excoriating Social Democratic initiatives to merge these organizations with economy-wide agencies. In its strongly antisocialist rhetoric, DVP campaign literature on this issue was virtually indistinguishable from that of the DNVP.[132]

Like other bourgeois parties, the DDP also supported the continuation of the distinct white-collar social services, though its appeals to white-collar employees were less stridently anti-Socialist. The party also attempted to maintain good relations with the liberal GdA. Although that organization refused to align itself officially with any political party in 1924, the GdA's principal allegiance, as its program for that year emphasized, was to the republican constitution. The translation of the constitution's social promise into concrete reality was defined as the GdA's primary goal,[133] and, as the bourgeois party that had most vocally defended the Weimar state, the DDP hoped to profit at the polls from the GdA's prorepublican orientation.

Given the stiff competition for the white-collar vote, the absence of a clearly articulated Nazi appeal to the *Angestelltenschaft* is quite remarkable. In sharp contrast to the vigorous National Socialist efforts to cultivate a constituency within the old middle class, the Nazis in 1924 demonstrated surprisingly little interest in formulating an appeal to white-collar employees. The social programs of neither the DVFP in the spring nor the NSFB in the fall dealt explicitly with white-collar concerns, and *völkisch* pamphlet literature was virtually silent on the specifically white-collar issues debated by the other parties.[134] Nazi appeals to white-collar personnel were either subsumed in more general appeals to middle-class voters or added, almost as an afterthought, to campaign literature addressed to civil servants.[135] At the same time, the party occasionally treated white-collar employees as components of the *Arbeitnehmerschaft* or as "workers of fist and brain," an appeal that certainly implied community of interest between white-collar personnel and the working class.[136] Although in subsequent camaigns the Nazis grew more forceful in their efforts to develop a white-collar constituency, the party's approach to this highly heterogeneous group never really overcame a fundamental ambivalence concerning its proper social position.[137]

That ambivalence appears to have been reciprocated by the white-collar electorate in 1924. As the figures of Table 2.5 suggest, the white-collar vote split along traditional liberal-conservative lines, with the DVP and DNVP exhibiting the most powerful coefficients. In marked contrast to the strong and consistent figures of these parties, the National Socialist coefficients begin and remain unexpectedly negative in May and December. Even when the white-collar variable is examined according to individual economic sectors, no positive relationship between the *Angestelltenschaft* and National Socialist voting emerges. White-collar discontent in 1924, therefore, appears to have been contained within the framework of the traditional parties. Lacking a clearly defined appeal and the good relations with white-collar unions enjoyed by their bourgeois and Social Democratic rivals,[138] the National Socialists, it seems, were unable to establish a significant constituency in this important segment of the middle-class electorate.

Although traditionally more insulated from economic vicissitudes than their counterparts in the private sector, civil servants could claim to be victimized by the economic woes of the period. Certainly unprecedented and extremely traumatic for civil servants were the austerity measures introduced by the Reich government in 1923, which resulted in a mass layoff of public officials. Forced into drastic budget slashing by the exigencies of stabilization, the Reich dismissed one hundred and fifty thou-

Table 2.5. *Party Vote and the New Middle Class (NMC), 1920–1924*

All NMC[a]

	Protestant (N=152)			Catholic (N=64)		
	1920	1924a	1924b	1920	1924a	1924b
NSDAP	NA	.121*	−.656	NA	−.268*	−.357
DNVP	−.555*	.212	.923	−.571	.309	.390
DVP	.321	.159*	.193	−.441	−.530	−.144*
DDP	.698	.115*	.196	−.988	−.126*	−.652
Z	−.210	−.105*	−.216	−.389*	.214	.209
SPD	−.292	.297*	−.158*	.393	−.456	−.548
KPD	−.131	−.118*	−.121*	.203*	.271*	.169*
Other	−.862	−.136	−.112*	.402	.997	.587

White Collar[a,b]

Protestant Subsample

	Commerce			Industry		
	1920	1924a	1924b	1920	1924a	1924b
NSDAP	NA	−.534	−.358	NA	−.548	−.376
DNVP	−.403	−.353	.236*	.322	−.737	−.193
DVP	.373	.606	.571	.207*	.287	.296
DDP	−.371	.221	−.325	.484	.336	.273
Z	−.196*	−.252*	−.247*	.194*	−.157*	−.122*
SPD	.102*	.244	.161*	.068*	−.463	−.201
KPD	.264*	.126	.243	.238*	−.131	.161*
Other	−.308	−.448	−.540	−.162*	.363*	−.612

Catholic Subsample

	Commerce			Industry		
	1920	1924a	1924b	1920	1924a	1924b
NSDAP	NA	−3.34	−2.25	NA	−.679	−.716
DNVP	.494*	−.626	−.832	.129*	−.992	−1.29
DVP	−.257	1.52	1.06	−1.61	.367	−.217
DDP	.254	.306	.268	.310	.921	.266*
Z	−1.21	−.747	.126*	.310	.795	.955
SPD	1.05	−.402	.168*	1.37	.549	1.04
KPD	−.703	.256*	.105*	−.100	−.898	.205*
Other	−.184*	1.06	.210*	−.882	.401*	−.310*

Table 2.5. (continued)

Civil Service[a,b]
Protestant Subsample

	Prof. Service			Transportation		
	1920	1924a	1924b	1920	1924a	1924b
NSDAP	NA	.372	.173	NA	.591	.808
DNVP	.444	.418	.550	.198*	.211*	.237
DVP	.106*	−.224	−.239	−.386	−.193	−.229
DDP	−.258	−.213*	−.555	.322	.109*	.995
Z	.322	.590	.291	.206*	.203	.216
SPD	.204	−.290	.196	−.200	−.124*	−.161
KPD	−.141	−.447	−.407	−.273	−.381	−.311
Other	−.815	−.178*	.302*	−.182*	.203*	.550

Catholic Subsample

	Prof. Service			Transportation		
	1920	1924a	1924b	1920	1924a	1924b
NSDAP	NA	−.490	.358	NA	.168*	−.239
DNVP	−.102	.631	.802	.228	−.921	.274*
DVP	1.01	.506	.415	−.653	−.518	−.551
DDP	−.810	−.571	−.829	.254	.306	.268
Z	1.67	1.52	1.75	−1.14	−.190	−.422
SPD	−1.03	−2.23	−2.39	.880	.826	.922
KPD	−.219	.275	.515	.224	.168*	−.113*
Other	.173*	.221*	.133*	.339	.286*	.214*

a. These figures are unstandardized regression coefficients (b), controlling for old middle class, *Rentnermittelstand*, blue-collar workers, religion, and urbanization (population size).

b. Presents coefficients for each component of the NMC, controlling for all remaining elements of the white-collar/civil service population in addition to those variables listed above.

*These coefficients are not significant at the .05 level.

sand public officials and government employees between November 1923 and April 1924. Moreover, state and local authorities were compelled to take similar measures. It is estimated that nearly seven hundred and fifty thousand public officials and civil employees lost their jobs as a consequence of the government's stabilization policy. Since civil servants enjoyed special legal privileges (*Beamtenrechte*), among which was a position of permanent tenure, the emergency measures of 1923–24 were viewed by the Reich's civil-service associations as a direct challenge to the unique legal and social status traditionally enjoyed by the German *Beamtentum*.[139]

Regardless of rank, dismissals came as a profound shock to civil servants presumably assured of job security. As one Reichsbank official put it, he was fired "in spite of lifetime tenure, conscientious service, and repeated assurances from competent government authorities that the rights of civil servants would not be infringed upon." As a result of the government's austerity program, he was "forced into retirement and thrown out onto the streets. If I had little faith in the regime up until then," he recalled, "a genuine hatred of the system set in at that moment."[140] Moreover, complaints were frequently voiced that the government had used the austerity measures to purge the civil service of officials with conservative political sympathies. "Old experienced men are . . . forced into retirement and replaced by politically reliable men, true to the system," another convert to National Socialism charged. "Qualification for a public position is not years of training in state service but the party book, pure and simple."[141]

The dismissals of 1923–24 also reinforced civil-service determination to maintain the *Berufsbeamtentum* as a professional and social estate clearly distinct from white-collar employees and other *Arbeitnehmer*. During the war, strains within the civil service had threatened its traditional ethos of social solidarity, and in the wake of revolution and the republic's efforts at "democratization" that homogeneity of political and social identity seemed severely eroded. Symptomatically, the politically neutral Civil Servants' League (Deutscher Beamtenbund—DBB), though still by far the largest public service union, suffered a steady hemorrhage of support between 1919 and 1922 as more and more officials turned to unions with explicit political orientations. Thus, the Social Democratic Allgemeiner Deutscher Beamtenbund (ADB), its strength centered primarily in the transportation sector, and the Christian-nationalist GDB made significant gains in this period, signaling an apparent political fragmentation of the *Berufsbeamtentum* and its transformation from a socially cohesive estate to a set of competing political and social interests. The shock of the personnel dismissals of 1923–24 reversed that trend.[142]

As the debate over the government's intention to reduce the size of the civil bureaucracy gathered momentum in the summer of 1923, the DBB took the lead in defending the traditional rights and privileges of the civil service. It conceded that the public payroll had swollen greatly since the war but was vehement in its position that professional civil servants should be protected at the expense of other occupational groups who did not enjoy the *Berufsbeamtentum*'s well-established right to lifetime tenure. If these extraordinary dismissals were, in fact, unavoidable, they should affect first and foremost public employees (*Angestellte* and *Arbeiter*) without civil-service status. For the DBB there was no question of social solidarity with other *Arbeitnehmer* to prevent the dismissals; the threat of layoffs called for unity *within* the civil service and a united defense of the *Berufsbeamtentum* at all costs.[143]

The politically oriented unions, but especially the Social Democratic ADB, found the issue far more problematic. The ADB was closedly linked with the socialist white-collar unions and was, therefore, hardly in a position to take an unequivocally pro-civil-service stance. Instead, it contended that the dismissals were an attempt by the upper echelons (the *Ministerialbürokratie*) to purge the lower and middle grades of pro-republican, progressive elements. The best protection of civil-service interests, it argued, was in a united front of all *Arbeitnehmer*—civil servants, white-collar employees, and workers—against the government's policy. One socialist white-collar publication charged that "the behavior of the DBB is reactionary and designed, as in the old authoritarian state [*Obrigskeitsstaat*], to create a gap between civil servants and other *Arbeitnehmer*," and it warned that such a strategy only aided the most conservative parties.[144]

That critique was as accurate as it was ineffectual. While the DBB staked out a narrow, pro-civil-service position, urging protection of the *Beamtentum* on the basis of traditional rights, the ADB was asking civil servants to forget that engrained elitism and join forces with other less privileged groups now competing with them for a position on the government payroll. In the highly charged atmosphere of 1923–24, this call for common action with such groups found little resonance with civil servants threatened with imminent dismissal. Indeed, the debate over the *Beamtenabbau* marked an important turning point in the fortunes of the DBB and in the sociopolitical orientation of the German civil service. It revived and greatly strengthened the long-standing but recently eroding tendency toward social exclusivity and internal solidarity within the *Berufsbeamtentum*, and it halted—if temporarily—its nascent political fragmentation. Beginning with this debate, the DBB not only reversed its declining popularity but began a period of sustained growth, while the politically oriented unions, especially the ADB, went into a tailspin from which they never recovered. In the period of relative stability that followed, the "nonaligned" DBB dwarfed the other civil-service organizations, reasserting its position as the paramount representative of the *Berufsbeamtentum*.[145]

Also contributing to the renewed sense of civil-service solidarity and to the rejuvenated leadership of the DBB in 1923–24 was the often bitter public debate on civil-service salaries. Unlike white-collar employees and workers, who collected their pay on a monthly or weekly basis, civil servants had traditionally received their salaries in prepaid quarterly installments. During the protracted period of hyperinflation, these quarterly installments were supplemented periodically by additional payments that were tied to the cost-of-living index. This meant that civil servants could not only count on a considerable lump of expendable income that permitted some form of financial planning but also expect favorable adjustments of that income from time to time. This arrangement became a matter of public debate during 1922–23, with some groups arguing that this manner of prepayment and the supplemental adjustments constituted preferential treatment for civil servants and acted to fuel inflation. Again the DBB took the lead in meeting these charges, denouncing the "persecution of civil servants" and defending these pay arrangements as a "well-deserved right." When at last, in November 1923, the government made civil-service salaries payable on a monthly basis—on the same day and for the same period as white-collar pay—the civil-service associations, with the DBB in the lead, condemned this measure as a blatant assault on the traditional rights of the *Berufsbeamtentum*.[146]

Civil servants also complained of a decline in real income as inflation gave way to stabilization in 1924. In the months before the spring election, the salary of a low-ranking civil servant stationed in a major urban area was even lower than that of a retail clerk, and job security, once a unique advantage of the public sector, was no longer a certainty. Although all ranks of the civil service suffered a decline in real income, the highest echelons were hardest hit. Beginning with the wartime inflation, officials in the top five grades had seen their real income shrink to between 27 and 35 percent of their prewar levels. This loss was considered even more onerous since, as one civil-service observer noted, "the higher officials were very poorly paid even before the war." These civil servants were also less able to rely on income from investments, since many had placed their money in government bonds with fixed rates of interest. Savings and investment income, often representing the crucial margin between proletarian and middle-class standards of living for status-conscious civil servants, had been lost.[147] As one municipal official, attracted by National Socialist propaganda, complained: "The inflation robbed us Mittelständler of the money saved from years of honest work. At the end of the inflation all I could call my own were my furniture and a small garden plot."[148]

Lower-level officials also experienced a contraction of real income, though to a lesser degree. During 1923 real incomes in the lower ranks mounted to between 43 and 82 percent of the prewar standards. Many schoolteachers and university instructors were forced to supplement their incomes with manual labor. Responding to a questionnaire on standards of living, many academics reported with considerable bitterness on their "difficult struggle for existence" during the inflation. One instructor, with an annual income of 190,000 RM in 1922, grumbled that he was "working for the railroad during vacations for day wages." Another complained that his school salary of 150,000 RM "has not even approached the minimum necessary to exist. I am forced to sell my personal belongings from time to time." At the German Natural Sciences Convention in 1922, another scholar voiced his fear that owing to the inflation, which at that time had not yet approached the fantastic proportions of the following year, "Germany's cultured middle class" was "about to disappear."[149]

After the election in May, salaries for public officials were boosted considerably, those of low-ranking civil servants climbing by about 28 percent between April and December, those for the higher grades even more.[150] These salary hikes, approved by the Reichstag in mid-summer, undoubtedly contributed to an improvement of civil-service morale, but they did not compensate for the shock of the massive dismissals or the loss of real income suffered particularly by the middle and upper echelons. Moreover, strains within the *Berufsbeamtentum* produced by the real income question tended to pale when civil servants were confronted with a serious challenge from the outside. The dismissals and the debate over civil-service salaries were symptomatic, many officials felt, of a "*Beamtenhetze*," and resentment remained rife within the *Beamtentum* throughout the election year.[151]

If the Nazis had little success in reaching the salaried employees of the private sector, their efforts to attract a civil-service constituency were considerably more forceful and more fruitful. In contrast to the indifference that characterized the National Socialist approach to white-collar employees, the party's campaign for the civil-service vote was both clearly articulated and highly aggressive. By stressing the low civil-service pay scale and the threat of additional dismissals, the party sought to manipulate civil-service anxiety over its diminishing economic security and social status. "Civil servants have been thrown out on the street by the hundreds of thousands, without consideration for family, war disability, or professional expertise," the Nazis charged.[152] These layoffs came in the middle and lower ranks, the Nazis claimed, "without planning and without saving the German people a single penny in taxes." With disdain the party noted that "salaries amount to at most 40 percent of their prewar value. . . . Vacation has been shortened, and working hours extended." While "the inflation, brought about by Jewish stock-market swindlers," had "pauperized the civil servants, white-collar employees, and pensioners of Germany," the Third Emergency Tax Decree was "a brutal unjustifiable act of violence" against those already threatened groups.[153]

Among those public officials who had survived the dismissals, the *völkisch* coalition attempted to exploit feelings of frustrated upward mobility. The party emphasized the republic's policy of "democratizing the civil service," which allegedly resulted in the appointment of unqualified personnel through the patronage of the government parties. While honest, well-trained civil servants were unceremoniously and unconstitutionally fired, "the politically clever November official," the Nazis contended, "remains at the feeding trough."[154] The career advancement of civil servants had been "infinitely delayed by the appointment of unqualified personnel," the *völkisch* coalition claimed, adding that "young German teachers have to make way for Jewish instructors." In fact, the Nazis maintained that the upper ranks of the civil service were "in ever greater numbers being staffed by Jews."[155]

To rectify this situation, the *völkisch* movement demanded the revocation of the emergency measures pertaining to personnel cutbacks and, in addition, called for the replacement of all "revolution officials" by "trained, professional civil servants." The party also endorsed a more just wage scale and a full schedule of pension benefits for retired civil servants. Finally, the Nazis reminded the civil-service electorate that "preservation of a professional *Beamtentum*" had been a plank of the original National Socialist platform adopted in 1920.[156]

The surprising emphasis on the plight of one of Germany's traditional social elites in Nazi campaign literature was, more predictably, duplicated in Nationalist electoral strategy. The conservatives had long commanded a strong following within the *Berufsbeamtentum*, and during both campaigns of 1924 the DNVP mounted major propaganda offensives to secure that traditional constituency. Untainted by responsibility for the emergency measures that had shocked the *Beamtentum*, the Nationalists, like the Nazis, played on the twin themes of declining economic fortunes and frustrated career ambitions. "Salary miseries and the nightmare of dismissals weigh heavily on civil servants," the DNVP declared. "Their workday has been extended from eight to nine hours without compelling justification and their vacation has been shortened. Like the rest of the middle class, civil servants have been hard hit by the Third Emergency Tax Decree which . . . robbed holders of war bonds of the hope of ever recovering a penny of the good money they lent the father-land." The party also complained that "years of loyal service, which the old *Obrigkeitsstaat* rewarded with decorations, titles, badges of honor, and promotions are recognized by the democratic republic with dismiss-als." Moreover, "it is an open secret," one Nationalist journal charged, that political considerations not infrequently have played a substantial role in the dismissals in the Reich and provincial governments, especially with regard to many rightist officials." [157]

While the DVFP and the DNVP pursued the civil-service vote with re-markably similar appeals, significant differences in tone and emphasis were also discernible. Like the Nazis, the Nationalists condemned the personnel cutbacks and charged that political favoritism threatened to ruin the traditions of professionalism and integrity within the *Berufsbe-amtentum*. However, Nationalist appeals tended to be more explicitly elitist in tone. The DNVP, for example, complained that "union secre-taries, ironworkers, bricklayers, bartenders, and cigar makers" were being appointed to high positions in municipal, state, and national gov-ernment. [158] Similarly, while the National Socialists tended to emphasize the effects of the cutbacks on the middle and lower ranks, the National-ists were particularly solicitous of the higher echelons. Following the Reichstag's passage of legislation to raise civil-service salaries during the summer of 1924, it was typical of the Nazis to argue that "since the high-est ranking officials have been granted really fabulous salaries, it is imper-ative that the lowest-ranking civil servants be given more than just the bare essentials of life." [159] The DNVP, on the other hand, charac-teristically warned voters that civil servants, but "especially higher offi-cials," as members of Germany's "intellectual and cultural aristocracy," simply could not be allowed to "decline socially in relation to other oc-cupational groups." [160]

The DVP also sought to appeal to the elitist orientation of the civil-service electorate, reminding officials that on the question of "democra-tization" the German People's party "stands in sharp opposition to the Social Democrats, who want to treat civil servants . . . like every private employee [*Arbeitnehmer*]." The DVP stood firmly against the "integra-tion of civil servants into the great front of *Arbeitnehmer*," which would mean the loss of the public servant's "privileged legal position, which they derive from their education and responsibility in the life of the state." If the Social Democrats had their way, the DVP contended, "the professional civil servant would hang suspended in constant danger of expulsion by alien elements." [161] The party's campaign literature also pointed to the DVP's basic principles, drafted in 1919, which demanded "permanent lifelong appointment of officials solely according to objective criteria without consideration of party membership and religious confession." [162]

Yet the DVP had maintained a high profile in the governments of 1923–24, and as a result, its appeals to white-collar and civil-service personnel possessed a palpable defensive quality. Referring to the unpopular decrees of the Marx-Stresemann cabinets, the party press asked plaintively: "Can one forget that at the close of the last year the German Reich stood before the imminent collapse of its finances and thus before hunger and turmoil? At that time it was imperative to take all measures without long deliberation that would balance the budget and protect the *Rentenmark* from deterioration." [163]

The DVP also sought to shift the responsibility for the unpopular government actions to the SPD. "The mismanagement of government finances, the planned economy, and the policies of unconditional fulfillment pursued by every government from Scheidemann to Wirth," had created a "swelling of the white-collar and civil-service body" and dictated "a painful intervention." The unavoidable reduction of government personnel "saved the Reich two hundred million gold marks," the DVP explained. As a last line of defense, the party also claimed that "the dismissals were unavoidable for reasons of foreign policy." The Dawes Plan, the DVP argued, "would not have been as favorable to us if it could be shown that the smaller and impoverished Germany employed *more* civil servants and white-collar personnel than the larger, more prosperous Reich of 1914." Given these considerations, the DVP contended that civil servants should regard their party's action as painful but patriotic. In one pamphlet addressed explicitly to civil servants, the party stoutly but defensively remarked that "the DVP has a clear conscience and confidently submits its work for *Volk und Vaterland* to the consideration of the sensible voter." [164]

The DDP also found itself on the defensive, owing to its role in cabinet decisions in 1923–24, noting bitterly that "the question of civil-service incomes and personnel cutbacks has been used by the Nationalists and *Völkischen* for ruthless agitation against the republic and the governing parties." In an attempt to explain the party's position to civil servants, one Democratic deputy maintained that the DDP had, in fact, "fought the ruthless reductions in government personnel" and had sought "only the release of superfluous officials. A reduction of such brutality," he conceded, "should never have been allowed." When the parties of the right assailed democratization of the civil service, the reduction of salaries, and cutbacks in personnel, linking these with the Versailles settlement, the Dawes Plan, and even the republican form of government, the DDP cautioned that "some shortsighted civil servants repeatedly forget that all these developments have their origins in the lost war and its consequences." The Democrats, therefore, felt that it was "quite incomprehensible that civil servants could be enthused for the rightist parties." [165] Nationalist demands for higher civil-service salaries were dismissed in the Democratic press as "grotesque" in view of the conservative support for "an increase in grain tariffs, a reduction of the tax burdens for the propertied, and an immediate termination of rent control." The Democrats also prided themselves on their concern for the problems of middle- and lower-ranking civil servants, advocating a decent minimum salary and a more equitable distribution of the tax burden. [166]

The figures of Table 2.5, however, strongly suggest that the liberals, implicated in the formulation and implementation of the unpopular austerity measures of 1923–24, proved unable to rebuff the vigorous assault of the conservative and radical right. The liberal/civil-service figures are low in May and remain weak even in the improved political and economic circumstances of the December election. The Nationalist coefficients, on the other hand, not only rise considerably between 1920 and May 1924 but remain high for the fall campaign as well. The conservative figures follow a steadily ascending curve through these first three Reichstag elections of the Weimar era. The conservative orientation of the German *Beamtentum* was, of course, long established. The civil service had been one of the traditional pillars of the Hohenzollern monarchy, and the revolution of 1918—despite all the complaints about "democratization"—had not been accompanied by a purge of rightist officials. Moreover, the restrictions on the size of the German military establishment by the Treaty of Versailles resulted in the transfer of many military men to other areas of public service. The reduction of civil-service personnel demanded by the government's stabilization program, however, severely curbed career opportunities for many ex-soldiers and graduating university students. Careers in the military and public administration, traditional avenues of social advancement in prewar Germany, were no longer readily accessible. In fact, unemployment among professionals—teachers, lawyers, and others whose hopes for a civil-service career had suffered a jarring setback—remained at gloomy levels throughout 1924. [167] Social ambitions nurtured during the Empire were thus rudely dashed in the crisis-ridden early years of the republic, driving many ex-military men into the numerous paramilitary organizations and others into less structured but no less vociferous opposition to the new "system." Perhaps no other group in German society was more directly affected by the loss of the war and the collapse of the Hohenzollern monarchy. In addition to the profound cultural shock experienced by many veterans and civil servants, especially of the older generation, the economic dislocations of the early postwar years produced, in Peter Merkl's words, "a whole crisis stratum in the military and public service."[168]

The figures of Table 2.5 reflect the extent of that crisis mentality. In the aftermath of inflation and stabilization, the growing discontent within the civil-service population could not be contained by the forces of the traditional right. The *völkisch*/civil-service coefficients are surprisingly strong for the May election in both public service sectors. Thereafter, as the political and economic crises abated, the *völkisch* coefficients fade in the professional services but remain strong in the smaller transportation sector. Nevertheless, given the conventional wisdom concerning the lower-middle-class origins of National Socialist support, it is noteworthy that the Nazi/civil-service coefficients are far stronger than the Nazi/white-collar figures. The National Socialists had made a major effort to win adherents within this traditional elite in 1924, and although these efforts met with only limited success, the party's scrupulous cultivation of this socially established and politially conservative element of the electorate reflected the surprisingly broad sociopolitical potential of National Socialism's appeal.

The Working Class

Despite the heavy emphasis traditionally placed on the plight of the *Mittelstand* in 1923–24, blue-collar workers were certainly among the biggest losers of the inflation, both individually and institutionally. The occupation of the Ruhr and the policy of passive resistance had cost thousands of workers their jobs, and the hyperinflation that followed greatly exacerbated that situation. Unemployment, which had remained relatively low in the early postwar years, began an irregular ascent in late 1922, reaching its apex in the bitter winter of 1923–24. In December of 1922, job-referral agencies recorded two applicants for every available position; twelve months later that ratio had jumped to nine to one. In December 1923, over half of all organized workers were either unemployed or working part-time.[169] Moreover, owing to the structure of the tax system, those workers who did find jobs were forced to bear a disproportionately heavy share of the government's financial burden. Unlike the self-employed, who paid their taxes in quarterly installments and hence in greatly inflated currency, blue-collar workers paid their taxes through withholdings from weekly pay.[170] As a result, inflation gnawed steadily away at blue-collar income, while the specter of unemployment loomed constantly in the not-so-distant background.

The inflation also severely weakened the institutional strength of the working class. As unemployment mounted, unions suffered serious losses in membership and in 1923 their funds evaporated in the heat of hyperinflation.[171] The extent of labor weakness was vividly demonstrated in December 1923, when a government ordinance eliminated one of the most prized achievements of the November revolution. In an effort to stabilize the economy and increase production, the Marx government—with the acquiescence of the unions and the SPD—revoked the eight-hour day. Thereafter, the work week for most laborers was extended to forty-eight or, in some cases, fifty-four hours.[172]

As the general economic recovery got under way in the spring of 1924, its effects were quickly reflected in the levels of blue-collar employment and wages. Although joblessness remained high in certain sectors, particularly in machine working, mining, and the chemical industry, unemployment among organized workers fell from approximately 27 percent in January to 9 percent in May. Despite some fluctuations in late summer, the rate remained stable for the remainder of the year, settling at 7 percent just before the December election. Wages also followed the same positive trends, as real wages for both skilled and unskilled labor rose gradually throughout the year. Between January and May average weekly real wages for skilled workers rose by approximately three marks (from 25.76 DM to 28.58 DM) and almost a mark and a half for unskilled labor (from 21.39 DM to 22.88 DM). Though these increases were small, both continued to improve during the summer and fall, with the gap between skilled and unskilled pay widening as the year progressed. After the massive problems and uncertainties of hyperinflation, 1924 proved to be a year of gradual recovery for the working class.[173]

In 1924 the National Socialists had managed to make significant though limited inroads into the constituencies of the major bourgeois parties. Unlike those parties, however, the völkisch coalition was not content to confine its electoral efforts to the diverse elements of the fractious Mittelstand. The vote of the blue-collar laborer was not seriously pursued by either the liberals or conservatives, and the Zentrum's working-class electorate was restricted to areas of heavy Catholic concentration. The National Socialists, on the other hand, refused to concede the blue-collar electorate to the Marxist left, and in both campaigns of 1924 sought to cultivate a labor constituency.

The major battle for the blue-collar vote was, of course, waged between the SPD and KPD, and although both directed some attention to the Nazi challenge, their campaigns were focused primarily on each other. In this bitter struggle, the Social Democrats developed two basic themes: defense of the republic against the increasing threat from the right, especially the DNVP, and the necessity of systematic legislative activity to protect and advance the interests of the working class. Since the Reichstag to be elected in 1924 would decide on issues such as "the eight-hour day, wage contracts, unemployment insurance, the right to organize, and distribution of the Reich's fiscal burden through taxation," it was imperative, the party pointed out, for the proletariat to have capable representatives to face the capitalist challenge. Social Democratic literature, therefore, repeatedly contrasted the "divisive agitation" of the Communists with the constructive parliamentary work of the SPD. "In this critical situation," *Vorwärts* asked, "should the working class entrust the representation of its interests . . . to the Communists . . . who must be fundamentally opposed to all parliamentary endeavors?"[174]

During 1923–24 the SPD had been dedicated to constructive legislative work aimed at improving the economic and political position of the working class, *Vörwarts* maintained, while the KPD had engaged in obstructionist tactics in the Reichstag and fomented unrest in the streets. The great fundamental difference between the two parties, the SPD contended, was that the Communists "desire the direst impoverishment of the workers because they believe that only in this way can they attain their objective"; the Social Democrats, on the other hand, "seek to prevent this misery," turning instead to "a moderate step-by-step improvement" as "the only way to free the path to higher goals."[175]

While the SPD presented itself as the only pragmatic and experienced representative of working-class interests, the KPD launched a vigorous assault on precisely this Social Democratic view of proletarian progress through parliamentary activity. Cooperation with the bourgeoisie in a bourgeois parliament, the KPD charged, had resulted merely in the cooptation of the SPD, a party "in which the majority of the German proletariat had once placed its hopes." Over the years the SPD had "become a middle-class party," the *Rote Fahne* maintained, "inextricably linked with the bourgeoisie . . . Social Democracy has deliberately and systematically delivered the proletariat . . . to the great wolves of capital."[176]

Throughout both campaigns, the Communists ridiculed Social Democratic emphasis on its pro-labor parliamentary activity, dismissing it as "a propagandistic swindle." After all, the KPD reminded blue-collar voters, the Social Democrats had supported the Dawes Plan, which meant "final elimination of the eight-hour day . . . massive unemployment in industry, and a complete break with all labor protection and social welfare."[177] Furthermore, in discussion of economic recovery, the *Rote Fahne* noted, "the Social Democrats no longer dare mention class struggle or nationalization. Social Democracy is totally oriented toward the continued existence of capitalism."[178] Liberation from this tyranny could obviously never be achieved by the revisionist strategy of the tainted SPD, the Communists charged. Only the destruction of Weimar's capitalist system and the establishment of a free state of soviets could accomplish that. Thus, in 1924 the KPD entered both campaigns under the antirepublican slogan: "Down with the black-red-yellow!"[179]

Despite the acrimonious conflict between the SPD and KPD, the National Socialists professed to find little to distinguish between the two parties of the Marxist left, both of which were assailed as frauds and enemies of the working class. Both of these parties, the Nazis charged, had pledged themselves for years to the eradication of capitalism but had acquiesced meekly in the continued exploitation of the German worker. The Marxists had bravely promised to abolish the capitalist system, but four years after the revolution German workers were "one hundred times more than ever before the slaves . . . of interest and dividend profiteers, of the great international bank Jews," the Nazis asserted. German workers had supported the SPD and the KPD because they had believed the Marxist promises of "the eight-hour day, international solidarity, freedom, equality, and fraternity."[180] But instead of the long-awaited workers' paradise, the "Marxist dominated republic" had allowed "capitalism to crack its whip over the enslaved workers," who "live in misery and despair, while facing an even grimmer future." What had happened to these Marxist promises, Nazi campaign literature pointedly inquired. "Why has the nationalization of the banks not begun? Why has the Social Democratic leadership so openly protected this lifeline of capitalism and why do these leaders ridicule us," the Nazis asked, "when we . . . strive to break interest slavery?"[181]

Not only had the SPD failed to deliver on its promises, but the KPD, the Nazis charged, was plotting to betray the German worker to international bolshevism. The Communists ultimately wanted to reduce the German worker to "the same fate as that of his counterpart in Russia. There one works twelve hours a day, and the right to strike has been revoked." If the KPD had its way, the German working man, the Nazis concluded, would find himself sentenced to the "very same prison state" that existed in the Soviet Union.[182]

The *völkisch* movement therefore called upon working-class voters to emancipate themselves from "Marxism and bolshevism, with their un-

German class hatred and their Jewish deception about the 'international solidarity of the proletariat.'" Instead of preaching class struggle, the National Socialists emphasized that their commitment was to the establishment of a true "people's community," in which social distinctions and class antagonisms would dissolve. "The curse of our *Volk*," the DVFP's platform explained, "has been this senseless division of employers and employees into antagonistic camps." The "ultimate cause" of Germany's collapse in 1918 lay precisely in this "hate-filled divisiveness," which had been "systematically fostered by Jewish Marxism." The creation of an "inner conciliation" between these mutually antagonistic groups and their integration into a "genuine *Volksgemeinschaft*" was, therefore, prominently touted as "the highest goal" of the *völkisch* movement in 1924. "Management and labor," the Nazis stressed, must become aware that they are "united by similar interests and by the common possession of German blood."[183]

To forge this new alliance, Nazi campaign literature called upon German voters to "leave all the small party squabbling behind. All decent people," they pleaded, "must stick together against the common enemy who exploits us all." The *völkisch* movement was to serve as the rallying point for the diverse social elements disgusted with the traditional divisions of German electoral politics. The National Socialists were uniquely qualified for this critical task because their movement "recognized no class differences. All *Stände* [!] that keep body and soul together in an honorable way belong with us," the Nazis explained, "whether workers, farmers, artisans, merchants, civil servants, factory owners—they all have the same interest in seeing the return of order and justice."[184]

This enervating division between "left and right, Nationalist and socialist," the Nazis argued, was artificial and a creation of "the Jewish press on both sides." While the "right demands love of the fatherland from the working people but wants to keep the treasures of the fatherland for itself, the left demands peace, freedom, and bread but hates those who are ready to give their lives for the attainment of freedom, for the maintenance of peace, and for the protection of our food supplies. And behind both camps," the Nazis warned, "the stock-market Jew sits and manipulates the people."[185]

For the National Socialists in 1924, "the resolution of the social problem" had "as its presupposition the resolution of the Jewish question."[186] Indeed, the linkage of Jews with both Marxism and capitalism constituted the ideological foundations of Nazi electoral strategy in 1924. When addressing workers, this linkage permitted the party to attack "Jewish international" or "interest capital" without necessarily demanding an end to the capitalist system. The workers had driven the kings from their thrones in 1918, only to have them replaced by the "kings of finance," the Nazis typically charged. Following the great suffering of the war, "international bank and stock-market capital" had "assumed absolute power," with the greatest financial clout resting "in the hands of the Jews, who maintain a powerful network extending over the whole world." Like the Marxists and their doctrine of class struggle, the forces of "international capitalism" were associated in National Socialist electoral propaganda with "rootless Jewry." The central issue confronting not simply the working class but German society as a whole, the Nazis warned, was not left or right, Nationalist or Socialist, but "for or against the Jews."[187]

Both the Social Democrats and Communists, of course, dismissed these Nazi appeals to blue-collar voters as hypocritical and self-evidently fraudulent. To the SPD, the *völkisch* coalition's campaign appealed to the worst in German political culture. The Nazis, like the Communists, were not interested in the welfare of the working class, the SPD charged, but were intent on destroying democratic government and throwing the country into civil war.[188] The Communists agreed that Nazi efforts to rouse a working-class following were nothing but "empty rhetoric and demagoguery," but the KPD was not above employing much of the same *völkisch* terminology in its own campaigns. Thus, while condemning the Nazi assault on "Jewish capital," the KPD argued that the goal of such attacks was "to divert the working class from the struggle against the entire Jewish and Aryan bourgeoisie." The Nazi campaign against the "Jewish Republic" was nothing but a big lie, the Communists charged. The only plank in the *völkisch* platform to be taken seriously was "not the battle against Jewish capital nor the clamor against the stock market, nor the ranting against parliamentarianism." The only policy that mattered to the Nazis, the KPD warned, was the "struggle against the revolutionary workers and against bolshevism."[189]

These counterattacks by the two major proletarian parties proved quite effective. The data of Table 2.6 would seem to indicate that Nazi efforts to secure a beachhead on the embattled shores of working-class politics were successfully thwarted by the Marxist parties. The Social Democratic vote is strongly related to the industrial blue-collar variable in both Protestant and Catholic samples, while registering mixed results in mining. The Communist vote, on the other hand, is related to the blue-collar variable in mining and metalworking, a sector where unemployment remained dismally high throughout the year,[190] and to the industrial variable in Protestant areas. In contrast, the National Socialist/blue-collar

Table 2.6. Party Vote and the Blue-Collar Working Class (BC), 1920–1924

All BC

	Protestant (N=152)			Catholic (N=64)		
	1920	1924a	1924b	1920	1924a	1924b
NSDAP	NA	.619	−.780	NA	−.792	−.378
DNVP	−.817	−.271	−.171	−.104	−.623	−.874
DVP	.210*	−.221	−.645	−.143	−.220*	−.332
DDP	.128*	−.297	−.118	−.279	−.353	−.320
Z	−.514	−.718	−.714	−.154*	.214*	−.393
SPD	.121	.370	.217	.210*	−.144*	−.988
KPD	−.254	.356	.630	−.309	.242	.169
Other	−.769	−.805	−.353	.150	.141	.140

BC in Industry[a]

	Protestant (N=152)			Catholic (N=64)		
	1920	1924a	1924b	1920	1924a	1924b
NSDAP	NA	.246*	−.815	NA	.448*	.362*
DNVP	.196*	−.334	−.193	−.202	−.358	.251*
DVP	−.221*	−.997	.129*	−.520	−.367	−.247
DDP	−.590	.251*	−.386	.101*	−.156	−.147
Z	−.100*	−.101*	−.982	−.964	.121*	−.333
SPD	.121*	.370	.217	.363	.418	.520
KPD	.254	.356	.630	−.385	.212*	.184*
Other	−.341	−.663	−.372	−.243	−.296*	−.112*

BC in Mining/Metalworking[a]

	Protestant (N=152)			Catholic (N=64)		
	1920	1924a	1924b	1920	1924a	1924b
NSDAP	NA	−.558	−.195	NA	.301*	−.329
DNVP	−.486	−.267	−.133	−.269	−.472	−.283
DVP	.199*	.147*	.274*	−.490	−.253	−.143
DDP	−.554	−.514	−.151	−.791	−.891	−.569
Z	−.332	−.610	−.379	−.368	−.928	−.262
SPD	−.473	.430	−.178	.224	.197	.366
KPD	.502	.217	.236	.322	.297	.323
Other	−.222	−.584	−.185	.126*	.114*	.186*

Table 2.6. (continued)

	BC in Handicrafts[a]					
	Protestant (N=152)			Catholic (N=64)		
	1920	1924a	1924b	1920	1924a	1924b
NSDAP	NA	.667	.600	NA	1.18	.220
DNVP	−.317	−.371	−.318	−.678	−.810	−.451
DVP	−.949	.190*	.235*	−.842	−.511	−.250
DDP	−.508	−.709	−.150	.742	.370*	.400*
Z	−.109	−.109	−.122	−.703	−.839	−1.32
SPD	.128	.213	.124	.852	1.24	1.76
KPD	.104*	.399	.114*	−.455	−.414	−.735
Other	.128*	−.533	−.180	−.506	−.227*	−.140*

	BC in Agriculture[a]					
	Protestant (N=121)			Catholic (N=125)		
	1920	1924a	1924b	1920	1924a	1924b
NSDAP	NA	−.138	−.283	NA	.211	.483
DNVP	.162*	−.104*	.362	.138	.153	.145
DVP	−.789	−.162	−.142	−.540	−.975	−.686
DDP	−.788	−.892	−.126	−.539	−.740	−.616
Z	−.906	−.156	−.149	−1.22	−.189	−1.11
SPD	.202	.130	.468	.358	.404	.418
KPD	.194	.178	.148	.948	.234	.105
Other	.106*	−.210*	.166*	−.610*	−.126*	−.164*

NOTE: The figures are unstandardized regression coefficients (b), controlling for old middle class, new middle class, *Rentnermittelstand*, religion, and urbanization (population size).
a. Presents coefficients for each component of the working class, controlling for all remaining elements of the BC population in addition to those variables listed above.

* These coefficients are not significant at the .05 level.

coefficients for both major industrial sectors are either strongly negative or insignificant in both elections.

Yet, in spite of these figures, the labor vote in 1924 was not the exclusive preserve of the Marxist parties, for the *völkisch* coalition also appears to have attracted a significant blue-collar following. Working-class support for National Socialism has been considerably underestimated in the past, primarily because researchers have traditionally worked within the confines of the official census categories. If, however, these rather amorphous categories are modified to differentiate between the handicrafts and industrial sectors,[191] a significant pattern of blue-collar support for National Socialism can be isolated. In both elections of 1924 the National Socialist vote is positively influenced by the blue-collar variable in handicrafts and small-scale manufacturing. The Nazi coefficients are strong and stable in the Protestant sample and surprisingly powerful—if less consistent—in the Catholic districts. Moreover, as developments after 1928 will indicate, these Nazi/blue-collar figures are both significant and portentous.

Employed in small businesses and often without special occupational skills, these workers represented the least organized elements of the blue-collar population. They also made up approximately one-third of the German working class. As assistants or journeymen in artisan shops, many such workers wandered between the well-established social fronts, belonging neither to the entrepreneurial *Mittelstand* nor the organized working class. The bitter social resentment engendered by this "in-between" status is vividly expressed by one such artisan worker who turned to National Socialism:

> I thought I would get ahead through honest labor, but when I realized how Marxism and liberalism had taken the soul out of work, how deceit, falsehood, and servility bring you material advantages, I turned away in disgust. The struggle of a young person for recognition and respect is greeted only with contemptuous smiles. He is just a "proletarian," a "worker." He has no connections. He is just "a number," used to get the job done. . . . On the one side [the worker encounters] the liberal entrepreneurs with their loot, for whom dividends are everything, and on the other side the Marxist workers and their representatives, for whom the pay envelope is all-important. On one side contempt, on the other fraternal conflict. Things must change." [192]

The National Socialists attempted to reach those workers not only by emphasizing their commitment to the establishment of a classless *Volksgemeinschaft* but by offering a number of proposals, most quite vague, some surprisingly specific, for social and economic reform. Despite regional variations in emphasis, the *völkisch* coalition remained outspoken in its support for the restoration of the eight-hour day, a position that certainly distinguished it from the liberal and conservative parties while linking it with Social Democracy. Similarly, the National Socialists espoused the establishment of *Werkgemeinschaften* in the plants, presumably giving labor a voice in the formulation and conduct of company policy as well as a profit-sharing scheme carrying the weight of law. The party also favored action to prohibit the hiring of women and juveniles in large plants. These demands, along with calls to "break interest slavery," to "nationalize the banks," to "crush stock-market and international capital," and to realize the principle of "the common good before the individual good," were always couched in a radical rhetoric that employed much of the political vocabulary familiar to German workers.[193]

Yet in spite of the efforts of the labor-oriented elements within the *völkisch* movement to place greater emphasis on the social revolutionary aspects of the Nazi appeal, National Socialism in 1924 maintained an ambivalent ideological posture. "Are we a workers' party or an employers' party?" one troubled member of the Stuttgart NSDAP had asked before the 1923 Putsch.[194] The campaigns of the following year did little to resolve that question. The appeals of the DVFP and the NSFB were not directed at a single social stratum or religious confession, and the social contours of the *völkisch* vote were not shaped by a single socioeconomic or religious group. The result was to engender considerable confusion concerning the appropriate position of the *völkisch* movement along the traditional lines of social and political cleavage. To the DNVP and its conservative followers, the Nazis appeared "leftist," and the movement was condemned as "bolshevism in nationalist wrapping." The Social Democrats and Communists, on the other hand, felt compelled to warn their blue-collar constituents against the counterfeit socialism of the Nazis.[195]

With its radical social rhetoric and its equivocal view of the nature of capitalism, the *völkisch* coalition in 1924 sought to carve out a new position between the well-notched columns of German electoral politics. "The DVFP is neither a right-wing party nor a left-wing party," one *völkisch* leaflet explained. "It is not an extension of the German Nationalists and has nothing to do with the Communists or any other existing party. It stands above parties, because it wants to destroy the party mentality."[196] In a confidential memorandum dispatched to local party functionaries in February 1924, the DVFP sketched the pose it would strike in the forthcoming campaign: "The *völkisch* movement represents a new political synthesis of seemingly contradictory and antagonistic currents. On national issues it stands on the far right, on social issues on the far left."[197] Although some variations in focus existed from region to region, the essential image the party sought to project in 1924 was that of "a great reform movement" determined to "fight the present economic system, which stands under the yoke of international Jewish finance capital."[198] As such, the party's electoral strategy did not follow the predictable social lines of traditional German electioneering but aimed at the disaffected, the frustrated, and the desperate, regardless of social or economic background. As one National Socialist pamphlet made clear, the party's appeal was directed at:

> those forced to sell or liquidate their property because of the inflation; those mortgagees and creditors, holders of savings accounts and insurance policies who have been swindled by bad legislation; those businessmen, whether large or small, whose existence has been threatened by the economic robbery of the government and the machinations of the powerful department store companies; those artisans whose economic floor has been ripped out from under their feet; those pensioners who have been reduced to charity cases and even to beggars; those disabled veterans before whom the "thanks of the fatherland" were once dangled; those civil servants and members of the free professions, workers, and white-collar employees whose constitutional right to work and bread has been taken from them by an inept economic policy.[199]

Religion

Just as the *völkisch* movement failed to conform to the accepted pattern of class politics in 1924, the confessional composition of its constituency also proved uncommonly diverse. The confessional lines of German electoral politics had been sharply drawn since the emergence of the party system in the nineteenth century, and voting in the new republic conformed neatly to the established pattern. In 1924, as in the past, the Zentrum, with rare exceptions, dominated the political stage in areas of Catholic concentration. In the sample of predominately Catholic communities, the party's vote averaged 40 percent, more than double its national figure. In the Protestant sample, on the other hand, the Zentrum's showing, with only 4 percent of the vote, was predictably weak. Whereas the major nonconfessional parties, from the DNVP to the SPD, found some support in Catholic areas, they fared much better with the Protestant electorate. Of the major parties participating in the elections of 1924, only the National Socialists and the Communists lacked a clearly definable confessional profile.[200]

In May, the DVFP scored its greatest victories in thoroughly Protestant Mecklenburg and in Lower Bavaria, an overwhelmingly Catholic district. Even in December, when the National Socialist vote plummeted, it is esti-

Table 2.7. Party Vote and Religious Confession, 1920–1924 (N=458)

	Protestant			Catholic		
	1920	1924a	1924b	1920	1924a	1924b
NSDAP	NA	.546	.445	NA	.540	.419
DNVP	.895	.889	.821	−.686	−.710	−.658
DVP	.620	.511	.369	−.111	−.610	−.486
DDP	.915	.416	.254	−.249	−.833	−.146*
Z	−.896	−.845	−.864	.943	.912	.919
SPD	.856	.610	.649	−.174	−.764	−.831
KPD	.156*	−.401*	−.402*	.153*	−.387*	−.401*
Other	.216	.233	.210	−.224	−.289	−.246

NOTE: The figures are unstandardized regression coefficients (b), controlling for old middle class, new middle class, *Rentnermittelstand*, blue-collar workers, and urbanization (population size).

* These coefficients are not significant at the .05 level.

mated that almost 17 percent of the votes won by the NSFB were cast by Catholics, ranking Nazi dependence on Catholic support second only to that of the KPD among nonconfessional parties.[201] But just as the KPD's Catholic spirit was confined largely to the party's coal mining constituency, Nazi success among Catholic voters was primarily a regional phenomenon, restricted for the most part to the nonindustrial areas of Bavaria where the party was best organized.[202] Still, the Nazi share of the vote in these Catholic regions remained well above its national figure for both elections in 1924.

In attempting to rebuff the Nazi challenge, the Zentrum consistently warned its voters that National Socialism was an enemy of Christianity in general and Catholicism in particular. The Nazis were driven by "a fanatical hatred of Christians and Jews," the Zentrum charged, and preferred "the old Wotan cult" to "Christian faith and Christian virtue."[203] This *völkisch* assault on Christianity was particularly dangerous for German Catholics, the party implied, since the Nazis seemed determined to revive the old antagonisms between the confessions. If one had any doubts about the Nazis' anti-Catholic attitude, the Zentrum suggested that he need only "read with what malice they repeatedly toss the old, long buried *Kulturkampf* slogans of 'ultramontanism,' 'Jesuitism,' and 'enemies of the Reich' at German Catholics. If you want revolution,

Kulturkampf, misery, and chaos," the Zentrum concluded, "then vote *völkisch.*"[204]

Along with condemning National Socialism as a threat to organized religion, the Zentrum attacked the party for its political radicalism and its failure to develop constructive approaches to the social and cultural problems confronting not only the Catholic population but the nation as a whole. "No party can survive for long," the Zentrum asserted, "solely on a rejection of the present state." *Germania* conceded that in May, "when the elections were held under the impact of general dissatisfaction and exasperation, the temptation to cast a radical vote was considerable." In December, however, the overriding goal of the election was "the establishment of a strong middle." Indeed, advocacy of a "middle course" between the extremes of right and left became the most prominent theme of the Zentrum's campaigns in 1924.[205]

Yet while advocating the politics of moderation and condemning the nascent fascist movement, much of the Zentrum's social and political rhetoric sounded quite similar to that found in Nazi electoral propaganda. Like National Socialism, the Zentrum sought to bridge the class cleavages emphasized in the electoral strategy of the traditional nonconfessional parties, appealing with almost equal emphasis to farmers, shopkeepers, salaried employees, and workers. Aside from the attainment of specific confessional goals, the Zentrum's primary social objective was "not to divide the German people into first- and second-class citizens but to lead them toward a true German *Volksgemeinschaft!*"[206] The party warned, however, that "no healthy people's community" could develop from class conflict, and, as in National Socialist propaganda, the Zentrum urged the blue-collar electorate to desert communism and Social Democracy. Similarly, the party dismissed liberalism, with its "materialistic *Weltanschauung,*" as bankrupt and condemned the DNVP for its shortsighted foreign policy and its desire to "rule the people, not to serve them."[207]

Given these apparent sociopolitical similarities, the Nazis moved to reassure Catholics, and indeed all Christians, that the *völkisch* movement was a friend of religion. Nazi electoral literature, especially those pamphlets and articles addressed to women, tirelessly pledged to "fight all enemies of the Christian faiths as well as all things in the press, in literature, in the cinema, and on the stage" that were "harmful to culture and religion." The *völkisch* movement desired "the healing of the *Volk,* the establishment of a new fatherland, and the creation of a greater German *Volksgemeinschaft* based on the Christian family."[208] Alluding to the vexing question of confessional education, the Nazi platform of 1924 espoused a system of "public education on a Christian and *völkisch* basis," while reiterating the movement's commitment to "freedom of conscience and the defense of the Christian religion." [209] Nazi pamphleteers even described National Socialism as "in its essence a religious movement," which recognized that "the German without religion is unthinkable." [210]

Above all, the Nazis strongly condemned the introduction of religion into the political arena, a tactic, they charged, employed by the Zentrum to frighten voters away from the *völkisch* movement. As a result, the National Socialists promised to "fight against the mixing of religion with Jewish . . . party politics." The *völkisch* goal, as it was presented to the voting public, was "to maintain the purity of religion by following the example of the Lord, who drove the usurers and charlatans out of the temple." [211]

To reassure Catholic voters, the Nazis explained that the *völkisch* coalition had no quarrel with the Church at all but with "ultramontanism" and "political Catholicism." "The pope and the Church, as representatives of the Holy Faith, are much too sacred to us to drag into the dirt of everyday political debates," the Nazis piously asserted. The party, however, could only regret that the Zentrum and its Bavarian ally, the Bavarian People's party (Bayerische Volkspartei—BVP) had not left "politics outside the Church." If, as the Zentrum alleged, religion was in danger, the responsibility lay with that party itself, the Nazis claimed, and its support for the Social Democratic governments of the Weimar Republic. Indeed, the Zentrum's endorsement of "Jewish parliamentarianism and modern democracy," the *völkisch* press charged, had proven to be a major factor in the erosion of religious values in Germany. [212]

National Socialist appeals to Protestant voters employed similar themes and provoked somewhat similar responses. The DNVP, which more than any other party viewed itself as the defender of traditional Protestant values, shared National Socialism's anti-Semitic orientation but deplored *völkisch* attitudes toward Christianity. In particular, the Nationalists were incensed at the Nazis' association of Christianity with Judaism. "The DVFP cries 'away from Christianity, away from Christ, for both are inseparable from *Judentum*,'" the Nationalists charged, and this attitude was simply indefensible. Such ideas, the DNVP lamented, had led to the *völkisch* movement's deplorable departure from the path of established Christianity. Some *völkisch* leaders had "gone so far as to call for a return to the pagan cults of the old Germans. They reject the Bible as 'un-*völkisch*' and speak of the heathen gods Wotan and Teut as the true symbols of *völkisch* cultural thought." No responsible Protestant, the DNVP concluded, could in good conscience cast his vote for such an enemy of Christianity. [213]

The Nazis responded to these charges by accusing the DNVP of an "outrageous abuse of religion." By falsely claiming that National Socialism intended to destroy Christianity, the DNVP was simply "using religion to mask its own political objectives." The Nationalists were actually guilty of engaging in the same sort of divisive confessional politics that they had traditionally condemned in the Zentrum, the Nazis charged, and the *völkisch* coalition again called on Protestant voters "to protect [their] faith against party politics."[214]

The ultimate aim of *völkisch* religious policy, according to the Nazi press, was to end confessional conflict in Germany and to bridge the fissure that separated the two major wings of the Christian faith. Just as the SPD had divided Germans into two classes and attempted to turn one class against the other, so, too, the *Kulturkampf* between Protestants and Catholics had turned Christian against Christian. While Protestants and Catholics fought, the moral fiber of the nation had disintegrated as Jews infiltrated German social, political, and cultural life. The Zentrum and DNVP might endlessly debate the merits of confessional schools, but the real danger to Christian values sprang from the expansion of Jewish influence in German society. Here lay the real issue confronting Germany, the Nazis argued, and "unconditional peace between both Christian confessions" was imperative if this Jewish threat was to be effectively countered. Among the major political parties concerned with religious issues, only the *völkisch* movement, the Nazis maintained, had identified the critical problem. Ultimately, they concluded, "the real test of a party's Christianity is its stance on the Jewish question."[215]

The extent to which voters from the two Christian confessions found these arguments convincing is, of course, difficult to ascertain in retrospect. An examination of the sexual composition of the Nazi electorate does, however, provide a very useful clue. Appeals emphasizing religious issues were almost invariably addressed explicitly to women voters. Efforts of the nonsocialist parties to reach the female electorate centered almost exclusively on religious, cultural, or educational issues, usually stressing the need to instill proper Christian values in German youth. In a typical Zentrum appeal to women, for example, the party reminded the female voter that "as wife and mother, you . . . are the protector of Christian morality in the state and in the family. Your highest ideal—the Christian education of youth—must, therefore, be secured at the ballot box."[216] The DNVP also emphasized the central role of women in the religious and moral upbringing of youth, but took the additional step of linking the inculcation of Christian values with another educational "mission" for women: "the perservation of German ways and German customs." The Nationalists welcomed women into the political arena, the

DNVP declared, "because of their essentially conservative orientation, which, by committing itself to the continuing organic development of the traditional, turns away from all violent revolution." [217]

Although certainly less religiously oriented in their electoral strategy than the Zentrum and DNVP, the two liberal parties also turned primarily to religious, cultural, and educational themes when addressing women voters. Neither the DVP nor DDP endorsed the confessional school, so close to the hearts of the Zentrum and DNVP, but, as they reassured women voters, both favored some form of religious instruction in the public schools. Rather than dwelling on the potentially troublesome school issue, the DVP preferred to stress the larger dangers of Marxism in German society. "Marriage, family, authority, religion, faith, conscience, and love of fatherland are not outmoded ideas," it declared in one typical appeal to women. "They still constitute the meaning, content, and value of life today." It warned that "the exclusively materialistic *Lebensanschauung* of socialism" had "already produced catastrophic effects on our youth" and urged women in particular to join the struggle against Marxist influences in German social and cultural life. "If we want to be healthy again," the party claimed, "socialism in our people must be overcome. . . . It is a struggle . . . from which women must not shrink," the DVP declared, "since it is above all a battle not over material values but over the future of the Christian, German culture." [218]

Although the DDP did not share this heavy emphasis on religious themes in its appeals to women, Democratic campaign literature targeted for the female electorate did stress the same cultural and educational issues. Its orientation toward those themes however, was decidedly secular, emphasizing, for example, the civic responsibilities of the educational system in the new republic. "We must have a school for our children that educates them to become loyal, upright republicans, true to the constitution," the DDP emphatically declared in an appeal to "wives and mothers." "Away with a faculty that calls itself Nationalist or *völkisch*, meaning antirepublican, and fosters hate and dissension instead of love and understanding in our youth." [219]

This emphasis on educational and cultural affairs, particularly when placed in a religious framework, proved quite effective for the bourgeois parties in their efforts to recruit women voters. Although women, like men, tended to vote along the same social and confessional lines that dominated German electoral politics, two significant variations emerged in the early Weimar years. Regardless of class, women tended to be underrepresented in the constituencies of radical parties and overrepresented in moderate parties, particularly those that had demonstrated a strong interest in religious affairs. Thus, working-class women were more inclined to vote Social Democratic than Communist, while among the nonsocialist parties, women voters were disproportionately represented in the DNVP, the Zentrum, or one of the small regional or special interest parties with a pronounced religious orientation.[220] Not surprisingly, the *völkisch* constituency was dominated by male voters in 1924, the percentage of women in the Nazi electorate being smaller than any other party's except the Communists'.[221]

National Socialist efforts to defuse the religious issue, therefore, appear to have failed. Still, if reservations about the movement's religious orientation cost the Nazis votes, the confessional composition of the *völkisch* constituency was remarkably varied in 1924. While religious confession played a very salient role in the electoral composition of the traditional parties, it was not a significant factor in shaping the contours of the National Socialist vote in either May or December. Just as the Nazis had sought and won the backing of a surprisingly wide range of social groups, the party's success was not confined to either Protestant or Catholic Germany. The *völkisch* constituency that emerged in 1924 was marked by its uncommonly diverse social and confessional composition. By actively seeking and winning significant support from the frustrated and discontented in virtually all walks of life, the *völkisch* coalition had become something unique in German political culture, a catchall party of protest.

III
Disintegration and Crisis: The Elections of 1928 and 1930

On 15 January 1925, the *Bürgerblock* government championed by the triumphant DNVP was at last established, and with its formation, the Weimar Republic entered a period of relative prosperity and political stability. Just as the early postwar years had been characterized by economic turmoil and political unrest, the years from 1924 to 1929 would be remembered as the Golden Twenties, a brief era of social and political tranquillity wedged tenuously between the seismic disruptions of the hyperinflation and the Great Depression. Economic recovery, based largely on a massive influx of short-term foreign loans, was accompanied by an unusual calm in the political arena. The Reichstag elected in December 1924 was able to serve virtually a full term, while changes in government amounted to little more than minor shufflings of the cabinet, never significantly altering its center-right orientation.[1] Even the death of Reich President Ebert in 1925 was followed by a relatively placid campaign, in which Paul von Hindenburg, the aging field marshal, prevailed on the strength of the same center-right coalition.[2] Moreover, as the traumas of the inflation and stabilization crises faded, the threat of political radicalism also subsided. The Social Democrats, with their strong showing in December 1924, seemed to have eclipsed the Communists, and the Nationalists (until 1924 the most vociferous opponents of the republic) not only vanquished the *völkisch* coalition but entered the cabinet, sharing government responsibility for almost three years.

For the National Socialists, in particular, the return of stability presented serious strategic problems. After Hitler's release from prison in early 1925, the party broke away from the *völkisch* coalition and announced a determination to pursue a path of legality to political power. In practical terms, this meant a drive to expand the party's membership and successful participation in the electoral process. In both areas, the party adopted what came to be known as "the urban strategy," focusing its propagandistic efforts on labor-oriented, anticapitalist themes calculated to attract the support of the urban working class. This strategy was naturally endorsed most enthusiastically by the National Socialists of north Germany, whose leading spokesman, Gregor Strasser, served as the party's propaganda chief from September 1926 until the close of the following year.[3] Yet even at the apex of the left's ascendance, the NSDAP's sociopolitical orientation remained blurred. While the northern faction continued to press for greater initiatives to woo the urban proletariat, National Socialists in the south persisted in stressing the radical nationalist and anti-Semitic themes characteristic of their stance in 1924. The future of National Socialism, they contended, lay not in the cities, where the Socialists and Communists held the allegiance of the working class, but among the *Mittelstände* of the towns and countryside.[4]

Throughout this period, Hitler's own position in the party's ideological debates remained characteristically vague. After his release from Landsberg, Hitler was determined to reestablish and formalize his control over the diverse National Socialist movement. His interests were primarily organizational, not doctrinal, and he was willing to tolerate considerable internal controversy in ideological matters so long as the contestants recognized his ultimate power to determine party policy. Although he had himself singled out "the mass of working people (*Arbeitnehmer*)" as the "reservoir from which the movement should recruit its followers," he preferred to refrain from direct intervention in doctrinal disputes unless his own position as Führer seemed threatened.[5] Consequently, the debate between the party's left and right wings persisted, and ideological opacity continued to plague the NSDAP as it entered the vigorous regional campaigns of the stabilization period.

Between 1925 and 1928 Hitler's first priority was to create a broadly based, centrally directed party organization necessary for the NSDAP's entry onto the stage of Weimar electoral politics. The party leadership (*Reichsleitung*) was in broad agreement that the *völkisch* coalition's conduct of the 1924 campaigns had been too disjointed, lacking clarity of focus and central direction. With the reestablishment of the party in 1925, Hitler hoped to concentrate responsibility for conducting nationwide propaganda in the *Reichsleitung* in Munich. He was convinced that if the newly reconstituted NSDAP was to compete effectively in electoral politics, it needed a national grassroots organization capable of both recruiting members and mobilizing voters. In the spring of 1926, the NSDAP, therefore, took the first steps toward creating such an organization. Its model, as a top secret communiqué of 20 March revealed, was the propaganda apparatus of the Marxist parties. "When we take a closer look at the propaganda system of these parties," the communiqué explained, "we see a network of cells spreading across the entire Reich." That network was "fed [information and directives] by a central head-quarters not only on a monthly but on a weekly basis . . ." and was ready for mobilization when the leadership chose to employ it. The communi-qué claimed that National Socialism had made great strides without such an organization, but the party could hardly expect local leaders to con-duct effective political agitation "without knowing the leadership's posi-tion and without the financial means of enlightening the public." To rem-edy this situation, a fundamental shift in the party's approach to political agitation was in order.[6]

The first step in this reform was to be taken at the grass-roots level. The party leadership ordered every local party chapter (*Ortsgruppe*) to estab-lish a propaganda cell by 26 March 1926. The cell was to serve as a com-mittee on propaganda and political agitation and was to be staffed by party members "infused with a fanatical, fiery spirit for our movement." In an effort to guarantee a broad social perspective within the cell, the party explicitly warned against selecting persons from the same occupa-tional background and dictated that one-third of the cell's participants should be women. Similarly, in an attempt to provide centralized direc-tion for local activities, the party also insisted that the propaganda cells bypass the regional leaders (*Gauleiter*) and establish direct contact with Munich. Specifically, they were instructed to report to the Propaganda Division of the *Völkischer Beobachter*, which would be responsible for providing leaflets, posters, and other information on the party's propa-ganda objectives.[7]

Although the creation of this network did get underway immediately, neither the state of the NSDAP's finances nor the level of the party's membership permitted the sort of national grass-roots activity that Hitler envisioned. In fact, by the summer of 1926 an alternative strategy was already being suggested by the ambitious executive secretary of the party's Ruhr Gau, Joseph Goebbels. Writing in Gregor Strasser's *Na-tional-Sozialistische Briefe*, Goebbels praised the NSDAP's expanding or-ganizational network, but he soberly warned that the party should have no illusions about its strength. "This network is ready to break in some places, in others is too finely spun, while here and there it is as delicate as a spider's web." On the other hand, Goebbels pointed out, the party was truly well organized in three or four areas, and rather than dispersing its propagandistic energies over the entire country, the NSDAP should con-centrate its resources in these places. Reflecting the party's largely urban orientation, Goebbels argued that "our objective in the coming winter must be to transform one, maybe two dozen large metropolitan areas (*Grossstädte*) into unshakable bulwarks of the movement." These cities should be carefully selected, and then, only after the most exhaustive and detailed preparation, subjected to an intensive propaganda barrage. Following centralized direction and uniform guidelines, these propaganda offensives would saturate the selected cities with leaflets, pamphlets, parades, rallies, and appearances by prominent National Socialist leaders. If these methods were employed, Goebbels concluded, the party could maximize its limited financial resources, make use of its very best speakers, and devastate its opponents in these targeted cities. Having secured such urban bulwarks, the NSDAP could then launch its assault on the surrounding countryside.[8]

Although Goebbels's strategy had much to recommend it to the fledgling NSDAP, the plan was not implemented in 1926. Instead, Hitler opted to continue the party's emphasis on national grass-roots expansion and to increase the central control over its burgeoning apparatus. That decision was formalized at the NSDAP's first national congress at Nuremberg in the following year, when Hitler officially clarified the chain of command within the party. The local party chapters were explicitly subordinated to the Gauleiters, who were, in turn, appointed directly by Hitler. Henceforth the *Ortsgruppen* were required to submit monthly reports on their propaganda activities to their regional superiors. These reports were processed at Gau headquarters and then passed on to the Propaganda Division of the *Reichsleitung* in Munich, where they could be analyzed and used in the formulation of party propaganda and campaign strategy. Using this institutional framework, the Propaganda Division, administered between 1927 and 1930 by Heinrich Himmler, was well on its way to establishing the national organizational network, grass-roots expertise, and uniform propaganda procedures that would be used in the national campaigns of subsequent years.[9]

The first opportunity for the NSDAP to test its national propaganda apparatus arrived in the spring of 1928, when the Reichstag that was elected four years earlier was dissolved and new elections set for 20 May. From the outset the *Reichsleitung* was determined to conduct a centrally directed campaign throughout the country. Following the party's recently established operational guidelines, the *Reichsleitung* was to determine the substance and strategy of the campaign. It would define the themes to be developed in the party's propaganda and the content of its electoral appeals. To guarantee that control, the *Ortsgruppen* were instructed to order all campaign leaflets, posters, pamphlets, and other propaganda materials direct from Munich. The Gauleiters, whose intermediary role between *Reichsleitung* and *Ortsgruppen* was extremely important, were to monitor all campaign activities within their region, to provide coordination between local groups, and to supply detailed instructions on the methods of electoral propaganda. Indeed, the Gauleiters focused their attention almost exclusively on the techniques of grass-roots campaigning. Communiqués from the Gau leadership to the *Ortsgruppen* offered a steady stream of directives on when and how to stage parades, conduct public meetings, arrange for the appearance of outside speakers, distribute leaflets, and post placards. The *Gauleitung* of the Ruhr, for example, emphasized to its locals that it was useless to distribute leaflets at polling places on election day since most voters would be weary of reading such material by then and just throw them away. Instead, the *Ortsgruppen* were instructed to distribute leaflets, on which the NSDAP placed enormous emphasis, steadily in the fourteen days before the election and then not on the streets but at private residences where they would be more likely to be read. Every *Ortsgruppe* was to see to it that its leaflets were "passed out in individual homes and apartment houses, starting on the top floor and working down." The major push, of course, was to come within the last days before the election.[10]

In spite of the NSDAP's obvious progress in establishing a centrally directed national organization, the propaganda apparatus of the party was still very much in a developmental stage when the 1928 campaign began. Although the Gauleiters provided important instructions on campaign techniques and the *Reichsleitung* offered the necessary printed matter, the *Ortsgruppen* were expected to finance their own campaign activities without aid from above. As a communiqué from the Brandenburg *Gauleitung* reminded its locals: "We again point out that the [local] groups cannot receive any funding from the Gau and must therefore cover the costs of propaganda, placards, travel expenses for outside speakers, and so on from admission fees, etc." The NSDAP, as a Ruhr Gau directive explained to financially strapped locals, "must make up for its lack of funds with a smooth functioning organization." That position did not change in the following years; the *Ortsgruppen* of the NSDAP were expected to develop election funds and to finance their own campaigns. In 1928, with the party's membership still low, its national reputation still cloudy, and its organization rudimentary, that task proved difficult indeed.[11]

In addition to financial problems, the party organization was beset with other difficulties in 1928. Lines of communication between Munich, the Gauleiters, and the locals were not always dependable, in spite of the party's new system of command. Indeed, to be sure of reaching the

Ortsgruppen at a critical stage of the campaign, the *Reichsleitung* felt compelled to publish propaganda directives in the *Völkischer Beobachter*, to which all locals were required to subscribe.[12] Moreover, despite the party's emphasis on the importance of leaflets, placards, and other printed matter, the Nazis still relied on the locals to order them from Munich. Efforts to synchronize their appearance on the streets with speeches on particular themes or rallies spotlighting a specific social group—an impressive tactic that would distinguish subsequent National Socialist campaigns—was simply beyond the party's grasp in 1928.[13] Indeed, the party's organizational structure was still too loose to guarantee the *Reichsleitung* the degree of control that it desired. Symptomatically, a directive from Munich late in the campaign warned the NSDAP's still small regional party press that "Adolf Hitler has recently called attention to the fact that the party line prescribed in the *Völkischer Beobachter* is to be followed in all speeches and in the press of the movement. Deviations from this line . . . will result in the offending paper's loss of its status as an official organ of the NSDAP."[14] In 1928, even one such loss would have been significant, since the National Socialist press could count only two dailies and a small number of regional weeklies.[15]

Relying on a campaign apparatus that was still far from the "smooth functioning organization" that Hitler envisioned and unwilling to anchor itself securely on the traditional lines of socio-political cleavage, the NSDAP had drifted listlessly through the Golden Twenties, faring poorly in each of the Landtag elections in which it participated. Indeed, the party's unimpressive performance in the December election of 1924 proved to be an adumbration of the coming years. The party did not participate in the 1925 presidential elections, and in none of the ten provincial campaigns between 1924 and 1928 could the NSDAP muster even 4 percent of the vote. In 1928, only six National Socialist deputies sat in the 450-member Prussian legislature, while in the party's traditional Bavarian stronghold the NSDAP held only nine seats.[16] The path of legality that the party had followed since the failure of the Munich Putsch had led to a dead end. In the four years since their promising showing in the "inflation election" of May 1924, the National Socialists had proven exceptionally maladroit in the democratic arts of electoral politics.

The national elections of May 1928 merely confirmed that verdict. With less than 3 percent of the vote, the National Socialists saw themselves relegated to the status of a minor curiosity on the radical fringes of German politics. Many analysts, using the performance of the NSDAP as a yardstick, have even interpreted the elections of 1928 as a triumph of Weimar democracy. The radical right had suffered a serious setback,

Table 3.1. The Election of 2 May 1928 (percentage of vote)

NSDAP	DNVP	DVP	Zentrum	DDP	SPD	KPD	Other
2.6	14.2	8.7	15.2	4.8	29.8	10.6	13.7

while the prorepublican SPD had registered substantial gains. For the first time since 1923 a Social Democrat, Hermann Müller, assumed the chancellorship and was able to form a broadly based coalition government extending from the SPD to Stresemann's DVP. "The most significant factor of the elections," one observer typically noted, "was the reendorsement of the republican form of government by a majority of the German people." [17]

Yet in spite of these developments, signs of nascent destabilization within the Weimar party system were also discernible in 1928. Examination of the returns from the regional elections of the mid-twenties reveals that a substantial segment of the voting public, particularly those strata that had traditionally formed the constituencies of the liberal parties, had become dissatisfied with the established alternatives of bourgeois politics. Whereas in 1924 much of this disaffection was reflected in defections to the DNVP, the period following the inflation and stabilization crises witnessed a phenomenal growth of special interest or single-issue parties that flourished under the republic's system of proportional representation. In the elections of 1919 and 1920, these small parties had accounted for only 3 percent of the vote. By May 1924, however, they represented over 10 percent of the German electorate. Significantly, that percentage did not decline during the period of relative political and economic stability in the mid-twenties. In the Landtag elections held between 1924 and 1928, these marginal splinter parties consistently gained ground while the liberals stumbled. [18]

The rise of the special interest parties, therefore, became a major issue of the 1928 Reichstag campaign. The liberals sought to prevent further splintering of the middle-class vote, arguing that continued fragmentation would only weaken the *Mittelstand* and strengthen the position of the Marxist parties. The DVP, for example, warned that support for the special interest parties would alienate "the other *Stände*" and result in a battle of "all against all." [19] Sounding a defensive note not uncommon in liberal campaign literature, the party contended that "it is not true, though often asserted, that the DVP has neglected the interests of the handicrafts and commercial middle class." Artisans, shopkeepers, and other merchants should not look to small special interest parties to represent their views but a large national party capable of exerting influence in the government and in the economy. "Handicrafts and commerce can be helped not by fragmentation but by consolidation," the DVP contended, and the party persistently underscored the ineffectiveness of the most prominent special interest parties.[20]

The DDP concurred with this assessment. "With their small number of deputies," the DDP argued, the regional or special interest parties were "condemned to impotence" in the Reichstag. The Democrats warned voters not to cast their ballots for "splinter parties, which may be motivated by the best of intentions but have neither the power nor the capability to attain their goals."[21]

These pleas, however, went largely unheeded. The returns of the 1928 Reichstag election merely extended the trend that had developed in the regional campaigns of the mid-twenties. While the liberal vote slipped from its 1924 level of 16.4 percent to 13.5 percent, the special interest parties continued to climb, winning 14 percent of all ballots cast. Moreover, while the political stock of German liberalism slumped in the relatively prosperous Golden Twenties, the DNVP was unable to take advantage of that decline. The conservative position also deteriorated strikingly. Between 1924 and 1928 the Nationalists, like the liberals, suffered surprising setbacks in a number of important regional elections.

Having assumed government responsibility for the first time in 1925, the DNVP found itself increasingly besieged by a variety of groups disappointed with its performance. The party offered a particularly vulnerable target for those organizations representing creditor interests,[22] and in the Landtag elections after 1925 the DNVP was compelled to defend its own cabinet record. Like the liberals, the Nationalists responded by condemning single-issue politics and demanding a united front against the dangers of advancing socialism.[23] These standard campaign tactics, however, failed to check the party's faltering popularity, and in 1928 the DNVP was staggered by the Reichstag returns. Four years earlier, Nationalist candidates had captured 20 percent of the popular vote; in May 1928 only 14 percent.

The pattern that had emerged in the regional elections of the mid-twenties was, therefore, thrown into vivid relief by the last national campaign of the predepression era. In 1928 German voters were hardly radicalized, but important groups within the electorate were turning increasingly away from both liberalism and conservatism toward special interest alternatives. Individually these splinter parties were small and insignificant, but together they had outpolled the two liberal parties and almost matched the conservatives. The Real Estate and Homeowners party, the Reich Association for Revalorization, the Tenants party, the Reich Party of the Middle Class, and so on, certainly represented different sets of interests within the highly fragmented *Mittelstand*. Nonetheless, these parties spoke for a sizable segment of the bourgeois electorate which had been alienated by the traumas of the inflation and stabilization period, and which thereafter drifted gradually away from their traditional political moorings. Rather than an endorsement of the Weimar Republic, the Reichstag election of 1928 reflected a fundamental breakdown of voter identification with the traditional parties of the bourgeois center and right. The Nazis, of course, did not profit immediately from this fragmentation, but without the destabilization of traditional voting allegiances within the middle-class electorate, the spectacular rise of National Socialist fortunes after 1928 is hardly conceivable.[24]

On the eve of the Great Depression the NSDAP was simply one of a number of small parties jostling to inherit these troubled voters, and its record in the regional campaigns of the mid-twenties had been nothing short of abysmal. As a catchall movement of protest, National Socialism had been unable to maintain its appeal in a period of sustained economic and political stability. A reorientation of its sociopolitical strategy was clearly in order if the party were to make a breakthrough into the mainstream of German political life. Thus, in the aftermath of the disastrous 1928 campaign, the party leadership began a reevaluation of the NSDAP's considerably muddled public image.

Especially dispiriting for Nazi strategists was the consistently poor National Socialist performance in cities and towns. Despite years of intense urban agitation, the party had made only marginal inroads into the working-class electorate. The urban plan, with its vision of an industrial working-class constituency, had clearly failed. In 1928, however, the NSDAP had done surprisingly well in a number of rural areas, notably the farm communities of Schleswig-Holstein, Lower Saxony, Thuringia, and Upper Bavaria. Almost immediately, influential party leaders renewed their calls for a greater cultivation of the rural electorate and a sharper focus on the urban middle class. While the SPD and KPD blocked the Nazi advance into the mainstream of working-class politics, the declining popularity of the traditional liberal and conservative parties seemed to offer a promising opportunity for a revitalized NSDAP, especially in the countryside. Evaluating the outcome of the election, the *Völkischer Beobachter* of 31 May 1928, signaled the party's new direction: "The results in the countryside have shown that greater successes can be achieved with less expenditure of energy, money, and time than in the large cities. National Socialist rallies with good speakers are real events in small towns and villages and are talked about for weeks. In the large cities, on the other hand, even rallies with three or four thousand people disappear and are forgotten." [25]

As a result of these considerations, a significant shift in the focus of National Socialist propaganda gradually became apparent. Without in the least reducing its efforts to attract a blue-collar constituency, the NSDAP intensified and broadened its campaign to win support in both the urban and rural middle class. Although the party's program remained essentially unaltered, the social revolutionary strategy advocated by the Strasser wing of the party assumed an increasingly subordinate role in Nazi policy. Hitler himself had actually presaged the party's reorientation by publicly reaffirming the NSDAP's strong support for private property during the 1928 campaign, broadly implying that Nazi demands for expropriation applied only to alien or antisocial—that is, Jewish—businesses. Building on this foundation, the party gradually intensified its vilification of the department stores and consumer cooperatives so resented by small business and launched a major campaign to enhance its appeal to the rural, landowning electorate. In addition to these propagandistic offensives, the party also accelerated its efforts to infiltrate existing middle-class organizations as well as to sponsor occupational associations of its own. Between 1928 and 1930, when the first national election of the depression era was held, the NSDAP organized formal Nazi associations for doctors, lawyers, and students, while creating the rudiments of a National Socialist farm organization as well. [26] The NSDAP had not abandoned its determination to become a party of mass integration, bridging the traditional cleavages of German electoral politics. It had, however, become increasingly clear that a solid base of support within the fractious *Mittelstand* offered the most promising foundation from which to construct that span.

Accompanying this shift in social focus was a significant alteration in the party's approach to political agitation. Recognizing the NSDAP's very limited resources and determined to attract maximum public attention, the party adopted a variation of the plan first suggested by Goebbels two years earlier. In a memorandum of 24 December 1928, the Propaganda Division of the *Reichsleitung* announced its intention of conducting intensive propaganda offensives "from time to time in every region of Germany" that would "surpass . . . our previous agitational activities." In these carefully prepared and coordinated "propaganda actions" seventy to two hundred rallies would be held in a single Gau within a period of seven to ten days. Motorized SA parades would be held, well-known party dignitaries would make appearances, and thousands of leaflets would be distributed in over a hundred villages, towns, and cities of the Gau. An official list of the party's most effective and popular speakers would be made available to the locals along with instructions on how to place requests for their favorites with the Gau and national headquarters. The effect of such saturation, Himmler's memorandum argued, would be to focus tremendous attention on the party in a given locale, encourage local Nazi activists, spark the growth of the party press, and stimulate recruitment for the SA and other party organizations. Moreover, these "propaganda actions" were not simply to be held during campaigns but were intended to provide the NSDAP with a high public profile in the fallow periods between elections. Propaganda actions were, in fact, already planned in the Gaus Ostmark, Halle-Merseburg, and Saxony.[27]

These propagandistic and organizational reforms coincided, of course, with the first tremors of the oncoming depression, but in late 1928 and early 1929 the NSDAP still desperately needed an issue that would thrust the party back into the center of public attention. The revival of the highly volatile reparations problem in 1929 offered the party precisely the opportunity it needed. The Young Plan, like the Dawes Plan before it, was an international attempt to settle the thorny question of Germany's reparations debt. Specifically, the new plan sought to establish what Germany owed and to arrange a final schedule of payments. Drafted by an international committee of economic experts under the chairmanship of Owen Young, a final report was released on 9 June 1929, and called for the republic to make payments over a period of fifty-nine years with annuities mounting gradually to a maximum of approximately 2.4 billion marks. Although the final figure was considerably lower than the original Allied claim of 132 billion marks, the plan provoked a storm of protest in Germany. When the Müller government accepted the report as the basis for negotiation, the Nationalists opened talks with the NSDAP, the Stahlhelm, the Pan-German League, and other right-wing organizations to form a "front of national opposition" against the proposed settlement.[28]

This "national opposition" hoped to initiate a referendum against the plan, and a draft bill, the so-called Freedom Law, condemning the experts' report, was composed for submission to the Reichstag and ultimately the general public.[29] Although some militant elements in the NSDAP opposed even limited cooperation with the Nationalists, Hitler convinced party leaders that a temporary alliance would serve Nazi interests. Utilizing its new organizational structure and drawing considerable financial support from Nationalist sources, the NSDAP played by far the most prominent role in the virulently abusive campaign waged against the plan. The Nazi press assailed the agreement as a *Teufelspakt* inflicted upon Germany by the victor states. The "insane indebtedness" produced by the plan would destroy "all economic credit," the Nazis warned, and thus eliminate "job opportunities for millions." The plan's implementation would quite simply mean "the ruin of Germany's economy, its agriculture, its middle class, and its small businesses."[30]

The Dawes Plan had not brought the relief its sponsors had promised, the Nazis contended, and the Young Plan would be no different. It would, in fact, represent merely "a third Versailles," which would enslave Germany for generations.[31] "Germany," Gottfried Feder commented, "has been cast into chains for nothing but empty promises." Through the "criminal blindness" of the government, Germany had "voluntarily assumed the unbearable burden" that would destroy it. "An injustice without parallel in world history," Feder melodramatically concluded, "has been committed against the German people."[32]

Although the Nazi propaganda barrage dominated Germany's national press for months, the anti-Young petition received barely enough signatures to insure its submission to the Reichstag. There the Freedom Law was decisively defeated in late November. When the national referendum was finally held on 22 December 1929, it received less than a third of the required votes.[33]

The anti-Young campaign failed to sabotage the new plan, but it had served its purpose for Hitler and the NSDAP. Nazi association with the DNVP lent the movement a touch of respectability in conservative circles that it had previously lacked and constituted a major step in revising public impressions of the party. Following the conclusion of the campaign, police reports on Nazi activities noted that "more and more frequently members of the *Mittelstand* and the so-called better classes [*bessere Stände*] are seen." Officials in Cologne and Koblenz, for example, reported to the Prussian Ministry of the Interior that "in contrast to previous observation," they had found "an increasingly strong participation by the middle class and respectable bourgeois circles [*gut bürgerliche Kreise*] in National Socialist meetings."[34] Equally important, the NSDAP had emerged as the most prominent and aggressive representative of the antirepublican right at a time when the beleaguered government parties were vainly attempting to cope with the onset of the world economic crisis.

In late 1929, industrial production in Germany began a steady slide, dropping by 31 percent between June 1928 and May 1930. As production fell, unemployment rose. By January 1930, over three million Germans were unemployed, an increase of more than 200 percent since 1928.[35] With tax revenue shrinking and the government deficit mushrooming, the Müller cabinet found it increasingly difficult to fund the now desperately needed unemployment insurance program.[36] While the DVP, supported by the major employers' associations, insisted on a reduction of benefits, the SPD countered by demanding greater government contributions to the fund.[37] Without the mediation of Stresemann, whose untimely death in October 1929 had greatly strengthened the influence of the DVP's industrial right wing, compromise proved unattainable. Thus, after securing Reichstag approval of the Young Plan, the Great Coalition dissolved in March 1930.[38]

With the collapse of the Müller cabinet, government based on a sound parliamentary coalition was no longer feasible. Reich President Hindenburg then called upon Heinrich Brüning, parliamentary leader of the Zentrum, to form a government "above parties." Although members of the DVP, DDP, Zentrum and, temporarily, the DNVP, held positions in the new cabinet, the parties were not bound by their decisions, and the government clearly rested on the confidence of the aging Reich president.[39]

Confronted with a rapidly deteriorating financial situation, Brüning viewed a balanced budget and thus a reduction of expenditures as the critical first step toward a reversal of the Reich's sagging economic fortunes. Between March and July the government submitted a series of fiscal reforms to the Reichstag, only to have each rebuffed, for quite different reasons, by a majority composed of Social Democrats, Communists, Nazis, and Nationalists. In late June, with a national deficit of more than one billion marks, Brüning presented a final budgetary plan, which, in effect, would have increased the government contribution to the unemployment fund but would also have ultimately reduced benefits. When the proposed legislation met with staunch resistance in the Reichstag, the chancellor moved to implement the plan by emergency decree. Shortly thereafter a motion calling for the abrogation of the decrees received majority support in the Reichstag, but Brüning refused to capitulate. Instead of resigning, he dissolved the legislature and called for new elections in September.[40]

Brüning's decision was ill-advised. Using its expanding organizational network and its strategy of political saturation, the NSDAP had scored disquieting gains in a series of regional elections in late 1929 and early 1930. The upward curve of Nazi electoral fortunes had begun in Baden in October with 7 percent of the vote, followed in November by Lübeck with 8 percent, and an ominous 11 percent in Thuringia during December. Then, less than a month before Brüning's announcement of new national elections, the Nazis stunned observers by winning almost 15 percent of the vote in Saxony, a traditional leftist stronghold where only two years before the NSDAP had attracted less than 3 percent of the voting public.[41]

The losers of these regional elections were not the parties of the Marxist left, nor were they the small splinter parties representing special interests. Instead they were, as they had been since 1924, the traditional parties of the liberal center and the conservative right. Voter dissatisfaction with the traditional alternatives of bourgeois politics, which had begun to crystallize before the onset of the depression, continued in 1929–30, accelerated by their apparent inability to deal effectively with the nation's deteriorating economic condition.

The crisis of bourgeois politics was perhaps the most severe within the conservative camp. The precipitous decline of the DNVP's popularity between 1924 and 1928 had caught party leaders off guard, and many attributed the recurrent electoral losses to three years of cabinet responsibility in a political system the DNVP had previously condemned with passion. In fact, the party had never established an unequivocal position regarding participation in the Reich government, and although fundamentally opposed to the republic on ideological grounds, the DNVP was under considerable pressure from agrarian, industrial, and civil service organizations to take an active part in government decisions that would affect their interests. As a result, the party was sharply divided between a moderate faction which favored government participation on pragmatic economic grounds and a radical right wing which maintained that such participation merely undermined the credibility of the conservative cause.[42]

Tensions between these factions had never really subsided since the divisive Dawes vote in August 1924, and participation in two center-right coalitions between 1925 and 1928 had only intensified the conflicting pressures on the party's beleaguered leadership. Following the disastrous Nationalist showing at the polls in May 1928, however, the internal conflicts escalated rapidly, as each faction blamed the other for the party's poor electoral performance. In October, after months of bitter debate, the moderate Westarp was replaced as party chairman by Alfred Hugenberg, the leader of the radical right wing, and the DNVP entered a protracted period of internal crisis.[43]

Within months, Hugenberg's immoderate attacks on the party's left wing had alienated important elements of the Christian-Nationalist white-collar unions, and his insistence on unswerving adherence to his commands greatly exacerbated the dissension within moderate ranks.[44] Opposition to Hugenberg's leadership, however, reached a crescendo during the campaign against the Young Plan. All elements of the DNVP were vigorously opposed to the new agreement, but moderates were concerned about the party's support for the Freedom Law. Since the fourth paragraph of the proposed law demanded the trial for treason of all German officials responsible for the adoption of the experts' plan, Reich President Hindenburg might conceivably be subject to this provision. As a result, resistance to the fourth paragraph of the draft law quickly developed not only among the moderates but in influential agrarian circles close to the party as well. Although the text was finally rephrased to eliminate Hindenburg's potential liability, the paragraph, at Hitler's insistence, remained in the draft when it was presented to the voters in the fall.[45]

To the moderates in the DNVP who were increasingly dismayed by the party's growing association with the National Socialists and by the new leadership's rabid conduct of the anti-Young campaign, Hugenberg's commitment to the controversial fourth paragraph came to symbolize his intransigent opposition to even a tactical modus vivendi with the existing state. Thus, at the Kassel party congress in late November 1929, Hugenberg's leadership was openly challenged by moderate and white-collar union representatives within the party who feared an irreparable breach with their former *Bürgerblock* coalition partners. Their efforts to effect a revision of the party's position were, however, unsuccessful, and when Hugenberg demanded unanimous Nationalist support for each provision of the Freedom Law, the stage was set for the party's first major schism.[46]

Despite Hugenberg's demand for parliamentary discipline, a number of Nationalist deputies abstained from the vote on the fourth paragraph and later voiced public opposition to it. Following an acrimonious exchange of charges, the first of three secessions from the party began in late December. Those dissidents close to the white-collar unions, distressed by Hugenberg's rigid antiunion views, left the DNVP and soon merged with a small regional party in southwest Germany, the Christian-Social People's Service (Christlich-Sozialer Volksdienst—CSV). Shortly thereafter, another group of moderates disenchanted with Hugenberg's close association with the NSDAP and his unbridled hostility toward a policy of tactical cooperation with the Weimar state, also withdrew from the DNVP. In July they were joined by a new wave of dissident Nationalists who bolted the party in response to Hugenberg's efforts to topple the newly installed right-center Brüning government. The result was the formation of yet another conservative splinter party, the Conservative People's party (Konservative Volkspartei—KVP). Other Nationalists with ties to moderate agrarian circles also withdrew from the party in July, some drifting to the Christian Peasants' party, others to the CSV. None of these seceding Nationalists had approved of the Young Plan, the republican form of government, or the policies of the Great Coalition. Each, however, was convinced that Hugenberg's uncompromising course would simply isolate the DNVP from the centers of power and that cooperation with the state, regardless of its form, was imperative if basic economic interests were to be protected.[47]

The defections from the DNVP in 1929 and early 1930 were initially confined to the Reichstag delegation, and Hugenberg maintained strong support in the party's regional organizations. However, the DNVP's ties with the white-collar trade unions, especially the powerful DHV, had been severely weakened, and its appeal in influential agricultural circles substantially reduced. Within eighteen months of Hugenberg's assumption of leadership, the DNVP had experienced three damaging schisms, and as the Reichstag campaign opened in the late summer of 1930, the forces of German conservatism were in considerable disarray.

Within the liberal camp the situation was equally confused. Between the campaigns of 1928 and 1930 the DDP, like its Nationalist rival, experienced the strains of mounting dissension. Following the party's disappointing performance in May 1928, the ideological and strategic rift separating those Democrats favoring a fusion with the DVP and those advocating a "regeneration from within" steadily widened. While the party's right wing energetically advanced the cause of bourgeois unity, urging in early 1930 the formation of a party extending from the DDP to the newly formed KVP, the party left contended with equal vehemence that such a concentration of "the propertied bougeoisie" was inconsistent with the social and political principles upon which the Democratic party had been founded.[48]

As the depression deepened and the party's position continued to deteriorate, the DDP began a perceptible drift toward the right. The party had long been under pressure from industrial interests to jettison its "socialist reform tendencies" and emancipate itself from "the influence of the free trade unions,"[49] and at the Mannheim party congress in October 1929 the DDP signaled a significant shift in its orientation. Setting the tone for the congress, one prominent speaker assailed "the radical metropolitan and cosmopolitan spirit of Berlin," which, he contended, had infested the DDP's left wing, and the party chairman, in a denunciation of "partyism" and "political horse-trading," called for greater governmental centralization, abolition of proportional representation, and an increase in presidential authority.[50] More significantly, the party also endorsed a new economic program that implicitly repudiated the DDP's commitment to the concept of "economic democracy." Long championed by the DDP left, economic democracy had aimed at an extension of democratic principles into economic and social relations by granting workers a greater participatory role in management and a share of corporate profits.[51] The DDP's new economic program emphasized instead the party's growing concern for the troubled *Mittelstand*. Gustav Stolper, who elaborated the party's new economic policy, explained that before the war the major concern of German social policy had been the condition of the industrial working class. Because of the momentous economic dislocations of the postwar period, however, the time had come for the state to turn its attention to "the mass of suffering farmers" and "the severely threatened middle class." "Oppressed by taxes, social burdens, and rising interest rates," these groups were "caught in a squeeze from two sides, the capitalist and the proletariat." Recognizing the perils of this situation, the DDP committed itself to the defense of capitalism and middle-class interests.[52]

Tensions within the party continued unabated into the spring of the following year, accentuated by the Württemberg DDP's entry into a coalition government with the DNVP, DVP, and Zentrum. While the party left complained bitterly about this participation in a *Bürgerblock* government, spokesmen for the party's right wing expressed resentment over the leadership's failure to take the lead in establishing a movement for bourgeois unity. Indeed, Willy Hellpach, the Democratic presidential candidate in 1925, left the party to protest the DDP's lack of initiative in this matter.[53]

The internecine strife that had been building within the DDP finally produced a serious political eruption in July 1930. Stung by a depressing series of losses in regional elections and convinced that the Democrats needed help in the upcoming Reichstag campaign, Erich Koch-Weser, the party chairman, announced that the DDP would join the rightist Young German Order in the formation of a new political party. The German State party (Deutsche Staatspartei—DSP), Koch-Weser hoped, would provide the nucleus for the much discussed bourgeois unity party.[54] The stated objective of the new party was to establish a solid "centrist bloc" that would reverse the splintering tendencies of the middle-class electorate and "preserve the state from the radicals of the right and left."[55] "The fragmentation of the parties is so far advanced," the DSP founders explained, "that the security of the state is threatened. The . . .

National Socialists and Communists want civil war and revolution. They want to erect a dictatorship and rob the German people of their self-government."[56] The special interest parties could neither protect middle-class interests nor save the state from extremism. "Whoever fights only for his own economic or social interests," the DSP warned, "shatters the free middle class and is responsible for its lack of power."[57]

The DDP left applauded this condemnation of special interest politics and political radicalism but was nonetheless dismayed by Koch-Weser's new creation. For while the DDP had traditionally focused its attention on individual rights and political democracy, the new DSP appeared to be more concerned with reestablishing the authority and stability of the state. From the very outset the DSP seemed determined to disassociate itself from what it referred to as "the politically bankrupt party system" of the Weimar Republic. Its leaders rarely spoke of defending the "republic" but rather of strengthening the "state." The party even called for the transformation of the ineffective republic into "a strong national German *Volksstaat*."[58] While the DSP refrained from the harsh language of class conflict employed by the DNVP and DVP, its political vocabulary was clearly borrowed from the right. Many provincial leaders protested this reorientation, but most ultimately acquiesced, hoping that the new DSP would reinvigorate the old party. Anton Erkelenz, the prominent chairman of the DDP's steering committee, and a number of his followers, however, resigned in protest and crossed over to the SPD. Such defections were held in check, but the rightward shift of the DDP had produced an unsettling effect on the party's organization at the very outset of the Reichstag campaign.[59]

The DVP was also beset with internal difficulties throughout 1929 and early 1930 and was suspicious of the newly formed DSP. It refused to interpret the establishment of the new party as the initial step in the formation of a middle-class unity party, viewing it instead as an attempt to divide the DVP by detaching the party's restive left wing. Like the Democrats and Nationalists, the DVP was wracked by internecine strife. Although Stresemann had been able to win the unenthusiastic consent of his party for the DVP's formal entry into the Müller government, opposition to this course remained strong in the party's influential right wing and constituted a source of perpetual tension. Following the Reichstag elections of 1924, elements of the right wing had reasserted their influence on the DVP's regional organizations in the Ruhr and other industrial areas and composed almost half of the Reichstag delegation elected in 1928. Since the representatives of small industry tended to ally with the right, the party's left wing had suffered a serious defeat.[60]

In the wake of the 1928 election Stresemann, therefore, encountered fierce resistance within his own party to a whole series of moves he considered essential. Aside from its opposition to the DVP's entry into the Great Coalition, the powerful right wing denounced the acceptance of the Young Plan and the maintenance of the unemployment insurance program. Although Stresemann, as Müller's foreign minister, was able to prevail on the first two issues and secure a temporary compromise of the third, he was increasingly disheartened by the mounting influence wielded by the industrial interests in the party. Writing to a colleague in 1929, Stresemann complained that the DVP was "no longer a party of Weltanschauung but merely a party of industrial interests" that lacked "the courage to come forth in opposition to the large employer and industrial organizations."[61]

Despite the discouraging attitude of his party, Stresemann had renewed his overtures to Democratic leaders in the fall of 1929, hoping to establish a viable basis for cooperation between the two parties. His sudden death in October and the subsequent election of Ernst Scholz as party chairman, however, insured the predominance of the DVP's rightist elements and terminated serious discussion of liberal unity within the party. Although Scholz did propose cooperation with the DDP and other bourgeois parties in an informal parliamentary coalition, he rejected the establishment of a united liberal party. Moreover, without Stresemann's tireless mediating activity, the party's left wing became isolated and was gradually deprived of significant influence in party counsels.[62]

The disappointing performance of the DVP in the Saxon Landtag election in June 1930[63] and the formation of the State party at last galvanized the leadership into action. Negotiations with the DSP were initiated but conducted in an atmosphere of mutual distrust and ended predictably in failure. The DVP was, however, successful in forming an electoral alliance with the Business party and the newly established KVP.[64] Nonetheless, after months of internal dissension and public recriminations between the liberal parties and the relentless bickering within the fragmented conservative camp, the parties of the bourgeois center and right were ill-prepared for the approaching battle for the middle-class vote.

That was not true of the NSDAP. In the autumn of 1930 the Nazis were better organized and better financed than at any time in their brief history. The factionalism that had plagued the party in the mid-twenties had been stifled, Hitler's leadership had been firmly established, and the organizational framework of the party both solidified and expanded. The transformed electoral orientation of the party and its prominent role in the anti-Young campaign had given the NSDAP a truly national profile and a growing sense of self-confidence. In 1929–30 the party had also initiated a set of organizational reforms intended to bolster Nazi campaign performance. The NSDAP's regional boundaries were redrawn to conform to the Reichstag electoral districts, and the authority of the Gauleiter was substantially increased in each area. It was the Gauleiter and his propaganda staff that were charged with executing the party's campaign directives. The position of the Propaganda Division in Munich was also greatly strengthened, formally concentrating in its hands responsibility for the direction of all Nazi propaganda activities throughout the Reich. In the spring of 1930 Joseph Goebbels, since 1926 the Gauleiter of Berlin, was appointed by Hitler to head the Propaganda Division.[65]

Shortly after the dissolution of the Reichstag, the NSDAP's propaganda organization moved into action. The general objectives and themes of the campaign were determined by Hitler at a meeting in late July attended by other members of the national leadership, the Gauleiters, and the NSDAP's Reichstag delegation.[66] The actual conduct of the campaign, however, the plotting of day-to-day strategy and the coordination of the party's campaign-related activities were left to the Propaganda Division under Goebbels's leadership.

His first concern, expressed in the stream of memoranda which followed that meeting, was that the party's campaign be carried out "in the most uniform possible manner."[67] Thus, at the very outset of the campaign, the Propaganda Division issued a lengthy circular to the Gauleiters outlining the NSDAP's objectives, explaining the major themes to be developed, and defining the slogans to be used. The central theme of the 1930 campaign was to be "For or Against Young," the circular noted, and the party's "entire electoral propaganda" was to be revolve around this theme. To insure conformity with its objectives, the Propaganda Division expressly forbade the *Ortsgruppen* to "make electoral propaganda of their own. They are to operate only according to the guidelines determined by the Propaganda Division and with the electoral materials provided to them." This centralization of control, the circular explained, was necessary to achieve the party's strategic goal: the uniform and systematic saturation of the public. "Everywhere in Germany the same placards will be posted, the same leaflets distributed, and the same stickers will appear." These propaganda materials were not, however, to be ordered from party headquarters or the NSDAP's publishing house in Munich, as in the past. Instead, the typewritten texts of all leaflets and other campaign literature would be wired or forwarded from Munich to the Gauleiters, who were responsible for their printing and distribution. In this way, the flow of material to the locals could be more closely monitored and coordinated.[68]

The circular also dealt extensively with the propaganda techniques and acquainted the party's functionaries with the services and propaganda aides that were available from either Gau or national headquarters.Locals were reminded that newspaper offprints, leaflets, flyers, stickers, brochures, and special *Bildplakate* were available. It recommended that direct mailings be undertaken by the *Ortsgruppen*, using a personally addressed form letter to every inhabitant of a given area. The party also printed special election postcards and swastika-bedecked stamps for correspondence or display on windows, books, briefcases, and so on. The distribution of leaflets, as usual, received special attention. "Flyers, leaflets, etc., should be passed out early on Sunday," the circular advised, "so that the worker, the civil servant, and the petit bourgeois (*Spiesser*) has them in hand before the expected flood of trash sets in." The use of propaganda parades led by trucks with large placards and filled with storm troopers was also recommended as "a propaganda device that should not be underestimated."[69]

Along with these forms of agitation, "the spoken word" also played an important role in the party's planning. Indeed, the circular noted that "the major burden of the party's campaign must be carried by the speakers since the means necessary to saturate the entire country with propaganda material are not available to us."[70] Thus, an official list of Reich speakers, each with a particular specialty—agriculture, the civil service, labor, etc.—was developed and guidelines established for their deployment. The appearances of these speakers were central to National Socialist campaign planning in 1930.[71]

In the weeks that followed the transmission of this circular, the Propaganda Division issued updates and reappraisals of the campaign, refining instructions, coordinating speaking dates, and announcing rallies or important appearances by Hitler. As the campaign developed, for example, the party raised the disintegration of German political life into a "heap of special interests" as a major theme, repeated often in the *Völkischer Beobachter* and the speeches of the party's traveling corps of speakers.[72] Goebbels was particularly determined to create the image of a dynamic, active, indefatigable party standing in sharp contrast to the dissipired, divided parties of the bourgeois center and right. Typically, on 18 August the *Völkischer Beobachter* announced that a total of thirty-four thousand rallies were planned for the final four weeks of the campaign,[73] and while that figure was probably ambitiously high, the energy and activism of the NSDAP could not be matched by the crumbling bourgeois parties.

Although the NSDAP's propaganda apparatus still was not the well-tuned instrument that Goebbels hoped to shape, his highly centralized organizational system proved remarkably effective in 1930, giving the National Socialist campaign the distinct advantages of speed, uniformity, coordination, and thoroughness.

In spite of the vigorous, often violent campaign[74] waged by the NSDAP in 1930 and the public discord within the liberal and conservative camps, few political analysts were prepared for the stunning magnitude of the Nazi surge. As the returns were tabulated on the evening of 14–15 September, it became increasingly obvious that the NSDAP had scored a shocking electoral victory. The Nazi vote lurched from a mere eight hundred thousand in 1928 to an astonishing six million, an increase of approximately 900 percent. With their aggressive campaign tactics, their thorough organization procedures, and their revised social focus, the Nazis had captured just over 18 percent of the national vote. When the new Reichstag convened in October, 107 National Socialists filed into the assembly, making the Nazi delegation second in size only to that of the SPD. Skillfully riding a mounting current of public discontent, National Socialism had swept into the mainstream of German politics.

Examining the district by district returns on 15 September, political observers noted that the Nazi breakthrough had come largely in the predominantly Protestant areas of the country. Catholic Germans, it seemed, had remained by and large loyal to the traditional party of their confession. Although the Zentrum's share of the vote slipped from 15.2 percent to 14.8 percent, the party's losses were minimal compared to the major nonconfessional parties. Among them, only the KPD was able to register gains. The SPD, DDP (DSP), DVP, and DNVP all stumbled, though losses were by far the greatest among the parties of the bourgeois center and right. Together the DVP and DSP polled less than 10 percent of the vote, while the Nationalist constituency was reduced by half. Among those parties seeking middle-class votes, only the small special interest parties were able to maintain their constituents against the Nazi onslaught. Indeed, these parties, augmented now by the new conservative splinter groups, actually drew five hundred thousand more votes than in 1928 and captured 14 percent of the national electorate.

A second factor that was immediately apparent to even casual political observers was that the portentous surge of the Nazi vote coincided with a dramatic increase in turnout at the polls. In 1928, approximately thirty-one million Germans had cast ballots in the Reichstag election; in September two years later, almost thirty-five million. In all, 82 percent of the eligible voters turned out on election day, the largest proportion since the elections to the National Assembly in 1919 and an increase of almost 7

Table 3.2. The Election of 14 September 1930 (percentage of vote)

NSDAP	DNVP	DVP	Zentrum	DDP	SPD	KPD	Other
18.3	7.0	4.9	14.8	3.5	24.5	13.1	14.4

percent over 1928. Contemporary analysts were, therefore, convinced that the Nazis had succeeded in tapping a reservoir of previous non-voters, Germans who in the past had been politically apathetic and only now, spurred by an increasingly ominous economic environment and mobilized by Nazi activism, entered onto the political scene.[75]

Who were these new voters? Despite advances in statistical techniques, little can be done to establish their social or demographic identity with any degree of confidence. Some inferences, however, can be drawn from a number of contemporary analyses. Studies of voter turnout conducted by the Reich Statistical Bureau in the mid-twenties consistently found that women tended to vote far less frequently than men and that younger voters—those under thirty—were less likely to cast ballots than older, particularly middle-aged voters. Rates of voter participation also tended to vary as one moved from town to countryside, with urban turnout consistently higher than rural. The Reich Statistical Bureau's comparative studies did not examine the role of occupation or income on turnout, but figures for occupation are available from a 1925 survey of a municipal election in Mainz. That study revealed that among the different *Berufs-gruppen*, artisan mastercraftsmen demonstrated the highest rate of voter participation (81.2 percent), followed by farmers (69 percent), workers (68 percent), civil servants and white-collar employees (60 percent), merchants and "industrialists" (57.8 percent), and surprisingly at the bottom, doctors, lawyers, and others in the free professions (39.7 percent). Unfortunately, no similar occupational findings are available for other municipalities or rural counties, and the Mainz figures must, therefore, remain merely suggestive. One limited survey of Nuremberg voters following the September 1930 election, however, was undertaken. It revealed that despite the sudden increase in turnout, the old demographic patterns continued to hold. Over half the non-voters of the Nuremberg sample in 1930 were young (59 percent under thirty), and 60 percent were women, findings that suggest that if the Nazi surge were the product of a sudden influx of new voters, those voters were more likely to be middle-aged and male rather than young and female, as is often asserted.[76]

More recent studies have even argued that the role of such new voters has been greatly exaggerated, claiming instead that the Nazis did not benefit disproportionately from the dramatic increase in turnout. Using a variety of statistical techniques, these analyses have concluded that crossovers from the traditional bourgeois parties, especially the DVP and DSP, constituted the greatest source of National Socialist growth in 1930. Theodore Meckstroth, whose study is both the most sophisticated and extensive, calculates that approximately 31 percent of the Nazi vote in 1930 was comprised by disaffected liberals, 21 percent by conservative crossovers, and 23 percent by previous nonvoters. Significantly, defectors from regional and special interest parties accounted for only 2 percent of the National Socialist constituency, the remainder being composed of former Nazi voters and crossovers from the other Weimar parties. Only 14 percent of the previous nonvoters who cast ballots on 14 September, Meckstroth estimates, selected National Socialist candidates.[77]

Charting the destination of crossover voters in a complex multiparty system, however, is a highly problematic endeavor, and the precision of these estimates may be questioned. Indeed, other studies have cogently argued that the NSDAP scored its greatest triumphs at the expense of the slumping DNVP.[78] Furthermore, even if the former political behavior of the emerging Nazi electorate could be established with confidence, important questions concerning the *social* identity of that constituency would remain. Which elements of the liberal electorate, for example, defected to National Socialism? Which conservatives? Similarly, from which social groups were previous nonvoters recruited and what was the appeal of the NSDAP to each? These difficult problems can be illuminated only by examining the fluctuating social composition of the National Socialist electorate as it emerged in the tumultuous years after 1928, and that examination must begin with the heterogeneous social groupings within Germany's troubled *Mittelstand*.

The Old Middle Class

In 1924 the old middle class had been severely shaken by the traumatic dislocations of the inflation and stabilization crises. The gradual restoration of economic stability in the summer and fall of that year, however, seemed to extend a fragile promise of renewed prosperity and social security for the troubled merchants and craftsmen of the old middle class. Four years later, despite pockets of continued discontent, that promise seemed largely fulfilled. Although legislation in 1926 raised the lowest level of taxable personal income from 1,100 RM to 1,300

RM, the number of persons with taxable gross income from business enterprises, excluding agriculture, rose 4 percent between 1925 and 1928. Moreover, while 44 percent of those entrepreneurs paying taxes on income from business enterprise were lodged in the lowest tax bracket in 1925, that figure declined to 38 percent by 1927.[79] Similarly, the index of turnover in retail trade (1925 = 100) indicates that between 1924 and 1928 retail sales had increased 36 points, rising from 87 to 123. Despite the widely publicized challenge from department and chain stores as well as consumer cooperatives, sales in traditional specialty shops composed 80 percent of that turnover in 1928.[80]

Proprietors of small shops nevertheless remained distressed about competition from their large corporate rivals. The contribution of personally owned retail business to the national income continued to decline, falling from 20 to 16 percent between 1913 and 1928. This was commonly explained as a result of the proliferation of large corporately owned firms.[81] Between 1924 and 1928 the proportion of retail turnover attributed to these large concerns, though still quite small, had expanded from approximately 6 to 8 percent, while the share of traditional one-item or specialty shops fell by 2 percent in the same period. Furthermore, the disparity in rates of growth appeared to be widening. Between 1924 and 1925, sales in specialty shops had risen by 19 percent, while department store sales had climbed at a rate of 14 percent. Three years later, however, that relationship was reversed, with turnover in department stores increasing by 12 percent, in specialty shops by only 7 percent.[82]

Other figures seemed to confirm the diminishing economic stature of small business in the mid-twenties. In 1923 almost 80 percent of all persons employed in retail sales worked in shops with fewer than five employees. Only three years later that figure had dropped to 66 percent. The number of persons engaged in small, family-operated shops or in one-man street sales had mushroomed during the inflation and stabilization crises and remained high throughout the late twenties. However, the annual per capita turnover in "market and street sales" fell from 600 RM in 1925 to 540 RM three years later.[83] Thus, while many of these small-scale entrepreneurs were able to extract a marginal livelihood from retail sales of some form, others were not. The annual number of bankruptcies also remained relatively high throughout the so-called Golden Twenties. Despite a generally favorable economic environment, over two thousand more bankruptcy petitions were filed in 1928 than in 1924.[84] Moreover, a survey of urban unemployment conducted in February 1929 revealed that whereas proprietors from handicrafts and commerce comprised only 3 percent of those collecting unemployment compensation, 27 percent of those former "independents" had been unemployed for over a year. Half had been drawing benefits for two years.[85]

Having survived the dislocations of the inflation, many small businesses fell victim to the contractions of stabilization. The trials of one such shopkeeper, a baker, were perhaps typical. "The inflation brought me into financial difficulties. Revenue fell off and business couldn't be maintained. I got a job as a manual laborer, working from seven in the morning until four-thirty in the afternoon, then walked back to the bakery so I wouldn't have to close my business. Still, in 1926, thanks to the Jewish business practices of my creditors, I had to give up my bakery and see my inventory and furniture repossessed." Unable to work, he moved to a nearby town and was eventually forced to accept poor relief as well as help from his wife's family. Finally, he found a job as a janitor. Overflowing with bitterness, he turned to the NSDAP, explaining:

> When you consider that during the prime of life I was denied the opportunity to make a living by the measures of the red regime, by the inflation, by unbearable tax burdens, etc., and that instead of the "gratitude of the fatherland" we veterans were ruled by a group of profiteers who used every possible means to reduce the starvation pennies we needed to live, then maybe you can understand why some of those who were swindled and gypped greeted the nationalist paramilitary organizations and particularly the Hitler movement with enthusiasm.[86]

With the onset of the Great Depression, the position of such small businessmen deteriorated rapidly. Between 1928 and 1930 real income from commerce and trade (*Handel und Gewerbe*), measured by 1928 purchasing power, plummeted by 16 percent. It is estimated that sales in handicrafts and retail commerce fell by approximately six billion marks in the same period, turnover in specialty shops declining by 11 percent in 1929–30 alone.[87] As a result, the number of persons with taxable income from retail commerce sank by 12 percent from 1928 to 1929, while the number of taxpayers from the major branches of the handicrafts sector plunged almost 20 percent.[88] In 1930, bankruptcies occurred with twice the frequency they had two years earlier, with business failures in retail commerce and in the major branches of the handicrafts sector representing just over half the total. Since 1928, bankruptcies in retail trade had risen by approximately 150 percent.[89] As the share of national income contributed by specialty shops shrank by 2 percent, that contributed by street and market sales rose slightly. Symptomatically, however, the per capita income from such marginal sales steadily diminished.[90]

The situation for farmers was even bleaker. The Golden Twenties had been badly tarnished for the old middle class in the countryside, and the economywide contraction of 1929–30 merely marked an intensification of agricultural decline. Farmers had been severely shaken by the traumas of stabilization in late 1923 and entered the postinflationary period in the throes of a deepening financial crisis. High taxes, increased production costs, dwindling sources of credit, and falling prices for farm products had created an atmosphere of mounting alarm in acricultural circles, an alarm effectively exploited by the DNVP's rural campaigns in 1924. Upon assuming power in January 1925, the *Bürgerblock* government had, therefore, moved to alleviate this distress in the countryside by facilitating access to credit, reducing taxes, introducing a new set of tariffs to protect agricultural products, and offering direct government subsidies to farmers. These measures were applauded by agricultural organizations and seemed to indicate a greater government sensitivity to farm interests than that evinced by the cabinets of the inflation and early stabilization periods.[91]

Yet, in spite of these promising signs, farmers, both large and small, found recovery elusive. Agricultural prices did rebound after reaching their nadir in the spring of 1924, but they again failed to keep pace with prices for industrial goods. As a result, production costs for farmers continued to mount during the Golden Twenties.[92] Moreover, with operating costs high, farmers faced renewed competition from abroad after 1926. Supported by a variety of urban interests, the *Bürgerblock* government concluded a series of international trade agreements in 1927–28 that resulted—despite the existing tariffs—in a surge of agricultural imports.[93] Aggravating this situation for farmers was the fact that neither the state nor private credit institutions could meet their escalating need for credit. Direct government assistance to agriculture had risen substantially over prewar levels, but it still accounted for less than 1 percent of the national budget in 1928.[94] Consequently, agricultural indebtedness rose dramatically during the twenties, and interest rates, despite unrelenting complaints from the countryside, remained unusually high. Between the stabilization of the currency in late 1923 and the onset of the world economic crisis in 1929, agricultural indebtedness soared by over 35 percent. Much of this debt took the form of short-term, high-interest loans, a development that would have serious consequences as the depression deepened in 1929–30. Yet, even at the height of Weimar prosperity in 1928, the average per capita income of farmers had fallen 44 percent below the national average.[95]

Agriculture as a whole suffered during this period, but the distribution of economic distress was highly uneven. While prices for all major categories of farm products rose between 1924 and 1928, prices for dairy and livestock products—the staples of peasant and family farming—failed to match the prices for grains and produce—the traditional strengths of estate production.[96] What is more, the increased volume of agricultural imports after 1926 had a far greater impact on small dairy farmers and meat producers than on the grain-oriented estates of the east. An index of agricultural trade (1913 = 100) reveals that while grain imports stood at only 87 percent of their prewar level in 1928, the importation of dairy products had jumped by 116 percent, meat and meat products by 154 percent.[97] Small farm indebtedness also rose by 15 percent between 1924 and 1928, and although this rate did not match that of the large estates (33 percent), the *Bürgerblock* governments, under the influence of the RLB, were far more willing to provide assistance to large-scale enterprises than to small family farms.[98] By the close of 1927, the government was already preparing an emergency aid program for heavily indebted East Prussian and Pomeranian agriculture, the first of a series of special assistance packages designed to rescue the estate-dominated agriculture of the eastern provinces. An extension of such aid to small and medium-sized holdings did not come into serious consideration until mid–1930.[99]

The depression, of course, vastly accelerated the deterioration of agriculture's already precarious economic position. Farm prices fell sharply in 1929 and continued to tumble in the following year. Agricultural indebtedness, already high in the years of Weimar prosperity, surged dramatically, followed by a rising wave of rural foreclosures. Between 1928 and 1930 agricultural indebtedness jumped by 13 percent, while foreclosures and the forced sale of agricultural property almost doubled.[100] Economic distress in the countryside was general and widespread, but the Great Coalition, like the *Bürgerblock* before it, proved far more receptive to pressure from the great grain producers than to small livestock and dairy farmers. With the support of the RLB and the DNVP, the government raised tariffs on grains in 1929 and continued, through a number of special arrangements and financial mechanisms, to maintain domestic grain prices at levels far above world prices. By 1930, grain prices in Germany were over two times higher than those on the world market.[101]

Meat and dairy producers, on the other hand, were far less sheltered. Prices for such goods remained much closer to the lower world market level, and although marginally protected by the government's increasing tariff legislation, meat and dairy products were still subject to intense international competition. This was particularly true after the conclusion of trade agreements with Denmark, Holland, Sweden, and France, treaties vehemently opposed by dairy and livestock producers. The effects of such differentiated agricultural protectionism were painfully obvious to small farmers by 1930. In that year, when the volume of grain imports had fallen to 48 percent of prewar levels, meat and dairy imports stood, respectively, at 188 and 158 percent of their 1913 volume.[102] Small farmers, therefore, not only continued to face stiff international competition but to pay higher prices for feed and other necessary grain products. In addition, direct government assistance to the estates of East Elbia mounted steadily as the depression deepened, while the peasant and family farms of Schleswig-Holstein, Hannover, Hessen, and elsewhere were forced to face hard times without significant government aid.[103]

Throughout the period peasant resentment had been largely contained within the established structure of agrarian interest politics. In 1928, however, smoldering peasant discontent at last ignited, erupting in mass demonstrations that revealed the extent of rural disaffection not only with the Weimar "system" but with the traditional representatives of agricultural interests as well. A new era of rural politics dawned on the morning of 28 January 1928, when over one hundred thousand farmers swarmed into the marketplaces of Schleswig-Holstein in a spontaneous protest against government indifference to the plight of agriculture. In speeches all across the province, peasants demanded higher tariffs, lower taxes, cheaper credit, and reduced social welfare expenditures. These demands were expressed regularly in hundreds of meetings, rallies, and mass demonstrations in the weeks that followed and, significantly, were usually accompanied by vitriolic denunciations of Versailles, reparations, the parliamentary system, "Jewish international finance," and the "Marxist welfare state."[104]

As peasant agitation spilled over into the neighboring north German states, both the DNVP and RLB sought to harness its obvious political energies for the approaching Reichstag campaign. It became increasingly apparent, however, that this grass-roots protest movement, the *Landvolk* or Rural People's Movement as it came to be called, could not be easily integrated into the traditional conservative fold. By 1928 the Nationalists and their supporters in the RLB were too prominently identified with big agriculture, East Elbia, and, after almost three years in power, with the government itself to be effective spokesmen for peasant protest. It was symptomatic of the widespread rural dissatisfaction with the DNVP's performance as "the party of agriculture" that a new peasants' party was founded in March to compete in the upcoming national elections. Expressing its dismay at the DNVP's failure to protect the peasant and family farm, the Christian National Peasants' and Rural People's party (Christlich-Nationale Bauren- und Landvolkpartei—CNBL) warmly embraced many of the demands and much of the rhetoric of the emerging peasant revolt.[105] Although it would never become a serious factor in national electoral politics, the formation of the CNBL and its regional successes in 1928 clearly illuminated the widening rift between the DNVP and a growing segment of its traditional rural constituency.

The magnitude of peasant disenchantment with the DNVP was further underscored by the returns of the May election. Although the DNVP's vote in the rural, Protestant communities of the sample remained substantially above its national average in 1928, it nonetheless dropped precipitously, falling from 39 percent to 27 percent. The Nationalists managed to hold their own in their traditional East Elbian strongholds, but they faltered badly in the farm communities of Schleswig-Holstein, Hannover, Hessen, Brandenburg, and Saxony. In Württemberg, where small peasant and family farms dominated the rural landscape, Nationalist losses were enormous.[106] The principal beneficiaries of the DNVP's rural decline were neither the established liberal parties, whose rural electoral base continued to shrink, nor the National Socialists, whose farm gains were isolated and marginal. Instead, the regional peasants' and middle-class splinter parties whose social orientation and economic demands paralleled those of the *Landvolk* movement experienced a sudden surge of electoral support. In 1928 these parties averaged 12 percent of the vote in the rural, Protestant communities of the sample, an increase of almost 4 percent since December 1924.

Rural unrest did not subside in the wake of the elections but steadily gathered momentum as the economic climate grew more and more menacing. By summer a widespread tax revolt was underway in the countryside, accompanied by acts of violence—sometimes by whole villages—against tax collectors and bank officials. Public buildings, especially finance offices, were rocked by bombs, and the black flag of the *Landvolk* movement appeared in village after village. Both the DNVP and RLB had hoped to divert this mounting fury at the republican authorities into conventional conservative channels, but their ability to manipulate rural opinion had eroded considerably since 1924.[107] The election of Hugenberg, a man widely identified with industrial interests, as Nationalist party chairman severely weakened the DNVP's influence with important elements of organized agriculture, and in the regional elections of 1929 and early 1930, the party proved unable to halt the erosion of its traditional rural constituency.[108]

Nor could the formation of an alliance of agricultural pressure groups under the sponsorship of the RLB disguise the serious fragmentation of agrarian interests. Founded in February 1929 by the RLB, the Organization of German Farm Associations, the German *Bauernschaft*, and the German Agrarian Council, the Green Front was intended to be a super pressure group that would guide peasant political energies while presenting a united agrarian front against the forces of industry and the urban consumer. The Green Front was presented to the peasantry as a powerful umbrella organization that would represent *all* farmers, large and small. Although it adopted positions similar to those of the *Landvolk*, the Green Front was soon recognized as a creation of East Elbian grain interests and never became an effective instrument for conservative political mobilization in the countryside. The RLB certainly continued to be a powerful interest organization after 1928, largely because of its considerable influence in the conservative circles around Reich President Hindenburg. That influence grew with the presidential governments after 1930 and paid important political dividends for East Elbian agriculture while contributing significantly to the collapse of the Weimar system.[109] The RLB did not, however, mold or direct peasant political behavior after 1928. Instead of leading peasant protest, the RLB found itself desperately trying to keep pace with shifting political sympathies within the peasantry, sympathies that ultimately led it away from the DNVP and toward the National Socialists.

The fragmentation of agrarian interests and the concomitant erosion of traditional rural electoral loyalties between 1924 and 1929 created the necessary preconditions for the stunning National Socialist successes in the countryside thereafter. The NSDAP had never ignored the peasantry as a potential reservoir of political support, but it was remarkably slow in taking the necessary organizational steps to cultivate a rural constituency. Between 1924 and 1928, National Socialist publications had dealt regularly with agricultural issues, formulating the set of demands and charges against the "system" that would remain the core of Nazi rural appeals in each of the campaigns of the depression era. In the pages of the *Völkischer Beobachter* and Gregor Strasser's *Der nationale Sozialist* the party called for the creation of an autarkic economic system in which the importation of foodstuffs would be drastically curtailed, new land opened for peasant settlement, taxes substantially reduced, interest rates slashed, social expenditures curbed, and the peasant returned to a position of economic security and social honor. Anticipating the positions of the *Landvolk* movement, the NSDAP invariably teamed these demands and promises with assaults on "international Jewish capital," the Dawes Plan and the financial burdens it imposed on agriculture, the Weimar party system, and the bourgeois parties—especially the DNVP—that had failed to provide adequate protection for farmers.[110] "Today [the farmer] must mortgage the grain that will stand on the stalk in summer in order to make the backbreaking tax and interest payments," the Nazis wailed in a typical appeal to farmers from this period. "His sons must migrate to the city as slaves of industry because the farm is mortgaged and arable land is shrinking." This situation was the result of "a senseless agricultural policy conducted by the regime and the parties in the interests of stock market capital," the NSDAP charged, and the result was "that the farmer sinks day by day deeper into debt and misery. In the end he will be driven from his hearth and home while international money and Jewish capital take possession of his land."[111]

Although this orientation was clearly consistent with that of the emerging peasant protest movement in 1928, National Socialist efforts to make inroads into the rural electorate had consistently encountered a major obstacle: the NSDAP's widespread identification with socialism. That association stemmed from point seventeen of the party's "unalterable" twenty-five-point program, a tenet that called for "the expropriation without remuneration of land for public uses." In early 1928, with peasant unrest mounting, the party moved to "clarify" its position on private property. In a highly publicized statement, Hitler explained that "expropriation without remuneration" would be confined to land "obtained illegitimately or administered without consideration for the good of the people." This attempt to refute "malicious distortions and ugly insinuations" about National Socialist policy did not have an immediate impact on Nazi electoral fortunes in May 1928, but it did mark the beginning of a more intense and sustained effort to reach the farm voter that would bear fruit in 1929–30.[112]

With this vague programmatic revision on the books, organizational measures to expand on the promising terrain of agrarian politics followed, though with surprising sluggishness. In 1929 the party leadership indicated an interest in establishing a department of agricultural affairs within the NSDAP, but no tangible steps were taken in that direction until the early summer of the following year. In May, however, the party issued a major policy statement on agriculture, the "Official Proclamation concerning the Policy of the National Socialist Party on the Rural Population and Agriculture." Signed by Hitler himself and published with much fanfare in the *Völkischer Beobachter*, the proclamation summarized the party's familiar views on tariffs, taxes, interest rates, and private property, while excoriating "the Jewish world financial monopoly" and praising farmers as "the main bearers of a healthy *völkisch* heredity, the fountains of youth of the people, and the backbone of military power." Whereas the original party program had been virtually silent about the rural population, this statement announced that "the maintenance of a productive peasantry" was "a cornerstone of National Socialist policy."[113] Although this certainly represented a significant addition to the original Twenty-five Points, the importance of the document lay less in its content, which largely elaborated on the party's already well-established agricultural views, than in the timing of its publication and its clear suggestion that the farm vote would be a major target of Nazi propaganda efforts in the coming months.

Shortly after the appearance of the party's agricultural program, R. Walther Darré, an agricultural theorist already well known for his "blood and soil" mysticism, was appointed as an adviser on farm matters to the party leadership and charged with the creation of a Department of Agrarian Affairs. In early August, Darré circulated a memorandum detailing a plan to establish an "agrarian organizational network throughout the Reich." Because of the great regional variations within German agriculture, Darré insisted on an organizational apparatus that would be both sensitive to local conditions and yet capable of implementing directives from party headquarters in Munich. Specifically, he proposed that every level of party leadership from the village to the Gau recruit a reliable member of the local farm community to act as a consultant on agricultural affairs. The primary task of these consultants would be to aid local Nazi leaders in the fields of propaganda and agitation among the rural population. Consequently, these consultants should be responsible, knowledgeable men capable of impressing local farmers. In addition, they would report regularly to Munich on their observations and activities, and this information, after being evaluated at party headquarters, would then be made "available to all agricultural consultants in the Reich as intelligence regarding agrarian policy for the political struggle on the home front." Although the creation of such an extensive network was not immediately possible, the first steps to implement Darré's design were taken in mid-August, and the rudiments of the National Socialist farm organization, the agrarpolitischer Apparat (aA) were in place for the first Reichstag campaign of the depression era.[114]

These intensified efforts to win support from alienated farm proprietors in 1929–30 were paralleled by the NSDAP's ongoing campaign to broaden the party's constituency within the urban old middle class. Despite some predictable variations in emphasis, Nazi appeals to shopkeepers and artisans were quite similar in both form and content to those addressed to peasant proprietors. The party's attacks on high taxes, usurous interest rates, wasteful government spending, and corrupt party politics were framed by the usual condemnations of big labor, big business, and international Jewish capital. Although discussion of tariffs as such was predictably sparse in appeals to urban retailers and craftsmen, calls for autarky and government protection of German business—especially small business—were plentiful. Similarly, the focus on the nefarious role of Jewish middlemen and the banks found in Nazi campaign literature addressed to peasants tended to be translated in a more urban environment to an emphasis on the threat to small business posed by Jewish department stores and socialist consumer cooperatives. Indeed, declamatory attacks against both became essential elements of the NSDAP's appeal to the beleaguered *Mittelstand* between 1928 and 1930.

The consumer cooperatives, the Nazis maintained, threatened not only small retail merchants but artisans as well and were, in the final analysis, socialist weapons to undermine the economic vitality of the old middle class. Department stores, on the other hand, were depicted as the tools of Jewish high finance, employed to dominate the economic and political destiny of the German people. The Weimar Republic, according to National Socialist literature, was controlled by international socialism and Jewish stock-market capital. Together these forces had "destroyed the middle class and robbed it of its role in the state and the economy." Nazi electoral propaganda repeatedly lamented that "vast sections of the middle class" were "already ruined," crushed between these rapacious, alien powers. "The department stores of big capital, the predominately socialist-oriented consumer cooperatives . . . the chain stores . . . and the penetration of mass production into the realm of commerce" had reduced the small merchant and artisan to a position of helplessness and despair. Germany was witnessing "the battle of the rich against the impoverished," the Nazis declared, and under the prevailing system it was inevitable that "this struggle will proletarianize more and more members of the middle class," bringing "the army of the unemployed ever greater numbers of reinforcements."[115]

"For years," one typical Nazi article explained, "the commercial middle class has fought a desperate battle against the excessively powerful great concerns and trusts which are supported with funds from the big banks and which not only . . . seek mass markets for their products, but, to an increasing degree, the markets of small business as well."[116] In this struggle the traditional parties of the bourgeois center and right had not only failed to protect the interests of small business from the Bolshevist challenge but had actually delivered the small merchant and craftsman into the hands of "Jewish finance capital."

The middle-class parties pledged to save the *Mittelstand* from destruction, but it is rapidly nearing its utter demise! The revalorization parties promised to introduce compensation for the crimes of the inflation. These parties live on, but the victims of the inflation are slowly dying. The parties for the salvation of small business promise to help the small craftsman, the shopkeeper, and merchant. But with their aid, the large department stores spring up and strangle hundreds of thousands of independent businessmen.[117]

As a result, this "process of alienation and expropriation," the Nazis warned, was "continuing its advance with a quickened pace." The "uprooted and expropriated" were "falling into the clutches of international capital," and the middle class was approaching the "end of its position in the state, indeed, of its existence as a class."[118] The only possible salvation for the *Mittelstand* was National Socialism, for it alone, the Nazis argued, had consistently supported "free German trade, an honorable handicrafts, the reestablishment of loyalty and trust in German economic life, the struggle against the pestilence of Jewish department stores, and the protection of small business."[119]

While the liberals and conservatives bickered over the formation of a *Bürgerblock* government or a middle-class unity party, the NSDAP had successfully employed these shibboleths in the regional campaigns of 1929 and early 1930, emerging as a credible bulwark against the anticipated surge of the Marxist parties. This won the National Socialists plaudits from middle-class interest groups, which previously remained skeptical about the NSDAP's sociopolitical orientation. The conservative *Nordwestdeutsche-Handwerks-Zeitung*, for example, while refraining from endorsing the party, expressed its considerable satisfaction with the surprisingly strong National Socialist showing in traditionally leftist Saxony: "Social Democracy, which set out to defeat the NSDAP decisively, itself lost fifty thousand votes!"[120]

Confronted by continued Nazi successes in these regional elections, the liberal parties, long identified with government responsibility, were hopelessly compromised and remained on the defensive throughout the Reichstag campaign. In an effort to retard the National Socialist advances into their own middle-class constituencies, the DVP and DSP attempted to brand the NSDAP as a party of the radical left. "Whether national or international," one DVP publication typically warned, "it is still socialism and, indeed, . . . of the most radical type." No one should be "fooled because the Nazis sit on the right in parliament or because they place the word 'national' before their socialist ideology," the DVP cautioned. "They have nothing in common with the bourgeois parties which stand on the foundation of the capitalist Weltanschauung." In fact, both the DVP and DSP agreed that the Nazis "would make a more compatible ally of Communism" than of the liberal or conservative parties.[121]

The DVP, which assiduously attempted to present itself to the middle-class electorate as the champion of the capitalist system, was particularly determined to link National Socialism with Marxism. "Whoever blindly assails 'capitalism' with ruthless proletarian phrases" and "talks of 'eliminating interest capital,'" the DVP charged, would simply "draw the life-blood from . . . the German economy," which was "so dependent on the international credit system." Such a policy would "not create new Lebensraum for the German people" but "immeasurably intensify the current malaise." Thus, in the struggle to prevent Social Democratic leveling that would "reduce thousands of self-employed proprietors" to the position of "economically dependent employees and workers,"[122] the *Mittelstand* should not expect help from the NSDAP. The Nazis "want socialism. They want to 'break interest slavery,'" the DVP warned in a pamphlet addressed to "merchants, shopkeepers, artisans, and rentiers." For a preview of economic relations in the Third Reich, small business need only look at the Soviet Union, "where interest slavery has been broken."[123] In the final analysis, the Nazis, with "their socialistic program, are not one penny better than the other Socialists," the DVP declared. The National Socialist program violated the principle of private property, and in the Reichstag the Nazis had supported "the most incredible Communist-sponsored proposals. But, of course," the DVP complained, "they don't tell the middle class and the peasants about this. In front of them they portray themselves as 'anti-Marxists.'" The German *Mittelstand* should, therefore, "beware of wolves in sheep's clothing."[124]

Though less equivocal in its defense of capitalism, the newly constituted DSP certainly shared the DVP's concern about the socialist threat. The old left liberals entered the campaign with a new electoral facade, contoured to enhance their attractiveness to the middle-class constituency that had been slipping steadily away from them since 1920. Determined to demonstrate its credentials as a savior of small business, the DSP vigorously condemned both the "trusts and cartels" of big business and the "idiotic leveling" of socialism. The party's most prominent assault, however, was directed against the socialist menace, and the DSP repeatedly emphasized its fundamental opposition to "all socialist experiments." The social structure of Germany, "in which millions of small and medium-sized businesses still exist, must be preserved," the DSP asserted, and the party promised to "fight all economic and tax policies that steadily reduce the number of self-employed entrepreneurs, so that one business after another must close and forfeit its independence."[125]

If the middle class were to save itself, however, it could not afford the fragmentation represented by the "economic egotism" of the special interest parties. Any further splintering of the middle-class vote, the DSP warned, would be disastrous, since this trend had already "allowed socialism greater influence in Germany" and increased the danger of "revolutionary disorders."[126] Nor could the NSDAP be counted on to protect middle-class interests since, the DSP contended, it had fallen increasingly under the sway of former socialists in its own ranks. "They determine the face of the party," the DSP's Artur Mahraun wrote, "bringing the party's Marxist agitation to a pitch not seen since the revolution." The task at hand was, therefore, to rally "all responsible German citizens" behind the DSP in order to protect "the people and the state" from the "torrent of radical Bolshevist elements from both the left and the right."[127]

The Nazi press responded to these charges with scorn and derision. To dispel worrisome doubts about the party's position on business and property, the *Völkischer Beobachter* restated the NSDAP's solemn commitment to protect private property and, of course, blasted Marxism in all its forms.[128] Turning to the liberal parties, the Nazis dismissed the DVP as little more than a party of "big capitalists," indifferent to the plight of the small proprietor.[129] The People's party, Goebbels wrote, had always been "the party of property and education," and as such "a typical class party of the bourgeoisie." Because of its social orientation, the DVP was a precursor of the proletarian class parties and hence just as guilty as the Marxists of fomenting the class conflict that had plagued Germany since the Industrial Revolution. The Nazis even maintained that the DVP was working hand in glove with the Social Democrats to destroy German society. Like the SPD, Stresemann's party had supported the policy of fulfillment and worked alongside the Social Democrats in the Great Coalition, Goebbels noted. The DVP's collaboration with Social Democracy" represented "the great united front of bourgeois and proletarian internationalism," which was eroding the traditional German values of "*Volk*, nation, marital virtue, personality, and blood. Take away the patriotic phrases from the DVP," Goebbels concluded, "and you have the SPD."[130]

Nor did the DSP escape Nazi abuse. The party was simultaneously condemned as a tool of Social Democracy and Jewish big business, and its belated and transparent turn to the right, the Nazis sneered, would fool no one. The party's new name and new electoral focus were merely reflections of the Democrats' ideological bankruptcy. Whether DDP or

Table 3.3. *Party Vote and the Old Middle Class (OMC), 1928–1930*

| | All OMC | | | |
| | Protestant (N=152) | | Catholic (N=64) | |
	1928	1930	1928	1930
NSDAP	.478	.646	.110*	.206*
DNVP	−.337	−.397	−1.40	−1.29
DVP	.174	−.453*	.824	.386
DDP	.962	.142	.627	.448
Z	.108*	.068*	−1.02	−.604
SPD	−.518	−.106	.316*	.277*
KPD	−.373	−.424	−.133	−.350
Other	.127	.915	.169	.592

| | OMC in Handicrafts[a] | | | |
| | Protestant (N=152) | | Catholic (N=64) | |
	1928	1930	1928	1930
NSDAP	.830	.597	.314	.635
DNVP	−.616	−.285	−2.32	−2.20
DVP	−.198	−.102	1.35	.360
DDP	.317	.372	1.21	1.55
Z	−.216*	.241*	−.150*	−.354*
SPD	−1.35	−.577	−.268*	−.301*
KPD	−.150	−.435	−1.86	−2.28
Other	.242	.186*	.125*	.443*

| | OMC in Commerce[a] | | | |
| | Protestant (N=152) | | Catholic (N=64) | |
	1928	1930	1928	1930
NSDAP	.851	1.07	2.59	3.52
DNVP	−1.23	−1.14	−1.97	−1.79
DVP	.122*	.152*	−1.93	.225
DDP	−.452	−.765	−.715	−1.57
Z	−.961	−.334	−.432*	−4.55
SPD	−1.93	−1.91	−.198	−.248
KPD	−1.64	−1.61	−.633	−.769
Other	.110*	−.397	1.21	.823

Table 3.3. (continued)

	OMC in Agriculture[a,b]			
	Protestant (N=121)		Catholic (N=123)	
	1928	1930	1928	1930
NSDAP	.302	.470	.112	−.152
DNVP	.492	.395	.246	−.102*
DVP	−.930	−.777	−.161*	−.263
DDP	.109	.124*	.438	.194
Z	.160*	.151*	1.02	1.62
SPD	−.700	−.564	−.577	−.490
KPD	−.166	−.294	−.241	−.561
Other	.341	.310	−.186*	.199*

NOTE: The figures are unstandardized regression coefficients (b), controlling for new middle class, *Rentnermittelstand*, blue-collar workers, religion, and urbanization (population size).
a. Presents coefficients for the OMC by economic sector, controlling for the OMC in all other economic sectors in addition to those variables listed above.
b. Size of farm has also been controlled.

* These coefficients are not significant at the .05 level.

DSP, the party remained "the facade of profiteer plutocracy." Thus, "the Jews should vote Democratic," the *Völkischer Beobachter* observed, "but the Germany of productive, working people will vote National Socialist and break the will of high finance, Marxism, and the bourgeoisie."[131]

Were these Nazi slogans effective with the craftsmen, shopkeepers, and farmers of the old middle class? The figures of Table 3.3 reveal that the Nazi/old-middle-class relationship in urban areas had not faded with the stabilization of the economy in the mid-twenties but had, on the contrary, grown stronger. Although the Nazi/old-middle-class figures slip in December 1924 as the nascent economic recovery gathered momentum, the ensuing period of relative prosperity did not precipitate a return to the liberal-conservative pattern of 1920. The liberal figures, though relatively strong in 1928, slip precipitously in 1930, while the conservative coefficients remain surprisingly low in both elections. The weakness of the conservative figures and the sharp decline of the liberal coefficients, however, stand in sharp contrast to those of the NSDAP, which are strong in both elections. It is particularly significant, given the harsh stabilization of the mid-twenties, that a substantial rise in the Nazi figures is already apparent by 1928, well before the onset of the depression. The Nazi/old-middle-class coefficients are almost as strong then as in the inflation election of May 1924. In 1928, however, the NSDAP was merely one of a number of small splinter parties benefiting from middle-class disenchantment with the traditional liberal and conservative partisan options. Only in 1930, as the effects of the depression spread beyond the pockets of chronic economic and social distress upon which the NSDAP had previously based its electoral support, did the appeal of National Socialism find wider acceptance within the entrepreneurial *Mittelstand*. In September 1930 the old middle class becomes for the first time a stronger predictor of the Nazi vote than of the liberal all across the sample.

An important variant of this same trend is also reflected in the figures of the rural sample. The erosion of the liberal/old-middle-class relationship, already evident in 1924, continues in 1928 and gathers momentum rapidly thereafter. After slipping steadily in the last of the predepression elections, the liberal coefficients plunge in the September elections of 1930. By 1930 the liberal vote in the rural sample was less than half its share in December 1924 and stood significantly below its urban figures. Indeed, the DVP vote stood at only one third its former strength. The DNVP, on the other hand, continued to command a significant following in rural areas. The Nationalist constituency within the old middle class had always been concentrated in the countryside, in villages and rural towns whose economies were intimately linked with the surrounding agricultural sector. Indeed, the Nationalists continuously tried to convince urban shopkeepers and craftsmen that their interests had not been hurt by the agricultural tariffs advocated so vocally by the DNVP. Although they produced higher food prices, these tariffs, the DNVP contended, also brought "an indirect and effective promotion of the handicrafts and small business" since they "secure a clientele with the necessary purchasing power."[132] Needless to say, these arguments were considerably more effective with farmers and rural merchants than with their urban counterparts, and the DNVP's appeal within the urban old middle class suffered as a result.

The relative rural concentration of conservative strength was again reflected in the elections of 1928 and 1930. In both those campaigns, the DNVP's rural vote was double that of its urban average. Yet, whereas the conservative vote averaged almost 25 percent in 1928 in the rural sample, it had fallen to only 13 percent two years later. That stunning collapse is also reflected in the sharp decline of the DNVP/old-middle-class coefficients for the two elections. By 1930 the Nationalists' once solid position in the countryside was crumbling fast, and that disintegration was not confined to a few disparate areas. Although the party continued to attract significant support in its traditional East Elbian strongholds, its position of dominance was clearly challenged by the NSDAP, which in 1930 made major breakthroughs in the rural counties of East Prussia, Pomerania, and the Mecklenburgs. In areas characterized by small peasant and family farms, on the other hand, the NSDAP clearly outmanned its conservative rivals. In 1930 the Nazis' greatest gains came in precisely such small-farming areas. In Schleswig-Holstein, Lower Saxony, and Thuringia, areas where the *Landvolk* movement had flourished, the NSDAP had clearly become the party of agricultural, and particularly small-farm, protest. The crisis of conservatism in the countryside was, in short, national in scope, and the NSDAP was the certain beneficiary of that crisis.

For the Nazis, the elections of 1930, therefore, represented a quantum leap forward, both in the towns and in the countryside. Although the party's most spectacular victories had come in rural areas, its urban constituency within the old middle class was firmly established. By 1930 the NSDAP, as its old-middle-class coefficients strongly suggest, had successfully bridged the urban-rural divide of German politics and was well on its way to becoming the long-sought party of middle-class integration.

The *Rentnermittelstand*

The dramatic National Socialist breakthrough into the traditional constituencies of the liberal and conservative parties was by no means limited to the disaffected artisans, shopkeepers, and farmers of the old middle class. In 1930 the NSDAP also trained its sights on a major bastion of conservative electoral strength, the rentiers, pensioners, and disabled veterans who had suffered most from the hyperinflation and its aftermath. By demanding a high revaluation of debts and mortgages during the campaigns of 1924, the DNVP had been particularly successful in garnering the support of creditor circles incensed by the government's Third Emergency Tax Decree. Condemnation of that measure, which set the rate of revaluation at 15 percent, had been a major leitmotiv of the DNVP's campaign strategy. Although the party had never formally bound itself to a figure, its campaign rhetoric had certainly raised hopes that under a Nationalist government the rate would rise dramatically, perhaps reaching 100 percent. Upon entering the cabinet in 1925, however, the DNVP came under increasing pressure from influential agricultural and industrial groups to temper its zeal on this issue. Thus, when the revaluation problem was raised in the Reichstag during the early spring, the DNVP found itself in a quandary. Torn between powerful organized interests and the party's creditor constituency, the

Nationalists moderated their demands and settled for an increase of the rate to only 25 percent.[133]

When details of the proposed legislation became public in May, leaders of the revalorization movement were predictably outraged at the DNVP's "perfidy." After consultations, the various regional groups decided to establish a Coalition of Revalorization Organizations and shortly thereafter launched a national campaign against both the legislation and its proponents. Meanwhile, the DNVP came under attack from the opposition parties (SPD, KPD, DDP, and NSDAP) for its failure to live up to the promises it had made for a full and equitable revalorization.[134]

Despite the wave of hostility generated by the new settlement, the DNVP gamely expressed its "firm conviction" that it had "fulfilled its promises" and attained "what was possible" for the victims of the inflation. It contended that "without the DNVP there would have been no revalorization at all" and implored those unhappy with its support for the new law to understand that as a great national party, "the DNVP could not assert itself in a one-sided manner for one group of its voters and thereby neglect the interests of the whole."[135]

As justification for their endorsement of the new legislation, the Nationalists pleaded economic necessity. Pointing to the extent of Germany's foreign debt, especially after acceptance of the Dawes Plan, the DNVP explained that promises made during the campaign of the previous year should be seen as "hopes and expectations" whose fulfillment was "dependent on later (international) developments." Moreover, the DNVP had never made extravagant promises, the Nationalists claimed. In contrast to the revalorization parties, the DNVP's approach to pensioners and small investors had always been sober and responsible, the party asserted. As soon as the impossibility of attaining their exaggerated goals became clear, "these splinter parties will collapse," the DNVP predicted, "leaving behind disappointment and bitterness." In the meantime, they would only have a "destructive impact on the bourgeois camp" and "strengthen those elements hostile to the fatherland."[136]

These admonitions failed to produce the desired effect, and in July, as the legislation passed the Reichstag, leaders of the revalorization movement began serious negotiations to create a strong national party to represent creditor interests. Two parties devoted to that task had already been established in 1924, and in early 1926 the Reich Party for People's Justice and Revalorization (Reichspartei für Volksrecht und Aufwertung—VRP) joined them. Like the other creditor parties, the VRP appealed to a middle-class constituency, not only by endorsing a higher rate of revalorization and the principle of private property, but also by condemning socialism, international capital, big business, department stores, and the "Americanization" of German society.[137]

Nationalist efforts to effect a reconciliation with the new party proved fruitless, and in late 1926 the DNVP's standing in creditor circles suffered another damaging setback. In October the Social Democrats and Communists launched a widely publicized campaign for a referendum to nationalize the property of Germany's princely families, and the DNVP quickly assumed the leadership of the opposition. Noting bitterly that the Nationalists had been willing to sacrifice the property of small investors, creditors, and rentiers but were eager to defend the wealth of the aristocracy, a number of revalorization organizations unexpectedly voiced their support for the referendum. Although the referendum clearly challenged the principle of private property, these groups hoped to dramatize the plight of the small investor and pensioner, while exposing the hypocrisy of the bourgeois parties, especially the DNVP.[138]

In exasperation, Count Westarp, the Nationalist party chairman, condemned this attempt to link the two issues and warned that a vote for the Marxist-sponsored proposal "would simply destroy the last claims . . . of all those with hopes for a revalorization." "If you help the Reds expropriate the princes today," the DNVP warned, "tomorrow they will take the property of the churches . . . and the next day all private property, down to the smallest."[139] These attempts to raise the specter of communism could not, however, disguise the fact that the DNVP found itself in an embarrassing political position. The party's defense of the princes must have struck many pensioners and rentiers as the worst sort of hypocrisy. In a leaflet addressed to "small investors, savers, and widows," for example, the Nationalists solemnly noted that "the Hohenzollerns once possessed assets of 88.5 million marks in mortgages, cash, and securities. But don't you know that, just like you, they lost their assets in the inflation? Only one million in cash remains. Is that too much for a big family of forty-nine?" Anyway, the party claimed, "the small investors, the pensioners, the widows, and disabled veterans" who "had lost their money to the Jewish international" would not benefit from the referendum. The only winners would be "the same Jews and exploiters . . . who have made so many Germans poor and unhappy."[140]

The DNVP's effort to shift attention away from its support for the revalorization law and its awkward role in the expropriation referendum met with only limited success. Throughout the provincial campaigns of the mid- to late twenties, the Nationalists were repeatedly forced to defend these policies against charges of sellout from the creditor parties and the National Socialists. Whether in Thuringia, Saxony, Hessen, or

Brunswick, the revalorization parties never allowed the electorate to forget the DNVP's "broken promises" to the victims of the inflation. Though never winning more than 5 percent of the vote in any of these Landtag elections, the creditor parties nonetheless detracted from the Nationalist electoral performance after 1925. In Saxony, for example, these parties had received only twenty thousand votes in December 1924. Two years later, however, they polled almost one hundred thousand, gaining just over 4 percent of the vote. Similarly, in Hessen, where in 1924 the revalorization parties had captured less than 1 percent of the electorate, they were able to attract a full 5 percent in November 1927. The DNVP, on the other hand, fell in both cases, slipping by a full 6 percent in the important Saxon elections.[141]

Kept alive by the VRP and other creditor organizations, the revalorization issue continued to haunt the DNVP into the Reichstag election of 1928. Throughout the campaign the Nationalists felt compelled to deny that they had made extravagant promises in 1924. The DNVP had promised to abolish the Third Emergency Tax Decree and create a legal framework for a just resolution of the revalorization issue, and *these* promises, the Nationalists emphasized, had been honored. Without the DNVP, small investors, pensioners, and other creditors would have lost everything, the Nationalists claimed, and the "counterproductive" single-issue parties had simply obstructed the DNVP's efforts on behalf of the inflation's victims.[142] In an appeal directed to all creditors, the DNVP contended that their interests could be protected only "by a strong organization, encompassing millions, a party that understands you and your desires, that has always stood up for you and will be able to fight for you in the future." To such assertions the VRP responded with a typically blunt retort: "How can a party with the revalorization law's mark of Cain on its forehead find the gall to say such things to the voters?"[143]

Although the Nationalists absorbed the brunt of the revalorization movement's ire, the other parties did not escape criticism. The SPD and KPD, though vocal opponents of the revalorization law, were condemned for their Marxist orientation, while the bourgeois parties were held responsible for the law which, according to the VRP, "had presented big business and the state with the hard-earned money of German savers and creditors, reducing the small investor and saver to penury."[144] According to the VRP, the liberals, conservatives, and Catholic Zentrum had "deprived the victims of the war and inflation of their constitutional rights and delivered them to the mercy of public charity." Borrowing a page from the Nazi notebook, the VRP claimed that the traditional bourgeois parties operated simply as the servants of big business and high finance and were, therefore, not inclined to help those ruined by the inflation and stabilization crises. The liberals and conservatives had "robbed [the small investor and pensioner] of their property and had "systematically violated their rights," the VRP charged, "beginning with the . . . wartime legislation" and continuing through "the economic war of 1919–25, which was planned and conducted by high finance behind the backs of the people."[145]

The DDP readily acknowledged that "all parties recognize the undeserved and bitter distress of the small investor" and that all had "promised to aid these victims of the war and inflation." The responsibility for their distress, however, the DDP laid squarely at the door of the DNVP and the right-center coalition that had held power in 1925. "The small investor can thank these parties," the Democrats declared, "for the fact that they must remain in the for them unbearable and shameful role of welfare recipients."[146]

As a prominent member of that coalition, the DVP attempted to rebuff these charges by appealing to "economic realism" and dismissing the demands of the revalorization parties as unfeasible. The DVP conceded that pensioners had "grown bitter" over "what was not achieved" and had lost faith in the traditional parties, but it appealed to those hurt by the stabilization experience "to think back to how things had been for them during the inflation and the period shortly thereafter." Perhaps then they would realize that the efforts of the DVP and other government parties "were not in vain" and that "some progress had been made." As usual, the party's campaign literature attributed the government's failure to achieve more satisfying results to the economic burdens forced on the republic by the victorious allies, burdens that had been partially alleviated only by the DVP's careful diplomacy. "Of course, we all had expected more," the party admitted, "but hardship and misery resulting from the Versailles *Diktat* have been the companions of the German people for years." Under the DVP's guidance, however, Germany was "slowly, all too slowly, rising once again," and with its recovery, pensioners could expect an improvement of their lot.[147]

These sober calls for "realism" and patience were, of course, loudly denounced by the National Socialists, who contributed to the shrill chorus of complaints against the liberals and conservatives. The party had won the support of some creditor organizations in 1924 for its opposition to the Third Emergency Tax Decree and had received a further boost in the following year when the DNVP's leading advocate of higher revalorization defected to the NSDAP.[148] Throughout the campaigns of the Golden Twenties the Nazis reminded pensioners that the NSDAP had opposed the revalorization law and had continued, even after its passage, to press for "a just revalorization." Exactly what constituted a just figure was never made clear, though Nazi campaign literature suggested that at least a rate of 50 percent would be in order.[149]

In spite of these blandishments, there was little compelling reason for a disaffected pensioner to choose the NSDAP in 1928. Its proposls were less concrete than those of the revalorization parties and its electoral orientation far more diffuse. Nor could it claim to wield significant influence in the Reichstag or the various provincial legislatures. Indeed, the figures of Table 3.4 suggest that while the DNVP's support among creditors showed serious signs of erosion in 1928, the NSDAP did not profit significantly from that slide. The Nazis certainly picked up some support from pensioners, small investors, and veterans, but the bulk of Nationalist defectors in 1928 were probably scattered among the different revalorization parties.

The campaigns of 1927–28, however, proved to be the high-water mark of the revalorization movement. The VRP never succeeded in becoming the effective instrument of creditor interests that its founders intended, and the movement's political energies continued to be divided among several regional organizations and parties.[150] Furthermore, with the onset of the depression, the number of persons earning taxable income from rents, capital gains, and other dividends declined, falling by 8 percent between 1928 and 1930.[151] As concern over the continuing slump mounted in investment circles, the revalorization issue faded and with it the parties that had made it the focus of their programs. During 1929 and early 1930 the revalorization parties tumbled in each of the provincial elections, clearly failing to extend their appeal beyond the narrow range of interests reflected in their programs.[152]

At the same time, the NSDAP, buoyed by its prominent participation in the anti-Young campaign, had acquired national recognition as the most vociferous non-Marxist critic of the Weimar "system." That new stature, coupled with the splintering of the conservative camp and the dwindling support for the revalorization parties, all contributed to a dramatic surge in Nazi popularity. In 1930 the NSDAP intensified its efforts to win the support of pensioners and veterans, capitalizing on the widespread fear that Brüning's austerity plans would lead to a reduction of insurance benefits and pensions—a fear confirmed by the government's first emergency decree on 26 July 1930. The reductions embodied in that decree touched a highly salient element of the electorate, since, aside from the widows, savers, and small investors already alienated by the revalorization issue, a survey conducted in 1930 disclosed that approximately 42 percent of the

Table 3.4. *Party Vote and the* Rentnermittelstand, *1928–1930*

| | Protestant (N=152) | | Catholic (N=64) | |
	1928	1930	1928	1930
NSDAP	.243	.686	.233	.405
DNVP	.624	.295	.514	.267
DVP	−.595	−.160	−.336	−.211
DDP	−.272	−.609	−.173	−.149
Z	.633	−.320	−.648	−.415
SPD	−.605	−.130	.133 [*]	.322 [*]
KPD	−.326	−.535	−.736	−.149 [*]
Other	.237	.119	.480	.498

NOTE: The figures are unstandardized regression coefficients (b), controlling for old middle class, new middle class, blue-collar workers, religion, and urbanization (population size).

[*] These coefficients are not significant at the .05 level.

officers discharged from the imperial army in 1918–19 were still unemployed and living on their pensions.[153] Making the most of the situation, the Nazis launched their Reichstag campaign by accusing Brüning of attempting to balance the budget at the expense of disabled veterans. Reductions in retirement benefits and services for veterans, the Nazis typically charged, had been undertaken "so that the department stores and banks can pay lower taxes."[154]

Divided and compromised by the festering revalorization issue, the Nationalists in 1930 failed to maintain their grip on the *Rentnermittelstand*, which had been one of the mainstays of their urban constituency since 1924. Meckstroth estimates that the DNVP suffered more defections in 1930 than did the liberals,[155] and the figures of Table 3.4 strongly suggest that many of those defectors came from disaffected pensioner and creditor circles. Although the DNVP/*Rentner* figures drop precipitously between 1924 and 1928, the *Rentnermittelstand* still is more highly related to the Nationalist vote than to that of any other party in the last election of the predepression era. The Nazi/*Rentner* coefficients also continue to fade from their highwater mark in May 1924, and the liberal figures for 1928 remain quite low. Between 1928 and 1930, however, the conservative figures plummet, dropping by over half, and unlike 1928, the Nationalist decline is matched by Nazi advances. While the liberal coefficients remain largely unchanged, the Nazi figures lurch strikingly forward in the first election of the depression period, easily surpassing their level of May 1924. In 1930, the *Rentnermittelstand* for the first time becomes a stronger predictor of the Nazi vote than of the conservative.

The New Middle Class

Like the pensioners, veterans, and rentiers alienated by the revalorization issue, the white-collar employees of the new middle class seemed to offer a rich potential for National Socialist recruitment, even before the onset of the depression. The Golden Twenties had brought neither prosperity nor social security to Germany's *Angestelltenschaft*. Instead, stabilization after 1924 produced retrenchment in many sectors of the economy and a rapidly expanding movement to rationalize traditional business practices. For white-collar personnel, rationalization meant streamlining sales and clerical techniques to eliminate superfluous positions, primarily through the introduction of business machinery such as typewriters, adding machines, and other bookkeeping devices. The result was the dismissal of thousands of employees. Union officials estimated that in the important commercial sector, one quarter of all white-collar personnel were laid off in 1924–25 alone, while in banking, the most prestigious white-collar occupation, one hundred and fifty thousand employees were unceremoniously dismissed between the close of 1923 and the spring of 1925.[156]

White-collar unemployment remained stubbornly high throughout the Golden Twenties and was particularly distressing for older employees. These veteran *Angestellten* were usually among the first to be laid off and had the most difficulty finding a new position. One union study compiled in 1925 revealed that 60 percent of those employees over forty who had lost their jobs remained unemployed for over six months. Older white-collar personnel, the unions lamented, were being dismissed after years of loyal service so that management could pay lower salaries to younger, often female newcomers.[157] Although the situation for older employees was grim in banking and other clerical posts, their prospects were even less promising in sales. In department stores, for example, one knowledgeable observer noted that "their higher salary rate and lower degree of efficiency are obstacles in their path; besides, the management's policy is to hire young girls of attractive and pleasing appearance."[158] Although conditions varied somewhat from sector to sector, the bitterness expressed by one former bank employee was perhaps typical of the wider discontent felt by many white-collar employees over these developments:

Everything collapsed like a house of cards, when I was discharged in 1924. I never had given it a thought. There was no other employee whose knowledge and practical experience was equal to mine. Still, I had to go. I ask myself: Why did I take courses evening after evening, and why did I give all my spare time to the bank? . . . Overnight the best employees are discharged and the new generation of bank employees needs to know nothing but correspondence and comptometry. Qualified employees are no longer needed. . . . Our places were taken by large American machines; one Powers machine threw twenty men out of their jobs. Mechanical manipulation is all that is required now; mental work on the part of employees is no longer necessary. Young girls are employed who, Heaven knows, work for lower salaries, and much quicker than we did with our stiff fingers. Their mechanical work is not blocked by worries as is the case with us old family men.[159]

Fear that women, particularly young women and girls, were swamping the white-collar job market was widespread during the period of stabilization and was reinforced by the findings of the 1925 census. Released in the late twenties, the census figures disclosed that the number of women holding white-collar posts had risen by 224 percent since the prewar era and that women, mostly under the age of twenty-five, made up over one-third of the white-collar labor force.[160] The conservative unions, especially the DHV, were quick to denounce "feminism," viewing the massive influx of women into white-collar positions as a symptom of the *Angestelltenschaft*'s declining social and economic status.[161] The Reich Association of German White-Collar Organizations (Reichsbund Deutscher Angestellten-Berufsverbände—RDV), for example, complained that "during the inflation almost anyone could become a white-collar employee" without completing the traditional apprenticeship or vocational training. Consequently, many people "who could never have attained this status in the past" had been allowed access, thus "lowering the *Stand*'s public stature."[162]

The conservative unions also contended that the entry of untrained employees into the job market had contributed to the decline in white-collar salaries. "In many cases," the RDV complained, "salaries for trained white-collar personnel are lower than the wages of unskilled workers." These factors and the ever-present threat of unemployment meant that white-collar employees were faced with "the danger of proletarianization." The simple but sad fact of the matter, the RDV concluded, was that "the social position of the *Stand* is not what it was before the war."[163]

The depression, of course, greatly intensified the economic and social anxieties that had beset the white-collar population throughout the late twenties. In May 1928 the ratio of applicants to jobs in white-collar occupations stood at nine to one; one year later it had risen to twelve to one. In 1930, however, the number of jobless white-collar employees soared abruptly, surging by 171 percent between January and September. Two weeks before the Reichstag election, the ratio of applicants to available white-collar jobs stood at twenty-six to one.[164] Meanwhile, as unemployment rose, salaries dropped. In 1928, an average Berlin bank employee earned 166 RM weekly. Two years later his pay envelope contained only 142 RM, a slippage of 14 percent. White-collar salaries in other sectors followed the same descending curve.[165]

For white-collar women, the situation was in many ways even bleaker. Although women continued to find jobs with greater ease than men, their salaries were predictably lower. As the depression deepened and fear of dismissal mounted, management was able to adopt practices that not only further reduced salaries but also exacerbated employee anxiety. Unpaid overtime became a commonplace, and because of the commission system in sales—a system which greatly intensified rivalry and tension among employees—"salesgirls" could be hired at salaries well below that stipulated by contract. One union survey conducted in 1929 disclosed that 15 percent of all saleswomen were paid less than the contract minimum, and the situation undoubtedly deteriorated thereafter. Moreover, many saleswomen, particularly in the large department stores, were under twenty years of age and received apprentice remuneration, which in some cases averaged less than eighty marks per month. With keen competition for each position, many department stores simply fired their saleswomen and immediately rehired them as assistants, paying them a correspondingly lower salary. The older the employee, the more readily she complied. Indeed, older saleswomen had even fewer prospects than their male counterparts, since a saleswoman over twenty-five was considered elderly. Being young and female, however, was no guarantee of a job. It was not uncommon for firms to fire young women who had just completed the three years of apprenticeship in order to hire a new set of younger, inexperienced, and therefore cheaper women employees. Thus, for white-collar women as well as men, the depression brought lower pay, deteriorating work conditions, and the constant threat of unemployment.[166]

Though occupying a far less exposed position than white-collar employees, civil servants were hardly immune to the economic pressures of the period. Legislation in late 1924 and again in 1927 had raised civil-service salaries, but even with these increases, pay continued to lag behind prewar standards. Moreover, the shock waves produced by the extraordinary layoffs in 1923–24 continued to reverberate through the Reich, state, and municipal bureaucracies, leaving considerable uneasiness about the sanctity of traditional civil-service rights and prerogatives. That uneasiness was further aggravated by the deteriorating economic situation after 1928. As unemployment lines lengthened and the financial burdens of government grew, the Müller cabinet openly considered a special surtax on civil-service salaries as a means of reducing expenditures. The plan failed to win the support of the DVP and was tabled temporarily, only to be revived upon Brüning's assumption of power. The new chancellor was already on record as an opponent of the 1927 salary schedule, and fears were widespread within the civil service that the government's new austerity program would result in reductions of salaries and pensions or even in additional dismissals. These fears quickly proved well-founded.[167]

In the early summer Brüning endorsed an emergency surtax of 2.5 percent on civil-service salaries and, when frustrated by the Reichstag, incorporated it into his first emergency decree of 26 July 1930. Euphemistically described as "Emergency Aid to the Reich by Persons in Public Service," the surtax was announced as a temporary measure, an "emergency sacrifice." The civil-service unions, however, correctly interpreted the decree not only as a permanent retreat from the long-fought-for 1927 schedule of pay but as an ominous prelude to further assaults on the once hallowed position of the *Berufsbeamtentum*.[168]

At the same time, many educators and university administrators were deeply concerned about the paucity of available positions for their graduates, many of whom had discovered their expectations for a career in government service destroyed by the stabilization measures of the midtwenties. Even before the depression exacerbated the problem, unemployment among professionals, especially teachers, had reached exorbitant proportions. By 1930 mounting public concern was expressed about "the emergence of an intellectual proletariat in the younger generation." Within just a few years, one troubled observer warned, an "army of 120,000 jobless scholars" would exist in Germany. These unemployed academics would constitute "battalions of agitators" who, "by . . . whipping up the masses," would "shake the *Volk* and the state to their foundations."[169]

Given these mounting pressures, civil servants and particularly white-collar employees appear to have been primed for radical political behavior. Yet in spite of these distressing economic developments, electoral support for the NSDAP within the new middle class appears far less ex-

Table 3.5. Party Vote and the New Middle Class (NMC), 1928–1930

	All NMC[a]			
	Protestant (N=152)		Catholic (N=64)	
	1928	1930	1928	1930
NSDAP	.165	.295	.068*	.154*
DNVP	−.312	−.115	.401	.527
DVP	.164	.103*	−.266	−.149
DDP	.104*	.243	−.652	−.857
Z	−.189*	−.438	.741	−.863
SPD	−.438	−.201*	−.543	−.368
KPD	.200*	−.122*	.368*	.331*
Other	−.319	−.311	.274	.149*

	White Collar[a,b]			
	Protestant Subsample			
	Commerce		Industry	
	1928	1930	1928	1930
NSDAP	.606	.157*	.156*	.192*
DNVP	.241*	.184*	−.543	−.472
DVP	.733	.851	.327	−.873
DDP	−.153	−.627	.133*	.168*
Z	−.258*	−.254	−.110*	−.128*
SPD	−.295	−.198	−.384	−.208*
KPD	.431	.253*	−.270	−.127*
Other	−.343	−.481	.300	.306*

	Catholic Subsample			
	Commerce		Industry	
	1928	1930	1928	1930
NSDAP	−1.28	−1.26	−.465	−1.96
DNVP	−.855	−.396	−1.38	−1.08
DVP	.707	.508	−.525	.198*
DDP	.837	1.47	−.772	.206*
Z	−.679	−.926	.631	.849
SPD	.106*	.211*	1.60	1.09
KPD	.107*	.400*	.200*	.166*
Other	−.315*	.626*	−.143*	.652*

Table 3.5. (continued)

| | Civil Service[a,b] Protestant Subsample | | | |
| | Prof. Service | | Transportation | |
	1928	1930	1928	1930
NSDAP	.157	.386	.489	.302
DNVP	.238	.192	.307	.494
DVP	−.205	−.208	−.269	−.383
DDP	−.211*	−.790	.122*	.273
Z	.239*	.340	.188*	.232
SPD	−.764	.204*	−.292	−.280
KPD	−.342	−.517	−.333	−.363
Other	.104*	.169*	.334	.285

| | Catholic Subsample | | | |
| | Prof. Service | | Transportation | |
	1928	1930	1928	1930
NSDAP	−.300	−.282	.855	.210*
DNVP	.424	.500	.788	.290
DVP	.111*	.376	−.562	−.256
DDP	−.483	−.624	.938	−.544
Z	1.11	.995	−.229*	−.412
SPD	−1.95	−1.57	.686	.584
KPD	.490*	.353*	.168*	−.345
Other	.221*	.407*	−.773	.113*

a. These figures are unstandardized regression coefficients (b), controlling for old middle class, *Rentnermittelstand*, blue-collar workers, religion, and urbanization (population size).

b. Presents coefficients for each component of NMC, controlling for all remaining elements of the white-collar/civil service population in addition to those variables listed above.

* These coefficients are not significant at the .05 level.

tensive than the traditional literature suggests. In the elections of 1924 the white-collar/civil-service variable proves a more reliable indicator of the liberal and conservative votes than of the Nazi, and that relationship does not change in 1928. Support for the NSDAP soars in 1930, but even in that election the Nazi/new-middle-class relationship remains surprisingly weak. Although the Nazi coefficients for the first time transcend those of the DNVP, the white-collar/civil-service variable remains as powerful a predictor of the liberal vote as of the Nazi. Moreover, the new middle class continues to lag far behind other social groups as a predictor of the National Socialist vote. Indeed, both the old middle class and the *Rentnermittelstand* prove to be much more strongly related to Nazi electoral performance than the white-collar/civil-service population, even after the calamities of the world economic crisis descended on the republic.

An equally surprising socioelectoral pattern emerges if the two component groups of the new middle class are examined individually. Most studies of Weimar politics acknowledge the antirepublican conservatism within the civil service, while emphasizing the more pronounced susceptibility of the white-collar population to National Socialism. According to the traditional interpretation, the steadily declining economic and social fortunes of the white-collar population exacerbated an already advanced case of status anxiety and resulted in a gradual radicalization of the *Angestelltenschaft*. Lodged between the entrepreneurial *Mittelstand* and the blue-collar proletariat, white-collar employees are said to have experienced a mounting fear of social decline, of proletarianization.[170] This determination to preserve a middle-class status rendered increasingly precarious by the economic dislocations of the Weimar years was certainly reflected in the programs of the non-socialist white-collar unions. These organizations tirelessly drew distinctions between white- and blue-collar labor, treating the *Angestelltenschaft* as a distinct and elevated social "estate" (*Stand*). Although the NSDAP maintained an ambivalent attitude toward the future of unions, whether white- or blue-collar, its espousal of a corporate economy and the concomitant preservation of a distinct white-collar *Stand* is said to have been a major factor in attracting white-collar support.[171]

In spite of this apparent attraction, however, the figures of Table 3.5 show the civil service variable to be a much stronger predictor of the Nazi vote in 1930 than its white-collar counterpart. Instead of rallying to the National Socialist banner, white-collar employees appear to have scattered their votes across the rich and varied spectrum of Weimar politics. Indeed, analysis of the election results offers little evidence to support the traditional thesis that the *Angestelltenschaft*, radicalized by stabilization and then depression, had turned to the NSDAP in 1930. Examination of the relative strengths of the white-collar unions, the most frequently cited evidence of this radicalization, does reveal that a rightward gravitation of white-collar sentiment had begun by at least 1925. In 1920 the socialist AfA accounted for 48 percent of organized white-collar labor, while the Gedag and its *völkisch* affiliate, the DHV, represented about 32 percent, and the liberal GDA 21 percent. By 1931, however, the Gedag had surpassed the AfA to become the largest white-collar organization.[172] Although not formally aligned with any political party, the Gedag had maintained close ties with the DNVP until 1928, when Hugenberg's rabid antiunionism alienated the DHV's leadership. In the ensuing period the Nationalists clearly suffered as a result of the highly publicized rift with the DHV, which actively campaigned against Hugenberg in 1930.[173] Although the leadership remained wary of the NSDAP, the Nazis were apparently able to infiltrate the union's rank and file after 1928. One DHV political specialist estimated that half of the union's members had voted Nazi in 1930.[174]

Still, it is important to remember that although the percentage of white-collar employees united in the DHV had climbed since 1925, the liberal and socialist unions still represented the majority of organized white-collar labor in 1930. Together the GDA and AfA encompassed approximately 60 percent of all organized white-collar employees. Though differing in political orientation and social composition, both unions steadfastly defended the republic and condemned radicalism of both the right and the left.[175] Thus, while membership trends favored the *völkisch* DHV, white-collar sociopolitical sympathies, as reflected in both union affiliation and electoral behavior, remained deeply divided, even after the onset of the depression.

This diverse social and political orientation was a clear expression of the complex demographic composition of the white-collar population, which in turn is perhaps the most important factor in explaining the surprisingly poor performance of the NSDAP among salaried employees. More than any other occupational group, the *Angestelltenschaft* lived in cities, included the largest proportion of working women in the urban economy, and its members possessed the most diverse social heritage. Two-thirds of the new middle class lived in cities with over twenty thousand inhabitants, over half in the *Grossstädten*, Germany's large urban centers with populations of over one hundred thousand. These large cities also contained the vast majority of organized white-collar employees, especially those in the liberal and socialist unions.[176] The Nazis had always found these cities less inviting than the small towns and villages of the countryside, and the depression did not alter that situation. Just as in 1924 and 1928, Nazi electoral performance in 1930 remained inversely correlated to the degree of urbanization.[177]

A second factor, all too often ignored in evaluations of white-collar political behavior, is the sexual composition of the *Angestelltenschaft*. As indicated above, women made up approximately one-third of the white-collar labor force and most of these working women lived in cities. While the SPD and DSP actively sought the support of working women, demanding "equal pay for equal work," the NSDAP prominently championed the traditional feminine role of *Kinder, Kirche, und Küche.* Typical of the Nazi approach to the employment of women in white-collar jobs was a 1928 article in the *Völkischer Beobachter* dealing with "the misery of older *Angestellten.*" Conceding that "today a girl who must earn a living should have the same claim for a job as a man," the article asserted that "a closer look at positions in state and local government, in the banks, and in large businesses reveals that with a little good will and without great hardship a number of young ladies *(jungen Dämchen)* who often don't know what to do with their not unsubstantial income could make room for suffering fathers of families." This view was perfectly consistent with DHV's condemnation of "feminism" and the advancement of women in white-collar positions.[178] Although National Socialism's hazy attitude on religious issues undoubtedly reduced the party's appeal to many women, its unregenerate antifeminism certainly detracted from its appeal to others. Without survey data, it is, of course, impossible to determine attitudes behind electoral behavior, but, for whatever reasons, women in 1928 and 1930 proved less inclined than men to cast ballots for the NSDAP. It seems quite likely that this was particularly true for white-collar women, many of whom lived in large urban centers and came from working-class backgrounds.[179]

The large number of salaried employees with such origins proved to be a complicating factor for any party attempting to ascertain white-collar political inclinations. While the majority of white-collar employees sprang from urban, middle-class homes, a substantial segment came from a working-class environment.[180] Many of these employees may have conformed to the upwardly mobile, status-conscious stereotype encountered so often in the literature, and for such persons fear of social decline was undoubtedly a powerful animating force in political decisions. Others, however, presumably continued to live in their old neighborhood, interacted with the same set of friends, and remained under the influence of their family's traditional political loyalties. Thus, many white-collar employees may have voted SPD or, if a nonsocialist party were chosen, the DDP/DSP, a longtime Social Democratic ally in Prussia and the Reich. Still others may have been attracted by the radical rhetoric of the NSDAP which allowed them to retain the anticapitalist attitudes of their upbringing without, however, voting Marxist. For the white-collar population, such variations were myriad.

This very heterogeneity of outlook made it extremely difficult for all parties to establish the sociopolitical locus of the *Angestelltenschaft*. The NSDAP, in fact, never developed a clearly formulated appeal to white-collar employees. While artisans, shopkeepers, farmers, pensioners, civil servants, and workers received prominent coverage in Nazi campaign literature, white-collar employees were usually treated more generally as subsidiary components of the *Arbeitnehmerschaft* or the endangered *Mittelstand*.[181] Moreover, much of Nazi propaganda was directed against institutions that were quite central to the economic survival of the *Angestelltenschaft*. In order to win the support of craftsmen and merchants, the NSDAP ruthlessly condemned the department stores where so many white-collar employees worked as well as the consumer cooperatives where many white-collar employees purchased their food or other necessities. In fact, National Socialist emphasis on the plight of small business and the farmer, its ambivalence, if not overt hostility, toward white-collar unions, and its prominent solicitation of the working-class vote were hardly calculated to attract white-collar support. National Socialist propaganda, therefore, remained uncharacteristically reticent in its approach to the *Angestelltenschaft*, and that reticence, it seems, was reciprocated by white-collar voters. While the NSDAP clearly made inroads into the white-collar electorate in 1930, the onset of the depression simply did not produce the coalescence of white-collar support for the NSDAP so often asserted in the literature.

A much stronger relationship between National Socialist voting and the new middle class is found when one turns from the white-collar population (*Angestelltenschaft*) to the traditionally conservative civil service. This is particularly suggestive since white-collar employees have commonly been seen as the classic representatives of an economically imperiled and politically radicalized lower middle class, while a more elevated and secure social status has been attributed to the *Berufsbeamtentum*. Civil servants, according to Ralf Dahrendorf, were much more likely to identify with the "ruling classes" than were private employees and would, therefore, be less inclined to engage in radical political activity.[182] Because of their well-established position in the state, civil servants, even in the middle and lower grades, enjoyed greater job security, often a higher level of education, and greater social prestige than the vast majority of their counterparts in the private sector. Indeed, this disparity in status, both legal and social, was keenly felt by the white-collar unions, which strove unceasingly to have their members recognized as *Privatbeamte*.[183] Despite efforts of the Weimar government to "democratize" the *Beamtentum*, the civil service, as Theodor Geiger pointed out in 1932, retained much of its former character as "a social caste."[184] Thus, while civil servants, especially of the middle and lower ranks, appear to have possessed a varied social background, pressure for conversion to the sociopolitical norms of the *Beamtentum* was probably much greater than in white-collar positions.

The special legal and social standing of the professional civil service had, however, absorbed a number of severe shocks since the collapse of the Hohenzollern monarchy in 1918. The republic's policy of democratization, however, feebly implemented, followed by the stunning dismissals of 1924, and the ongoing controversy over civil-service pay scales, were seen as unwarranted assaults on the privileged position of the *Berufsbeamtentum*. Mistrust of the Weimar system was, therefore, widespread within the civil service, even in the predepression period. As the republic's financial situation deteriorated in late 1929 and early 1930, civil servants became increasingly convinced that they would be forced to shoulder a disproportionately heavy burden in the state's struggle against the depression.[185]

These anxieties played a prominent role in National Socialist electoral propaganda in 1929–30. In contrast to the party's ambivalent approach to the white-collar electorate, Nazi pursuit of a civil-service constituency was both aggressive and direct. The NSDAP had assiduously courted the *Beamtentum* in each of the predepression elections, but the campaign against the Young Plan in 1929 offered the party a particularly promising opportunity to mobilize civil-service support. Along with the DNVP, the Nazis attempted to exploit widespread fears that the plan would require cuts in domestic spending and hence more economic sacrifices by the civil service. During the campaign, the NSDAP and DNVP vigorously contended that the acceptance of the plan would certainly result in a reduction of civil-service salaries, and both parties sought to organize civil-service opposition to the plan.[186]

Despite a directive from the Prussian minister president demanding that civil servants refrain from active participation in the campaign, Prussian authorities in late 1929 acknowledged their concern that support for the referendum was growing among public officials.[187] Government efforts to repress public expression of civil-service support for the referendum naturally drew heavy fire from the NSDAP. The Nazis charged that the Prussian government realized that "large numbers" of civil servants wanted to join the referendum movement and had, therefore, initiated a campaign of "terror" against them. Those who had shown support for the referendum, the Nazis asserted, were persecuted and threatened with disciplinary action, and as a countermeasure, the NSDAP began organizing "National Socialist protective associations" to defend civil servants sympathetic to the movement. Similarly, when the Prussian government declared membership in the NSDAP and KPD to be incompatible with public service, the Nazi press once again raised the banner of political freedom for the civil servant. This "latest abomination of the system," the Nazis piously commented, had been committed by a state infamous for its promotion of "Socialists, Democrats, and notorious incompetents." [188] Although these measures were never rigorously enforced, the Nazis were quick to convert them into political capital. By repeatedly developing variations on this theme of discrimination and harassment, the NSDAP by 1930 had—ironically—become a leading advocate of greater political freedom for the German civil service.

At the same time, Nazi campaign literature continued to stress the economic burdens forced on civil servants by the Weimar system. Playing on civil-service anxiety about Brüning's retrenchment plans, the party blasted the surtax on civil service salaries, claiming that the responsibility of meeting Germany's reparations obligations had been foisted onto the already overworked and underpaid *Beamtentum*. Worse still, those affected by the surtax, the Nazis grumbled, were not simply high-ranking officials but "all civil servants and employees of the Reich, state, and municipal governments, the Reichsbank, the Postal Service, and even members of the military." These measures, the Nazis intimated darkly, were merely the first of many that civil servants could expect from the Brüning government or from any other produced by the corrupt Weimar state. [189]

While the DNVP echoed these sentiments, the liberal parties condemned National Socialist assaults on the "system" and warned civil servants that an attack on the state was an attack on the *Berufsbeamtentum* itself. The election of 1930 represented a struggle to preserve the state and with it the civil service. While continuing to stress its support for the traditional elitist status of the *Beamtentum*, the DVP explained that its endorsement of the Brüning surtax had been "dictated by state-political necessity" and admonished civil servants to recognize their higher responsibilities in this time of crisis. [190] The DVP's campaign, one party publication explained, could not be focused "on the special interests of the civil service, though we by no means misunderstand or deny their validity." Instead, the duty of all responsible and patriotic citizens was to "strengthen those parties . . . ready to work with Hindenburg for the preservation of the *Berufsbeamtentum* and the state." [191]

The DSP agreed. The new State party also endorsed the traditional rights of the civil service, emphasizing in particular the DSP's support for a secure lifetime tenure, but called on civil servants to rise above the particular interests on their *Stand*. The great political task of the 1930 campaign, the party stressed, was "to create a Reichstag that is able to defend the state against the assault of radical and economic interest groups."[192]

The figures of Table 3.5 suggest that, in spite of these pleas, a radicalization of the civil service was under way by 1930. Before the onset of the depression, the Nazi/civil-service relationship had been significant only in the immediate aftermath of the massive layoffs and salary reductions in the spring of 1924. With the general recovery of the mid-twenties, the Nazi/civil-service coefficents quickly fade. While the Nazi figures drop considerably from May 1924 to May 1928, the conservative figures remain relatively stable. In 1930, however, the Nazi/civil-service coefficients rise significantly, clearly challenging the supremacy of the DNVP and exceeding the NSDAP's white-collar figures.

What, then, do these figures suggest and what are their implications for an interpretation of fascism? Above all, they indicate that the startling thrust of National Socialism between 1928 and 1930 cannot simply be attributed to a traumatized lower middle class of peasants, shopkeepers, and white-collar employees threatened by proletarianization. Although low-ranking civil servants lived on virtually proletarian incomes, the *Beamtentum*, regardless of rank, enjoyed greater job security, usually a higher level of education, greater social standing, and quite often higher pay than their counterparts in the private sector. The evidence, therefore, suggests that, contrary to the traditional interpretation, support for the NSDAP within the new middle class was far less extensive than in other segments of the bourgeois electorate and that that support was not merely the product of a sociopolitical panic by a lower-middle-class population. By 1930 the NSDAP had begun to transcend its lower-middle-class origins, establishing itself on an electoral terrain traditionally occupied by the conservative right. Although their degree of success varied from group to group, the National Socialists in 1930 had achieved a remarkable breakthrough into each of the major components of the middle-class electorate. As the liberals and conservatives gradually disintegrated, the NSDAP was well on its way to becoming the long sought-after party of middle-class integration.

The Working Class

During the 1930 campaign, the NSDAP concentrated its propagandistic efforts on the middle-class electorate. The labor-oriented "urban plan" had been revised after the disastrous 1928 election, but the party by no means ceased to court working-class voters. Indeed, among the non-Marxist parties, only the NSDAP and the Catholic Zentrum made serious efforts to elicit support from the blue-collar electorate. Throughout the campaigns of 1929 and 1930 the NSDAP continued to present itself as a "people's party," above class and confessional considerations. "It is the movement," one typical Nazi appeal to working-class youth explained, "that does not narrow-mindedly represent the interests of one class [*Stand*] but serves the entire *Volk*."[193] The people of Germany, Goebbels argued, were demanding a union of nationalism and socialism because they had at last come to realize that "the German fate is less a matter of classes and more—even exclusively—a matter of the entire *Volk*." Therefore, "the class parties of the right and left must be overcome and a new way opened for the creation of a genuine people's party." This difficult task could be accomplished only by replacing "the false patriotism of the bourgeoisie" with "a steely nationalistic toughness" and "the false socialism of the Marxists with a true and unsentimental socialist justice."[194]

In addition to these typically vague rhetorical endorsements of "German" or "true" socialism, the usual litany of charges against the Versailles settlement, the Locarno Pact, and the Dawes Plan was encanted with ritualistic regularity. Each of these international agreements marked another dismal milestone in Germany's decline and in the republic's unconscionable exploitation of the working class. Indeed, Socialist support for the Young Plan, the burdens of which, the Nazis insisted, would be "borne exclusively by the broad mass of working people," was only the latest manifestation of Marxist infamy.[195]

Social Democracy could easily be linked with government responsibility for the "infamous" treaties of the period and was, therefore, relentlessly vilified for its alleged sellout of German labor. The SPD had produced nothing for the workers in the twelve years of Weimar democracy, the Nazis charged, "but hunger, misery, and slavery." During the revolutionary days of November 1918 there had been much talk about smashing capitalism and erecting the socialist state. Where, Nazi propagandists wanted to know, was this "workers' paradise"? What had happened to the pillars of the capitalist economic system that the SPD had pledged to nationalize? "The extortionist capital of the profiteering stock market and the banks remains untouched," the Nazis noted with scorn. In fact, finance capital had "strengthened and extended its powers . . . under Marxist rule to such a degree" that it was "now the true ruler of the German people and not just of the proletariat."[196] Meanwhile, the SPD had prospered, but not the German workers. "Their party bosses have become big and fat," the Nazis carped, "while the workers lead a dog's life on the unemployment lines of this glorious republic." [197]

Nor were things better for the worker in the Soviet Union. In fact, the KPD's "slavish dependence" on Moscow constituted, in Nazi estimation, merely another form of foreign treachery. If the German working class wanted to free itself, it would have "to break the chains" of both capitalism *and* Marxism. "Marxism," the NSDAP explained, "is democratic . . . and thus destroys all creative powers in the *Volk* . . . by the immoral terror of the majority," while its international character "obliterates *Volk* and nation and severs the roots of our organic existence." Only National Socialism offered the working people of Germany genuine liberation. In the coming Nazi state, workers would be "integrated into the nation with full rights and obligations" and guaranteed "social justice, work . . . a decent living. . . , and bread." [198] "The working people will put their stamp on the Third Reich," the Nazis promised. "Bourgeoisie and proletariat, however," would "remain in the past." Obviouly no class-based party could achieve this solution. [199] "Only a new movement, which rejects the distinction between bourgeois and proletarian," could liberate German society from its tradition of class conflict. The Nazis proclaimed that many young workers, disillusioned with the traditional parties, had already discovered "genuine comradeship" in the NSDAP as well as "the honest desire of their 'bourgeois' comrades to put aside the old prejudices and to build hand-in-hand with them a new *Volksgemeinschaft* in which character, not money, will be the decisive factor in judging a human being." [200]

These accusations and lofty promises were, of course, hardly new in 1930. In both 1924 and 1928 the NSDAP had employed similar tactics without demonstrable success. The vast majority of the blue-collar electorate had remained unmoved by such Nazi appeals. The National Socialist foothold in the working class was largely confined to unorganized workers in handicrafts and small scale manufacturing. Industrial workers had remained firmly anchored in the troubled waters of the Marxist left. [201]

Yet in spite of past failures, the prospects for Nazi gains in the industrial working class seemed increasingly bright after 1928. As the 1930 campaign got under way, blue-collar unemployment in the major industrial and manufacturing sectors was rampant. In September 1929, just over 17 percent of all organized metalworkers were either unemployed or working part-time. A year later, that figure had soared to almost 45 percent. Joblessness and part-time employment in the chemical, paper, and glass-producing industries almost tripled in the same period. In leather, clothing, and textile production over half of the organized labor force had to rely on unemployment compensation or accept reduced hours. Nor were these industries exceptional. No matter where one looked, the economic landscape yielded the same desolate view.[202] Furthermore, since these figures reflect unemployment among organized workers only, they actually understate the increasingly desperate condition of blue-collar labor. The highest rates of unemployment were recorded among unskilled and unorganized day laborers who flooded the job-referral and unemployment agencies in 1929–30.[203] Even for those workers fortunate enough to hold a full-time job, the contraction of the economy produced a steadily declining standard of living. Between 1928 and 1930, as one index revealed, average real net wages for blue-collar workers fell by 11 percent.[204]

Yet these economic trials, coupled with the mounting threat of National Socialism, did nothing to reduce the rift between the parties of the Marxist left. In fact, as the economic situation deteriorated, the deeply rooted enmity between the SPD and KPD seemed to blossom with renewed vigor. As in previous campaigns, both the SPD and KPD dismissed Nazi "socialism" as an obvious fraud, claiming that the NSDAP was nothing more than "the last bulwark of big capital."[205] Both parties warned working-class voters that fascism could be defeated only by proletarian unity, but then they proceeded to accuse each other of sabotaging that unity. Indeed, the Social Democrats charged that Communist attacks on the SPD represented "the last hope of the Reaction." Fascism had triumphed in Italy because the proletariat had been divided, the SPD contended, and the Communists were now determined to "divide the workers' movement" in Germany.[206] The Communists, for their part, charged the SPD with collaboration with the forces of monopoly capitalism and concluded that the Social Democrats were not worthy of working-class allegiance. "Nazis and Social Democrats stand on the foundation of capitalist private property," the KPD argued, and were, therefore, "slaves of capital and enemies of the workers."[207]

Adding to the already intense conflict between the two working-class parties was the KPD's adoption of the theory of "social fascism" at its Wedding party congress in June 1929. According to this theory, which was to dominate the Communist campaign for the blue-collar vote in the following years, the rationalization of industry, designed to maximize profits for monopoly capitalism, had instead produced massive unemployment and a new crisis of the system. It had also created a new aristocracy of labor, which had assumed control of the unions and was seeking to gain a predominant position in the state as well. Since it attempted to preserve the capitalist system and thus did not act in the interests of the proletarian masses, this aristocracy of labor, most clearly represented in the SPD, constituted "the vanguard of fascism." The defeat of Social Democracy, "the strongest support of fascism within the working class," therefore became the principal objective of Communist electoral strategy.[208]

Although the Communists vigorously condemned the Brüning government for its "reduction of salaries and wages" and its "brutal taxation of the working class," the first priority of the KPD's campaign was to link Social Democracy with "the capitalist enemy."[209] The Young Plan served as a convenient issue for accomplishing that goal. Just as the Communists in 1924 had portrayed Social Democratic support for the Dawes Plan as a betrayal of the proletariat, the SPD's endorsement of the Young Plan was depicted as "high treason against the interests of Germany's working class." With a typically dramatic flourish, the KPD press charged that the Social Democrats had "only one enemy, the working people; only one goal, to shift the burdens of the Young Plan onto the shoulders of the proletariat; and one fear, the workers' struggle against the rapacious Young Plan."[210]

Expanding on this theme, the KPD assailed the entire policy of fulfillment, long a fixture in Social Democratic thinking on foreign affairs. In terms strikingly familiar to those seen regularly in the Nazi press, the Communists blasted the SPD for "utterly capitulating to the imperialists of France and Poland." The KPD persistently stressed that it had always stood against "the territorial dismemberment and pillage of Germany resulting from the brutal Treaty of Versailles." Indeed, Ernst Thälmann, the party's leader, proudly argued that the KPD had "led the struggle against the Versailles treaty of shame at a time when no one had even heard of the Nazis."[211] So stridenly nationalistic in tone and content was this Communist rhetoric in 1930 that *Vorwärts* branded the KPD "more National Socialist than Hitler."[212]

While the extent of nationalist phraseology represented something of a departure for the KPD, the party's electoral appeal contained the familiar denunciation of the parliamentary system. The Brüning government and the rise of National Socialism, the KPD asserted, amply demonstrated the "bankruptcy of bourgeois democracy." The SPD's efforts to gain influence in the Reichstag were ridiculed as "a maneuver of social fascism to spread confusion and disunity in the masses." The situation was actually quite simple, the KPD maintained: "As long as capitalist private property exists and bankers, monopoly magnates, and wealthy landowners control the factories, the mines, and the land, every government of the capitalist state, with or without SPD ministers, will help management against the workers and never the workers against management."[213]

In a more positive vein, the KPD advocated "higher wages, the seven-hour day, bread and work for the jobless, higher unemployment benefits, inexpensive housing for workers, . . . and a higher standard of living for the proletariat." These objectives, however, could only be attained in a Communist Germany. The KPD, therefore, called upon working-class voters to remember that it was "the only revolutionary, Marxist anti-Fascist power" and that "only the overthrow of capitalism, . . . the dictatorship of the proletariat, . . . and a Soviet Germany in alliance with the Soviet Union" could save them. The choice confronting the working-class electorate in 1930 was simple: "Fascist dictatorship or proletarian dictatorship? Fascism or bolshevism?"[214]

The Social Democrats, of course, urged working-class voters to reject both these alternatives. Although clearly on the defensive after two years of government leadership, the SPD entered the 1930 campaign in its more comfortable role as opposition party. In such a position the SPD had scored impressive electoral gains in December 1924 and in 1928. In fact, considerable skepticism concerning the political wisdom of entering the Reich government had circulated within the party in 1928, especially since the SPD was firmly ensconced in a powerful coalition government in Prussia. Whereas the party's leadership consistently warned of the alternatives to a Social Democratic cabinet, especially in 1929 and early 1930, the left wing insisted that the party should "not place an imaginary interest of state above the class interests of the proletariat."[215] The SPD "should not be willing to take responsibility for the state," one leftist spokesman argued, "but only for the working class we represent."[216] When confrontation with the DVP developed over the unemployment insurance plan, the party's left wing, with the vigorous support of the trade unions, had refused to accept a compromise solution. Fearing a desertion by the unions and the defection of disgruntled blue-collar workers to the KPD, the party leadership reluctantly concurred, and the Great Coalition had disintegrated. The unions were appeased and party unity had been preserved. Moreover, the SPD could again enter the field of electoral politics as the embattled but staunch defender of proletarian interests.[217]

The situation of the working class in the fall of 1930 was grim and threatened to grow worse, *Vorwärts* conceded, but the SPD stubbornly defended the record of the Müller cabinet. Under the Great Coalition, Social Democracy had succeeded in "repelling dangerous plots of the reaction while obtaining valuable concessions for the working class," the party maintained. The Müller government had prevented an erosion of

Table 3.6. *Party Vote and Unemployment, 1930*

	Protestant (N=114)	Catholic (N=31)
NSDAP	.379*	−.555*
SPD	.444	−1.97
KPD	.791	1.38
Z	.126*	.266*

NOTE: The figures are unstandardized regression coefficients (b), controlling for old middle class; new middle class; *Rentnermittelstand*; blue-collar workers in mining/metalworking, industry, and handicrafts; religion; and urbanization (population size).

* These coefficients are not significant at the .05 level.

SOURCE: Calculations are based on unemployment figures from every city of over twenty-five thousand inhabitants. These figures taken on 31 August 1930, include those receiving *Arbeitslosenversicherung* or *Krisenfürsorge*. The figures are reported in *Statistische Beilage zum Reichsarbeitsblatt*, Nr. 13, 1931, pp. 7–8.

the unemployment insurance, and wages had been protected. The Brüning regime, on the other hand, had "given the signal . . . for a general reduction of wages and salaries without . . . the promise of price rollbacks." The establishment of his government "above parties" really represented little more than an attempt by "the propertied class, with the aid of the bourgeois parties, to expunge the influence of the working class from the state and the economy by eliminating formal political democracy." The Müller government had not fallen because of an unreasonable Social Democratic stance but because the SPD had chosen to defend the interests of the working class. By its actions, the SPD, in *Vorwärts'* view, had once again demonstrated that "it alone is the true representative of the political, economic, and social concerns of the *Arbeiterklasse*."[218]

The Social Democrats also stoutly defended their determination to pursue "the path of peaceful evolution" toward socialism, arguing that parliamentary democracy was "the foundation on which a balance of competing forces can be achieved without harming society as a whole." The SPD warned, however, that "only a large united workers' party ready to accept responsibility for the state" would be capable of providing effective resistance to the Fascists and reactionaries. A vote for the KPD, the party cautioned, "only helps the reaction and serves the interests of management." The KPD "loathes the workers and does not fight for their betterment and welfare," *Vorwärts* charged. "It views them only as cannon fodder for world revolutionary experiments that are no less criminal than the imperialist experiments of the militarists." The establishment of a "Soviet Germany" would "mean the loss of the social and cultural achievements of the working class, economic chaos, and an era of the most horrible and hopeless misery for the working population of Germany." The SPD, on the other hand, did "not want a deformed socialism that creates a mass prison!" The SPD's goal was the establishment of "a socialist society of peace and equality." "We want to liberate," the party proclaimed, "not oppress." [219]

The years of government responsibility had, however, been too much. The Social Democratic vote slipped from almost 30 percent in 1928 to 24 percent in 1930, while the Communists jumped from 10 to 13 percent. The figures of table 3.7 further suggest that Social Democratic popularity skidded in the blue-collar population, regardless of economic sector. The principal beneficiary of this slump was not, however, the NSDAP but the KPD. Building on an already solid foundation of support in mining and heavy industry, the KPD appears to have extended its appeal to a somewhat broader industrial electorate in 1930. Moreover, unemployment in 1930 is far more strongly related to the Communist than to the Nazi vote. The KPD/unemployment coefficients are quite powerful and the Social Democratic figures marginal. The Nazi/unemployment relationship, however, is strongly negative. This is perhaps less surprising when one considers that the vast majority of the unemployed in 1930 were blue-collar workers drawn from the major industrial and mining sectors.[220] Yet even when the blue-collar variable in those sectors is controlled, the Nazi/unemployment figures remain negative. The ever-lengthening lines of jobless workers and the concomitant specter of serious social unrest may have prompted some nervous shopkeepers to support the staunchly anti-Marxist NSDAP, but it is quite clear from the figures of Table 3.6 that rising unemployment in a town or city generally meant a rising Communist, not Nazi vote.

The NSDAP had not suspended its efforts to attract a working-class constituency after 1928, but its intensified solicitation of the middle-class vote in a period of deepening social conflict may have substantially reduced its potential appeal to dissatisfied workers in the major industrial and mining sectors of the economy. It did not, however, diminish its appeal to that large body of workers in handicrafts and small-scale manufacturing. The NSDAP/blue-collar coefficients for the handicrafts sector had been solidly positive in the elections of 1924, before dropping to a level of virtual insignificance in 1928. In the first election of the depression era, however, they jump dramatically, especially in predominantly

Table 3.7. *Party Vote and the Blue-Collar Working Class (BC),*
1928–1930

| | All BC | | | |
| | Protestant (N=152) | | Catholic (N=64) | |
	1928	1930	1928	1930
NSDAP	.178	.201	−.210*	−.489
DNVP	−.198	−.189	−.691	−.249
DVP	−.431	−.912	−.229	.231*
DDP	−.107	−.101	−.320	−.360
Z	.131*	−.631	−.238	−.186*
SPD	.450	.213	−.111*	−.182*
KPD	.115	.217	.275	.206
Other	−.263	−.713	.193*	.147*

| | BC in Industry[a] | | | |
| | Protestant (N=152) | | Catholic (N=64) | |
	1928	1930	1928	1930
NSDAP	.504*	.379*	−.310*	−.489
DNVP	−.236	−.199*	−.641	−.249
DVP	.368*	−.401	−.229	.231*
DDP	.133*	.168*	−.664	−.148
Z	−.509	−.779	−.868	.133*
SPD	.929	.851	.644	.402
KPD	.258	.226	.275	.206*
Other	.155*	.126*	.389*	.102*

| | BC in Mining/Metalworking[a] | | | |
| | Protestant (N=152) | | Catholic (N=64) | |
	1928	1930	1928	1930
NSDAP	−.797	−.735	.301	−.329
DNVP	−.233	−.235	−.363	−.300
DVP	−.735	−.278	−.227	−.727
DDP	−.141	−.564	−.131*	−.181
Z	−.198	−.630	−.526	−.288
SPD	−.386	−.120	.371	.184
KPD	.383	.198	.423	.361
Other	.215*	−.459	.149*	.203*

Table 3.7. (continued)

| | BC in Handicrafts[a] | | | |
| | Protestant (N=152) | | Catholic (N=64) | |
	1928	1930	1928	1930
NSDAP	.165	.840	.448	.362
DNVP	−.234	−.187	−.709	−.637
DVP	.193 *	.168 *	−.118	−.664
DDP	−.129	−.114	.117 *	.188
Z	−.745	−.105	−1.24	−1.00
SPD	.298 *	.889	1.52	1.46
KPD	.164	.694 *	−.847	−.291
Other	−.777	−.112	−.675	−.404

| | BC in Agriculture[a] | | | |
| | Protestant (N=121) | | Catholic (N=125) | |
	1928	1930	1928	1930
NSDAP	−.525	−.280	.480	.166
DNVP	.162 *	.197	.144	.409
DVP	−.106 *	−.265	−.377	−.566
DDP	−.713	−.811	−.428	−.527
Z	−.161	−.153	−1.12	−1.24
SPD	.217	.273	.481	.458
KPD	.133	.106 *	.687	.217
Other	.161 *	.124 *	−.321 *	.298 *

NOTE: The figures are unstandardized regression coefficients (b), controlling for old middle class, new middle class, *Rentnermittelstand*, religion, and urbanization (population size).
a. Presents coefficients for each component of the working class, controlling for all remaining elements of the BC population in addition to those varibles listed above.

* These coefficients are not significant at the .05 level.

Protestant areas. Indeed, among the different social variables considered, the surge of the Nazi/blue-collar coefficients in handicrafts is the most pronounced. In 1930, the Nazi figures again quite easily surpass those of the KPD, seriously challenging the high Social Democratic coefficients. At the same time, the blue-collar variable in handicrafts and small-scale manufacturing becomes one of the most powerful predictors of the National Socialist vote, a position it would not relinquish in 1932. The strong coefficients in both Protestant and Catholic samples suggest that the NSDAP's efforts to recruit a significant working-class following, to cross the great social divide of German electoral politics, had not been the dismal failure so often depicted in the traditional literature.

Religion

Just as the social contours of National Socialist voting had conformed to the traditional divisions of German electoral politics in 1930, so too did its confessional composition. In the elections of the pre-depression era, support for the NSDAP had not followed the usual lines of religious cleavage. Despite efforts by the DNVP, and Zentrum, to persuade voters—especially women voters—that the NSDAP was an enemy of Christianity, the Nazis had won support from both Christian confessions in 1924 and 1928. In 1930 the party again won followers from both denominations, but the great National Socialist surge occurred primarily in Protestant Germany.

The Nazi breakthrough was achieved despite the usual Nationalist campaign against the "pagan" nature of the NSDAP. In 1930 the credibility of that assault may have been substantially reduced by the prominent Nationalist collaboration with the Nazis in the only recently completed anti-Young campaign. Having promoted the NSDAP as a respectable member of the "National Opposition," the DNVP found it difficult to dismiss the Nazis as a menace to Christian civilization just a few months later. Indeed, the successes of the NSDAP in 1929 and early 1930 left the Nationalists not only presenting themselves as pious defenders of Christian family values, but groping to associate themselves with National Socialism's vehement anti-Semitism as well. While the DSP mildly rebuked the Nazis for their anti-Semitic propaganda, the Nationalists strove to assure the electorate that the DNVP and NSDAP were in fundamental agreement on "the Jewish question." Some differences existed, the Nationalists conceded, but these were centered on a few "radical demands of the NSDAP" which were, in the DNVP's estimation, "hardly important since in practice they cannot be implemented."[221]

As in all previous elections, the vast majority of campaign literature dealing with religion, education, the family, and contemporary values was addressed to women, and in 1930, as in the past, women tended to be underrepresented in the National Socialist constituency. Even in Protestant Germany, women, much more than men, were inclined to cast their ballots for parties that emphasized religious themes. In Protestant

Table 3.8. *Party Vote and Religious Confession, 1928–30 (N = 462)*

	Protestant		Catholic	
	1928	1930	1928	1930
NSDAP	.248	.581	.258	.497
DNVP	.671	.437	.557	.374
DVP	.295	.272	−.385	−.320
DDP	.968	.214	−.583	−.521
Z	−.754	−.874	.817	.931
SPD	.430	.611	−.620	−.783
KPD	−.701 *	−.547 *	−.706 *	−.552 *
Other	.211 *	.268 *	−.681	−.612

NOTE: The figures are unstandardized regression coefficients (b), controlling for old middle class, new middle class, *Rentnermittelstand*, blue-collar workers, and urbanization (population size).

* These coefficients are not significant at the .05 level.

areas that meant above all the DNVP and the CSV; in Catholic districts the Zentrum or Barvarian People's party. In 1930, however, the NSDAP greatly expanded its female constituency, particularly in Protestant areas. While men still dominated in the party's electorate, women were rapidly closing the gap.[222] With their enthusiasm for traditional family life, their unrelenting defamation of "cultural bolshevism," and their endorsement of *Kinder, Kirche, und Küche*, the Nazis may have seemed less threatening to middle-class women in 1930 than in previous years.[223] Qualms about the NSDAP's religious orientation certainly seemed to be receding as the economic and political dangers of the depression mounted.

The Nazis also scored sizable gains within the Catholic electorate, but the Church, with its extensive network of social and political organizations, greatly impeded Nazi progress.[224] The Church was, of course, aided in this task by the Zentrum, which, unlike the DNVP, was neither uncertain of its constituency nor compromised by collaboration with Hitler's party. The Zentrum could, therefore, condemn the National Socialists as "deadly enemies of Christianity" without equivocation.[225] Thus, while the nonconfessional parties of the bourgeois center and right suffered grievous losses at the polls, the Zentrum's share of the vote remained relatively stable in the regional and national elections of 1929–30.

A vote for the Zentrum in 1930 was not, however, an unequivocal endorsement of Weimar democracy. Like the DVP, DDP, and DNVP, the

Zentrum had gradually drifted toward the right after the elections of 1928, when its leadership was assumed by the conservative prelate Ludwig Kaas. In October 1929 Kaas contended that future governments should possess "greater independence from the unpredictable parliamentary climate," and in early 1930 Eugen Bolz, an influential Zentrum politician, condemned "the impotence of our whole system of government."[226] Thus, while the party denied "participation in a conspiracy against the SPD" and excoriated Hugenberg's "desire to destroy the democratic constitution and, along with the NSDAP, to erect a dictatorship" in Germany, the Zentrum's position on parliamentary government was laced with reservations. It defended Brüning's reliance on emergency powers, arguing that "the welfare of the people stands above parliamentary form." The principal task of the Zentrum in the new Reichstag, one prominent party leader asserted, was "not the protection of democracy" but "the salvation of the economy."[227] On the other hand, Catholic voters were warned not to cast their ballots for either the Communists or National Socialists since both were "revolutionary . . . and enemies of the faith and of Christianity." Political and social progress, the Zentrum maintained, demanded "evolution, not revolution."[228] Thus, relying on an extensive network of social, cultural, and political organizations to reinforce voter allegiance to the party, the Zentrum entered the campaign of 1930 espousing "a healthy, conscientious democracy, unity, the *Volksgemeinschaft*, and a stronger governmental authority."[229]

At a time when the precarious foundations of Weimar democracy were perceptibly eroding under the pressure of adverse economic developments and a rising tide of political extremism, the priorities reflected in the Zentrum's appeals were symptomatic of the malaise afflicting Germany's traditionally prorepublican parties. The elections of 1928 had revealed a disquieting lack of voter identification with the liberal DVP and DDP, as middle-class voters defected to the plethora of small bourgeois parties representing special economic interests. Confronted with an extremely aggressive National Socialist campaign for the middle-class vote, the DVP and DDP gravitated steadily to the right after 1928. The establishment of predominance by industrial interests in the DVP was indicative of the changing political currents within the troubled liberal community. The transformation of the Democratic into the State party was highly symbolic of the political metamorphosis of liberal values. By 1930, protection of the state from political extremism and defense of the capitalist system had superseded preservation of democratic government. In 1930, however, even this new electoral orientation proved unable to revive the allegiance of liberalism's dwindling constituency.

Though never reconciled to the republic, the DNVP also moved sharply to the right after the elections of 1928 in an attempt to reserve its sagging electoral fortunes. Hugenberg's radical antidemocratic course and his close association with Hitler's NSDAP, however, merely intensified the party's internal strife and weakened the DNVP's relations with powerful agrarian and white-collar interests. Moreover, Nationalist cooperation with the NSDAP in the anti-Young campaign, and especially the prominent coverage devoted to it in the DNVP press, not only immensely increased voter recognition of the NSDAP but served to legitimize National Socialism to the conservative electorate. Thus, in 1930, some of the NSDAP's most impressive gains appear to have come from those groups that traditionally constituted the Nationalist constituency, farmers, civil servants, and, to a lesser extent, white-collar employees.

Less spectacular, though hardly less ominous for Weimar democracy, was the sharp contraction of the SPD's base of electoral support within the blue-collar working class. Concerned that, after two troubled years of cabinet responsibility, a compromise on the politically and socially charged issue of unemployment compensation would undermine the party's standing with blue-collar voters, the Social Democrats had permitted the Great Coalition to disintegrate. Yet despite the party's apparent readiness to withdraw to the security of its position in the powerful Prussian cabinet, the SPD's campaign, more than any other, reflected a fundamental commitment to the preservation of parliamentary democracy. Communist inroads into the SPD's industrial constituency, therefore, did not augur well for the republic's already imperiled future.

In the fall of 1930, with an electorate traumatized by rising unemployment, falling prices, and failing businesses, the social bases of Weimar democracy appeared to be shrinking ineluctably, compacted by an intense and unremitting pressure from the extremes of both left and right. In May 1924 a similar electoral pattern had developed, only to dissolve in the ensuing period of economic stability. The elections of 1930, however, did not mark the crescendo of political crisis in Germany but the end of that transient stability.

IV
Polarization and Collapse:
The Elections of 1932

The dramatic National Socialist breakthrough in September 1930 produced a staggering effect on the already embattled Weimar Republic. The outcome of the Reichstag election rendered the formation of a viable parliamentary coalition almost impossible and vastly enhanced the public standing of Hitler and his party. The devastating losses suffered by the bourgeois parties dashed Brüning's hopes of reviving a *Bürgerblock* coalition, and efforts to coax the NSDAP into some form of government participation were neither seriously undertaken nor seriously entertained by the Nazi leadership. Hugenberg also quickly informed the chancellor that the DNVP was not interested in serving in another Weimar cabinet but was determined to pursue its increasingly radical antigovernment course. Thus, after only desultory efforts to find a workable majority in the Reichstag, Brüning opted to continue the convenient presidential government based on emergency decrees. Afraid that a failure of the Brüning cabinet and new elections would result in a government of the radical right, the parties of the bourgeois center and the Social Democrats were reluctantly willing to tolerate Brüning's rule by article 48. As a consequence, the Weimar political system, so denigrated by its foes, underwent a profound metamorphosis in 1930–31. As the chancellor's use of emergency powers escalated, jumping from five decrees in 1930 to over forty in the following year, the role of the Reichstag shrank concomitantly. In 1930 the Reichstag held ninety-four sessions. In 1931 that number dropped by more than half. By 1932, government by emergency decree had become the norm. In that year, three successive Reich governments enacted no fewer than fifty-seven such measures, while the Reichstag convened only thirteen times. Almost three years before Hitler assumed the reins of power, Brüning had embarked on a course that resulted in the termination of parliamentary government in Germany.[1]

Most of Brüning's profoundly unpopular decrees were designed to remedy the republic's economic woes. Following the 1930 elections, the deterioration of the already grave economic situation accelerated. Between 1929 and 1932, industrial production plunged by almost 50 percent, the most precipitous drop coming in 1931. In roughly the same period, individual savings dwindled, bankruptcies soared, and unemployment lines grew steadily.[2] In the winter of 1929–30, three million Germans had been out of work. During the following year that figure almost doubled, climbing to six million in early 1932. As grim as these official statistics apeared, they were certainly conservative. By 1932 perhaps a million jobless men and women had exhausted their eligibility for unemployment compensation and, in their despair, no longer bothered to register at the job-referral agencies. In the midst of the pervading economic gloom, the banking crisis of 1931, during which several major banks appeared on the verge of insolvency, exacerbated the already palpable crisis of public confidence in the beleaguered "Weimar system."[3]

As joblessness increased, public expenditure on unemployment compensation and related benefits began an inexorable rise, while tax revenues continued to shrink. Afraid that growing government deficits would lead to a recurrence of the disastrous inflation, Brüning implemented a series of stringent austerity measures that he believed to be the preconditions for recovery. The chancellor also hoped to score a major foreign-policy success by convincing the Allies to reduce or even terminate Germany's reparations obligations, and a balanced budget, he felt, was necessary to demonstrate Germany's commitment to fiscal responsibility. Thus, the decrees of 1930–32 systematically reduced wages, prices, rents, pensions, and social services, while raising some existing taxes and introducing new ones to cover the government expenditures. These measures failed to reverse the debilitating trends of the escalating economic crisis, but they did inflame political passions, providing a prominent target for antirepublican protest.[4]

Fresh from its impressive showing at the polls in 1930, the NSDAP led the assault. Although the party's now imposing Reichstag delegation could, and did, exploit parliamentary proceedings as a forum for National Socialist propaganda, the NSDAP's political energies continued to be directed at extraparliamentary activities. Between the Reichstag elections of 1930 and 1932, the Nazis did not relax or slacken the pace of their agitation. Instead, the party continued to centralize its propaganda apparatus and to pursue its revolutionary strategy of "perpetual campaigning."[5] This strategy had evolved gradually since the adoption of Goebbels's "propaganda action" campaigns in 1928–29 and was facilitated by a number of interrelated sociopolitical developments. As the depression deepened, the party's membership began to swell. Between 1928 and September 1930, it almost tripled, rising from 108,717 to 293,000. Then in the aftermath of the 1930 Reichstag campaign, applications for membership jumped dramatically. Between September and the end of the year, almost 100,000 new names were registered on the party rolls. Without the benefit of a national campaign in 1931, the NSDAP still doubled its membership again. Indeed, the SA claimed to have inducted 100,000 new members in two months alone during the harsh winter of 1931–32. By the close of 1932, a year dominated by a plethora of national and regional elections, the NSDAP boasted a membership of almost 1.5 million.[6]

As the membership rose, so did the level of Nazi agitation. In every region of the country the party was now able to organize mass rallies, stage elaborate parades of the uniformed SA, and engage in widely publicized street battles with the Communists and Social Democrats.[7] These activities, at which the Nazis excelled, were intended to create a dynamic and peripatetic public image for the party, bridging the temporal gaps between national and regional elections. To cover these activities, the Nazis vastly expanded the scope of their party press in 1930–31. Before the great electoral breakthrough in September 1930, the party controlled 49 newspapers, only 6 of which were dailies. By 1932 that number had expanded to 127, with a circulation in excess of a million. The party's *Völkischer Beobachter*, published in both Munich and Berlin, saw its circulation soar from 26,000 in 1929 to over 100,000 in 1931, and Goebbels's own paper, the Berlin-based *Der Angriff*, became a daily for the first time in November 1930.[8]

Perhaps most important for the success of the party's electoral efforts, however, was Hitler's creation of the Reich Propaganda Directorate (Reichspropagandaleitung—RPL) in early 1931. Goebbels had been directing Nazi propaganda since the previous year, but in 1931 his staff was expanded and his responsibility for National Socialist propaganda activities throughout the entire Reich formalized in the RPL. The RPL provided the Gauleiters with secret monthly reports on national political developments, propaganda techniques, and an outline of Nazi propaganda for the coming month. Beginning in April 1931, the RPL also distributed a monthly publication, *Unser Wille und Weg* (*Our Will and Way*), a journal for local Nazi functionaries that explained the party's position on key political and economic issues.[9] To keep the RPL in touch with popular attitudes, the Gau organizations were required to submit monthly reports on local political activities and to provide assessments of grassroots sentiment. The RPL urged the Gauleiters to send their functionaries into "the bakeries, butcher shops, grocery stores, and taverns" to sample public opinion and find out for whom the people had voted and why. This information could then be used by the national leadership in developing the party's campaign literature.[10] Similarly, propaganda techniques that had originated and worked well in one locale were reported to the RPL and then incorporated into the monthly reports to all the regional offices. In this way a circular flow of valuable information was created that would serve the party well in the following campaigns.

Utilizing their expanding membership and their increasingly sophisticated propaganda apparatus, the Nazis marched aggressively through the regional elections of 1931. In Oldenburg, Hamburg, Hessen, and Anhalt the NSDAP scored sizable gains, while the traditional bourgeois parties faltered badly.[11] Moreover, the strategy of perpetual campaigning was considerably aided in 1931 by another referendum controversy in which the National Socialists played by far the most salient role. Initiated by the DNVP and supported by both the Nazis and the Communists, a referendum campaign was launched to unseat the democratically elected Prussian Landtag, which was controlled by the parties of the Weimar Coalition (SPD, DDP/DSP, and Zentrum). Beginning in April 1931, the campaign raged across the Reich's largest state until August, when the Prussian public was at last summoned to the polls. Although the referendum failed, it did attract considerable support, and more importantly, allowed the NSDAP to continue its high visibility campaign against the "Weimar system" in a period of growing public unrest.[12]

Shortly after the conclusion of the Prussian referendum, the party was given another important boost by a revival of the anti-Young Plan alliance. Organized by Hugenberg, the alliance was intended to mobilize the National Opposition under DNVP leadership. The NSDAP was thus invited to join the Stahlhelm, the Reichslandbund, and Pan-German League, and other rightist organizations in a mass demonstration of anti-republican unity at Bad Harzburg in October. At that highly publicized rally and in the months that followed, it became absolutely clear that Hitler, not Hugenberg, was the dominant figure in the alliance, and the Harzburg Front quickly turned into yet another vehicle for National Socialist propaganda. The loose cooperation between the Nazis and their Harzburg allies lasted only until the presidential election of the following spring and ended in considerable bitterness. Nonetheless, the Harzburg Front had served its purpose for Hitler, providing him with extensive national exposure and marking another stage in the legitimation of National Socialism in traditional conservative circles.[13]

The growing popularity of the NSDAP also paid handsome financial dividends to the party. The reorientation of National Socialist propaganda, particularly its rigid anti-Marxist stance and its intensified solicitation of middle-class support, had gradually opened important new sources of revenue for the party. Until 1932 the NSDAP had relied almost exclusively on membership dues to finance its activities. During 1931, however, as the financial demands on the party escalated, Hitler began to court representatives of the business community. Impressed with the NSDAP's militant anti-Marxism but concerned about its vague socialist rhetoric, business leaders had, with some notable exceptions, remained aloof from the party. In January 1932, however, Hitler was invited to speak at the influential Düsseldorf Industrial Club, and his success there signaled an important breakthrough for the NSDAP. Although business leaders continued to prefer the more predictable bourgeois parties, the Nazis were henceforth recognized as a plausible if problematic alternative to the DNVP and DVP. The extent to which business contributed to the financial strength of the party in 1932 remains a matter of controversy, but Hitler's visit was certainly calculated to enhance the party's respectability and to emphasize its utility as a reliable bastion against the anticipated surge of the left.[14]

That image was certainly reinforced by the first election of 1932 in the tiny state of Lippe. With over 30 percent of the vote, the NSDAP surpassed the combined totals of the bourgeois parties and exceeded the Socialist vote as well. Confident of success, the Nazis looked forward to the upcoming elections in Prussia and Bavaria, scheduled for the early spring. At the same time, a much more exalted goal loomed on the horizon. Hindenburg's term as Reich president was due to expire in May, and at eighty-five, Hindenburg hoped to avoid a campaign. In an effort to forestall a new election, Brüning sought Nazi support for a plan that would extend the president's term by a mere vote in the Reichstag. When Hitler demanded the dismissal of the chancellor and new Reichstag elections in return, Hindenburg balked, and a presidential campaign became inevitable.[15]

Hitler did not relish the prospect of campaigning against the highly venerated Hindenburg, and Nazi opinion was divided on the issue. In late February, however, Hitler decided to risk his rising prestige and enter the campaign. The decision also meant a break with the party's Harzburg allies, who favored the Stahlhelm's Theodor Duesterberg as the Harzburg Front's candidate. The Nazis were nonetheless confident that the party was well prepared for the campaign. With its propaganda machine well organized and well financed, the NSDAP launched a massive media blitz the likes of which the voting public had never witnessed. For weeks

the country was saturated with pamphlets, rallies, and theatrically orchestrated appearances by Nazi leaders. Over thirty thousand party-
sponsored meetings took place and eight million leaflets were distributed
as the campaign progressed.[16] Although Hitler did not emerge triumphant on 13 March, his strong showing (30.1 percent) devastated the
Harzburg candidate (6.8 percent) and prevented Hindenburg (49.6 percent) from achieving the required majority on the first ballot.

In the runoff that followed in April, Hitler confronted Hindenburg and
the Communist candidate, Ernst Thälmann. While the Reich president
was again supported by a bizarre coalition extending from the SPD to the
KVP, the Harzburg parties urged their voters to abstain rather than endorse Hitler. Undaunted, the NSDAP launched a vigorous campaign
against Hindenburg, branding him the candidate of the Social Democrats
and "system parties." The Nazi press sought to associate the Reich president with Brüning's unpopular emergency decrees, warning voters that
"if you vote for Hindenburg, then you're voting for Brüning, and whoever votes for Brüning casts his ballot for the emergency decrees."[17] In the
campaign's most dramatic stroke, Hitler took to the skies in a highly publicized *Deutschlandflug*, appearing in twenty-one cities in six days. He
was the first German politician to incorporate air travel into campaign
strategy, and the image of a daring and innovative leader descending from
the heavens spearheaded the RPL's propaganda offensive.[18] In spite of
these efforts, Hitler's bid to unseat the Reich president again fell short.
With over thirteen million votes (36.6 percent), however, Hitler had
dwarfed the other leaders of the antirepublican right and emerged as a
political force of the first magnitude.

Aside from vastly increasing Hitler's public stature, the presidential
campaigns also allowed the RPL to perfect the techniques it would use to
such tremendous advantage in the following months. Indeed, the procedures adopted by the RPL in both the planning and conduct of the presidential campaigns were prototypical of those the party would employ in
each of the subsequent national campaigns of 1932 and in the most important regional contests. At the outset of each campaign the RPL circulated a lengthy position paper that defined the party's strategy, isolated
the themes to be emphasized, and explained the NSDAP's posture toward
leading personalities, parties, organizations, and current issues.[19] As in
1930, the RPL dictated the principal themes and slogans that would
serve as the leitmotivs of each campaign. In the first presidential election,
for example, the RPL informed all Gauleiters:

The thrust of our slogan for this campaign is roughly the following: It must be made clear to the masses of German voters that . . .

the National Socialist movement is determined to use the presidential elections to put an end to the entire system of 1918. The two words *Schluss jetzt!* represent the most direct and forceful formulation of that determination. As the final words of every leaflet and every placard this slogan must be relentlessly hammered into the heads of the reader and voter. In ten days no one in Germany should be talking about anything but this slogan.[20]

As the campaign progressed, the RPL circulated regular propaganda updates, designating new themes and social groups for particular emphasis. A new slogan or theme was specified for each week of the campaign and the regional party offices were flooded with an endless flow of leaflets, placards, and other printed materials to be distributed or posted on specified dates. These printed materials were accompanied by the usual reminders about other propaganda aids available from the national or Gau headquarters. The party's list of such aids and services had grown considerably since 1930, including now films, phonograph records, loudspeakers, motorcycles, trucks, and, for the most affluent and important Gaus, even airplanes. The RPL also continued to offer detailed instructions on virtually all aspects of campaigning from the sort of music to play at rallies to the colors of campaign placards and the frequency with which they should be changed to keep public attention. In each of the 1932 campaigns, the NSDAP continued to concentrate on what the RPL referred to as "systematic work at the grass-roots level."[21] No detail seemed too small for Goebbels and his propaganda staff.

In addition to these suggestions on the techniques of campaigning, the RPL also targeted specific elements of the electorate for particular attention during the campaign. Between the first and second ballots of the presidential elections, for example, the RPL was convinced that the party had failed to attract sufficient support from civil servants, pensioners, and women. Hindenburg's strong showing, Goebbels averred, could be "traced to the typical mentality of certain bourgeois circles, especially the German *Spiessbürger* whose vote was won with sentimentality and the fear of the unknown; the woman whose vote was swayed by appeals to the tearducts and the fear of war; and the pensioner and public official who were misled by references to inflation, benefit cuts, and National Socialist hostility toward civil servants [*Beamtenfeindseligkeit*]."[22] To counter such charges and reassure these important groups, the RPL deluged the Gauleiters with drafts of leaflets directed to precisely these elements of the electorate during the second presidential campaign. Similarly, during the important Prussian state elections in April—a campaign directed not by regional officials but by the RPL—Goebbels targeted the blue-collar voter for special attention. An RPL memorandum of 2 April instructed the local organizations to do all they could to remove working-class mistrust of the NSDAP, "to interest the worker in us, to bring him into our rallies, to win him." [23] To help in this task, the RPL provided the locals with an almost ceaseless flow of leaflets addressed explicitly to working-class voters, detailing Nazi positions on labor-oriented issues and assailing the parties of the Marxist left. In the Bavarian state elections, on the other hand, the party was concerned less with the working-class vote than with the Catholic electorate, and the Bavarian locals were therefore instructed to focus primarily on the NSDAP's defense of religious values against the onslaught of godless Marxism. There the party's campaign theme was to be "a National Socialist Bavaria as a bulwark against Centralization and Godlessness!" [24]

Perhaps most impressive in the National Socialist campaigns of 1932, however, were the RPL's extraordinary displays of nationwide propaganda coordination. Since the radio had not yet become an effective propaganda tool for the party and film was still in its political infancy, Nazi campaign strategy relied heavily on public rallies and the distribution of printed matter. Thus, in addition to the mass of leaflets and posters provided to regional leaders on an almost daily basis, the RPL in 1932 earmarked some for public distribution on specific dates. Their appearance on designated dates was designed to dovetail with important speeches or rallies devoted to a particular social group or political issue. An RPL memorandum of 4 July 1932, for example, announced that the drafts of eighteen placards would arrive shortly and that each was scheduled to be posted on a specific date. "The placards must appear, whether in the press, as leaflets, or as posters on exactly the date for which they are marked," the RPL stressed to the Gauleiters. "The end effect must be that on the same day all over Germany our attack on the system and its parties has been launched as a unified assault." [25]

Similarly, during the fall Reichstag campaign, the RPL informed regional leaders that the party's Battle Front of the Commercial Middle Class had designated 3 November as a day of nationwide mass meetings devoted to National Socialist *Mittelstandspolitik*. The purpose of these meetings was to discuss "the inadequacy and drawbacks of Papen's economic policies" and to educate proprietors in "handicrafts, retail commerce, and trade" in the National Socialist approach to their problems. On 26 October the RPL, therefore, instructed all Gauleiters to arrange such meetings and to provide qualified Nazi speakers from the commercial middle class. To set the stage, the *Völkischer Beobachter* would publish an appeal to the commercial *Mittelstand* on 2 November and on 4 November each Nazi newspaper was to give extensive coverage to the meeting in its locale.[26] Such coordinated propaganda assaults were common in the National Socialist campaigns of 1932, and the desired effect was obvious: on a given date Nazis from Königsberg to Aachen would be on the streets distributing roughly the same leaflets, posting similar placards, and holding widely publicized speeches or rallies on the designated topic of the day. The degree of nationwide coordination provided by the RPL was unmatched by the other parties of the Weimar era and gave the NSDAP a tremendous advantage in the day-to-day conduct of national campaigning.

If the displays of national coordination reflected the RPL's firm, centralized control over the NSDAP's campaigns, the party also demonstrated a greater sensitivity to regional variations than it had two years before. During each of the 1932 campaigns the RPL furnished the Gauleiters with drafts of electoral appeals on an almost daily basis. These appeals covered virtually every group, with farmers, civil servants, and workers in that order leading the list, and every theme of the campaign.[27] As in 1930 these drafts were composed by the RPL and dispatched to the *Gauleitungen* several times a week for the duration of the campaign, sometimes arriving fifty at a sending. Yet, unlike 1930, Goebbels, who after 20 February 1932 directed the campaigns from Berlin, did not insist that these drafts be adopted without change. In fact, the RPL repeatedly emphasized that these drafts were intended as models that could be altered somewhat to suit local tastes. A memorandum of 23 March 1932, for example, contained fifteen such drafts but stressed that they be "selected for use on an individual basis. Each Gau should take what is appropriate for its situation." The RPL communique noted that "it is impossible for the Propaganda Directorate to publish uniform leaflets for the whole Reich. Since the mentality of the North German is different from that of an East Prussian or a Badener, etc., the drafts composed by the RPL must be modified to conform to the mentality of the local population."[28]

This decision to insure greater flexibility at the local level, however, had its limits. Under no circumstances, the RPL repeatedly warned, were the local parties, the *Ortsgruppen*, to compose their own leaflets or posters. Only the Gauleiters and their propaganda staff were entrusted with this review and revision authority.[29] Moreover, as a systematic examination of the leaflet collections in Berlin, Potsdamm, Munich, and Koblenz indicates, many Gaus simply adopted the RPL wording of this campaign literature verbatim. The upshot of this shift in RPL strategy was, therefore, not to change the substance or thrust of the party's national campaigns but to allow the regional leadership greater flexibility in presenting the NSDAP's case to the voters of a particular region. After all, the RPL concluded, "it is senseless to press a leaflet addressed to peasants into the hand of a worker and vice versa."[30]

The conduct of National Socialist campaigns in 1932 was not always the smooth-running operation that a reading of the RPL files might superficially suggest. As some of its correspondence with the Gauleiters reveals, signals were sometimes crossed, communiqués ignored, and instructions improperly executed. The RPL sometimes found it necessary to goad regional leaders on, complaining of flagging enthusiasm and energy, especially by the close of the year.[31] Yet, by and large the RPL's organization and direction of the 1932 campaigns proved astonishingly effective. The RPL had shaped an extraordinary propaganda organization that assured the national leadership firm control over the substance and strategy of the campaigns while providing a uniform but flexible framework within which regional variations could be addressed. Despite its centralization, the National Socialist propaganda machine was remarkably responsive to shifts in the political topography of the country. Local issues, local personalities, and local organizations clearly played important roles in the NSDAP's impressive electoral performance in 1932, but it was the party's—actually the RPL's—ability to link those local activities together, to coordinate them, and give them a uniform appearance and direction all across the Reich that made National Socialism such an imposing political phenomenon to contemporaries.

Using this extensive propaganda apparatus and pursuing a policy of what might be called coordinated saturation, the NSDAP rolled up impressive gains in the regional elections that followed hard on the heels of the presidential campaigns. Despite efforts by the Reich government to reduce the party's public presence, particularly Brüning's ban on the SA and SS, the NSDAP captured 36 percent of the vote in the extremely important Prussian elections, 32 percent in Bavaria, 26 percent in Württemberg, and 31 percent in Hamburg, all in April. In the following month, the parade of Nazi triumphs continued. In Oldenburg the Nazis took 48 percent of the vote, while in Hessen, long a Social Democratic stronghold, the NSDAP secured 44 percent of the electorate.[32]

As the list of Nazi electoral successes lengthened, pressure on the Brüning cabinet mounted. Business had become increasingly disenchanted with the chancellor's failure to use his emergency powers to dismantle the social legislation of the Weimar Republic, while powerful agrarian interests were alarmed at Brüning's plan to resettle the unemployed on large estates in East Elbian Germany. At the same time, influential military leaders, especially General Kurt von Schleicher, were disappointed in

Brüning's apparent unwillingness to reach an understanding with the National Opposition. Schleicher believed that the time had come to jettison
the Weimar constitution and establish an authoritarian regime backed by
the army. Such a regime would enjoy the support of business and agriculture, while the troublesome NSDAP, Schleicher argued, could be "tamed"
and used to draw popular support for the government's new authoritarian course.[33]

Convinced by his conservative entourage that a new government with a
strong rightist orientation could secure the support of both the DNVP
and NSDAP, Hindenburg stunned the public and the Reichstag by unceremoniously dismissing Brüning in late May and, largely at Schleicher's
suggestion, installing the osbcure Franz von Papen in the Reich chancel-
lery. Papen was charged with the formation of a "government of national
concentration," which would stand "above parties," and the new cabinet,
composed almost exclusively of conservative aristocrats without formal
party ties, left little doubt about the chancellor's orientation. "The cabinet of barons," as it was popularly dubbed, was quickly denounced by
the left, the DSP, and even the Zentrum, Papen's own party. This left the
new government with an even smaller nucleus of parliamentary support
than its predecessor had enjoyed, but Papen and Schleicher, who was now
serving as defense minister, were not concerned with parliamentary ma-
jorities. They were determined to make the transition from presidential
government to authoritarian state, relying on the backing of Hindenburg
and the Reichswehr. The Nationalists and perhaps the DVP could be relied upon to support such a regime, while the Nazis, Schleicher hoped,
could be outmaneuvered. In fact, the general believed that he had struck a
bargain with Hitler, according to which the NSDAP agreed to "tolerate"
a Papen cabinet in exchange for a revocation of the ban on the SA and SS
as well as a promise of new Reichstag elections.[34]

The Papen era, therefore, began with a concentrated effort to court
both the business community and the forces of the political right. Appealing to industrial and business leaders, Papen described his government as the last "great chance" to reestablish the primacy of private enterprise and halt Germany's slide into state socialism. The chancellor
indicated that tax credits for industry and a retreat from the binding nature of wage contracts, a step long demanded by business, lay ahead, and
he promised a reduction of government spending on social programs. As
a sign of his determination to dismantle the Weimar "welfare state," Papen used his first emergency decree in June to introduce substantial
reductions in unemployment and health benefits, while suggesting that
government spending in certain areas—transportation and housing con-

struction, in particular—might spur economic activity in the private sector. Predictably, these measures outraged labor, while finding considerable resonance in the wary business community.[35]

While sending these signals to management, Papen also moved to win the support of the political right. Throughout the early summer he courted both Hugenberg and Hitler, hoping to bind them in one manner or another to his regime. As a sign of his good faith, Papen lifted the ban on the SA and SS, despite strong objections from several state governments. Moreover, he used his emergency powers to dissolve the Reichstag and call for new elections to be held on 31 July. Papen apparently hoped that the campaign would further discredit and weaken the center and left, while providing a broad popular base for his authoritarian regime. The culmination of this strategy came on 20 July, when the chancellor used a violent clash between Nazi and leftist supporters in Altona as a pretext to eliminate the most stable institutional power base of Social Democracy in the republic. Claiming that he was forced to act to preserve public order, Papen dissolved the Social Democratic government of Prussia and imposed martial law. With the election only eleven days away, Germany seemed poised on the verge of civil war.[36]

Papen's bold intervention in Prussia had been, in part, a maneuver to rally public support for his regime, and it did win praise in conservative, nationalist, and anti-Marxist circles. The new government, however, still lacked an established electoral constituency. The parties of the bourgeois center and the left were unalterably opposed to the new course, and while both the DNVP and DVP applauded the move against Prussia, neither was enthusiastic about conducting a pro-Papen campaign. Moreover, Nazi toleration of the new regime did not imply support. In a secret communiqué dated 4 June 1932, Goebbels did instruct regional leaders that "all party officials are to refrain from any discussion of the Papen cabinet during the campaign."[37] Two weeks later, however, the RPL, in a confidential memorandum on campaign strategy, stressed that the party must "refuse most strenuously to be associated with this cabinet." Any suggestion that the NSDAP either tolerated or supported the Papan government was to be vigorously condemned as a "great fabrication." Nevertheless, the RPL explained that the primary target of all National Socialist propaganda was not Papen but the "bankrupt system parties," which were trying to divert attention from their own history of failure by attacking the newly established government. The Nazi goal in the campaign was, therefore, "to destroy the bourgeois splinters, to make inroads for the first time into the Zentrum's electorate, and to drive the Marxists from power once and for all."[38]

Of the bourgeois parties, the DSP was both the most outspoken critic of the Papen government and the most vulnerable to attack from the right. A skein of electoral disasters reaching back to the 1928 Reichstag elections had almost exhausted the party's funds and destroyed its organization. The Prussian Landtag elections in April had been particularly devastating. Until then, the DDP/DSP had maintained a sizable bloc of deputies in the Prussian Landtag, and the new elections, the first since 1928, were viewed as a crucial test of the party's uncertain future. The DSP's hopes had been buoyed by the outcome of the presidential elections in March, in which the party had lent its support to Hindenburg, but the Prussian campaign proved disastrous. Having conducted a campaign directed against the NSDAP, emphasizing that "the socialism of Hitlerism is no less dangerous for the bourgeois world than any other form of socialism,"[39] the DSP suffered grievous losses. With only 1.5 percent of the vote, the number of its deputies was reduced from twenty-eight to two and its last claim to influence was lost.[40]

The DSP, however, refused to fold. The party had been a minor parliamentary prop for the Brüning government, and when Papen assumed power in May, the DSP attempted to secure an alliance with the Zentrum and SPD for the anticipated Reichstag elections. When these bids failed, the party again entertained a DVP proposal for the creation of a bourgeois unity party. As usual, the negotiations quickly encountered difficulties, particularly when the DSP insisted that this new party take an unequivocal stand "against fascism and for parliamentarianism." Cooperation with the DVP again proved impossible, since the DSP, as one of its campaign statements put it, refused to ally itself with a party that had "as its only slogan 'private enterprise' and nothing more."[41] As a result, the DSP entered the campaign without allies and without hope.

The central theme of the DSP's campaign was "the preservation of the republic and democracy," warning its middle-class constituents that they "must fight hard for the republic and against the cabinet of Junkers."[42] It acknowledged the attractions of a National Socialist vote, but dismissed them as superficial and illusory. "National Socialism embodies an amorphous mass of the most diverse feelings and instincts," the DSP explained, "which can be grouped under the rubric: 'things have to change!' The 'how' and 'with what means' remain unanswered."[43] The party hotly denied that, given its recent record, a vote for the DSP was a wasted vote,[44] but in the aftermath of the Prussian debacle even its foremost supporters in the press, the *Frankfurter Zeitung* and the *Berliner Tageblatt*, questioned its viability as a party. Indeed, the former urged its readers to cast their ballots for the Zentrum or the SPD to prevent the election of a National Socialist majority in July.[45]

The prospects of the DSP's liberal rival were hardly more promising. In the wake of the September elections in 1930, Edward Dingeldey had assumed leadership of the DVP with a mandate to halt the progressive erosion of the party's electoral support. Convinced that the DVP's dwindling electoral fortunes resulted from its public image as an "interest party" for big business, Dingledey hoped to prevent further National Socialist incursions into the DVP's constituency by transforming the party into a genuine *Volkspartei*. As a prerequisite for a successful revival of voter allegiance, Dingeldey hoped to dismantle the loose network of district organizations, often controlled by a small clique of local notables, and replace it with a tightly knit hierarchical structure capable of combatting the well-organized Nazis at the grass-roots level.[46]

These plans, however, encountered stiff resistance from the party's right wing. The industrial interests within the DVP had initially expressed hope that Brüning's "Socialist-free" presidential government would provide great opportunities for business to influence economic and social policy. However, as the depression deepened and Brüning's measures proved largely ineffective, the DVP's right wing grew progressively disenchanted. By 1931, rightist elements within the party were demanding the withdrawal of the DVP ministers from the cabinet.[47]

In an effort to mollify the industrialists and establish the party's public credentials as a rightist party, Dingeldey enlisted the DVP in the right-wing referendum campaign to unseat the Prussian government in 1931. He also opened negotiations with Brüning and Hitler to effect a National Socialist entry into the Reich government. When these initiatives failed, the DVP lodged a vote of no confidence against the Brüning government in October and again in February of the following year. The latter vote was accompanied by a disavowal of the two moderate DVP members serving in the cabinet, but this was not enough to prevent the secession of the party's right-wing-dominated district organizations in Westphalia and the Lower Rhine.[48]

With its organization disintegrating, the DVP suffered repeated setbacks in the regional elections of 1931 and early 1932, but the Prussian campaign proved particularly humiliating. With less than 2 percent of the vote, the DVP, like its left-liberal rival, had been reduced to the status of an insignificant splinter party. Faced with the catastrophic returns from Prussia, Dingeldey redoubled his efforts to create a broadly based unity party ranging from the DNVP to the right wing of the DSP. When this plan miscarried in mid-July, rightist elements within the party intensified their agitation for renewed negotiations with the National Opposition. Desperate to avoid the utter decomposition of the party at the outset of the Reichstag campaign, Dingeldey, with the enthusiastic endorsement of the party's right wing, entered an electoral alliance with Hugenberg and the DNVP.[49]

The purpose of this cooperation, Dingeldey assured the party's dwindling constituency, was "to prevent the splintering of the bourgeois, nationalist vote." In a circular distributed to local party officials, the DVP leadership stressed that the party had to prevent "our members and voters from forming the impression that things can be achieved only in the framework of the radical parties." The DVP, therefore, escalated its antirepublican rhetoric, condemning not only "Marxism and pacifism" but "the party state, whether black, red or brown."[50] Echoing the views of the new chancellor, the party recommended a constitutional reform that would end the "mass rule" of "party democracy" and replace it with "a strong national state."[51] The DVP was "fighting for a new Germany" and would not "tolerate" a situation in which this new state would be "bound from the start by the shackles of a misconceived democracy." Whereas the DSP had failed to perceive the changing realities of the period, the DVP's opening to the right had reflected a genuine political perspicacity.[52] "The Democrats have become a sect in Germany because they pray to a god long dead. Today democracy and the republic are no longer the issues of debate," the DVP argued. The struggle facing the German middle class in 1932 was for "the preservation of German culture," which was "threatened everywhere by radicalism and destruction." As the bearers of that culture, the middle class had to be protected, and in the context of 1932 that required "alliance with the political right." The party had preferred "the formulation of a broad national front," its Executive Commitee explained, and regretted that it had not materialized. The objective, nevertheless, remained the establishment of "a right-wing government but not the sole rule of the National Socialists. . . . When a new era dawns," the DVP warned, "we do not want another state of subjects [*Untertanenstaat*] to emerge."[53]

Hugenberg, too, hoped that the new combination would pay dividends in July. The DNVP, however, might have offered a striking object lesson to Dingeldey, since the radical, antidemocratic course it had pursued after Hugenberg's assumption of power in 1929 had proven to be an ineffective shield against voter disaffection. Although the party maintained a solid core of support in predominantly Protestant rural areas,[54] the DNVP's national constituency had receded steadily from its high-water mark in 1924. Following the disastrous 1930 Reichstag elections, Hugenberg had accelerated his efforts to transform the DNVP into a mass movement capable of competing with the aggressive NSDAP. In 1931 the party's numerous paramilitary organizations were consolidated into a united Bismarck League, which, it was hoped, would rival the NSDAP's rowdy SA. Moreover, the Nationalist press was increasingly employed to depict Hugenberg as a dynamic, charismatic Führer. Purged of its numerous dissident elements by 1931, the DNVP, as one Nationalist commentator enthusiastically observed, had been transformed under Hugenberg's leadership into a "modern activist social movement." It had, he concluded with satisfaction, become "the Hugenberg movement." [55]

Along with this activist strategy, the DNVP had also endeavored to harness the greater dynamism of the NSDAP through collaboration in the National Opposition. Yet, while the two parties had joined forces in the anti-Young campaign, the Prussian referendum, the Harzburg Front, and in numerous demonstrations of antirepublicanism in the Reichstag,[56] cooperation between them was largely an illusion of Nationalist propaganda. Hitler's desertion of the Harzburg Front, the humiliating failure of Duesterberg's presidential candidacy, and the Nationalists' dismal showing (6.9 percent) in the Prussian Landtag elections were all vivid reflections of the limitations of this strategy and were bitter pills for the DNVP leadership.

With the sudden exit of Brüning and the installation of the Papen government, Nationalist electoral strategists once again took heart. After two years in opposition, the party threw its support behind the new chancellor and loudly endorsed his attack on the Socialist government of Prussia. The Nationalists hoped to transform the Reichstag campaign into a referendum on socialism, presenting themselves to the electorate as the only dependable bulwark against the Marxist menace. Thus, while the DNVP blasted the Nazis for their failure to cooperate with the new government and accused the NSDAP of sabotaging "the antiparliamentary front," [57] the central thrust of the Nationalist offensive against the NSDAP was directed at the dangers of Nazi "socialism." The NSDAP could hardly be counted on in the struggle against Marxism, the Nationalists repeatedly asserted, since the Nazis were "not rightist but leftist in their orientation." [58] Although "socialist tendencies" had always been present in the Nazi program, they had recently been gaining influence within the movement, the DNVP charged. This was a particularly ominous development, the Nationalists warned, since "hundreds of thousands of property-owning farmers, shopkeepers, artisan masters, and other proprietors have decided *emotionally* for National Socialism without realizing that its economic program is ultimately a socialist one which ignores the principle of free enterprise just as the socialism of the Marxists does." [59] In fact, the Nazis "want revolution and preach it openly," the Nationalists charged, and although the NSDAP formally condemned Marxism, the Nazis were working "arm in arm" with the Communists, pushing German society into class conflict with unparalleled public violence.[60] In this dangerous situation, the country needed "an anti-socialist counterweight," and the DNVP, its campaign literature persistently stressed, was ideally suited for the role since it was "unalterably opposed to Bolshevist radicalism" and was committed to "the salvation of middle-class free enterprise."[61]

The Nazi press, of course, sought to counter these charges, reassuring middle-class voters of the party's commitment to private property, but the NSDAP was much more concerned about Social Democratic and Zentrum accusations linking National Socialism to the Papen government. Almost every RPL communication during the campaign exhorted regional leaders to rebuff these "cowardly lies." The NSDAP had "neither formed the Papen regime nor ever tolerated it," one secret RPL memorandum asserted, and this "chief lie of our opponents must be refuted in the sharpest possible terms!"[62] When addressing "bourgeois circles," regional functionaries were instructed to "stress the heightened danger of civil war, pointing out the growing threat of Socialist and Communist unity," but it was also imperative, Goebbels emphasized, to rebuff SPD efforts to brand the party as "reactionary and unsocial."[63] Condemnation of the government's emergency decrees, therefore, became a major theme in the leaflets and placards that streamed steadily from the RPL to the party's regional offices during the campaign.[64]

Although the RPL was compelled to spend a great deal of time and energy responding to the conflicting charges that rained on the party from left and right, the leadership maintained high expectations for the approaching election. From the outset the party's objective had been to convince voters that "after 31 July no government is possible without the NSDAP" and that "National Socialism should, therefore, be given the majority and power."[65] In light of the strong Nazi showing in the presidential and regional elections of the preceding months, attainment of this goal certainly seemed within the party's grasp. Indeed, as 31 July drew near, concern was frequently expressed in the non-Nazi press that the NSDAP might actually gain a majority of the popular vote.

The Nazis did not attain that lofty pinnacle, but the results of the summer election were nonetheless menacing. With 37.3 percent of the vote, the NSDAP, which only four years earlier had attracted only 2 percent of the national electorate, emerged from the bitter and often violent campaign as Germany's largest party. While sustaining some losses, the SPD and Zentrum, two parties that had opposed both Papen and the NSDAP, managed to maintain a stable core of electoral support, and the Communists actually gained votes. The parties of the bourgeois center and right, however, were decimated. The DNVP's constituency was cut in half, falling to its lowest level since 1920, and the two liberal parties together

Table 4.1. The Election of 31 July 1932 (percentage of vote)

NSDAP	DNVP	DVP	Zentrum	DDP	SPD	KPD	Other
37.3	5.9	1.2	15.7	1.0	21.6	14.3	3.2

failed to attract even 3 percent of the vote. The special interest and regional parties, which had totaled 14 percent in 1930, also suffered enormous losses, falling to a mere 3 percent of the votes cast. (See Table 4.1).

In the wake of the election, the NSDAP appeared to stand on the threshold of power. Yet Hindenburg refused to consent to Hitler's demand for full power, and negotiations between the NSDAP and Zentrum concerning a possible coalition government failed to dispel their mutual distrust and enmity.[66] Still, the NSDAP and KPD together held over half the seats in the new Reichstag, rendering government by a coalition of moderates impossible. The parties of the bourgeois center and right controlled fewer than fifty of the Reichstag's roughly six hundred seats, and the Papen government, which found its only parliamentary props in the DNVP and DVP, could actually depend on only approximately forty-four of the newly elected deputies. Thus, in the first working session of the Reichstag a vote of no confidence, initiated by the KPD, was supported by an overwhelming 84 percent of the chamber's deputies, and the Reichstag was dissolved before the Papen government had even delivered its opening declarations. New elections were set for 6 November. It would be the fourth national campaign of the year.[67]

As the new campaign got under way, the NSDAP was determined to dispel any lingering doubts about its relationship to the Reich government. "Papen is already finished," Goebbels wrote to regional leaders in October. This was the message the party had to carry to the voters in November. "A feeling of utter panic about Papen must be awakened in the broad masses," he continued, "a feeling so strong that Papen and his cabinet will be utterly discredited and can no longer be seen as a bulwark by the wavering middle class." With the liberals in disarray and the special interest parties fast dissolving, the battle for the middle-class vote, Goebbels felt, would be fought between the NSDAP and DNVP, and he cautioned the regional leaders to proceed carefully against the Nationalists. Although the NSDAP could expect "hateful attacks" from the DNVP, National Socialist propaganda would show restraint and "objectivity." The party's "struggle against the DNVP must be continued with objective trenchancy but without personal insults or calumny." This tactic, Goebbels hoped, would draw attention to the contrast between the "reasoned" arguments of the NSDAP and "the bitter assaults of the DNVP and Stahlhelm."[68]

For their part, the Nationalists hoped to inflict losses on the NSDAP and clear the way for "a national presidential regime. . . . If this goal is reached," one confidential Nationalist memorandum explained, "the Papen government will have nothing more to fear from the Reichstag. The objective of our entire propaganda and advertising efforts must be to further the disenchantment with National Socialism that is already setting in."[69] Thus, during the ensuing campaign the DNVP repeated its charges of "narrow-minded party egotism" and "Marxist tendencies" within the NSDAP, claiming at one point that "the NSDAP has worked against . . . the Papen government because it did not receive any ministerial positions."[70] As a result of this exclusion, the Nazis had sabotaged the antiparliamentary front led by the DNVP and Stahlhelm and was playing the parliamentary game by negotiating with the Zentrum for the formation of an alliance. The DNVP conceded that the NSDAP had performed some important services for the revival of nationalist sentiment in Germany, but Hitler and his associates lacked experience, were impatient, and as the exesses of their storm troopers demonstrated, too radical.[71] Both the DNVP and DVP implored voters to give the new regime a chance. Papen's plans to create new jobs and revive the economy had not yet had time to take effect, the Nationalists argued. "Does anyone seriously believe that it is possible to overcome in just a few months the consequences of a misconceived economic and social policy that has oppressed our people for years?"[72] Sounding a similar refrain, the DVP asked voters "to give the men of the government, the deputies of Hindenburg, the opportunity to do their job. Don't destroy the last hope of peace and order by supporting those parties that only tear down but can never cooperate and build together."[73]

The NSDAP, as usual, waged an aggressive, often violent, campaign, blasting the Marxist left and condemning the DNVP for its support of "Papen's reactionary *Herrenklubsystem*." However, after months of intense, almost ceaseless campaigning, signs of strain had begun to surface within the party's organization. An RPL memorandum to the regional leadership in October expressed concern about flagging energy in the midst of an important Reichstag campaign and urged the Gauleiters to press on with the expected vigor. Although Hitler's new *Deutschlandflug* had recently brought some of the party's "old verve" back into the campaign, the RPL complained that "the entire movement must display more activity. . . . From now on the National Socialist press must concentrate entirely on the election. . . . Every article and essay must close with the

Table 4.2. The Election of 6 November 1932 (percentage of vote)

NSDAP	DNVP	DVP	Zentrum	DDP	SPD	KPD	Other
33.1	8.5	1.8	15.0	1.0	20.4	16.9	4.7

conclusion that Adolf Hitler is the only salvation and that one must therefore vote NSDAP."[74]

When the vote was tabulated on the evening of 6 November, the results held a number of surprises. For the first time since 1928, there had been a drop in voter turnout. Perhaps wearied by the incessant political turmoil and frightened by the ever-present street violence, two million fewer voters ventured to the polls in November than had in July, a decline of 4 percent. More predictably, the polarization of German political life that had been gathering momentum since 1929 continued unabated. While the Social Democratic vote fell again, dropping to just over 20 percent, the Communists continued their steady ascent. With almost 17 percent of the vote, the KPD surpassed the Zentrum to become the third largest party in Germany. At the opposite end of the political spectrum, the NSDAP continued to hold its position of dominance. The Nazis had again emerged at the top of the electoral ladder, far outpolling the parties of the Marxist left, the bourgeois parties of the center and right, and the Catholic Zentrum. However, for the first time since its remarkable string of electoral triumphs began in 1929, the NSDAP had suffered a potentially significant setback. With 33 percent of the ballots cast, the party's share of the vote had slipped by 4 percent since July. While the liberal and special interest votes, abysmally low in the earlier campaigns of the year, remained almost unchanged, the DNVP had reversed its slumping electoral fortunes by registering a modest gain of almost 3 percent. Nazi losses had not signaled even a minimal revival of political moderation. Instead, the disintegration of the *bürgerliche Mitte* was completed, and the struggle for the middle-class vote in both July and November was waged on the increasingly congested terrain of right-wing politics.

The Old Middle Class

The economic situation of the old middle class in 1932 was bleak. An index of retail turnover (1925 = 100) indicates that the downward spiral of sales which had begun in 1929 continued throughout

1931 and into the following year. Whereas turnover in 1930 was indexed at 113, a decline of ten points from 1928, retail sales, at 98, plunged to a six-year low in 1931. This dreary trend showed no signs of abatement in early 1932, monthly figures for the quarter ending in July averaging a dismal 79. The late summer and fall brought no relief. In November the index of retail trade stood at 77.[75]

As the depression deepened, the percentage of retail turnover derived from traditional specialty shops continued to decline, dropping from 79.7 percent in 1929 to 77.3 percent at the close of 1931. Although gains were small, sales from department stores, consumer cooperatives, and other chain establishments contributed to an ever-greater share of the total retail turnover. Between 1929 and 1931, that contribution rose from 8.6 percent to 10.1 percent. Symptomatically, the percentage of turnover from street and market peddlery also edged upward as the unemployed turned in desperation to various forms of small-scale retail enterprise. At the outset of 1932, sales from such sources constituted 7.4 percent of Germany's retail turnover.[76]

As retail trade plummeted, bankruptcies increased with mounting regularity. Between 1930 and 1931, the number jumped by 20 percent. Although the frequency of bankruptcy proceedings diminished significantly in 1932, falling by 21 percent, this reduction was not a sign of improving economic conditions. In many cases, the debtor's financial situation had so thoroughly deteriorated by 1932 that a favorable court settlement, creditors discovered, would not even cover the cost of bankruptcy proceedings. In fact, 40 percent of all petitions for bankruptcy in 1932 were rejected owing to lack of debtor assets.[77] Moreover, business failures occurred with the greatest frequency in commerce and handicrafts. In 1931, almost 35 percent of all bankruptcies were registered in retail trade, while the major branches of the handicrafts sector contributed another 17 percent. In the three months prior to the July election, bankruptcies in retail commerce and handicrafts represented 51 percent of the national total.[78]

The radicalizing impact of these economic developments is perhaps best reflected in the experience of a middle-aged florist who, after years of apprenticeship, had opened his own business in October 1927 only to see it fail in the early months of the depression. After closing his shop in 1929, he was unable to find work for almost two years. A brief stint as a municipal gardener ended with his dismissal in late 1931, and he remained unemployed during the politically turbulent months of the following year. "As the misery in Germany . . . grew worse and my wife had to earn our living while I, the real breadwinner of the family, sat idly at home, this [period] became the most bitter time of my life." What political conclusions did he draw from his situation? "Because of everything I had experienced," he later explained, "I became sympathetic to the [National Socialist] movement and voted for the NSDAP."[79]

In order to defuse this swelling discontent within the beleaguered *Mittelstand*, the presidential governments from 1930 to 1933 implemented a number of measures designed to protect small business. In April 1930, the first Brüning government raised taxes on retail establishments with an annual turnover of more than one million marks, a blatantly discriminatory measure directed against the department and chain stores. While smaller enterprises paid a tax of 8.5 percent on every thousand marks of turnover, the larger firms were charged 13.5 percent. In 1931, taxes on house rents and commercial transactions were substantially reduced by emergency decree, and in March of the following year, the establishment of department stores in cities of fewer than one hundred thousand inhabitants was prohibited until 1 April 1934.[80]

Yet rather than mollifying small business interests, these measures merely precipitated greater demands. Handicrafts and retail organizations were convinced that their members had borne a disproportionately heavy share of the burden under the emergency decrees of both the Brüning and Papen regimes and were adamant in their calls for a reduction of government expenditure on social welfare, especially unemployment benefits, the total elimination of taxes on house rents and commercial transactions, and the appointment of artisan and retail representatives to the Reich government. Furthermore, influential spokesmen in both handicrafts and retail organizations renewed their demands for the creation of some form of representation by occupational estates (*Berufsstände*) that would either replace or augment the Reichstag. This demand for a chamber of *Berufsstände* represented a clarion call not only for a return to the protectionist, authoritarian social regulation of the Empire but the establishment of a corporative economic system as well.[81]

These demands found immediate resonance in the NSDAP and were skillfully employed as leitmotivs in campaign literature. The burdens of "the November system," the Nazis charged, had been "carried on the backs of the commercial middle class." During the war the *Mittelstand* had made "great, difficult, and voluntary sacrifices, only to be robbed of all its property by the inflation." Then, "having barely recovered a bit," it had been devastated again by "rationalization, competition with mass production, . . . the emergency decrees, and finally the deflation."[82] The NSDAP, therefore, called on shopkeepers and artisans to join with it in "the decisive battle against the system and for the revitalization of the German *Mittelstand*." The "traitorous burgeois parties," the Nazis maintained, had "forgotten the rights of their middle-class constituents and delivered the handicrafts and retail commerce . . . to the liberals and Marxists," who had "destroyed the German economy." [83] Indeed, "the system and the parties which support it," the NSDAP argued, had "brought the ruin of the *Mittelstand*. . . . the department stores and chains, creations of . . . Jewish international finance capital, had ruined thousands of retail merchants and . . . condemned even more retail employees to joblessness." With the depression showing no signs of abatement, the ruthless expansion of the chain stores threatened to bring the virtual extinction of small business, the Nazis claimed. "Capitalism," one party spokesman typically contended, "has prevailed over the small businessman and the small homeowner." [84]

In contrast, the Nazi economic program, as the party's campaign literature tirelessly pointed out, was consistent with the demands of small business. The party vigorously denied that its economic policy was a form of veiled Marxism, reassuring proprietors that the NSDAP endorsed the principle of private property. Its only departure from this position, Nazi spokesmen emphasized, was in the party's demand for the communal expropriation of department stores and the leasing of their buildings to small businesses. [85] The NSDAP also promised the most scrupulous consideration of small firms in the distribution of government contracts on the Reich, state, and communal levels. In addition the erection of a strong autarkic economic system would eliminate foreign competition for German agricultural and industrial products. Ultimately, however, only the establishment of a National Socialist corporative state, embracing all productive occupational estates, could revive the stagnating middle class. In this "organic *Ständestaat*," the Nazis promised, "handicrafts and commerce would again find justice and honor." [86]

This message was carried to shopkeepers and craftsmen not only through the extensive Nazi propaganda apparatus but through an expanding network of middle-class organizations. The Artisans' and Merchants' Group of the NSDAP, for example, had been founded in 1930 by individual party members from the major handicrafts sectors. Although the extent of the group's activities varied from region to region, many built up extensive organizations. By June 1932, for example, sixty Nazi trade groups with over one thousand members were active in the city and surrounding county of Hannover. The Nazis also worked within existing artisan organizations, and by 1932 the party was increasingly able to dominate their activities. Thus, in January 1932 a Nazi sympathizer was elected president of the influential Northwest German Handicrafts Association and two party members became vice-presidents. In 1930 the organization had recommended that its members vote for the bourgeois parties of the political center. In July, two years later, the association threw its support to the NSDAP.[87]

The intense activity aimed at artisans and shopkeepers was more than matched by the party's vastly expanded agrarian agitation in 1932. From its creation in the summer two years earlier, Darré's agrarpolitischer Apparat (aA) had essentially two objectives: first, the aA was determined to win grass-roots support from farmers all over the Reich, and second, to infiltrate and ultimately dominate the established agricultural interest organizations, especially the RLB.[88] Those objectives were spelled out to regional aA functionaries in an instruction sheet circulated by Darré shortly after the September 1930 elections. The party's new agrarian organization was

> to penetrate into all rural affairs like a finely intertwined root system . . . embed itself deeply in them, and seek to embrace every element of agrarian life so thoroughly that eventually nothing will be able to occur in the realm of agriculture anywhere in the Reich which we do not observe and whose basis we do not understand. Let there be no farm, no estate, no village, no cooperative, no agricultural industry, no local organization of the RLB, no rural equestrian association, etc., etc., where we have not—at the least— placed our agents in such number that we could paralyze at one blow the total political life of these structures.[89]

Ambitious as these objectives seemed, the aA's organizational efforts were so successful that Darré could report at year's end that an extensive network of National Socialist agents had been established in almost all of the party's thirty-five districts.[90]

Along with the aA's intense grass-roots activities, the NSDAP took a number of steps to draw public attention to its increased interest in agricultural affairs. In February 1931, as the climax to the party's first convention of agrarian agents, the aA orchestrated a highly publicized mass rally of farmers in which Hitler and other prominent party dignitaries participated. Shortly thereafter, a weekly party newspaper devoted to farm matters, the *Nationalsozialistische Landpost*, began publication under Darré's editorship, and the *Völkischer Beobachter* and other Nazi papers began to carry a regular supplement on rural life, "Our Struggle for Blood and Soil."[91]

Tremendously encouraged by their rural triumphs in the 1930 Reichstag campaign and their subsequent success at rural organization, the Nazis stepped up their efforts to infiltrate the major farm organizations.

In the summer of 1931, Hitler publicly urged Nazi farmers to join the RLB, explaining that "unquestionably valuable forces are at work in this great organization, which, once put to work in the proper places, will also be able to accomplish much in the Third Reich." Although the RLB leadership remained understandably wary of this Nazi "Join the RLB" movement and resisted National Socialist efforts to influence its political orientation, it became increasingly obvious that the Landbund's hold on its own rank and file was slipping. By late 1931 the RLB's regional and local organizations were honeycombed with National Socialists, an increasing number of whom actually held pivotal leadership positions.[92]

The extent of Nazi grass-roots influence in the countryside was dramatically demonstrated to the RLB in the fall and winter of 1931–32. Refusing cooperation with the Landbund, the NSDAP submitted its own list of candidates for the elections to the chambers of agriculture in Prussia. These elections resulted in an impressive string of triumphs for the Nazis. The party made major breakthroughs in Hannover, Brandenburg, Hessen-Nassau, and in such varied locales as Lower Silesia, the Rhine Province, Provincial Saxony, Oldenburg, and East Prussia. The strong Nazi performance in these elections not only revealed the diverse regional appeal of the party but also its broad generational base. Only landowners (*Hofbesitzer*) were permitted to vote in these occupational elections, meaning that the NSDAP's victories had been produced not by the younger, landless, and supposedly more radical peasants but by their more established elders.[93]

In the wake of these elections, the resolve of the RLB broke. It formally recognized the NSDAP as "a farmer's party," and in December 1931 named Darré's deputy Werner Willikens as one of its four presidents. In less than two years the NSDAP had undermined the largest and most influential farm association and co-opted its national leadership. Opposed to the Weimar system but disappointed with Hugenberg, wary of Hitler but unable to prevent the defection of its rank and file to the NSDAP, the RLB joined the other organizations of the old middle class that in 1931–32 were drawn into the orbit of the rising National Socialist star. In the runoff election for Reich president, the RLB openly supported Hitler, and in the critical Reichstag campaigns that followed, it served as a drumbeater for the NSDAP among the rural electorate.[94]

The National Socialist penetration of the countryside in 1931–32 was made possible by the continuing deterioration of agriculture's economic position and the divisions within the agrarian sector that had widened steadily since 1928. Between the September elections of 1930 and the Reichstag campaigns two years later, agricultural income continued to plummet, while indebtedness soared and foreclosures almost doubled again. Imports continued to plague small producers, while grains were accorded special protection, and East Elbian estate owners were the beneficiaries of truly massive state aid under the 1931 Eastern Assistance (*Osthilfe*) program. Mounting economic distress, therefore, heightened the already substantial conflicts within the agricultural sector, particularly between grain producers and small dairy and livestock farmers. Two years of presidential government under Brüning had merely convinced peasants and family farmers that their interests had been sacrificed in favor of antitariff export industry and subordinated in agricultural policy to the desires of East Elbian grain.[95]

With their traditional supporters drifting away in frustration, the major agricultural organizations, united in the Green Front, sought to regain their fading credibility with small farmers by attacking the Weimar system and presenting demands to save the *Bauernstand*. Although emphasis varied from association to association, the major peasant and farm organizations demanded that the government establish a stringent quota system on food imports, revoke the commercial treaties so despised by dairy and livestock farmers, declare a moratorium on repayment of debts, lower taxes, extend credit, and reduce public spending on social welfare programs that benefited only the urban, working-class population.[96] To dramatize their opposition to the hated system, leaders of the Green Front joined Hugenberg and Hitler at Bad Harzburg, and even the Catholic Bauernvereine, generally of a more moderate orientation, now openly stressed their preference for some form of radical-corporatist economic and political order to replace the discredited parliamentary system of Weimar.[97]

When Brüning refused to accept these demands, he was viciously attacked by the agricultural organizations, and when he sought to rally some peasant support by advocating increased settlement on the land of bankrupted estates in the East, he was accused of "agricultural bolshevism" by influential estate owners who contributed directly to his dismissal.[98] Papen, on the other hand, moved with surprising dispatch to meet many of these demands. He instituted import quotas on a wide range of agricultural products, halted the public sale of defaulted agricultural property everywhere in Germany—not just in the East—reduced taxes, and made clear his intention to slash spending on welfare programs. This program, however, quickly ran afoul of important industrial interests, which were surprisingly united in their negative evaluation of the program's core, and therefore created a serious strategic problem for the Papen regime.[99] More important for rural grass-roots reaction to the program, however, was the fact that it simply came too late. Years of economic hardship, social distress, and political frustration had convinced a growing mass of peasants and family farmers that the government, the traditional parties, and the agrarian organizations were not interested in their plight. The *Bauernstand*, they believed, had been crucified in order to save the urban proletariat, the traditional agrarian elite, and the capitalist interests of big business.

These, of course, were precisely the sentiments on which the NSDAP had so effectively played since 1928. The dramatic National Socialist gains in the countryside were not the result of the party's superior agricultural program, which in its essentials differed very little from those of the DNVP, the RLB, the Green Front, or even the Papen regime. Nazi calls for agricultural autarky, revival of rural purchasing power, and a reduction of taxes, interest rates, and wasteful social expenditure [100] did not distinguish the NSDAP from any of its serious competitors for the farm vote. Yet unlike the DNVP and the Landbund, the NSDAP was not identified with big agriculture or, like the Zentrum and the liberal parties, with the Weimar government. Finally, the NSDAP after 1930 was clearly a major national party with a growing electorate in all parts of the Reich, setting it off from the regional or peasants' parties whose limited ability to advance farm interests were obvious to all by 1932.

This state of affairs was not lost on Darré or campaign strategists in the RPL. Local branches of the party were, therefore, instructed to avoid specifics in their appeals to farmers and to focus instead on large issues within a clearly defined framework that assailed liberalism, Marxism, the corrupt parliamentary system, and the Jews who stood behind it all. [101] Of course, the party made the usual claims, asserting that the NSDAP would halt agricultural imports, while channeling funds to peasants that would be "used for soil improvement, creation of excellent seed-corn, the purchase of necessary machinery, and the payment of better wages." [102] In addressing peasant women, the NSDAP vigorously denied that the party was pagan or an enemy of Christianity, and it ridiculed the frequent charge that the party wanted to expropriate the farmer. "The truth is," the Nazis claimed, "that the German peasant has already been expropriated by this system and is just a mortgage administrator for the big banks who already own the land." Perhaps more important than these particulars, however, was the pervasive tone of confidence and determination with which the NSDAP flatly stated, "Under a National Socialist regime no German farm will be permitted to be auctioned off owing to foreclosure and no peasant will be driven from his hearth." [103]

Capping these familiar pillars of Nazi rural propaganda was the usual ideological cornice: the ritual assault on both liberal capitalism and Marxist socialism. German farmers faced two real dangers, the Nazis typically warned. One was "the American economic system, or big capitalism [*Hochkapitalismus*]" that "wants to take the independent farmer from his hearth and transform him into a rationally functioning employee of a gigantic concern." Capitalism, the Nazis charged, "enslaves human beings under the slogan of progress, technology, rationalization, standardization, etc.," while "recognizing only profits and dividends . . . and placing the machine above man." The other threat to the *Bauernstand* was Marxism. That system, the Nazis explained, "recognizes only one class, the proletariat, while institutionalizing the controlled economy [*Zwangswirtschaft*]. It creates the domination of the tractor, bureaucratizes farm work, destroys the family, faith, morality, and the sacred traditions of a people." [104]

Aside from this prominent attack on technology,[105] which was far more pronounced in the traditional countryside than in the towns and cities, National Socialist appeals to farmers followed the same guidelines and were reinforced by the same organizational activity that characterized the Nazi campaign for the urban old middle class. If anything, Darré's organizational apparatus was even more active than its urban counterparts, and the RPL, as its directives to regional leaders throughout 1932 make clear, was determined to exploit its organizational and propagandistic advantages in the countryside to the hilt.

Outflanked by Nazi rhetoric and overwhelmed by Nazi organization, neither the traditional bourgeois parties nor the regional peasants' parties proved able to capitalize on the mounting discontent within the urban and rural old middle class. In appealing to artisans, shopkeepers, and farmers, the DVP soberly presented itself as "the opponent of nationalization, the bulwark of private property, and the friend of the most restrained government spending." [106] Yet under the influence of the great industrial interests that had shaped its politics since the death of Stresemann, the DVP continued to stress its commitment to free enterprise. Although the party conceded that "excesses in the private sector must be eliminated at all costs," it expressed the conviction that "whoever fights for a free economy" must be prepared to "accept the risk of crisis." Thus, the protectionist schemes of the NSDAP were condemned as "veiled socialism," and some elements within the party were accused of desiring the nationalization of all large enterprises.[107]

The role of the state, DVP representatives stressed, should be reduced, and private enterprise should again receive "the freedom curtailed by state-socialist coercion." Government should not seek to establish "some form of state socialism . . . or a planned economy," but should guarantee economic freedom. The DVP, therefore, rejected proposals of economic autarky or government protection of business and agriculture by the introduction of a quota system on foreign imports. The step from such regulation to "a state import-export monopoly," Dingeldey warned, "would not be great."[108] The DVP could, therefore, enthusiastically support Papen's commitment to the concept of private enterprise. "Personal economic initiative and the free exercise of the rights and duties of property ownership are essential for a healthy economy," the chancellor asserted. "The private sector must, however, affirm its right to exist without expecting public support.[109] In concurring, the DVP not only shunned the increasingly shrill pleas of small business and the peasants but did little to alter its image as the party of corporate capitalism.

The DSP, on the other hand, sought to reach the small shopkeeper, craftsman, and farmer by attacking the government's "one-sided preference for big agriculture at the expense of small and medium-sized enterprises." The party charged that the Brüning and Papen governments had undertaken "an unlimited and unsystematic subvention of economic monopolies," channeling to the East Elbian latifundia and gigantic corporation funds that were derived from the taxes paid by small business. Moreover, the corporate and agrarian giants routinely received credit "for which small business waits in vain." The DSP promised to reverse this policy, rerouting government contracts and credit to the small farm and business community.[110]

Although the DSP was receptive to the demands of small business, it steadfastly refused to accept the widely held thesis that the Weimar system was responsible for the miseries afflicting the old middle class. "The monstrous economic crisis," the DSP asserted, was rather the product of "the lost war and far-reaching changes in the private sector that had led to the concentration of enterprises into . . . enormous conglomerates and thus to the ruin of countless independent businesses."[111] Although the party resolutely opposed the autarkic and corporatist designs of National Socialism, the DSP was prepared to accept government intervention for the protection of small business. The DSP had even endorsed the discriminatory taxation of department stores, and the Democratic finance minister of Württemberg had been the first government official to propose restrictions on the establishment of chain stores.[112] Nazi schemes for the expropriation of these businesses, however, were firmly rejected. Such proposals, the party maintained, "had finally provided the evidence" "that Nazi 'socialism' is 'the worthy brother of bolshevism.'" With their confused rantings about autarky, public works projects, and a new domestic currency, the Nazis could "force the economy into a new strait-jacket," the DSP charged, "which would make the unpopular restrictions of the wartime economy seem mild. The *Mittelstand* should be fully aware that "dictatorship and the *Ständestaat*, with its confining chains, cannot save the German middle class and lead it forward again." The restoration of the *Mittelstand*, the DSP warned, could be achieved only by "a free economy in a free state," and it was toward this end that the DSP—alone among the middle-class parties, its campaign literature suggested—was working.[113]

The DNVP concurred with the liberal assessment of National Socialist economic policy, and its appeals to the old middle class in both town and country were laced with warnings about the dangers of Nazi socialism.[114] The Nationalists, on the other hand, presented themselves to the electorate as champions of "bourgeois private enterprise," adding the usual condemnation of Marxism and the planned economy. The party also attacked the department stores and consumer cooperatives, called for tax relief for small business, and proposed the creation of a special government department of "commerce, handicrafts, and trade."[115] In addition, the DNVP intimated that Hugenberg, unlike the leaders of the other parties, could exert considerable influence on the Papen regime to protect the interests of small business and small farming.[116] As in the past, the main thrust of the party's electoral appeals to the entrepreneurial middle class was directed at the agricultural sector, where the Nationalists had traditionally found widespread support. Although the NSDAP had made great strides in the countryside since 1928, especially among small farmers, the DNVP had maintained a sizable rural constituency. Consequently, its campaign literature, unlike that of the DVP or DSP, displayed a pronounced agrarian orientation. This strong association with agriculture, and particularly with large agrarian interests, had been effectively exploited by the NSDAP and others to reduce the DNVP's appeal to the urban middle class.[117]

In the highly charged atmosphere of 1932, neither the DNVP nor the liberals could mount an effective challenge to the NSDAP's campaign for the middle-class vote. Their repeated warnings about Nazi socialism, Nazi radicalism, and Nazi inexperience clearly failed to deter middle-class voters. The Nazis appear to have extended their already substantial constituency within the old middle class both in the towns and the countryside. The figures for 1932 represent the apex of a relationship that had constituted the social mainstay of the Nazi vote since 1924. The depression, as the coefficients of Table 4.3 indicate, undoubtedly strengthened the correlation between the National Socialist vote and the self-

Table 4.3. Party Vote and the Old Middle Class (OMC), 1932

	All OMC			
	Protestant (N=152)		Catholic (N=64)	
	1932a	1932b	1932a	1932b
NSDAP	.648	.681	−1.02	−.869
DNVP	−.237	−.351	−.164	−.289
DVP	.339	.866	.163 *	.302
DDP	.405	.438	.584	.661
Z	−.448	−.413	.333 *	.108 *
SPD	−.306	−.290	.104 *	.121 *
KPD	−.256	−.259	.280 *	−.421 *
Other	.630	.842	.825	.996

	OMC in Handicrafts[a]			
	Protestant (N=152)		Catholic (N=64)	
	1932a	1932b	1932a	1932b
NSDAP	.606	.658	−2.13	−1.65
DNVP	−.175	−.320	−.303	−.577
DVP	.587	−.129 *	.256	.412
DDP	.698	.773	.158	.234
Z	.102 *	.101 *	.155 *	.292 *
SPD	−.619	−.530	−.261 *	−.439
KPD	−.331	−.376	−1.43	−.843
Other	.187 *	.202 *	.752	.748

	OMC in Commerce[a]			
	Protestant (N=152)		Catholic (N=64)	
	1932a	1932b	1932a	1932b
NSDAP	.923	1.28	1.44	1.46
DNVP	−.342 *	−.581	−.556	−.516
DVP	−.298	−.216 *	.382	.511
DDP	−.232	−.915	−.380	−.408
Z	−.466	−.394	−.410	−.338
SPD	−2.03	−1.94	−.421	−.336
KPD	−1.81	−1.64	−1.71	−.516
Other	−.200 *	−.496	.770	.250

Table 4.3. (continued)

| | OMC in Agriculture[a,b] | | | |
| | Protestant (N=121) | | Catholic (N=125) | |
	1932a	1932b	1932a	1932b
NSDAP	.841	.837	−.655	−.562
DNVP	.552	.723	−.161	−.223
DVP	−.210*	.166*	.212	.150*
DDP	.402	.539	.186*	.306
Z	.141*	.155*	1.40	1.50
SPD	−.609	−.522	−.334	−.292
KPD	−.337	−.370	−.369	−.614
Other	.234*	.168*	−.268*	−.310

NOTE: The figures are unstandardized regression coefficients (b), controlling for new middle class, *Rentnermittelstand*, blue-collar workers, religion, and urbanization (population size).
a. Presents coefficients for the OMC by economic sector, controlling for the OMC in all other economic sectors in addition to those variables listed above.
b. Size of farm has also been controlled.

* These coefficients are not significant at the .05 level.

employed, especially in agriculture and the troubled handicrafts and commercial sectors. Moreover, Pratt's analysis of the July election reveals that the Nazi vote was highly correlated to the proportion of businesses with only one employee, a strong indication that National Socialism found its most solid support among small, perhaps marginal proprietors threatened by economic collapse.

Yet, while the economic trials of the depression certainly radicalized elements of the commercial *Mittelstand*, the consistency displayed by the coefficients from 1924 to 1932 suggests that Nazi sympathies within the old middle class were not merely spasmodic reactions to short-term economic ills. Instead, the durability of the Nazi/old-middle-class relationship reflects a profound opposition to long-term structural trends in the German economy, trends that were resisted by small business and attacked with unflagging violence by the NSDAP in each election of the Weimar era. The ability of the NSDAP to articulate the anticapitalist, protectionist demands of small shopkeepers and artisans as well as the vigor with which the party combated the socialist labor movement constituted the key ingredients in the persistent and strong appeal of National Socialism within the urban old middle class.

These same appeals, with a somewhat different twist, were also of critical importance in the countryside. The NSDAP's support in rural areas was far more pronounced than in the cities, but it had been slower to develop. In the countryside the party played on the familiar themes indicated above but also on the widespread bitterness that had grown steadily since the imposition of the wartime *Zwangswirtschaft* by the imperial authorities. That bitterness was directed first against the state, against the liberal and Social Democratic parties that maintained those controls in the immediate postwar period and finally introduced a stringent stabilization on the economy in late 1923 and early 1924. In the elections of 1924 the DNVP had played masterfully on this resentment, but the party's entry into the government in January 1925 failed to halt the mounting economic crisis within the agricultural sector. The years of Nationalist participation in the *Bürgerblock* government merely exacerbated the latent tensions between the mass of small farmers who made up the DNVP's rural constituency and the landed agrarian elite who exerted considerable influence on DNVP policy. Disappointed with the Nationalist performance as the party of agriculture, many peasants turned to regional alternatives in 1928, convinced that their interests had been sacrificed to the urban consumer and the East Elbian estate owners. With the intensification of the economic crisis, however, and with the increasing solicitation of the peasantry by the expanding National Socialist organization, the stream of peasant defectors from the regional and conservative parties became a torrent.[118] By 1932 the NSDAP had vanquished even the Conservatives, whose rural constituency continued to shrink ineluctably, even east of the Elba. Having destroyed the liberals in their urban strongholds, the NSDAP succeeded in replacing the DNVP as the party of agriculture, playing particularly on the anticapitalist, anti-Marxist, and antiliberal sentiments that had been voiced by virtually all the agrarian organizations in Germany. By 1932 the NSDAP stood alone in the Protestant countryside as a party unsullied by participation in the hated Weimar regime and uncompromised by association with either major urban interests or the forces of big agriculture.

The *Rentnermittelstand*

For the pensioners, small investors, and rentiers traumatized by the inflation and stabilization crises of the mid-twenties, the depression had again raised the specter of financial ruin. With the sharp decline in economic activity after 1928, stocks fell steadily and with them the number of persons commanding taxable income from rents, capital gains, and other dividends. Between 1929 and 1932, the number of persons with taxable earnings from their investments decreased by 16 percent, while savings deposits dropped by over 23 percent.[119] Moreover, the danger of bank failures, particularly in 1931, brought widespread fear that savings might once again be lost. Most importantly, however, the stringent deflationary measures of both the Brüning and Papen governments had slashed pensions and other benefits, the most serious cuts coming in health insurance and related services. The curtailment of these benefits, the sharpest of which came in Papen's emergency decree of 14 June 1932, replaced revalorization as the central political issue for the *Rentnermittelstand* in the elections of 1932.[120]

The NSDAP had traditionally devoted considerable attention to pensioners, disabled veterans, widows, and so on, but in 1932 the party was particularly determined to extend its constituency among these voters. During the presidential campaigns, the party leadership felt that gains had to be made within three important and traditionally conservative groups if the NSDAP were to emerge successful. As the RPL saw it, these groups were pensioners, civil servants, and women, and during the subsequent campaigns of the year, the NSDAP assiduously wooed all three.[121]

In electoral appeals to pensioners, the overwhelming majority of whom were women, the Nazis lamented their declining standard of living, ascribing it to the insensitivity of the Brüning government and the parties that had either supported or tolerated it. Pensioners had "saved and paid for decades in order to have a secure retirement," only to be swindled by the system, the Nazis charged. "With one stroke of the pen," Brüning had "taken away the rights of pensioners," reducing their benefits to little more than "beggars' pennies." The NSDAP also denounced the cuts imposed by Papen's emergency decree of 14 June and demanded a restoration of the funds for retirees. While these cuts had reduced benefits to millions of needy pensioners, the social insurance administration, the Nazis charged, was riddled with corruption. Payments to the elderly might be slashed, but "the salaries of the bosses go right on rising," the party claimed indignantly. Indeed, according to the NSDAP, the history of the republic had been a dishonorable series of broken promises to pensioners and veterans, and with the depression deepening, the party warned pensioners that "the bourgeois parties . . . no longer have either the strength or the will to help you." Only National Socialism could save the *Rentnermittelstand* from destitution, only National Socialism could "bring you the revalorization of your savings and just and adequate retirement care."[122]

Throughout the campaigns of 1932, the NSDAP barraged pensioners and veterans with promises of a better future in the Third Reich. Nazi campaign appeals to the *Rentnermittelstand* were filled with assurances that the party would not only preserve retirement and health benefits but would increase payments and services. The party press also laid heavy stress on the need to extend veterans' benefits. "Only a front soldier knows how to help a comrade from the front," the *Völkischer Beobachter* asserted, pointing out that the National Socialist Reichstag delegation boasted the greatest number of combat veterans. In the future Nazi state, the party promised, "victims of the war will be given their due instead of the degrading alms of the present." [123] In the meantime, however, the NSDAP complained that "the poorest of the poor, the small pensioners, war victims, widows, and surviving dependents must not be stripped of their pitiful support. . . . They must know that the gratitude of the fatherland is certain, and not just in theory. The state should come to the aid of widows, and orphans, old mothers, and careworn fathers," the Nazis piously intoned. Veterans and war widows were, therefore, called upon to join with other pensioners in the NSDAP's battle against the emergency decrees and the corrupt system that had produced them. [124]

Opponents of the National Socialists, particularly the DNVP and DVP, agreed that more should be done for pensioners and veterans but cautioned that the Nazi economic program, with its many promises, would only result in "a new inflation." Nazi plans, vague as they were, to create a new domestic currency and increase government spending would have a serious inflationary impact on the economy. "Should the already gravely weakened *Mittelstand* bear the costs of new currency experiments?" the DVP asked. [125] The Nationalists agreed, condemning the Nazi proposals as "socialist experiments" which would ruin the state and the economy. Although Hugenberg distanced himself and the DNVP from the measures contained in the emergency decree of 14 June, he urged voters to be patient with the Papen regime which had, after all, inherited "an empty treasury and a bankrupt government." Its sober and difficult course would certainly demand sacrifices from everyone, but it was nonetheless preferable to the irresponsible and inflationary plans advanced by the NSDAP. [126]

Responding to these charges, the National Socialist press launched a massive counterattack, claiming that it was "the November parties" that had destroyed Germany's economic and political life. The Weimar system, not National Socialism, had hurled the country into financial chaos ten years before, and the parties of that system had "not yet made reparation for the crime of the inflation." [127] Moreover, the Nazis never tired of reminding pensioners and small investors that the DNVP, though not responsible for the inflation, had nonetheless betrayed its victims. By failing to honor their alleged 1924 campaign pledge of a 100 percent revaluation, the Nationalists were guilty of "robbing savers and pensioners while clashing with the fundamental principle of the sanctity and inviolability of private property." The NSDAP also pointed out that while the Nationalists had fought fiercely in the Reichstag against Marxist attempts to expropriate the princes in 1927, they had abandoned the mass of small investors and creditors. "They robbed the poorest people in the Volk of their property and savings," the Nazis charged, "but they protected the princes."[128] Moreover, the Papen government, with the support of the DNVP, had "continued Brüning's disastrous pension and retirement policies, reducing the benefits of the unemployed, pensioners, and veterans . . . to a level that isn't enough for either living or dying," while "on the other hand granting billions upon billions in subventions to the big banks and corporations."[129]

In defending its own economic program, the NSDAP conceded that the party's plans would require greater government expenditure, but assured pensioners and investors that it was committed to fiscal responsibility. To insure tight control over money supply while at the same time stimulating the economy, the party proposed "strict regulation of the banks, a reduction of interest rates, a draconian law to prevent the flight of capital out of Germany, and a revitalization of the domestic market." Together with a systematic public works program, these measures, the Nazis argued, would revive the economy without triggering a recurrence of the inflationary spiral that had wreaked havoc ten years before.[130]

In spite of its reputation as a youth-oriented movement, the NSDAP had made a systematic and sustained effort to win support among pensioners, rentiers, widows, and veterans in 1932. The figures of Table 4.4 strongly suggest that the party's appeal to such groups found considerable resonance. Indeed, of the major socio-occupational groups examined, the Rentnermittelstand emerges as the strongest predictor of the National Socialist vote in July 1932. In contrast to the NSDAP's appeal to the old middle class, however, the Nazi-Rentner relationship was highly crisis-related. While the coefficients for the old middle class remain relatively stable from 1924 to 1932, the Rentner figures faithfully follow the curve of economic crisis. The coefficients are surprisingly high in the inflation election of May 1924 but fade in the relatively tranquil Golden Twenties. Until the onset of the depression, the Rentnermittelstand had been far more strongly related to the Nationalist than to the Nazi vote. In 1928, however, the Nationalist figures slip, and as they tumble, those of the NSDAP begin a dramatic ascent. While in 1928 the Nazis had been able to make little headway against the conservatives and the revalorization parties, the Nazi coefficients surge in 1930, for the first time surpass-

Table 4.4. Party Vote and the Rentnermittelstand, *1932*

	Protestant (N=152)		Catholic (N=64)	
	1932a	1932b	1932a	1932b
NSDAP	.710	.728	.318	.249
DNVP	.984	.194	.737	.289
DVP	−.369	−.453	−.373	−.107*
DDP	−.211	−.365	−.433	−.206*
Z	−.356	−.572	−.352*	−.334*
SPD	−.124	−.117	.116	.230*
KPD	−.547	−.650	−.957	−.260
Other	−.187	−.106	.660	.713

NOTE: The figures are unstandardized regression coefficients (b), controlling for old middle class, new middle class, blue-collar workers, religion, and urbanization (population size).

* These coefficients are not significant at the .05 level.

ing those of the DNVP. Then, in 1932, the gap widens spectacularly as the Nazi figures reach their apex in the November election, far outstripping those of the other parties. Cultivation of a *Rentner* constituency was a very important component of Nazi electoral strategy in the campaigns of 1932, allowing the NSDAP to transcend the confines of its youth-oriented public image and giving the movement a surprisingly broad generational base for its assault on the crumbling Weimar system.

The New Middle Class

Like the pensioners and veterans of the *Rentnermittelstand,* civil servants of the new middle class were among the groups targeted for intense Nazi solicitation in 1932. The NSDAP had actually devoted a considerable amount of attention to this traditional social elite in past campaigns, relentlessly stressing the erosion of the *Berufsbeamtentum's* elevated status in the politically corrupt Weimar system. It had assailed the "democratization" of the civil service as a shabby device for Social Democratic patronage, condemned the massive layoffs in 1924 as a breach of the *Beamtentum's* traditional right to lifetime tenure, and decried the "discriminatory" tax on civil-service salaries in the early days of the Brüning cabinet. The party's opposition to the Young Plan and the threat of severe budget cuts that its acceptance implied, as well as the party's splashy stand for the political freedom of public officials during the anti-Young referendum, had struck responsive chords in 1930, and the NSDAP hoped to extend its civil-service constituency in 1932.

In each of the 1932 campaigns the Nazis endeavored to exploit mounting resentment over the repeated reductions of salaries and benefits imposed by the Brüning and Papen governments. The systematic lowering of the *Beamtentum*'s standard of living had begun with Brüning's imposition of a special surtax on civil-service salaries in the summer of 1930. Before the end of the year an emergency decree slashed civil-service pay by 6 percent, and an additional 8 percent followed in June 1931. That same June decree also reduced the salaries of state officials, and shortly thereafter communal pay scales were revised downward to match the decreases at the Reich and Land levels. Brüning's economy measures were profoundly unpopular within the *Beamtentum*, and the advent of the Papen regime, far from heralding a new age for the civil service, merely continued the process of the decline. Although no new pay reductions were announced, the government added a surtax on civil-service salaries that would furnish contributions to the unemployment fund. In all, civil-service salaries had been slashed by about 20 percent in less than three years. Moreover, as the government's financial situation deteriorated, fears that cutbacks in personnel, reminiscent of the mass layoffs of 1924, were widespread at all levels of government.[131]

By 1932, signs of strain and, concomitantly, of rising support for National Socialism surfaced with increasing regularity within the civil service. In Württemberg, for example, where curtailment of salaries and benefits was particularly sharp, government officials were shocked at the "tone" of protesting civil servants. It was disturbing, one state minister remarked after hearing protests from university faculties, that the "professors have made their relationship to the state dependent on a triviality such as the abolition of emeritus status."[132] In the district around Trier, police reports noted that interest in National Socialist rallies had become "very great not only among the small and middle businessmen but also among many civil servants of the court, customs, finance, and railroad administration."[133] More ominously, however, investigators in Chemnitz discovered that an informal Association of National Socialist Police Officers had been founded, and Reichswehr officers reported an increase of Nazi sympathizers in the ranks of the army.[134] As Nazi activities within the civil service increased, and political violence in the streets became more acute, government at all levels determined that at least police salaries should not be further reduced. "In these times," one troubled official confided, "we need a civil service closely bound to the state."[135] Yet, by 1932 a severe crisis of confidence had developed between government and the public officials who served it, and the NSDAP was ready to capitalize on that growing malaise.

As the scattered reports of Nazi infiltration into the *Beamtentum* suggest, the NSDAP had launched an intensive recruitment drive within the civil service. Although the party was quite active in existing civil-service organizations, the Nazis preferred to form their own "working groups." In these *Arbeitsgemeinschaften*, the Nazis proudly proclaimed, "officials from the upper ranks sit together with those from the middle and lower grades." Enjoying the *völkisch* solidarity of these Nazi organizations, civil servants could "forget for a moment that they belong to a particular branch of government and hold a certain rank." On the outside they might be "superior and subordinate," but in such National Socialist communities "they are simply German civil servants . . . fighting shoulder to shoulder . . . to regain their lost rights."[136] Nazi organizational appeal, therefore, promised a classless fraternity within the group while pledging a determination to reestablish the traditional position of the *Berufsbeamtentum* in the society at large.

While mounting this drive to organize public officials, the NSDAP also sought to cultivate a wider civil-service electoral constituency. During each of the campaigns of 1932, the RPL unleashed a torrent of leaflets and placards addressed to *Beamten* at all levels of government, and the party press was particularly sensitive to civil-service-related issues. At the same time, the party staged numerous assemblies and rallies devoted to the civil service. In Brunswick, for example, the NSDAP sponsored six rallies specifically for civil servants during a single week in early 1932, with separate meetings for officials in municipal, state, and Reich administrations. The party also held meetings for officials in the postal and customs services and for employees of the state and private banks.[137] In pursuing the civil-service vote, the NSDAP therefore employed the same techniques of political saturation that characterized its solicitation of other targeted social groups.

Nazi appeals to the civil-service electorate sounded two major themes in 1932. First and most prominently, the party attacked the government's harsh deflationary program, which had substantially reduced the public official's standard of living. Nazi campaign literature meticulously catalogued the pay reductions and curtailments of benefits imposed by the Brüning and Papen regimes, while reminding civil servants that the NSDAP had steadfastly opposed these measures and condemned the "system parties" that had made them possible. The Nazis relentlessly criticized Brüning's "irresponsible financial policy, which has taken away all security for the future" and imposed extraordinary hardships on the civil service.[138] It also warned that Papen's new regime would be no better. "The economic program of the Papen government has restored the stock market and the banks with premiums and tax credits, while demanding monstrous sacrifices from workers and white-collar employees in the private sector." The government had, however, remained "silent about civil-service salaries before the election," the Nazis noted, "and for good reason." More brutal emergency decrees, the party intimated broadly, were on the way.[139]

To prevent a further deterioration of the *Berufsbeamtentum*'s economic and legal status, civil servants were urged to join with the NSDAP in its battle against "the present system of starvation." Because of the party's uncompromising hostility to the "reign of emergency decrees," the government at both state and national levels, had initiated a campaign of persecution against the NSDAP, the party charged, in an attempt to intimidate the movement's growing legion of followers within the civil service.[140] This restriction of political freedom, was merely the most obvious symptom of the system's utter disregard for the rights of the *Berufsbeamtentum*, the Nazis claimed. Pointing to the installment of the "November officials" following the revolution, the mass dismissals of 1923–24, and the unprecedented reductions in civil service benefits between 1930 and 1932, the NSDAP accused the republic of systematically dismantling the traditional rights of the professional civil service.[141]

Condemnation of the "steady deprivation of civil service rights," therefore, became the second major theme of the National Socialist campaign for civil service support in 1932. "Where are your well-established constitutional rights?" one typical Nazi leaflet inquired. "Where is your secure income? What has happened to the political liberty guaranteed to us all?"[142] The humiliating position of the civil service in 1932 was the product of fourteen years of inept and corrupt republican leadership, the Nazis charged, and if civil servants wanted to avoid "a total loss of their rights," their only choice was to join the NSDAP's crusade "to overthrow the current democratic, internationalist system of domination."[143]

Turning to more specific matters, the party promised a radically new personnel policy that would restore the high standards of the German civil service. In the Third Reich there would be no place for *Parteibuchbeamten*. While the party ostentatiously endorsed freedom of political expression for civil servants, it simultaneously demanded "the dismissal of 'revolution officials'" and "the removal of all members of the Jewish race" from the public payroll. The vacancies created by these actions would permit the party to rehire officials unjustly dismissed by the republican governments and to name "competent disabled veterans" to administrative posts. The NSDAP also promised higher pay, especially for the lower grades, and assured civil servants that pensions would not be slashed.[144] The NSDAP was not content simply to preserve existing privileges and benefits, the Nazis emphasized, but would do everything it could to "reestablish all the rights that have been taken from the civil service." Officials were reminded that Hitler himself was the son of a civil servant and therefore "knows the great misery to which the *Beamtenschaft* has been brought and in which it still finds itself today. He knows all the cares of the civil servants from their perspective, whether it be income, promotion, or other concerns." His party, Nazi propaganda emphasized, also understood and would "act with all its might for the *Beamtentum*."[145]

As the Nazis' most serious competitor for the civil service vote, the DNVP hoped to convince voters that while Nazi sentiments were often in the right place, the NSDAP was both too radical and too inexperienced to be trusted. Like the Nazis, the Nationalists bemoaned the civil servant's reduced circumstances, assailed the "monstrous" decrees that had cut salaries and pensions, and denounced the harassment of rightist officials. The DNVP continued to demand the "cleansing" of the civil service and the return to a "professional" *Beamtentum*. Nationalist leaders were particularly upset by the presence of "uneducated" persons in government service and blamed the decline in standards on the "democratization" of public administration after the war.[146] Yet while agreeing with the NSDAP on these issues, Nationalist propaganda intimated that the Nazis were wild-eyed radicals without a proper understanding of the importance of law. With unintentional irony, the DNVP charged that in several states the NSDAP had acted in civil-service related matters "without regard for current law." In Prussia, for example, the Nazis had "proposed . . . the immediate dismissal without pension of civil servants with whom they were uncomfortable" and "in defiance of the Reich constitution, demanded the dissolution of an unfriendly civil service union." In Mecklenburg-Strelitz, where the National Socialists were in power, they had even adopted "the principles of Marxist salary and pension policy." These actions, the Nationalists implied, constituted a pattern of behavior that "disregarded the law on which alone the security of the civil service's position rests."[147]

Although neither the DVP nor the DSP agreed entirely with the Nationalist analysis of civil-service problems, they shared the DNVP's distrust of the NSDAP. In addressing civil servants, the DVP lauded itself for having fought against "the ruinous [Social Democratic] economic and financial policies for years," and claimed that "if we had been listened to, the austerity policies of the emergency decrees would not have been necessary to this extent." While sympathizing with the impatience of many civil servants, the DVP warned disaffected officials not to permit "the old domination of the party book to be replaced by a new and even worse one."[148] The DSP echoed these concerns, cautioning civil servants about the nature of National Socialist intentions. Following a seizure of power, the Nazis would simply remove officials from their posts and install their own followers, the DSP charged. "We're not talking about a few high positions," the party warned, "we're talking about your position, about middle and lower-ranking positions that will be occupied by SA men who are expecting appointments."[149] The DSP, therefore, called on civil servants to ward off the Nazi challenge by "protecting the republican state that guards and advances your rights and thus maintains the civil service on the basis of public law."[150]

While the parties waged a vigorous campaign for the civil service vote in 1932, pursuit of the white-collar electorate was conducted on a much more modest scale. Throughout the various campaigns of the year, the RPL spewed appeals to civil servants, pensioners, farmers, artisans and workers, but campaign literature dealing specifically with white-collar issues was comparatively rare. This remarkably low level of attention was, in fact, characteristic of all the major parties. White-collar employees tended to be approached as either a subspecies of the civil-service electorate or as a somewhat elevated component of the working class. This uncertainty, reflective of a general confusion about the sociopolitical orientation of white-collar employees, became particularly acute during 1932 as signs of a growing radicalization within the *Angestelltenschaft* and its organizations steadily increased.[151]

White-collar unions were gravely concerned about the inexorable rise of joblessness among their members and outraged by the government's emergency decrees, which had lowered salaries and loosened the binding nature of wage contracts. White-collar unemployment, high even before the depression, had soared since 1930, rising by 150 percent. Joblessness among sales personnel was particularly high, with women making up roughly 40 percent of those seeking jobs. Although unemployment among blue-collar workers subsided mildly during the summer of 1932, white-collar figures continued to climb, reaching a new high as the Reichstag campaign got under way. For those *Angestellten* fortunate enough to hold a job, salaries were low and continued to fall throughout the period. In banking and retail commerce, the largest employers of white-collar personnel, salaries shrank by 12 percent in 1931–32.[152] For female employees, the situation was even worse. As the depression deepened and jobs became scarce, women were casually hired and fired, while for those who were regularly employed, fear of dismissal routinely meant submission to the most burdensome work.[153] Moreover, pay for women employees remained substantially lower than for their male counterparts. In Cologne, Leipzig, Magdeburg, and Hamburg, for example, wage contracts stipulated that base pay for female sales personnel fall roughly 10 percent below that of male employees. Because of the weakening of such contracts, however, actual pay often lagged behind this standard for both sexes.[154]

Responding to these grim developments, the white-collar unions, from the socialist ZdA to the *völkisch* DHV, roundly condemned the Brüning and Papen governments and took an increasingly militant stand against the forces of management. On the left, the ZdA predictably viewed the ongoing crisis as an inevitable product of "a failed economic system." Because of "a lack of planning" and "a thirst for profit," the "capitalist system has become the graveyard for hundreds of thousands of white-collar existences," the union lamented. While "small but politically powerful groups" reaped handsome economic rewards, "it was the white-collar employee who above all paid the price for the concentration of monopoly capitalism. . . . Over six hundred thousand white-collar employees are jobless," and more would soon "stand before the void," the ZdA warned, "if the Reaction is allowed to go unchallenged."[155]

While less willing to denounce the capitalist system, the liberal GdA was no less vociferous than the ZdA in its condemnation of Papen's sociopolitical course. The union called on white-collar employees to fight "against the Reaction, which wants to make Hellots of you; against the government, which is interested only in imposing the most brutal burdens on labor; and against the parties that stand for this." The Papen regime had "cut pensions from the white-collar insurance plan and spoken disparagingly of government as a welfare institution for labor." When the regime "preaches the reestablishment of economic responsibility," the GdA warned, "it really means the reestablishment of the old rights of domination. Big agriculture and monopoly capital, as wielders of power in the new regime, think their time has arrived." These groups "want to use the opportunity to dismantle the structure of state social policy, to free wages and salaries from any government regulation, and to dictate the standard of living of the masses by exploiting unemployment," the union angrily charged. "The relations between labor and management are to be set back at least fifty years, and decades of progressive sociopolitical work are simply to be extinguished."[156]

The *völkisch* DHV was equally incensed. In a report on its activities in 1931, the DHV described the year as one in which organized labor had "stood in a fierce defensive struggle against the outrageous demands of management." The depression had "given the powers of social reaction and their . . . bosses a favorable field of battle for an assault on our basic social and political rights," the DHV complained. The goal of management was to eliminate "all government influence on the conditions of labor" in Germany, and Papen had "even attempted to mobilize the forces of the National Opposition for this plan."[157] So far the chancellor had succeeded in seducing only the reactionary DNVP, but organized white-collar labor would have to be increasingly vigilant to protect its rights, the union warned. The DHV, therefore, pledged to continue its campaign against the regime and the emergency legislation that was "a brutal slap in the face to all white-collar employees."[158]

While the white-collar unions appeared united in their renunciation of government economic policy, their political views continued to follow divergent paths. All denounced Papen and the Reaction and all were either uneasy or actively opposed to the NSDAP, but long-standing sociopolitical divisions still remained within the ranks of white-collar labor. The largest of the three organizations, the DHV, found itself in a particularly sensitive position in 1932. Alienated from the DNVP since 1928 and concerned about the disintegration of the moderate right, the DHV, had been left without a strong political ally. Throughout the campaigns of 1932, the union remained on the offensive against the DNVP, charging that "the Hugenberg party has persistently piled proof upon proof that it is the bitter enemy of any sort of free, independent labor movement."[159] Under Hugenberg's leadership, the DNVP had become the party of the Reaction and had grown increasingly hostile to white-collar labor, the DHV complained. Yet even as the union adopted the language of class conflict, it continued to deny any community of interest with the socialist movement. The DHV repeatedly expressed its contempt for the SPD's "leveling tendencies" and declared its determination to defend the unique status of white-collar labor. The DHV, its leaders promised, would remain a bulwark "against Marxist fanatics and their attempts at proletarian egalitarianism."[160]

Having rejected the reactionary right and the Marxist left, the DHV seemed a likely ally of the rising NSDAP. Relations between the two had, however, been strained for years. The union leadership resented National Socialist efforts to recruit within the *Verband*, beginning with the party's drive to "conquer the DHV" in 1928–29, while the Nazis chided the union for its close ties with other parties, particularly Westarp's *Volkskonservativen* and "the pro-Jewish, high-finance DVP."[161] Nazi-DHV relations had shown signs of improvement in the fall of 1931 when the union publicly proposed the inclusion of the NSDAP in a government of national concentration and encouraged the party to clarify its stand on organized labor. Meetings between union and party representatives were held in Munich, and Hitler appeared before union leaders in Hamburg during November, but this incipient reconciliation quickly dissolved when the DHV threw its support to Hindenburg in the subsequent presidential elections.[162] During those campaigns, the DHV praised Hitler's anti-Marxism but remained skeptical about his positions on labor-management relations. Nazi acceptance of "the union idea" simply wasn't enough, the DHV explained. The party had to acknowledge the independence of organized labor as well, and this the NSDAP had shown little inclination to do. In the months that followed the presidential campaigns, relations between the DHV and the NSDAP eroded steadily. The union complained of Nazi efforts to disrupt its activities and claimed that the NSDAP did not want to cooperate with the *Verband* but to subvert and control it.[163] At the DHV's annual convention in June, Hans Bechly, the organization's chairman, conceded that the *Verband* supported many National Socialist objectives and reiterated the union's enthusiasm for Nazi participation in a nationally oriented government. The DHV, however, refused to endorse the party in the upcoming Reichstag election, and Bechly stressed once again that the union's course would not be dictated by any political party.[164] Although the DHV briefly attempted to promote the formation of a Nazi-Zentrum alliance following the July election, relations between the *Verband* and the party did not improve. Thus, despite the persistence of strong sociopolitical affinities, the DHV was unable to find a suitable modus vivendi with the NSDAP in 1932.[165]

Neither the GdA nor the ZdA shared this ambivalence about National Socialism. Both abhorred Nazi extremism and were committed to a defense of the Weimar constitution. "The political radicalism of our times lives on the rejection of all present conditions," the GdA observed. "It hinders organic development and seeks its own growth in indiscriminate destruction." Urging political moderation, the GdA argued that "the promotion of class conflict or one-sided party dictatorship" would "do nothing to improve the situation of white-collar labor." The interests of the *Angestelltenschaft* could only be maintained, the union asserted, if the elections "result in a Reichstag capable of forming an adequate counterweight to the fundamentally antiparliamentary and socially reactionary powers."[166]

While agreeing with the necessity of preserving the democratic state, the ZdA was much more adamant in its condemnation of National Socialism. It urged white-collar employees to give no votes to a party that "cooperates with the sworn enemies of white-collar rights, the great capitalists Hugenberg and Papen, the representatives of a paper-thin upper crust." [167] The NSDAP's socialist phrases were counterfeit goods, the ZdA continued, noting that Nazi social demands proceeded from "an expressly middle-class economic policy." "The Nazis have nothing to offer white-collar employees," the union claimed. "Indeed, white-collar-interests are endangered by this unjustifiable Nazi preference for the commercial and agricultural *Mittelstand*." Nazi efforts to forge an alliance of shopkeepers and white-collar employees against big business was a sham, the union contended, since "the competition between small business and corporate capitalism prevents neither the artisan nor the merchant from joining monopolistic conglomerates in an antilabor front on sociopolitical questions." White-collar employees could best defend their interests by recognizing their comrades in the working class and lending their support to the traditional representative of both blue- and white-collar labor, the SPD. [168]

These appeals were loudly echoed in the Social Democratic press. The party warned that "under the 'new system,' all the social gains made by the *Angestelltenschaft* stand in the gravest peril." According to the SPD, the new regime was bent on "destroying the unemployment insurance while maintaining high premiums"; on "degrading legitimate white-collar claims to unemployment compensation" by instituting a "need test"; on "curtailing retirement and invalid pensions," and on "reducing salaries by refusing to enforce the binding nature of wage contracts." This "Hitler-Papen system" had come to power because "millions of people, indeed, thousands of white-collar employees had, in their desperation and anticapitalist yearning, been fooled by the National Socialists." Instead of the liberation they sought, white-collar employees had been subjected to a regime dominated by "monopoly capital and big agriculture." The "attempts of the bourgeois unions to represent white-collar interests within parties controlled by management have failed," *Vorwärts* asserted, and "the bourgeois parties of the center have been historically surpassed." The political lines had, therefore, been clearly drawn, the party declared, and white-collar employees were called upon to join with the SPD in its struggle for "democracy and socialism" and "against capitalism and fascism." [169]

Given the deteriorating economic condition of the *Angestelltenschaft* and the increasingly militant rhetoric pouring from the unions, the middle-class parties were deeply concerned about the radicalization of their white-collar constituencies. This was reflected in the heightened emphasis placed on the "socialist menace" in campaign literature addressed to *Angestelleten* in 1932. In an appeal to "workers and employees," the DVP typically argued that "unemployment and bad pay" had become their lot "because socialism was the law of the government and much of the economy for too long." White-collar employees were again reminded that "the DVP rejects socialism, whether red or brown," and were urged to turn away from the siren call of simplistic socialist solutions.[170] DSP campaign literature also warned white-collar employees about the dangers of socialism, whether Marxist or Nazi. While pledging itself to "the preservation of the economic existence of civil servants and white-collar employees" and to "the maintenance of their well-deserved rights," the DSP charged that "National Socialism is the pacesetter of bolshevism."[171]

Not to be outdone, the Nationalists took the hardest line on socialism, attempting to link all organized labor with socialist subversion. The DNVP warned white-collar employees that "Marxist party and union politics will not liberate us from this situation." White-collar participation in union activities merely obscured the line between white- and blue-collar labor, detracting from the special status of the *Angestelltenschaft*. If white-collar employees were to improve their economic situation, they "must engage in *Stand*-oriented politics and liberate themselves from all union Marxism." Only by pursuing such a *Standespolitik* could "the significance of white-collar employees as the most important and numerically largest stratum of the German *Mittelstand*" be recognized.[172]

The NSDAP, of course, joined the anti-Marxist crusade for the white-collar vote, claiming that the *Angestelltenschaft* had been betrayed by the bourgeois parties and their social position undermined by Socialist economic policies. "Once the *Angestelltenschaft* was a proud occupational estate," the Nazis observed, but no longer. "Marxism coined the term 'stiff-collar proletariat' not to help the white-collar employee but—after the proletarianization of artisans into industrial slaves—to fit yet another productive *Stand* into the gray army of the nameless industrial proletariat." The white-collar unions were powerless to prevent this proletarianization, the Nazis asserted. Their indifference to white-collar interests had been amply demonstrated during the presidential elections, the RPL charged, even when the unions supposedly opposed to Marxism had thrown their support to the SPD-backed Hindenburg.[173]

Yet although the party did pursue the white-collar vote in 1932, Nazi appeals to *Angestellten* were far fewer in number than to any other major social group. RPL leaflets addressed to civil servants, for example, outnumbered those to white-collar employees by approximately ten to one,

and articles dealing with specifically white-collar issues remained remarkably rare even during the politically turbulent campaign months.[174]
In its electoral literature addressed to white-collar problems, the party
dwelt on two interrelated themes: the National Socialist jobs program,
which would put white-collar employees back to work, and the role of
women in the labor force. Indeed, the Nazis spent considerable energy
attempting to rebuff charges that a National Socialist victory would
result in mass layoffs of female personnel. Throughout the year the party
was repeatedly accused of seeking to deprive women of an opportunity to
earn their livelihood. "In the Third Reich your right to work will be taken
away," the DVP predicted in a typical warning to women voters. "Do you
want to sit at home, a burden to those to whom you used to be a support?
Do you want your impoverished parents to rot because you are not
allowed to earn money? Do you want your abilities to atrophy because
the single woman in the Third Reich is treated as an inferior and is forbidden to exercise her talents?"[175]

The Nazis, of course, denied these accusations, declaring that in the
Third Reich women would become citizens with equal rights.[176] Yet while
the party admitted the necessity of women in the job market, it clearly
regarded the home as the proper area of female endeavor. National Socialist campaign literature sought to depict the entry of women into the
labor force, especially after 1918, as a blatant deprivation of woman's
"most fundamental right," that of having a family. "Millions of German
women have been denied the opportunity to establish a family by the
parties of the present system," the Nazis charged. "Millions are either
unemployed . . . or condemned to indecent starvation wages in big department stores or in some similar achievement of the Revolution." Thirteen years of "progressive" republican legislation had advanced women's
rights but had produced "millions of men without work" and "millions
of women without familial happiness." Still, the party vigorously denied
that National Socialism would "throw working women out onto the
street."[177] Far from being *frauenfeindlich*, as its critics claimed, the
NSDAP wished to *restore* the lost rights of women, the party contended.
"We demand the right to life and family for the German woman and
mother," the Nazis declared, "and if she goes her way alone, the right to
work and decent pay." In the future National Socialist state, "surplus
women who cannot function in the family or in the home will be given
extensive career opportunities," the Nazis promised.[178] In other words,
the NSDAP was reluctantly prepared to accept single women in the labor
market but intimated that job opportunities for married women should
be curbed, or even eliminated. While reassuring some working women,

this position, repeated throughout the campaigns of 1932, certainly did little to diminish the party's already well-established antifeminist reputation—and this, in fact, may have been precisely the point.

Just as the NSDAP's pursuit of the white-collar vote was comparatively lackluster, the results of its organizational efforts within the *Angestelltenschaft* were decidedly mixed. For years the party had attempted to infiltrate the white-collar unions, especially the DHV, but by 1931 those efforts appeared to be flagging. Alfred Krebs, the Nazi Gauleiter of Hamburg and an influential DHV member, reports that in 1931 Nazi political agitation within the union diminished, while criticism of the party increased among the union's rank and file. Dissatisfied with its recruitment within the existing white-collar unions, the NSDAP founded its own organizations in 1931 as part of the National Socialist Shop-Cell Organization (Nationalsozialistische Betriebszellenorganisation—NSBO). From that time on, the NSBO competed with the other white-collar unions in shop council elections, proposing its own list of candidates and publishing its own political journal. However, the NSBO, as Krebs noted with disappointment, simply divided votes with the *völkisch* DHV.[179] Although the NSBO was more successful among white than blue-collar workers, the party candidates still received only about 25 percent of the white-collar ballots cast in the shop council elections in 1931.[180]

There is little convincing empirical evidence to support the traditional view that white-collar employees flocked to the NSDAP in 1931–32. The Nazi/white-collar coefficients do rise in the elections of 1932 as the figures of Table 4.5 indicate, but that rise is surprisingly modest. In both elections of 1932 the National Socialist new middle-class coefficients remain substantially lower than the figures for either the old middle class or the *Rentnermittelstand*. Moreover, the civil service, as in 1930, continues to be more strongly related to the Nazi vote than is white-collar labor.

Given the traditional emphasis on the lower-middle-class locus of the Nazi constituency, the surprisingly strong civil-service coefficients and the equally surprising weakness of the white-collar figures are particularly significant. As noted earlier, members of the *Berufsbeamtentum* enjoyed far greater job security, often a more advanced level of education, generally higher salaries, and certainly greater social prestige than most white-collar employees. The *Beamtentum* had suffered a number of social and economic setbacks since the collapse of the Empire, but it still retained much of its former elitist identity. The NSDAP, in all its campaigns, had been careful to appeal to civil servants on precisely that basis. The potentially alienating effects of the NSDAP's radicalism may have been considerably offset by the prominent attention paid to civil-service

Table 4.5. Party Vote and the New Middle Class (NMC), 1932

| | All NMC[a] | | | |
| | Protestant (N=152) | | Catholic (N=64) | |
	1932a	1932b	1932a	1932b
NSDAP	.144*	.204	.389	.443
DNVP	−.346	−.736	.197	.196
DVP	.353	.654	−.134*	−.431
DDP	.443	.109*	−.234	−.454
Z	−.205	−.337	−.108*	−.544
SPD	−.958	−.135*	−.406	−.331
KPD	−.804	−.827	−.381	−.185
Other	.104*	−.470	.106*	−.132*

	White Collar[a,b]			
	Protestant Subsample			
	Commerce		Industry	
	1932a	1932b	1932a	1932b
NSDAP	−.443	−.593	.403	.701
DNVP	−.620	.310*	−.400	−.609
DVP	.139	.306	−.522	−.410
DDP	.350	.402	.185	.429
Z	−.239	−.257	−.497	−.632
SPD	.251	.175*	−.264	−.400
KPD	.300*	.366*	−.845	−.652
Other	−.184*	−.256	−.166*	.227

| | Catholic Subsample | | | |
| | Commerce | | Industry | |
	1932a	1932b	1932a	1932b
NSDAP	−.213	−.124	−1.91	−1.64
DNVP	.184*	−.189*	−.211*	−.641
DVP	.502	.305	−.106*	.201*
DDP	.294	.299	.171	.284
Z	−.778	−.843	1.15	.822
SPD	−.615	−.147*	.708	1.00
KPD	.122*	.112*	.216*	.166*
Other	.229	.118*	.102*	−.272

Table 4.5. Party Vote and the New Middle Class (NMC), 1932 (continued)

| | Civil Service[a,b] Protestant Subsample | | | |
| | Prof. Service | | Transportation | |
	1932a	1932b	1932a	1932b
NSDAP	.252	.257	.427	.690
DNVP	.146	.162	.103 [*]	.151 [*]
DVP	−.521	−.803	−.568	.100 [*]
DDP	−.252	−.339	.262 [*]	−.991
Z	.295	.271	.241	.244
SPD	.172	.205 [*]	−.352	−.416
KPD	−.462	−.501	−.375	−.408
Other	.214 [*]	−.155	.639 [*]	−.981

| | Catholic Subsample | | | |
| | Prof. Service | | Transportation | |
	1932a	1932b	1932a	1932b
NSDAP	−.127	−.202	.218	.343
DNVP	.372	.196 [*]	−.500	−.210 [*]
DVP	−.119 [*]	.378	−.232 [*]	−.109 [*]
DDP	−.721	−.103 [*]	−.373	−.191 [*]
Z	.978	.943	−.310 [*]	−.251 [*]
SPD	−1.69	−1.34	.525	.502
KPD	.453 [*]	.232 [*]	−.357	−.452
Other	−.150	.122 [*]	.169	−.193

a. These figures are unstandardized regression coefficients (b), controlling for old middle class, *Rentnermittelstand*, blue-collar workers, religion, and urbanization (population size).

b. Presents coefficients for each component of the NMC, controlling for all remaining elements of the white-collar/civil service population in addition to those variables listed above.

[*] These coefficients are not significant at the .05 level.

issues in Nazi campaign literature and by the party's elitist approach to the civil-service electorate and its problems. That elitist appeal paid considerable political dividends, for National Socialist sympathies within the *Beamtentum* were hardly confined to the lower echelons. Although the NSDAP commanded a considerable following among lower ranking officials, Kater's analysis of the party's membership indicates that support for National Socialism in the middle and higher grades had grown substantially since 1929. By 1932, civil servants in both the upper and middle grades were slightly overrepresented in the party's membership.[181]

This forceful solicitation of civil-service support provided a sharp contrast to the party's murky approach to white-collar employees. While the NSDAP carefully cultivated the *Beamtentum*'s self-image as a wounded elite, white-collar employees continued to be treated as components of the "*Arbeitnehmerschaft*" or as "workers of the hand and brain."[182] This Nazi linkage of blue and white-collar labor was consistent with the party's evocations of a classless *Volksgemeinschaft*, but the social leveling implied in the concept certainly ran counter to the sociopolitical orientation of the nonsocialist white-collar unions. Moreover, the party's difficulties with working women, who composed over a quarter of the white-collar labor force, were greatly exacerbated by the depression, as other parties, particularly the SPD, relentlessly assailed the NSDAP's position on female labor."[183]

Fear of social decline, or proletarianization, was undoubtedly a powerful motivating force in the radicalization of some elements of the salaried population, particularly after the onset of the depression. The Nazi/white-collar coefficients in industry, for example, jump sharply from their 1930 levels, perhaps reflecting the high degree of white-collar unemployment in industry. This would be consistent with Pratt's finding of a high correlation between white-collar joblessness and Nazi voting in 1932.[184] Yet, the *Angestelltenschaft* in industry represented only 13 percent of all white-collar labor, and the Nazi/white-collar figures for the much larger commercial sector remain negative in 1932. It seems quite likely that some unemployed white-collar employees turned to the NSDAP in 1932, but the extent of that movement appears to have been far more limited than traditionally assumed. The figures of Table 4.5 strongly suggest that the depression simply did not bring the sharp crystallization of National Socialist support within the new middle class so often assumed in the literature. Equally significant, that support appears to have been far more concentrated in the traditionally elitist civil service than in the socially heterogeneous but largely lower-middle-class *Angestelltenschaft*.

The Working Class

Despite its obvious concentration on the middle-class electorate, the NSDAP refused to abandon its efforts to cultivate a working-class constituency. While posing as the staunch defender of private property to the beleaguered *Mittelstand*, the Nazis sought to convince working-class voters that their lot could be improved only if they deserted the chimeric Marxism of the left for the *Volksgemeinschaft* of National Socialism. The major ideological themes of Nazi propaganda were, of course, already familiar to working-class audiences, but by 1932 the blue-collar population had endured over three years of extreme economic hardship, and the NSDAP hoped that the bonds that bound them to their traditional leftist parties could be severed on the lengthening unemployment lines.

Despite some seasonal improvements, those lines continued to grow in 1932, forming a grim backdrop for the campaigns of that year. At the peak of the crisis, over six million Germans, the overwhelming majority of whom were blue-collar workers, were out of work, while millions more scrambled to make ends meet on part-time wages. By the summer of 1932 over 40 percent of organized labor was either unemployed or working reduced hours. In many of the major industrial and manufacturing sectors, the situation was even worse. Over half the labor force in the metal-working industry was jobless or working part-time in July, while the unemployment figures for the construction workers, woodworkers, and garment workers reached from 54 to 77 percent.[185]

While umemployment continued to creep steadily upward, wages continued to sink, reaching their nadir during the fall campaign. On 1 November 1932, wages for skilled workers stood at only 84 percent of their 1928 level, having slipped by almost 20 percent since early 1930. Pay for unskilled labor, always considerably lower, followed a similar downward curve. Although the cost of living also dipped in the same period, it is estimated that the real net wages in 1932 had fallen to 64 percent of their prewar level. Indeed, organized labor continuously complained that, under the system of forced reductions dictated by the emergency decrees, wages fell faster than prices. Moreover, the emergency decrees had slashed unemployment compensation, reduced the duration of eligibility, and undermined the binding nature of wage contracts, allowing employers to hire at lower rates than those agreed upon in labor-management negotiations. Although both unemployment and real wages, when seasonably adjusted, showed some signs of improvement in the late summer and fall, this mild recovery was not enough to halt the progressive radicalization of the blue-collar electorate.[186]

Undaunted by their failures in the past, the Nazis moved to tap this working-class discontent. Beginning early in the previous year the party had intensified its efforts to attract working-class support by launching its own labor organization, the NSBO. Not intended to function as a trade union, the NSBO had as its sole objective the dissemination of political propaganda for the party. A forerunner of the organization had actually been in existence for over a year, operating in Berlin and other areas of industrial concentration, but it had received little encouragement and even less funding from the party. It had scored some minor successes among municipal and government workers, especially in railroad administration, but its impact on party strategy was minimal until the national leadership decided to participate in the factory council elections in the spring of 1931.[187] Thus, on 1 January 1931 the NSBO was formally established and charged with the duty of "spreading the National Socialist Weltanschauung in the factories and winning important sectors of the working class for the party." The organization was even encouraged to adopt Marxist terminology and tactics if they were useful in gaining an audience, and a bimonthly paper, *Arbeitertum*, was published to help in the NSBO's recruitment campaign.[188] As the year progressed, the NSBO expanded its activities, gradually taking public positions on purely economic issues and even supporting strikes, if they were economically motivated. Although the NSBO had little success in the factory council elections and its membership drive was slow to gather momentum, the organization counted over one hundred thousand members by May 1932.[189]

With this organization in place, the NSDAP targeted the blue-collar electorate for special attention in the campaigns of 1932. Nothing could be farther from the reality of National Socialist electoral strategy than Bracher's assertion that "in the final phase of the republic, National Socialist propaganda was directed almost exclusively toward the middle classes."[190] Indeed, in 1932 the Nazis were determined to make a dramatic breakthrough into the ranks of the SPD's traditional working-class constituency. As an RPL memorandum of 2 April emphasized, the NSDAP intended to launch a major campaign among blue-collar workers to clarify the party's position on labor-related issues and to discredit the SPD's anti-Nazi propaganda. "One Social Democratic lie in particular must be refuted more sharply than ever," the memorandum stressed: "the attempt to portray the NSDAP as a party of management."

> The great majority of the Social Democratic–oriented working class has long recognized that they have been betrayed and sold out by their leaders. They know they've been cheated and lied to by the bosses. But their mistrust of the National Socialists, who for years have been described in their press and meetings as "the mercenaries of capitalism" holds them to their party. Not confidence in victory, not belief in the triumph of the SPD—the worker hasn't possessed

these things for years—but rather mistrust of others is the bond
that holds them to the SPD. We must remove this mistrust by
making clear to the worker that the assertion that the Nazis are
"mercenaries of capital" is a Social Democratic lie intended to divert attention away from their own betrayal of the working class.[191]

While much of the National Socialist propaganda addressed to blue-
collar workers dealt explicitly with the party's image problem, attempting to discredit Social Democratic "lies" and to underscore the failures of
the Marxist parties, the NSDAP's central appeal to the working-class
electorate in 1932 revolved around a dramatic demand for "work and
bread." It was the first obligation of the state to guarantee every German
a job, the party declared. Breaking with the other parties, the NSDAP
endorsed a massive "crash program" of public works, including the construction of roads, dams, canals, and much-needed housing. However,
just as the state was morally bound to provide work for the jobless,
young able-bodied Germans should be prepared to labor for *Volk und
Vaterland*, the party asserted. The NSDAP, therefore, advocated the introduction of compulsory labor service to remove the jobless from the
streets and to inspire them with the selfless virtues of the people's
community.[192]

Whereas the other parties attacked such plans as "irresponsible and
inflationary," the NSDAP loudly proclaimed its commitment to the idea
that "the right to work" was a moral imperative outweighing strictly economic considerations. Besides, the Nazis contended, the cost of providing
jobs would ultimately be less than the financial and psychological strain
of financing the current system of unemployment compensation.[193] The
party criticized the republic's social welfare system, which, the RPL
maintained, acted as a serious drain on the government's finances without providing adequate care for the public. The purpose of this criticism
was not, however, to destroy government welfare institutions, the Nazis
explained, but "to make them superfluous by breaking capitalist exploitation and putting the worker back on his own two feet."[194] This could be
done with comparatively little cost to the government, the party maintained, if the tyranny of international and Jewish finance capital could be
broken. Lower interest rates would free capital for productive investment
in projects to benefit the entire *Volk* and not a handful of "stock-market
swindlers."[195] Breaking the financial stranglehold of the Jews at home
would, of course, have to be coordinated with the emancipation of Germany from foreign exploitation. Above all, this meant establishing an
autarkic German economy, self-sufficient and free of all foreign influence.

The NSDAP, Nazi propaganda emphasized, was determined to restore "the right of economic self-determination for the German people so that international capital can no longer decide whether or not Germans work and live." [196]

Although National Socialist publications provided their readers with rather detailed analyses of the economic situation and the party's prescribed remedies, the RPL warned local organizations not to worry about specifics. "These things don't need to be discussed in propaganda," it explained. "Currency questions, autarky, and financial issues don't belong in rallies. They are technical problems to be handled by specialists." Party functionaries were, therefore, instructed to confine themselves to the general campaign slogans developed at the Munich headquarters: "work and bread," "the right to work," and "economic self-determination." [197]

These formulas were particularly evident in Nazi appeals to labor in 1932. Party spokesmen even contended that the Nazi program, based as it was on the principle of full employment, represented the essence of true socialism. According to the NSDAP, socialism was "a moral not an economic imperative." It "demands justice, the common good, and security from exploitation. The right to work is socialism," one Nazi economic specialist typically explained. By the same token, capitalism had little to do with the ownership of private property. "Capitalism," in the Nazi lexicon, was "the exclusive control by capital over the opportunity to work." Under such a system, "it is the exclusive right of capital to decide whether or not one works." The guarantee of the right to work in a National Socialist state would thus produce a metamorphosis of the system. It would "turn the capitalist social order around." In the Nazi *Volksgemeinschaft*, the party claimed, "capital will no longer decide, labor will." [198] This definition of capitalism was particularly useful to the NSDAP since it allowed the party to embrace "socialism" without demanding the expropriation of private property. Indeed, the Nazis rejected "senseless expropriation" just to benefit "a small clique of bosses." Rather than expropriating the propertied, the NSDAP demanded "the deproletarianization of the propertyless and the participation of the working class in the ownership of property." [199]

While elaborating its own definition of socialism, the NSDAP relentlessly lambasted the inadequacies of Marxism, claiming that the workers of Germany were coming at last to recognize the bankruptcy of the Marxist solution. "The Social Democratic voters of the Free Trade Unions are in confusion," the party asserted. "They have grown doubtful that Marxism is really the socialism for which they have struggled." [200] After all, what had become of the SPD's promises to be proletariat, Nazi leaflets were fond of asking. "Where is the nationalization of industry? Where are your contract rights?" Instead of the highly touted workers' paradise, "Marxism," the Nazis charged, "has lifted the most brutal capitalism into the saddle." Thirteen years of Marxist-dominated republican policy had only brought "six million unemployed, hunger and misery" to the working class.[201]

Because the NSDAP had dared to point out the bankruptcy of Marxism, the party and its leader had been savagely vilified in the leftist press, the Nazis complained. The National Socialists were accused of being the lackeys of the Reaction and enemies of the working class, but the NSDAP was hardly responsible for the loss of the eight-hour workday, skyrocketing unemployment, and the emergency decrees that reduced wages and social insurance benefits. These were the work of the SPD, which had supported the governments of the early republic and tolerated the Brüning cabinet.[202] Social Democratic bosses were to blame for low pay, the weakening of wage contracts, and for the election of Hindenburg who had, after all, appointed Papen.[203] Hitler, who had challenged the reactionary Reich president and led his party's determined opposition to the disastrous economic policies of the Brüning regime, had nonetheless been ruthlessly assailed in the leftist press. "No banker, no great capitalist, no industrialist has been so accused, so ridiculed, so slandered, and so abused before the working class as Adolf Hitler," a typical Nazi leaflet asserted. Yet "in spite of this persecution, millions of workers are flocking to him and are ready to lay down their lives for him," the party press maintained. Only Hitler had correctly foreseen the misery and suffering that Marxism had brought to the working class in the thirteen years of republican politics, and only Hitler and the NSDAP could possibly rescue the German worker from the bitterness and disillusionment spawned by Marxist rhetoric and republican corruption.[204]

This assault on the electoral bastions of Marxism did not, however, provoke a united leftist front against the National Socialist challenge. Despite the alarming gains of the NSDAP in 1931 and 1932, the Communists continued to cling to a strategy directed primarily against the SPD. On instructions from Moscow, the party had participated in the right-wing referendum against the Social Democratic government of Prussia in 1931 and continued to emphasize that the KPD was prepared to form a united front against fascism only "from below," with "Social Democratic workers."[205] Although Papen's action against that same Prussian government in July 1932 was condemned as a "naked fascist coup," the KPD lambasted the Social Democratic leadership for its failure to retaliate. "The SPD wants to destroy the proletarian united front," the Central Committee maintained, "and capitulates to fascism." A vote for the Social Democrats, the KPD reasoned, would, therefore, only strengthen "the Hitler-Papen dictatorship."[206]

A successful struggle to eradicate this "bourgeois dictatorship," party chairman Thälmann argued, was predicated on the Communist conversion of working-class supporters of the SPD and the Socialist unions. "As long as they are not emancipated from the influence of the social-fascist leaders, these millions of workers are lost to the antifascist struggle. The isolation of the SPD and ADGB leaders within the working class, remains our most important strategic objective." This strategy did not mean a weakening of the Communist struggle against the NSDAP, he explained, since "Hitler-fascism" could not be destroyed without first eliminating Social Democratic influence within the working class. "The battle against the chief enemy, the bourgeoisie, the Papen government, and its National Socialist lackeys," Thälmann concluded, "cannot be waged successfully without . . . the primary offensive against Social Democracy . . . without this struggle for the majority of the working class."[207]

Social Democratic opposition to the Papen government was, therefore, dismissed as a ruse, an effort to undermine proletarian unity. "Because the SPD leaders stand on the basis of defending the bourgeois order," the KPD contended, "they will always attempt to enlist the proletarian masses . . . for the suppression of the revolutionary mass movement."[208] When the SPD responded that these attacks only prevented proletarian unity and strengthened reactionary forces, Walter Ulbricht, speaking in Berlin, replied that "it would be a crime against the working class if we did not use every opportunity to expose the 'state-preserving policies' of the SPD leadership that only help maintain the Papen government."[209]

While condemning the Social Democratic leadership, the KPD announced the formation of an antifascist front, which, it hoped, would secure the support of the SPD rank and file. This "Anti-Fascist Action," as its manifesto of 12 July 1932 declared, sought "the honest coalescence of all class comrades and working people who are ready and willing to lead the struggle against the dictatorial emergency decrees, against National Socialist terror, and against the establishment of a fascist dictatorship by the Papen regime."[210] Thus, while Communist campaign literature accused the SPD of betraying its working-class constituents, it depicted the NSDAP as little more than a tool of high finance and monopoly capitalism. National Socialism, the *Rote Fahne* charged, could "be comprehended only if one recognizes that the German capitalist class created the Hitler party and nurtured it so that its exploitive capitalist profits could be protected against the revolution of the working people."[211] During both Reichstag campaigns the Communist press, therefore, labored to identify the NSDAP with the Papen government, warning workers that this "Nazi-supported regime" had only one objective: "to reduce further the starvation rations of the working class, thus freeing more billions to subsidize bankrupt capitalists."[212]

The KPD was, nevertheless, clearly concerned about possible National Socialist penetration of the blue-collar electorate. During July, a series of articles appeared in the party press carefully examining Nazi policy. According to the *Rote Fahne*, "compulsory labor service," and "autarkic national trade policy," and "the creation of jobs through inflation" constituted the essence of Nazi economic thought. "These three points," the KPD concluded, "reveal the cloven hoof of the servants of capital. Each of these demands means the enrichment of the wealthy and the continued robbery of the poorest of the poor."[213] The only way to create millions of jobs, the party argued, was to "take the necessary means away from the capitalists, away from the exploiters." Specifically, the KPD called for the "cancellation of . . . compensation and indemnities to the former princely houses, reduction of salaries and pensions for high-ranking civil servants and publicly employed white-collar workers, . . . elimination of obligations to foreign creditors, abolition of all military expenditures, initiation of a 'millionaires' tax,' a tax on dividends, and . . . a special tax on gigantic incomes."[214] The party also renewed its standard demands for a seven-hour workday, a forty-hour work week, elimination of overtime, an expanded public works program, construction of additional housing for workers, free food for the jobless, higher unemployment compensation, and a halt to wage cuts.[215] The ultimate objective, of course, remained the establishment of a soviet Germany, and in Communist estimation realization of that goal required above all the eradication of "social fascism."

Greatly compromised in the eyes of many working-class voters for its "toleration" of the Brüning government, the SPD in 1932 found it increasingly difficult to rebuff the vitriolic assaults of the KPD. Although the Social Democrats had been unwilling to participate in a Brüning cabinet, they had, ironically, proven to be the government's most reliable source of parliamentary support since 1930. Fearful that a collapse of the Brüning government would only result in more ominous National Socialist and Communist gains, the SPD had elected to adopt a policy of toleration. To do otherwise, the party argued, would merely expedite the disintegration of the already gravely endangered republic.[216] Sounding the theme that would be elaborated again in the campaigns of 1932, the SPD attempted to underscore the vital nexus between preservation of the republic and protection of working-class interests. "We fight for this state," the party explained, "because we know that the moment the black-red-gold flag [of the republic] sinks, the red flag of socialism will fall along with it. It must be clear . . . that the republic and the working-class are bound together for life and death."[217] The policy of toleration, however, proved costly at the polls. Unable or unwilling to step beyond the bounds of traditional capitalist economic orthodoxy, the SPD reluctantly accepted the harsh deflationary measures of the Brüning government without offering a substantive alternative. The program of deficit spending and extensive public works drafted by the ADBG in early 1932 elicited little enthusiasm from a party leadership still fearful of renewed inflation.[218]

If they could offer little in the way of innovative solutions to the nation's economic difficulties, the Social Democrats could present themselves to the voters as the most formidable bulwark against "social reaction and fascism." Stressing that the "solidarity of the proletariat" was "more crucial than ever before," the SPD warned that the fascist challenge could be repelled only "if a truly common desire for proletarian unity is present."[219] Responsibility for past failures to achieve a united front was attributed to the KPD's myopic vilification of the Social Democratic leadership and its persistent efforts to undermine all constructive legislative initiatives proposed by the SPD. The Social Democrats were conducting "a passionate battle against the impudence of the Reaction," *Vorwärts* stated, and were bitterly disappointed that the "Communists, rather than offering support," were "interested only in the struggle between the socialist workers' parties."[220]

The SPD's approach to campaign strategy in 1932 appeared to have been considerably simplified in May when Brüning was replaced by Papen and the party's policy of "toleration" came to an abrupt end. No longer burdened by the need to defend its reluctant support for the regime, the party hoped to go on the offensive against Papen's "cabinet of barons."[221] The Prussian coup of 20 July and the party's restrained reaction to it, however, complicated that strategy. When confronted by an authoritarian government determined to eliminate the last vestiges of Social Democratic institutional power, the SPD would not mobilize the party's well-organized street units for a direct confrontation. Despite the recommendations of representatives of the Reichsbanner and the Iron Front for a more active resistance, the leadership refused, preferring to entrust the party's and, indeed, the republic's future to the courts and to the ballot box.[222] The party condemned Communistic agitation for a proletarian uprising and rejected past efforts at "Communist revolution" as "crimes against the working class and socialism," which "had only strengthened the reaction and fascism." Instead, the Social Democrats reaffirmed their commitment to parliamentary democracy, urging the electorate to make 31 July "a day of reckoning for the misgovernment of the barons and their National Socialist helpers." All the party's energy was, therefore, to be concentrated in achieving "a victory for the SPD in the forthcoming campaign."[223]

While conceding that elements of the working-class electorate had been radicalized by almost three years of rising unemployment and falling wages, the party contended that radicalism was "hollow, unfruitful, and an impediment to the struggle of the working-class movement." The way to socialism, *Vorwärts* argued, required the proletariat to "overcome this radicalism" and to employ its strength in the slow and arduous task transforming German society from within. National Socialist and Communist electoral successes, *Vorwärts* acknowledged ruefully, simply proved that "it is obviously easier to intoxicate the voters with tempting calls for the Third Reich or a soviet Germany" than to engage in difficult, constructive legislative work for the betterment of the working class. The SPD, however, would opt for the latter course.[224]

The party was convinced that a strong and widespread anticapitalist sentiment had been awakened by the miseries of the depression, and its campaigns in 1932 sought to mobilize that discontent for the SPD. Social Democratic campaign literature, therefore, attempted to "spread the awareness that the capitalist economy has passed its zenith, that it is no longer capable of fulfilling its tasks, that it can no longer feed, clothe, and house the people, that it must be replaced by a new, higher form of economy."[225] At the same time, however, *Vorwärts*, like the *Rote Fahne*, repeatedly warned its readers against the "false socialism" of the NSDAP. "A party with Hohenzollern princes, barons, former generals, and other 'workers' at its summit . . . is not a workers' party but an antiworkers' party," the SPD charged. Similarly, the Papen cabinet with its emergency decrees, which brought "no new burdens for the well-to-do, the rich, but more misery and distress for the poor and the oppressed," was presented as "the fruit of National Socialist victories."[226] Still, the "anticapitalism of today," the SPD argued, could "be the socialism of tomorrow if the German workers remain true to their old flag and use their millions and millions of votes . . . to construct the social *Volksstaat* on the will to freedom of the German working class and on the political power of the unions and Social Democracy." The party could "calmly trust that sooner or later the voting masses, to the extent that they are truly filled with anticapitalist longing and the desire for socialism, will turn in disappointment from the Nazis and Communists and find their way to Social Democracy."[227]

As the election returns of both July and November were to show, these hopes proved considerably optimistic. In both elections the Social Democratic vote continued to slide, dropping from 21.6 percent to 20.4 percent, while the Communist electorate expanded from 14.3 percent to 16.9 percent. Examining the individual economic sectors, it would appear that the KPD not only managed to maintain its remarkably stable constituency in mining and metal producing, but to make significant inroads into the strongholds of Social Democratic strength in other industrial sectors. Although the Social Democratic-industrial coefficients are strong in both samples, the Communist figures surge in the Protestant districts, actually exceeding those of the SPD by November (see Table 4.6).

While charting the shifting sociopolitical relationship between the Marxist parties and blue-collar labor, the figures of Table 4.6 also strongly suggest that the NSDAP's continuing efforts to penetrate the industrial working class had failed to produce significant results. In the major industrial categories, the Nazi coefficients are either strongly negative or simply insignificant. Moreover, just as in 1930, the Communist, not the Nazi, vote proves to be the strongest correlate of unemployment (see Table 4.7). Although the Social Democratic vote is also positively related to unemployment in the first election of the year, the SPD coefficients for the November campaign drop to a marginal level of statistical significance. The National Socialist figures, on the other hand, remain weakly related to unemployment for both elections, a reflection, no doubt, of the preponderance of industrial workers in the ranks of the unemployed.

Although the Nazis were unable to make significant inroads into the industrial blue-collar electorate, recent studies of party membership uniformly contend that the NSDAP's appeal to working-class Germans was much stronger than traditionally assumed.[228] Certainly, the NSBO's membership tripled in 1932, rising to over three hundred thousand just after the July election, and regional analyses of the party's rank and file indicate a rising "worker" interest in the party as the year progressed.[229] The NSDAP's official statistics are, however, extraordinarily vague about what constituted a "worker" and the NSBO, which had never made distinctions between white- and blue-collar labor, even admitted entrepreneurs and independent craftsmen.[230] Who, then, were these workers? Although the Nazi/industrial-labor coefficients remain largely negative throughout the Weimar period, an important pattern of working-class support for the NSDAP does emerge, as we have seen, if nonindustrial

Table 4.6. Party Vote and the Blue-Collar Working Class (BC), 1932

| | All BC | | | |
| | Protestant (N=152) | | Catholic (N=64) | |
	1932a	1932b	1932a	1932b
NSDAP	.691	.229	−.123*	−.932
DNVP	−.183	−.271	−.643	−.123*
DVP	−.928	−.222	−.964	−.122*
DDP	−.197	−.279	−.664	−.148*
Z	−.831	−.735	−.684	−.738
SPD	.891	.761	.982	.740
KPD	.776	.849	.231	.197
Other	−.171	−.413	−.420	−.410

| | BC in Industry[a] | | | |
| | Protestant (N=152) | | Catholic (N=64) | |
	1932a	1932b	1932a	1932b
NSDAP	.156*	.109*	−.564	−.496
DNVP	−.227	−.292	−.166	−.215
DVP	−.801	−.746	−.146	−.282
DDP	−.241	−.196	−.496	−.493
Z	−.840	−.791	.141*	.222*
SPD	.606	.368	.401	.389
KPD	.684	.626	.191*	.326
Other	−.774	.366*	.154*	.291*

| | BC in Mining/Metalworking[a] | | | |
| | Protestant (N=152) | | Catholic (N=64) | |
	1932a	1932b	1932a	1932b
NSDAP	−.488	.176*	−.402	−.352
DNVP	.164*	−.234	−.132	−.186
DVP	−.359*	−.421*	.104*	.125*
DDP	−.291	−.340	−.407	−.401
Z	−.509	−.488	−.171*	−.232
SPD	−.989	.119	.219	.207
KPD	.260	.291	.387	.471
Other	.176*	−.118	.100*	.199*

Table 4.6. (continued)

| | BC in Handicrafts[a] | | | |
| | Protestant (N=152) | | Catholic (N=64) | |
	1932a	1932b	1932a	1932b
NSDAP	.975	.216	.499	.239
DNVP	−.246	−.293	−.354	−.346
DVP	.202*	.243*	.393*	−.158*
DDP	−.378	−.408	.242*	.224*
Z	−.112	−.114	−1.07	−1.05
SPD	.819	.961	1.03	.859
KPD	.131	.984	−.244	−.222
Other	−.207*	−.499	−.969	−.962

| | BC in Agriculture[a] | | | |
| | Protestant (N=121) | | Catholic (N=125) | |
	1932a	1932b	1932a	1932b
NSDAP	−.674	−.787	.518	.478
DNVP	−.625	.156*	−.168*	−.385
DVP	−.195	−.247	.115*	−.119
DDP	−.161	−.132	−.438	−.411
Z	−.147	−.178	−1.13	−1.17
SPD	.339	.265	.315	.310
KPD	.187	.177	.122	.230
Other	−.261*	−.154*	−2.10*	−.196*

NOTE: The figures are unstandardized regression coefficients (b), controlling for old middle class, new middle class, *Rentnermittelstand*, religion, and urbanization (population size).
a. Presents coefficients for each component of the working class, controlling for all remaining elements of the BC population in addition to those variables listed above.

* These coefficients are not significant at the .05 level.

sectors are examined. Throughout the predepression period the Nazi vote is positively, if modestly, related to the blue-collar variable in handicrafts and small-scale manufacturing. In 1930 that relationship becomes far more powerful, and in the elections of 1932 the Nazi/blue-collar coefficients for this sector surge once again. For the first time they surpass the Nazi/new-middle-class and Nazi/*Rentner* figures, becoming one of the most powerful predictors of the National Socialist vote. Yet, by No-

Table 4.7. Party Vote and Unemployment, 1932

	July Protestant	July Catholic	November Protestant	November Catholic
NSDAP	.106*	−.657	.293	−.210
SPD	.199	.249	1.00	.266
KDP	.395	.899	1.15	2.64
Z	.166*	.222*	.214*	.266*
N=	(138)	(35)	(138)	(35)

NOTE: The figures are unstandardized regression coefficients (b), controlling for old middle class, new middle class, *Rentnermittelstand*, blue-collar workers in industry, mining, and handicrafts, religion, and urbanization (population size).

* These coefficients are not significant at the .05 level.

SOURCE: Calculations are based on unemployment figures from every community of over twenty-five thousand inhabitants. These figures, taken on 31 May 1932 and 30 November 1932, include those receiving either *Arbeitslosenversicherung* or *Krisenfürsorge*. The figures are reported in *Statistische Beilage zum Reichsarbeitsblatt*, Nrs. 19 and 22, 1932, pp. 9–10.

vember this relationship weakens, dropping sharply in both samples, while the SPD/KPD figures surge upward. The very volatility of these figures may indicate that it was in this socially amorphous element of the working class that Nazi-SPD/KPD crossovers, so often speculated about in the literature, were most likely to occur.

Although the Abel Collection does not constitute a valid statistical sample of all National Socialist workers, it is nevertheless signficant that by far the great majority of the workers included there were employed in the handicrafts sector or sprang from artisan backgrounds. Carpenters, plumbers, tinsmiths, gardeners, painters, and locksmiths abounded, as did laborers from rural origins who discovered, as one new factory worker reported, that "the small farm didn't provide income or employment for the entire family."[231] Some Nazi workers were employed in municipal or other government enterprises, such as the Reichsbahn or public utilities,[232] while another prominent group changed jobs frequently, some enduring protracted periods of unemployment.[233] Those in industrial occupations, however, were fewer in number and almost unanimously stressed their alienation from their Marxist coworkers. "When my fellow workers found out about [my political views]," one Nazi worker complained, "their hate knew no bounds."[234] The tremendous political and professional difficulties encountered by a worker with National Socialist sympathies provided a common theme in the biographies of virtually all the workers in the Abel Collection. One electrician, employed in a municipal utility, typically explained that "the tremendous resistance from the employers as well as from the workers, ninety percent of whom were infected with Marxism, . . . made it extremely difficult for the small group of National Socialists to achieve success."[235] Nazi workers not only had to contend with hostility from management and the authorities but from the "Marxist workers and their shop councils," which "greatly complicated our propaganda activities." "The struggle to win working-class converts was particularly difficult," another municipal worker argued, since "attitudes held for decades had to be swept away and the Marxist worker had to be taught that everything he had believed and expected was only theory and could never become reality."[236]

Although some Nazi workers indicated that their recruitment efforts were not without some success, most dwelt on their political isolation within the working class. "I was the only National Socialist-oriented worker in the plant," one shoe factory employee stated, "and remained so until the [Nazi] assumption of power."[237] These personal impressions of the party's limited success were by and large substantiated by the results of the shop council elections, especially in industrial areas. Despite considerable blue-collar-oriented propaganda and the party's support for labor in a number of strikes, especially the widely publicized strike of Berlin transportation workers in 1932, the NSBO never achieved any appreciable success in the shop council elections. Moreover, while the NSBO's membership grew rather spectacularly in late 1932, its three hundred thousand members were dwarfed by socialist Free Trade Unions, whose members numbered over five million.[238] The NSDAP undoubtedly won some crossovers from both the SPD and KPD, as a number of Abel biographies attest,[239] but the Marxist vote remained remarkably stable throughout the depression years, fluctuating between 36 and 38 percent. Nonetheless, the NSDAP *had* attracted a blue-collar constituency in 1932 and was not merely a middle-class party. Although National Socialist penetration of the working-class electorate remained clearly circumscribed by organized industrial labor, which remained firm in its commitment to the Marxist parties, a substantial part of the blue-collar population remained aloof from those parties. Indeed, the NSDAP, with its blend of anticapitalist, anti-Marxist rhetorics was clearly attractive to a significant portion of the German working class that felt neither accepted by the entrepreneurial middle class nor a part of the organized working class.

Religion

Just as the industrial working class remained by and large immune to the National Socialist "contagion," areas of Catholic concentration continued to be relatively impervious to Nazi electoral advances. The National Socialist breakthrough in 1930 had come primarily in Protestant Germany, and the party was determined to weaken the Zentrum's hold on its Catholic constituents in 1932. "The battle against the Zentrum demands extraordinary agility and . . . political sensitivity," the RPL wrote early in the year. Local party leaders in Catholic areas were therefore warned against making any statement or taking any action which would provoke charges that the NSDAP was reviving the anti-Catholic *Kulturkampf.* "The Catholic religion and Church . . . must never be attacked or abused from our side," the RPL cautioned. Local functionaries were, however, encouraged to emphasize the Zentrum's contemptible misuse of religion . . . to promote its own partisan interests."[240] The party strenuously denied that its attacks on the Zentrum were in any way animated by anti-Catholic bias. On the contrary, the party argued, the NSDAP's criticism was inspired by the Zentrum's "wanton mixture of religion and politics." The Zentrum's willingness to align itself with "godless Marxism" was given particularly prominent treatment in National Socialist campaign literature in 1932. "For years," one typical Nazi leaflet charged, "the Zentrum has collaborated with antireligious organizations whose equivalents rip down the churches in Russia, while murdering priests and burning convents in Spain."[241] When the Zentrum responded by suggesting that National Socialism was essentially a pagan movement interested in resurrecting ancient German cults, the party counterattacked, arguing that the Zentrum, not the NSDAP, had been a coalition partner with "atheistic Marxism" for thirteen years, during which time "German Christian culture" had "been poisoned by Jewish pestilence."[242]

In addressing the Protestant and Catholic audiences in 1932, the Nazis linked their own commitment to Christian principles with a warning about the threat to religion posed by advancing Marxism. "A people without faith in God will fall," the party preached. "Religion is not an opiate but sustenance for the soul of the *Volk.*" The atrocities committed against the Christian faith in Spain and Russia could happen in Germany as well, the Nazis warned, if the forces of Marxism remained unchecked. "The enemies of religion are fighting with all their might to rip that most holy thing, faith, from your heart," the party asserted, and they would use "the most despicable means to mock and ridicule your God and religion, branding you with atheism, blasphemy, and anti-Christian materialism." The NSDAP, therefore, had an obligation "to erect a dam against the filthy torrent of atheism" that endangered Christian values everywhere.[243] The party stated its desire to "help the Christian confessions gain their rights" and restated its commitment to the equality of the churches. At the same time, however, the Nazis insisted on the removal of religion from the political arena. "Christianity is too important to this party," the NSDAP piously intoned, to allow "church and religious affairs to be tied up with partisan politics." Instead, the party stressed that the NSDAP, "like Christ, demands that God should be given what is God's and the state what is the state's."[244]

In spite of these efforts to reassure Christians, and particularly Catholics, of the NSDAP's support for Christianity, the party continued to fare far better in Protestant Germany than in Catholic areas. Although the Nazis registered sizable gains throughout the country in 1932, their vote in Catholic towns and villages lagged far behind their totals in Protestant communities. As in previous campaigns, electoral literature dealing with religious issues tended to be addressed primarily to women, and non-Marxist appeals to women tended to focus on the home, family, and religious values. Moreover, those parties that stressed religious themes in their platforms and campaigns—the Zentrum, the BVP, the DNVP, and a number of conservative splinter parties—had traditionally done quite well with female voters. On the other hand, women had been consistently underrepresented in the radical parties, especially the NSDAP and KPD.[245]

The elections of 1932, however, brought a significant transformation of this well-established relationship. Attempting to widen its appeal, the NSDAP, in particular, had intensified its efforts to recruit women for the movement. Just as the party established its own organizations for artisans, farmers, civil servants, and veterans, the NSDAP, in the summer of 1931, announced the formation of a new national women's organization to supersede and unite the various Nazi women's auxiliaries. The Nationalsozialistische-Frauenschaft (NS-F), as its first declaration of principles emphasized, stood for "a German women's spirit which is rooted in GOD, nature, family, nation, and homeland," and its strongly religious, anti-Marxist stance was presented regularly in a new magazine for women, the *Nationalsozialistische-Frauenwarte*, which began publication in July 1932. Although the NS-F tended to be underfunded and encountered some resistance from regional party leaders, the NSDAP lavished increasing publicity on its new women's organization, especially during the campaigns of 1932. Acutely conscious of National Socialism's poor performance among women voters in the past, the RPL saturated the female electorate with political literature throughout the election year, relentlessly pledging the party's support for traditional religious and cultural values.[246]

These efforts were not without effect. Although women still tended to favor parties with a strong religious orientation, the NSDAP made enormous gains among the female electorate in 1932. In those areas where votes were tabulated by sex, women for the first time outnumbered men in the National Socialist constituency.[247] Exactly what role religion played in this shift is unclear, but an important division within the female electorate quickly emerges when its vote is broken down geographically. While women in Protestant districts outnumbered their male counterparts in the Nazi electorate, women in Catholic areas did not. Indeed, Catholic women remained strikingly underrepresented in the National Socialist constituency throughout 1932. Significantly, female support for National Socialism proved weakest in rural Catholic areas where the influence of the Church was strongest.[248] While the NSDAP's efforts to dispel worries about its religious and moral character clearly enjoyed a considerable degree of success in Protestant Germany, the Catholic minority obviously remained skeptical. Thus, despite some erosion, Catholicism, like the "Marxist political church," continued to act as a serious impediment to the rising tide of Nazi electoral success, even when that tide reached its crest in the summer of 1932.

Yet, while the presence of a substantial Catholic population retarded the advance of National Socialism, a vote for the Zentrum can hardly be interpreted as an endorsement of the Weimar Republic. The Zentrum's antisystem campaigns of 1932 vividly reflected the authoritarian orientation of the party under Kaas and Brüning, a man "whose true national feeling attempted to liberate the German people from the system of party domination and from the chains of Versailles." While others only "pretended to fight the system of party rule," Germania gloated, "Brüning translated talk into action." The Zentrum explained that it was not opposed to Nationalist or Nazi participation in the Reich government. Brüning had, in fact, sought their support. "The question was not if they were to be integrated into the action but how and when."[249] Although the party rejected dictatorship and radicalism, it hoped to achieve a "true national concentration" that would reestablish authority and discipline in public affairs. The choice confronting the German electorate, Germania maintained, was not "party state or authoritarian state but authoritarian state with or without the people." The Zentrum "rejects the boundless domination of the parties," its press repeatedly explained, but unlike the NSDAP and DNVP, "it had never sought power for only one party." The

Table 4.8. Party Vote and Religious Confession, 1932 (N = 462)

	Protestant		Catholic	
	1932a	1932b	1932a	1932b
NSDAP	.690	.649	.460	.484
DNVP	.361	.476	.302	.388
DVP	.462	.164	−.834	−.177
DDP	.299	.298	−.418	−.391
Z	−.879	−.877	.931	.933
SPD	.637	.578	−.789	−.724
KPD	−.491	−.598	−.483	−.588
Other	−.211*	−.246	−.411	−.386

NOTE: The figures are unstandardized regression coefficients (b), controlling for old middle class, new middle class, *Rentnermittelstand*, blue-collar workers, and urbanization (population size).

* These coefficients are not significant at the .05 level.

Zentrum's goal in 1932 was, therefore, "the concentration of all responsible national forces, which only together can provide the indispensable foundation for a truly authoritarian government."[250]

By the summer of 1932 the disintegration of the political center was, therefore, complete. The parties of the *bürgerliche Mitte*, their constituencies decimated by massive defections, had ceased to be a significant factor in German electoral politics. The progressive rightward drift in liberal policies and propaganda had failed to slow the deteriorating appeal of the DVP and DSP, and the conservatives, too, despite their flirtations with the NSDAP, had been unable to maintain their traditional electorate. Even the Zentrum, with its stable constituency, had undergone a profound political metamorphosis. Although it had withstood the National Socialist infection, it was not immune to the political malaise of which the NSDAP was a symptom. By 1932 the Zentrum, a participant in all but one of the Weimar governments, no longer represented a solid bulwark of the now virtually moribund republic (see table 4.8). Indeed, only the Marxist SPD continued to offer steadfast allegiance to the endangered Weimar constitution, but its constituency was also receding, eroded by an intractable economic crisis. Together the antirepublican parties represented the majority of German voters. It was a constituency that knew few social boundaries.

Conclusion

From its first campaign in the spring of 1924 to the pinnacle of its electoral fortunes eight years later, the NSDAP remained an enigma in German political life. Unlike their more established rivals, the National Socialists were never content to anchor their movement securely along the traditional lines of social, religious, and regional cleavage that had structured the German party system since its formation in the last half of the nineteenth century. Instead, they were determined to transcend those widely accepted restrictions on their potential constituency to become the first genuine party of mass integration in German political history. National Socialist electoral strategy, with its consistent efforts to mobilize support in every sector of the economy, in every occupational group, in every region, and in the major Christian confessions, vividly reflected that ambition. Although the party shifted the emphasis of its campaign strategy after 1928, revising the urban plan and concentrating more pointedly on the middle-class electorate, it never abandoned its efforts to cultivate a broader constituency.

The NSDAP's heightened focus on the middle-class voter coincided with the onset of the depression, and as economic conditions deteriorated, the Nazis achieved significant breakthroughs into each of the major elements of the *Mittelstand*. By the summer of 1932 the NSDAP had succeeded where the traditional parties of the bourgeois center and right had repeatedly failed, becoming the long-sought party of middle-class concentration. The miseries of the depression radicalized voters, contributing directly and powerfully to the rise of National Socialism after 1928. Yet, the dramatic Nazi victories during the depression era are hardly conceivable without the erosion of traditional loyalties within the middle-class electorate that had been under way since the inflation and stabilization crises of the mid-twenties. Those interrelated crises had not produced an immediate radicalization of the middle-class electorate but seriously destabilized traditional bourgeois voting patterns. That destabilization was most clearly reflected in the sudden electoral successes of the middle-class special interest parties between 1924 and 1928. The growing appeal of those parties cannot be interpreted simply as the triumph of interest politics and "the eclipse of ideology." Although they represented different sets of interests within the socially diverse *Mittelstand*, these parties shared a number of social and political assumptions that lent their programs an implicitly ideological dimension.

Above all, the middle-class *Interressenparteien* were rabidly anti-Marxist. Although each found fault with the liberal and conservative parties, their hostility toward the SPD and KPD was almost unbounded, and condemnation of "Bolshevist experiments" assumed a prominent position in their programs. At the same time, they took a strong stand against the forces of "big capitalism." Resentment toward the "captains of trusts and corporations, department stores, and consumer cooperatives" was repeatedly stressed in the campaigns of the special interest parties. Although most of these parties looked to the state for protection against both big business and big labor, they nevertheless remained mistrustful of big government as well. Government was usually associated with Social Democratic spending programs and high taxes. Consequently, most special interest platforms called for strict budgetary restraint, curbs on government spending, particularly for social programs, and a reduction of state intervention in the economy. Finally, most expressed disappointment with the Weimar parliamentary system which, in their view, permitted large corporations and organized labor to exert inordinant influence on public life. No agreement on an alternative emerged from these programs, but almost all special interest parties couched their critiques of the Weimar system in highly moralistic terms, some explicitly advocating a return to "Christian virtue" in both public and private affairs.

These views were stated with different degrees of intensity, and emphasis varied from party to party. Yet, taken together they reflected a fundamental distaste for the basic social, economic, and political foundations of the Weimar Republic. Special interest voting was, therefore, not ideologially neutral but instead represented an antisystemic protest that quickly transcended the confines of narrow interest politics. Middle-class voters before 1929 were clearly not yet ready to embrace the radical solutions proposed by the NSDAP, but in turning to special interest alternatives, they displayed a strong affinity with the sociopolitical appeal that the Nazis would perfect in the following years of economic crisis. Catalyzed by the inflation and mobilized in opposition to the harsh stabilization which followed, a large and steadily expanding percentage of the middle-class electorate rejected the traditional parties of the bourgeois center and right after 1924, setting in motion an electoral realignment that would end with the National Socialist triumphs of 1930 and 1932.[1]

Although the NSDAP succeeded in exploiting the widespread disaffection with the traditional liberal and conservative options, support for the party was unevenly distributed among the different groups of the middle-class electorate. Indeed, support for National Socialism varied in duration and degree and sprang from a wide variety of motives. It was, however, by no means confined to the lower middle class or to socially marginal de-classés. The nucleus of the NSDAP's following was formed by the small farmers, shopkeepers, and independent artisans of the old middle class, who constituted the most stable and consistent components of the National Socialist constituency between 1924 and 1932. It was among these groups that the fear of social and economic displacement associated with the emergence of modern industrial society was most pronounced, and it was among these groups that the NSDAP's corporatist, anti-Marxist, and anticapitalist slogans struck their most responsive chord. Nazi sympathies within the old middle class certainly intensified and broadened after the onset of the depression, but the persistence of those sympathies even in the period of relative prosperity between 1924 and 1928 strongly suggests that this support did not represent a spasmodic reaction to immediate economic difficulties but expressed a congenital dissatisfaction with long-term trends in German economic and social life.

In periods of economic crisis this hard core of Nazi electoral support was augmented by protest voters from the new middle class and the *Rentnermittelstand*, both of which had been battered by the economic traumas of the era. Living on proletarian incomes and threatened with the imminent prospect of unemployment, some white-collar employees turned to National Socialism after 1928 as did pensioners, rentiers, and others who had seen their savings, investments, and retirement benefits dissolve. Yet, the Nazi/white-collar relationship remained far weaker than traditionally assumed, even after the onset of the depression, and *Rentner* support for the party was as shallow as it was broad. The depression simply did not produce the oft-asserted concentration of support for the NSDAP within the socially heterogeneous *Angestelltenschaft*, and the Nazi-*Rentner* relationship was clearly crisis-related, waning again at the close of 1932 as it had between 1924 and 1930.

Although National Socialist sympathies among lower-middle-class white-collar employees were less developed than expected, the NSDAP found a surprisingly large following in more established social circles. By 1932 the party had won considerable support among the upper middle-class student bodies of the universities, among civil servants, even in the middle and upper grades, and in affluent electoral districts of Berlin, Hamburg, and other cities.[2] Motivations were myriad, including fear of the Marxist left, frustrated career ambitions, and resentment at the erosion of social prestige and professional security. Yet, while sizable elements of these groups undoubtedly felt their positions or prospects challenged during the Weimar era, they cannot be described as uneducated, economically devastated, or socially marginal. They belonged, in fact, to the established elites of German society.

Just as the Nazis were winning support from elements of both the upper- and lower-middle classes, they also secured a significant constituency within the blue-collar working class. Usually ignored or dismissed as unimportant, the NSDAP's prominent solicitation of a working-class following and its success in the endeavor, were exceptional in the context of German electoral politics. Aside from the confessionally oriented Zentrum, the NSDAP was alone among the non-Marxist parties in its efforts to establish an electorate within the blue-collar population. Even after 1928, the party refused to concede the blue-collar electorate to the left and continued to invest a surprising amount of energy to win working-class voters. Nor were those efforts—which led the traditional bourgeois parties to denounce the Nazis as Bolsheviks—without effect. Despite hostility and indifference from the organized industrial *Arbeiterschaft*, the party's appeal found considerable resonance among that sizable body of workers in handicrafts and small-scale manufacturing. These workers were usually employed in small shops or in government enterprises and were rarely integrated into either the organized working class or the entrepreneurial *Mittelstand*. Their support was loudly trumpeted in the Nazi press and was extremely important in establishing the public image the Nazis sought to project, allowing them to maintain, with some degree of credibility, that they had succeeded in bridging the great social divide of German electoral politics.

The generational and sexual composition of the Nazi constituency was also broader than traditionally assumed. Usually treated as the party of youth, the NSDAP, in fact, found its greatest electoral support among groups composed of older voters. The party effectively pursued the vote of the *Rentnermittelstand*, 53 percent of whom were over sixty years of age. Similarly, less than 10 percent of the shopkeepers, self-employed artisans, and other entrepreneurs in the old middle class were under thirty. In addition, the male-dominated NSDAP attracted a steadily increasing percentage of women voters after 1928. In the final elections of the Weimar era, women appear to have surpassed men in the Nazi electorate.

By 1932 the NSDAP could, therefore, approach the German electorate claiming the coveted mantle of a *Volkspartei*. Its constituency was certainly broader than that of the traditional bourgeois parties or of the Marxist left. Yet, even after the NSDAP's dramatic surge between 1929 and 1932, the limits of its expansion were clearly defined by the two most prominent predictors of German electoral behavior, class and religion. Although the Nazis had won adherents within the blue-collar electorate, they proved unable to establish a significant foothold within the industrial working class. Among workers in the major industrial sectors, electoral sympathies continued to be divided chiefly between the SPD and KPD. Even as unemployment soared after 1928, working-class radicalism found political expression in a Communist vote, not in support for National Socialism. The fragmentation of political loyalties that had increasingly splintered the middle-class electorate after 1924 did not infect the constituencies of the Marxist left. While the liberal, conservative, and special interest parties virtually collapsed between 1930 and 1932, the Marxist parties maintained a remarkably strong and stable electoral base. Despite their efforts to cultivate a working-class constituency, the Nazis were confronted by a solid bloc of blue-collar support for the Marxist left that showed no signs of disintegration even at the apex of Nazi electoral fortunes.

The NSDAP also encountered a major obstacle to its ambitions in the Catholic population. Although the party won an increasing percentage of the Catholic vote after 1928, its electoral base remained far smaller in Catholic Germany than in Protestant areas. Catholic support for National Socialism was by and large concentrated in the same occupational and social groups that formed the mainstays of the party's constituency in Protestant areas, but the NSDAP was never able to undermine the solid foundation of Catholic support for the Zentrum. Backed by the Church, the Zentrum, like the Marxist parties, offered its followers a well-defined belief system vigorously reinforced by an extensive network of political, social, and cultural organizations. Although a vote for the Zentrum after 1930 was hardly an enthusiastic endorsement of the Weimar system, the strong Catholic support for the party continued to impose a solid barrier to the potential expansion of the National Socialist constituency.[3]

Given these limitations to the appeal of National Socialism, what does the composition of the Nazi constituency reveal about the social foundations of fascism in Germany? First, the most consistent electoral support for the party was concentrated in those social and occupational groups that harbored the greatest reservations about the development of modern industrial society and that expressed, through their organizations, socially exclusive, corporatist views of their socioeconomic position. By the same token, its appeal was weakest in that segment of the population most prominently identified with modern industrial society, the industrial working class. Even within the new middle class, where electoral sympathies were scattered across the political spectrum, support for National Socialism was concentrated to a surprising extent in the traditionally conservative civil service. Although not directly affected by industrial change, bitterness over the erosion of the *Berufsbeamtentum*'s elevated social and political status under the republican regime was endemic in all ranks of the civil service, and Nazi campaign literature assiduously cultivated precisely that sense of elitist resentment.

The Nazi appeal to women also carried powerful antimodernist overtones. With its enthusiastic espousal of *Kinder, Küche, und Kirche*, National Socialist literature addressed to women voters represented a sharp reaction to the feminist movement and to the introduction of women into the labor force. The much-heralded emancipation of women, the Nazis fiercely contended, had simply produced greater economic exploitation of both sexes while at the same time denigrating traditional feminine roles in the home and family.

Nazi antimodernism was, therefore, not a simple assault on modern technology or a promise to dismantle one of the world's most advanced industrial economies and return to a romanticized agrarian past. It was instead a fundamental rejection of the social and political implications of modernization, a rejection that found its most vivid expression in the NSDAP's visceral attacks on both Marxist socialism and liberal capitalism. It was in the party's relentless offensive against these manifestations of modern political and economic life that the NSDAP's anti-Semitism was most prominently displayed before 1933. While Rosenberg and other party theorists continued to develop—and publish—the radical racial doctrine that formed the true core of National Socialist ideology, the party's day-to-day political literature tended to emphasize a more familiar form of social and economic anti-Semitism. This strategy of linking Jews with both "supercapitalism" and bolshevism proved doubly effective for the Nazis. On the one hand, it allowed the NSDAP to exploit an already deeply engrained form of anti-Semitic sentiment in German political culture during a period of protracted economic distress; on the other, it lulled even those parties that took public stands against the NSDAP's obsession with "the Jewish question" into the mistaken assumption that it was merely another ephemeral manifestation of that traditional anti-Semitism which had surfaced periodically in the German party system since 1890. "Like a fire made of straw," the DDP hopefully and mistakenly asserted, "it burns brightly and then dies out."[4]

Antimodernism was not, however, the only cohesive factor in the appeal of German fascism, and those voters attracted to the movement were not necessarily the "losers of the modernization process." Except within the old middle class, where such antimodernist sentiments were widespread, electoral support for the NSDAP followed a pristine pattern of protest voting, surging in periods of economic distress, subsiding upon the return of "normal" times. While long-standing discontent with the social and economic evolution of modern Germany rendered elements of the *Mittelstand* particularly receptive to the antimodernist appeal of National Socialism, economic crisis in 1923–24 and between 1929 and 1933 proved the necessary catalyst for Nazi success at the polls.

Drawn from the *Rentnermittelstand*, the civil service, the *Angestelltenschaft*, and marginal elements of the working class, this crisis-related support represented a protest against a political system that had produced a seemingly endless series of social and economic shocks. Each of the elections of the Weimar era, and particularly those after 1928, ultimately assumed the character of a referendum on the system itself, a system identified above all with Social Democracy, even when the SPD was not represented in the government, and, to a lesser extent, with a set of powerful, organized interests. The NSDAP was able to exploit this increasingly widespread dissatisfaction with the system after 1928 by skillfully and often brutally demonstrating its militant anti-Marxism and by emphasizing its independence from the major industrial and agricultural interests. Whether in addresses to farmers, shopkeepers, or workers, the party's assault on Social Democracy and communism was by far the most conspicuous and consistent aspect of Nazi electoral literature. The other bourgeois parties had, of course, also established their anti-Marxist credentials, but unlike the DVP and DNVP, the Nazis were not associated with either big business or big agriculture, and unlike the DDP and Zentrum, they were not tainted by collaboration with the Social Democrats. Moreover, because the NSDAP was not saddled with government responsibility before 1933, the party could make extravagant and often blatantly contradictory appeals to mutually hostile groups without having to reconcile those promises.[5] This freedom from government responsibility and from association with discredited special interests allowed the Nazis to spurn the traditional practices of *Interessenpolitik*, while appealing to an unusually broad spectrum of social and occupational groups. Using these advantages, the NSDAP by 1932 had become a unique phenomenon in German electoral politics, a catchall party of protest, whose constituents, while drawn primarily from the middle-class electorate, were united above all by a profound contempt for the existing political and economic system.

Yet, even at the height of its popularity at the polls, the NSDAP's position as a people's party was tenuous at best. If the party's support was a mile wide, it was at critical points an inch deep. The NSDAP had managed to build a remarkably diverse constituency, overcoming regional divisions, linking town and country, spanning the social divides, and shrinking the gap between confessions. Yet, the basis of that extraordinary electoral alliance was dissatisfaction, resentment, and fear. As a result, the Nazi constituency, even at the pinnacle of the party's electoral popularity, remained highly unstable. Indeed, the fragmentation of the NSDAP's volatile electorate was already underway in November 1932. Whether the Nazis would have been able to maintain their appeal under improving economic conditions remains, of course, a moot question, but for a party of protest such continued success is doubtful. Even in the flush of their victories in 1932, Nazi leaders were aware of the party's vulnerability. "Something has to happen now," Goebbels noted in his diary following the NSDAP's victory in Prussia during April. "We have to come to power in the near future or we will win ourselves to death in these elections."[6] It therefore remains one of history's most tragic ironies that at precisely the moment when the party's electoral support had begun to falter, Hitler was installed as chancellor by representatives of those traditional elites who had done so much to undermine the parliamentary system in Germany and who still believed that the National Socialist movement could be safely harnessed for their reactionary objectives.

Appendix I
Methodology

The statistical procedures employed in this study are easily explained and require no previous knowledge of statistics. As indicated in the introduction, the greatest obstacle encountered by a researcher interested in electoral behavior in the age before polling became common is the lack of survey data. The researcher cannot ask voters for whom they cast their ballots and why. Only aggregate figures are available and, therefore, all analyses of historical voting are ecological in nature, whether they take the form of neighborhood case studies or are based on a broad national sample. Although a number of procedures have been suggested over the years to cope with the "ecological problem," there is no completely satisfactory way of solving it. Increasingly, however, researchers have settled on some form of regression analysis as the most effective means of examining a large number of social, confessional, and political variables in a large sample of electoral units.[1]

Traditionally historians have used visual comparisons to examine voting behavior in the prepolling era, noting, for example, that as the percentage of Catholics increased across a particular sample, the National Socialist vote fell. This technique allowed researchers to determine rather obvious trends, but its limits were quickly reached.[2] What if one were interested in the interaction of several social and confessional variables and their impact on voting behavior? What if one wished to measure more precisely the strength of a relationship, isolating the impact of a particular variable—the percentage of white-collar employees in a given sample, for instance—on Nazi voting in a complex social environment. Although religiously homogeneous neighborhoods or communities are relatively easy to locate, occupationally or socially homogeneous electoral units are not. Moreover, individuals in such homogeneous environments may behave quite differently from their counterparts in the mixed society at large. As expected, the researcher interested in white-collar employees quickly discovers that no clearly homogeneous white-collar neighborhoods or towns exist. Instead, each community is composed of a variety of occupational groups, economic sectors, religious confessions, and displays a different combination of other demographic features. In this common situation, visual comparisons are virtually useless. This is, however, precisely the problem for which multivariate regression analysis is designed.

Regression analysis provides a measure of the strength of the relationship between two or more variables, the so-called R^2 indicating the amount of change in one variable explained by the change in another. Thus, an R^2 of .30 would mean that 30 percent of the variance in variable A (the Nazi vote, for example) is accounted for by the change in variable *B* (the percentage of white-collar employees in a *Gemeinde*). Multiple regression is particularly valuable when a great many variables are involved and the researcher wishes to determine the incremental and cumulative impact of a set of variables on another variable.

Unstandardized regression coefficients, however, are of particular utility in ecological analysis, since they indicate the exact amount of change to be expected in one variable for every unit of change in another, while the effects of a third or fourth or fifth are controlled. Using multivariate techniques, an equation is constructed in which all relevant independent variables—those variables that are related to either the independent variable in question (white-collar employees, in this case) or the dependent variable (the Nazi vote)—are included. The values generated by this equation are coefficients that reveal the influence of each of these independent or "explanatory" variables on the Nazi vote, while simultaneously controlling statistically for the impact of the others. Thus, the researcher can determine the influence of the white-collar variable on the Nazi vote, while controlling for the influence of the blue-collar, self-employed, civil service, *Rentner*, Protestant, and Catholic variables. The coefficients may be positive or negative, indicating the exact amount of change to be expected in the Nazi vote for every unit of change in the white-collar variable, when the effects of the other independent variables are controlled. If, for example, the coefficient for the relationship just described is .60, it would be interpreted to mean that as the percentage of white-collar employees increases (by 10 percent) across the sample of roughly five hundred communities and counties, the Nazi vote could be expected to rise by 6 percent, when the Catholic, blue-collar, and other variables are held constant at their statistical mean. This is what is meant by the predictive power of the white-collar variable. Unless otherwise stated, the figures found in the tables of this study are such unstandardized regression coefficients.

Leaving aside possible sampling or measuring errors, the effectiveness of such coefficients depends on the inclusion of all relevant variables in the equation. For this reason, a wide range of explanatory or independent variables should be employed in the regression equation. Thus, as in the example above, variables expressing occupation, religion, economic sector, and urbanization have been used in the regression equations. That list is, of course, hardly as extensive as one would like. Education, income, age, and sex are all factors of obvious importance in electoral behavior and should be taken into consideration. Comparable figures on education, however, are not available for the *Gemeinden* and *Kreise* used in the sample, and data on income are both incomplete and of a very indirect nature. Income and withholding-tax figures in many of the electoral units employed here are available for 1928 and 1932 and were coded for inclusion in the analysis. In every instance, however, they produced insignificant and statistically unreliable results. Similarly, figures on age and sex, though available in 1925 and 1933, do not vary sufficiently across the sample to permit statistically significant measurement of their impact. The percentage of women or persons between twenty and thirty years of age in one community tends to be quite similar to that in all others, and without significant variance, the influence of these variables cannot be adequately evaluated. Figures on both age and sex were, nonetheless, coded and included in equations, but, as in the case of income, produced a statistically insignificant impact on the coefficients. Fortunately, a number of Weimar localities actually tabulated returns by sex, and although the resulting figures do not represent a valid statistical sample, they—uniquely for the Weimar era—are not ecological in nature and they do provide a variety of regional, religious, and urban-rural contrasts that are quite useful. For these reasons, they have been preferred to the less reliable coefficients produced by the corresponding demographic variables in this study.

The statistical validity of the coefficients generated by regression analysis can also be tested by an examination of standard errors. In established statistical analysis, convention rules that coefficients, in order to be statistically reliable, must be significant at the .05 level. Baldly stated, this means that there must be less than one chance in twenty that the coefficients produced by the equations drafted are the result of random or unconsidered factors. No coefficients, on which arguments in this study are based, exceed that level; most fall well below it.

As noted above, these procedures are well-established in electoral sociology, though they have never been applied to the campaigns of the Weimar era. Even in those instances when similar techniques—correlation analysis for example—have been used, they have concentrated on a particular region or a particular election. More significantly, correlations between socioeconomic variables and voting behavior are determined in the existing studies on the basis of the broad economic categories (*Wirtschaftsabteilungen*) employed by the Reich Statistical Bureau.[3] Thus when examining the Reichstag election of July 1932, Rudolph Heberle presents correlations between Marxist voting and workers employed in "Industry and Handicrafts," Wirtschaftsabteilung-B of the 1925 census. While this may produce potentially significant relationships, far more informative results can be attained if instead of the six major economic categories, the twenty-three economic groups (*Wirtschaftsgruppen*) of which they are comprised[4] are taken as the basic units of analysis. For if only the category "Industry and Handicrafts" is used to calculate correlations or regressions, miners and steel workers are lumped indiscriminately together with plumbers and bakers, carpenters and railroad workers. Indeed, the census classification contains a wide range of occupational endeavors in which the scale, organization, and modes of production are quite different. Only by subdividing this amorphous economic category into more homogeneous groups on the basis of the twenty-three *Wirtschaftsgruppen* can the social structure emerge. In those branches characterized by large plants and mass production, the percentage of self-employed proprietors is disproportionately low, while the percentage of blue-collar workers is unusually high. In those branches dominated by artisan or small-scale production, however, these relationships are reversed. Indeed, in such branches the number of self-employed proprietors and "assisting family members" vastly exceeds the average for the economy as a whole.[5]

In eight branches of the Industry and Handicrafts classification, the ratio of *Arbeitnehmer* (blue- and white-collar employees) to self-employed exceeds ten to one and these have, therefore, been selected to form two new categories in this study. Mining, industries of stone and earth, and iron, steel, and metal production have been grouped together to form a new category designated as "Mining and Heavy Industry," while machine and automobile production, chemical production, the paper industry, rubber and asbestos production, and the public utilities have been placed under the simple label of "Industry." The social composition of these new sectors is reflected in Table A.I.1

A second set of economic branches contained in *Wirtschaftsabteilung*-B does not, however, conform to the industrial pattern depicted above. These branches, in which the ratio of employees to entrepreneurs was less than ten to one are: (1) woodworking, (2) production of musical instruments, (3) food production and processing, (4) clothing production, and (5) the construction trades.[6] The Subcommittee for Trade, Industry, Commerce and Handicrafts disclosed in 1930 that 94 percent of all handicrafts establishments and 80 percent of all employed artisans were contained in those branches.[7] The social structure of these branches, which together are designated as Handicrafts and Small-Scale Manufacturing in this study, is presented in Table A.I.2.

Finally, the official Industry and Handicrafts classification contains several branches in which industrial and artisan modes of production and distribution were so intertwined that their inclusion in either of the new categories proposed above is highly problematic. They are: (1) production of iron, steel, and metalwares; (2) electrotechnical and precision instruments production; (3) textile production; and (4) leather and linoleum production. The difficulties presented by these branches are best illustrated by the iron, steel, and metalwares group, in which plumbers and locksmiths are classified together with industrial metalworkers. Thus, in communities with little heavy metal industry, the artisan element would dominate, whereas in other communities the presence of a large metal-producing or processing plant would lend the sector a distinctly industrial character. In this study, each of these branches has been treated on a community to community basis, their inclusion in the industrial or handicrafts categories being determined by the ten-to-one ratio of *Arbeitnehmer* to entrepreneurs. The social composition of these important swing branches is presented in Table A.I.3.

This reclassification of economic sectors does not, of course, eliminate potential sources of error. Each new category contains some anomalous elements that cannot be isolated and removed. However, by restructuring the original census classifications along the lines charted above, economic sectors can be attained that are both more precise and more homogeneous, thus permitting a more differentiated analysis of the socioelectoral dynamics of Weimar voting.

Unlike the economic categories of the census, the occupational classifications (*Stellung im Beruf*) do not require extensive reorganization. The *Selbständige* classification consists of four subgroups: (1) self-employed proprietors (*Eigentümer*); (2) tenants (*Pächter*), a group of very little significance outside the agricultural sector; (3) executives (*Administratoren, Direktoren, Geschäftsführer, leitende Beamte und sonstige Betriebsleiter*); and (4) cottagers (*Hausgewerbetreibende und Heimarbeiter*). The first of these subgroups, comprised of shopkeep-

Table A.I.1. The Social Structure of the Industrial Sectors (by percentage)

| | Mining and Heavy Industry | | |
	Self-Employed	White Collar	Blue Collar
Mining	0.3	7.0	92.7
Earth and stone	5.0	7.6	87.4
Metal production	1.0	13.4	85.6

| | Industry | | |
	Self-Employed	White-Collar	Blue Collar
Machine	2.9	18.0	79.1
Chemical	3.9	26.5	69.5
Paper	7.8	12.4	79.8
Rubber	2.5	19.5	78.0
Utilities	1.6	25.9	72.5

SOURCE: *Das deutsche Handwerk*, pp. 54, 69, 125, 146, 155, and 167.

Table A.I.2. The Social Structure of the Handicrafts and Small-Scale Manufacturing Sector (by percentage)

	Self-Employed	White Collar	Blue Collar
Construction	13.8	0.3	78.2
Woodworking	21.0	6.5	72.5
Musical instruments	21.4	10.1	68.5
Food production	28.4	12.2	59.4
Clothing	40.9	5.6	53.5

ers, wholesale merchants, independent artisans, and other entrepreneurs represented 83 percent of all "independents" in the Weimar Republic. Of these, 80 percent were male, and less than 10 percent were under thirty years of age. The overwhelming majority were active in handicrafts and commerce.[8]

Ranking second in numerical significance in 1925 were the cottagers, remnants

Table A.I.3. The Social Structure of the Swing Branches (by percentage)

	Self-Employed	White Collar	Blue Collar
Metalwares	14.9	8.9	76.2
Electrotechnical	9.1	19.6	71.3
Textiles	11.1	10.4	78.5
Leather	29.0	9.6	70.4

SOURCE: *Statistik des Deutschen Reichs*, 408:123, 130–32.

of the preindustrial "putting-out system." Concentrated primarily in textile and clothing production, cottagers represented 8 percent of the nonagricultural independents in the Weimar era. Moreover, 69 percent of all those independents involved in cottage industry in 1925 were women. Thus, while female entrepreneurs composed 63 percent of all independents in textile production, 90 percent of them were cottagers. Although technically entrepreneurs, the socioeconomic position of cottagers was more closely related to that of the wage-earning populace than of the self-employed proprietors of the first group.[9]

Just the opposite was true of the executives, administrators, and high-ranking civil servants of the third subgroup. While formally *Arbeitnehmer*, these officials of private corporations and government agencies commanded the social prestige and often an economic position associated with independent status. Representing 7 percent of the nonagricultural independents, the executives were distributed rather evenly across the industrial and commercial sectors. By far the largest concentration (46 percent of all executives) was found in the administrative and professional services sector, where most held civil-service or military posts.[10]

The distribution of independents among the different economic sectors is found in Table A.I.4.

While these groups form the "old middle class" category used in this study, the census classification *Beamte und Angestellte* clearly reflects the sociological essence of the much-discussed "new middle class." This census group consisted of three subgroups: (1) technical personnel and specialists (*technische Angestellte und Beamte, Fachpersonal*); (2) supervisors (*Werkmeister und Aufsichtspersonal*); and (3) clerical and administrative personnel (*kaufmännische Angestellte und Verwaltungsbeamte, Büropersonal*). Technical specialists, constituting 31 percent of the nonmanual population, included teachers, military enlisted personnel, railway conductors, postmen, telegraph operators, and others. They were found most frequently in commerce, transportation, and the professional services sector. Supervisors, who comprised only 7.3 percent of the new middle class, were, for the most part, former skilled blue-collar workers now placed in charge of fellow employees. Not surprisingly, 82 percent of these white-collar employees were found in the major industrial sectors, especially in metal production. Cleri-

Table A.I.4. The Dispersion of Self-Employed Proprietors and Other Selbstständige *across the Economy (by percentage)*

	Self-Employed	All *Selbstständige*
Industry	3	4
Handicrafts	40	39
Swing branches	8	10
Commerce	37	34
Transportation	2	2
Professional services	3	5
Health services	6	5
Domestic services	1	0
	100	100

SOURCE: *Statistik des Deutschen Reichs*, 408 : 139–73.

cal personnel, representing 62.6 percent of the white-collar labor force, were certainly the most numerous *Angestellte* in 1925. The majority of these salesmen, typists, stenographers, and other office employees were active in the commercial and transportation sectors, forming the core of the German *Angestelltenschaft*. Together, these salaried employees were rather evenly dispersed among the different economic sectors. The percentages of this dispersion are as follows: industry, 13%; handicrafts, 9%, swing branches, 7%; commerce, 29%; transportation, 14%; professional services, 23%; health services, 4%; and domestic services, 1% (*Statistik des Deutschen Reichs*, 408 : 186). Although the 1925 census did not differentiate between civil servants and white-collar employees, it is estimated that those salaried personnel employed in the commercial, industrial, and handicrafts were mainly white-collar employees, whereas those in the professional services and transportation sectors were largely public officials.[11]

The self-employed entrepreneurs and salaried nonmanuals constituted the major elements of the German middle class; pensioners, rentiers, and others living on accumulated assets, investments, and rents composed the so-called *Rentnermittelstand*. Although Category G of the census, "Persons without Occupation," contained a number of socially amorphous groups, three-quarters of those included among these *berufslose Selbstanständige* were pensioners or rentiers. More than half (53 percent) were over sixty years of age, and 78 percent were women, the overwhelming majority of whom were either widowed or divorced. Together with their dependents, these *Rentner* represented approximately 12 percent of the population. Although most lived on proletarian incomes, the majority were certainly considered elements of the middle class and have, therefore, been treated in conjunction with the *Mittelstand* in this analysis.[12]

Least problematic among the occupational categories of the census is the *Arbeiter* classification. In 1925, blue-collar workers and their dependents composed approximately 45 percent of the German population. Over three-quarters of all *Arbeiter* were male, and over half (57 percent) were under thirty years of age. Although the census did not differentiate between skilled and unskilled laborers, the *Arbeiter* category was composed of three subgroups which, in a general way, express those levels of occupational rank. "Workers in characteristic occupations" and "plant artisans" correspond approximately to skilled and semiskilled workers, while the "remaining workers" clearly represent the unskilled. Although the proportion of skilled and unskilled workers varied substantially between the various branches of the industrial and handicrafts sectors, skilled laborers tended to be most heavily concentrated in the major artisan and swing branches, whereas unskilled workers were found most frequently in the industrial sectors.[13] The distribution of blue-collar workers by percentage among the different economic sectors is as follows: industry, 32%; handicrafts, 32%; swing branches, 19%; commerce, 6%; transportation, 6%; professional services, 1%; health services, 2%; and domestic services, 2% (*Statistik des Deutschen Reichs*, 402:106–9).

These major categories, restructured from the 1925 census, constitute the fundamental social and economic variables employed in the statistical analysis of Weimar voting found in this study. Despite some anomalies and inconsistencies in the census data, these structural variables, when supplemented by figures on religious affiliation, on income, savings, and unemployment do provide a more accurate and differentiated picture of the major social characteristics and economic trends of the Weimar era than those traditionally employed in electoral analyses of the period.

The sample from which all inferences are drawn in this study is also far larger and more diverse, both geographically and socially, than samples found in the existing literature. The sample is composed of 212 Gemeinden—towns and cities—drawn from every electoral district in Germany ranging in size from just over six thousand inhabitants to over four million. More specifically, the sample includes every German town of over twenty thousand inhabitants and all smaller Gemeinden for which electoral and economic data are available for the entire Weimar period. Only those towns that underwent significant population changes owing to incorporations or other boundary adjustments have been eliminated from the sample. Along with this largely urban sample, 266 rural counties have been included in the study. These are counties in which no village exceeded ten thousand in population. Most contained only one sizable village, almost half being without a community of over five thousand inhabitants. Again, only those counties that experienced significant redistricting have been deleted from the sample. Together the towns and communities of the sample contain over half the electorate of the Weimar Republic.

Appendix II
Summary Tables

The summary tables presented in this appendix reflect the cumulative explanatory power of the major structural variables employed in this study. As the figures for the elections of 1924–28 reveal, the National Socialist vote in the predepression era lacked a clearly discernible demographic profile. The party's constituency was small and displayed a considerable social and religious diversity. Ironically, it may have been in this period, when the party's organization was hardly national in scope, its strength varying tremendously from region to region—indeed, from town to town—that local, organizational, and personality factors had their most pronounced impact on Nazi electoral performance. With the onset of the depression, the relationship between the major structural variables and the National Socialist vote grows steadily stronger. Although still influenced by a wide variety of socio-occupational variables, the Nazi vote after 1928 acquires clearly defined structural contours. By July 1932, the apex of Nazi electoral fortunes, the major structural variables employed here account for over 60 percent of the variance of the party's vote in the urban sample, over 70 percent in the rural.

The format of Table A.II.2 is notably less occupationally differentiated than that of Table A.II.1. This is a consequence of the far greater structural uniformity within the rural counties examined than in the urban units of the study. Virtually no counties in the rural sample possessed significant numbers of miners, industrial workers, white-collar employees, or even civil servants. The mean for the new middle class in the rural sample is 6 percent, compared to 22 percent in the urban areas. Breakdown by occupational sector would, therefore, produce occupational categories too small for reliable statistical analysis. The occupational structure of the rural counties was dominated by agricultural and artisanal proprietors, "assisting family members," and agricultural and artisanal workers. The variables of Table A.II.2 reflect that more traditional configuration.

*Table A.II.1. National Socialist Vote and Major Structural Variables,
1924–1932, Urban Sample (N=212)*

	1924a	1924b	1928	1930	1932a	1932b
OMC-Hndcrf	.672	.473	.291	.883	.402	.387
OMC-Comm	2.01	.538	1.06	1.09	.568	.718
Rentner	.662	.200	.221	.449	.474	.509
NMC-Prof Srv	.394	.164*	.146*	.156	.166	.122
NMC-Trans	.238*	.117*	.160*	.236	.366	.593
NMC-Comm	−1.23	−.557	−.356	−.822	−.158	−.372
NMC-Ind	.914	.359	.723	.636	.902	1.25
BC-Ind	.149*	−.183	−.107*	−.610	−.142	−.131
BC-Min	.101*	−.282	.120	−.674	−.181	−.850
BC-Hndcrf	.512	.199	.210	.182	.125	.195
Cath	.593	.399	.271	.538	.364	.368
Prot	.592	.421	.261	.625	.595	.563
Pop	.269	.101	−.790	−.625	−.163	−.611
R^2	22%	17%	26%	28%	60%	51%

NOTE: The figures are unstandardized regression coefficients, controlling for the effects of all variables in the equation.

* These coefficients are not significant at the .05 level.

Table A.II.2. *National Socialist Vote and Major Structural Variables,*
1924–1932, Rural Sample (N=246)

	1924a	1924b	1928	1930	1932a	1932b
OMC	.112*	.523	.707	.761	.518	.312
Rentner	.672	.161	.182	.112*	−.468	.256
WC	−.716	−.340	−.145	−.179	−1.00	−1.18
CS	−.822	−.102*	.229	.381*	.123*	.802*
BC	.707	.128*	.127	−.382	−.139	.161
Prot	−.533	−.103	−.959	.618	.615	.605
Cath	−.580	−.403	−.234	−.140	−.333	−.289
Farm size	.748	.138*	−.261	−.375	−.410	−.398
R^2	36%	25%	34%	52%	71%	64%

NOTE: The figures are unstandardized regression coefficients, controlling for the effect of all variables in the equation.

* These coefficients are not significant at the .05 level.

Appendix III
Weimar Electoral Leaflets

"Handwerker, Kaufleute, Gewerbetreibende!" = "Artisans, Merchants, Shopkeepers!" (DNVP leaflet, 1924)

"Handwerker! Gewerbetreibende! Kaufleute!" = "Artisans! Shopkeepers! Merchants!" (BVP leaflet, 1928)

Alle Bauern wählen „Schwarz-Weiß-Rot"!

Deutschbewußte Führung! Alle Stimmen des Landvolkes für „Schwarz-Weiß-Rot"!

„Schwarz-Weiß-Rot" ist deutschnational!

Darum wählt

deutschnational!

"Alle Bauern wählen 'Schwarz-Weiss-Rot'!" = "All Peasants vote 'Black-White-Red'!" (DNVP leaflet, 1924)

An die Beamten und Angestellten Groß-Hamburgs!

Die Deutsche Staatspartei ist die einzige Partei, die sich vorbehaltlos für das Berufsbeamtentum einsetzt.

Liste 8
die Deutsche Staatspartei.

Dr. Gustav Stolper, Andreas Lorenzen, Paul Maack.

"An die Beamten und Angestellten Gross-Hamburgs!" = "To the Civil Servants and White Collar Employees of Greater Hamburg!" (DDP/DSP leaflet, 1932)

Wen wählt der Beamte am 20. Mai?

Zentrum?

Deutsche Volkspartei

die Demokraten?

die Sozialdemokraten?

Liste 4 Deutsche Volkspartei **Liste 4**

"Wen wählt der Beamte am 20. Mai?" = "Who is the Civil Servant voting for on May 20?" (DVP leaflet, 1924)

Beamte!

für die Aufrechterhaltung des Berufsbeamtentums,

für die Reinigung des Beamtenkörpers von ungeeigneten und unwürdigen Elementen,

für eine angemessene Besoldung,

für den Schutz der verfassungsmäßig gesicherten Rechte,

für zeitgemäße Reform des Beamtenrechts.

Deshalb, Beamte, her zur Fahne Hugenbergs, hinein in die

Deutschnationale Volkspartei!

Wählt am 31. Juli

Liste 5, Deutschnational!

"Beamte!" = "Civil Servants!" (DNVP leaflet, 1932)

Rentner, Rentnerinnen.

Jahre bitter Not, schwerer Enttäuschungen liegen hinter euch, und noch seht ihr nicht, ob und wann nachhaltige Hilfe kommt.

Voller Zweifel steht ihr bei den Wahlen den Parteien gegenüber und fragt euch, ob ihr noch einer vertrauen dürft, daß ihr euch helfe im Kampf um das nackte Leben. Einer geworben, — wer wollte das nicht verstehen — seht ihr in erster Linie, was nicht erreicht wurde.

Denkt aber zurück, wie es um euch in der Inflationszeit und noch vor einigen Jahren stand, als der letzte Reichstag zusammentrat. Dann werdet ihr erkennen, daß die Bemühungen im Reichstag nicht ganz vergebens waren, daß geringe Fortschritte gemacht wurden.

Gewiß, noch immer habt ihr mit Not und Elend als Folge des Berliner Diktats zu kämpfen, noch lange nicht ist das Ziel erreicht.

Laßt euch nicht betören

von den Versprechungen kleiner Splitterparteien, die Hoffnungen zu erwecken verstehen, daß durch ihren Eintritt in den Reichstag ein Umschwung erfolgen werde.

Gebt darum eure Stimme diesmal geschlossen der Deutschen Volkspartei.

alle Kapitalrentner wählen am Wahltage die

Deutsche Volkspartei

Liste Nr. 4

"Rentner, Rentnerinnen" = "Male and Female Pensioners" (DVP leaflet, 1928)

Hypothekengläubiger, Sparer, Rentner!

Wie war der Hergang?

Ein neuer Vorstoß.

Die Arbeiten des Ausschusses.

Ein neuer Antrag Düringer.

Die Haltung der Regierung.

Unberechtigte Angriffe.

Was daraus zu lernen ist!

An alle Interessenten!

wählen alle Sparer und Hypothekengläubiger auch diesmal die bewährten Vertreter der Deutschen Volkspartei.

Wählt Liste 5

"Hypothekengläubiger, Sparer, Rentner!" = "Mortgagees, Savers, Pensioners" (DVP leaflet, 1924)

Kleinrentner!
Hypothekengläubiger!
Sparkasseneinleger!

"Kleinrentner! Hypothekengläubiger! Sparkasseneinleger!" = "Small Pensioners! Mortgagees! Savings Depositors!" (DNVP leaflet, 1924)

Adolf Hitler
und
der Arbeiter!

"Adolf Hitler und der Arbeiter!" = "Adolf Hitler and the Worker!" (NSDAP leaflet, 1932)

Seine Ziele

in sozialistischer Gemeinschaft
untereinander verbunden fühlt.

Wiedererweckung des

nationalen Stolzes auf die eigene Bedeutung
als Volk gegenüber dem Nationalismus der anderen Völker.

**6 Millionen Arbeitslose,
Hunger und Elend sind das Ergebnis!**

Adolf Hitler

der, aus diesem Begriff rüstend, in hartem Ringen die nationalsozialistische Bewegung zur heutigen Größe führte, um mit ihr für das deutsche Volk Freiheit und für jeden einzelnen dieses Volkes Brot zu erkämpfen.

Nationalsozialistische Deutsche Arbeiterpartei
(Hitlerbewegung)

Liste 1

Der meint es ehrlich,
der kämpft aus tiefster Ueberzeugung für uns
und unser Schicksal

(continued) "Adolf Hitler und der Arbeiter!" = "Adolf Hitler and the Worker!" (NSDAP leaflet, 1932)

Frauen und Mütter!

Soll alles anders werden?
Ihr könnt es herbeiführen!

LISTE 2

Wieso kam das?

sechs Millionen Menschen aufs Pflaster geworfen.

das Ende des Kapitalismus, das Ende der Not

wurden die Nazis zu Rettern der Reichen,
zu Schützern der Barone und Kapitalisten.

die Rüstungsfreiheit.

auf den Kasernenhof stellen, sie zum nächsten Krieg drillen,
das kann und will man wieder!

Wird da nicht euer Gewissen aufgerüttelt?

Klagt nicht, sondern handelt!

Am 6. November habt ihr zu wählen!

Wendet euch ab

von den bürgerlichen Parteien, die Papen stützen,
von den Nazis, die ihn in den Sattel gehoben haben,
von den Kommunisten, die den Hauptkampf nicht gegen die Reaktion, sondern gegen
die Sozialdemokratie und damit gegen die Interessen der Arbeiterschaft führen.

Entscheidet euch

gegen Ungerechtigkeit, kapitalistische Ausbeutung und Not, für den Aufbau einer sozialistischen
Gesellschaft.

Ihr wollt Freiheit, Wohlfahrt und Frieden!

Deshalb kämpft aufrecht im Zeichen der drei Pfeile und gebt am 6. November eure Stimme
der einzigen Partei, die unbeirrt für diese Ziele eintritt, der

Sozialdemokratie

Liste 2

"Frauen und Mütter!" = "Women and Mothers!" (SPD leaflet, 1932)

Notes

Introduction

1. Karl Dietrich Bracher, *Die Deutsche Diktatur*, pp. 166–67.

2. This theme is widely developed in the literature. Among the more prominent examples are: Theodor Geiger, "Panik im Mittelstand," pp 637ff.; Harold D. Lasswell, "The Psychology of Hitlerism," p. 374; Franz Neumann, *Behemoth. The Structure and Practice of National Socialism 1933–1944*, p. 411; Hans Rudolf Roeske, *Faschismus: Soziale Herkunft und Soziale Funktion* p. 54; Svend Ranulf, *Moral Indignation and Middle Class Psychology*, pp. 8–9. Marxist examinations of fascism have traditionally shown little inclination to investigate the popular bases of the NSDAP, preferring instead structural analyses of interest conflict in the capitalist system. Yet, while rejecting the conceptual framework of the major bourgeois interpretations, Marxist analysts, too, have isolated the social locus of Nazi support in the lower middle class. See, for example, Manfred Clemenz, *Gesellschaftliche Ursprünge des Faschismus*, p. 96; and David Abraham, *The Collapse of the Weimar Republic*, p. 324.

3. William Kornhauser, *The Politics of Mass Society*, p. 180.

4. Hannah Arendt, *The Origins of Totalitarianism*, p. 323.

5. Seymour Martin Lipset, "Fascism—Left, Right, and Center." See also Alexander Weber, "Soziale Merkmale der NSDAP-Wähler. Eine Zusammenfassung bisheriger empirischen Untersuchungen und eine Analyse in den Gemeinden der Länder Baden und Hessen" and Sammuel A. Pratt, "The Social Bases of Nazism and Communism in Urban Germany. A Correlation Study of the July 31, 1932, Reichstag Election in Germany."

6. Proceeding chronologically, see David A. Hackett, "The Nazi Party in the Reichstag Election of 1930"; Loren K. Waldman, "Models of Mass Movements—The Case of the Nazis"; Dee Richard Wernette, "Political Violence and German Elections: 1930 and July 1932"; James P. Madden, "The Social Composition of the Nazi Party, 1919–1930"; Thomas Childers, "The Social Bases of Electoral Politics in Urban Germany, 1919–1933"; Childers, "The Social Bases of the National Socialist Vote"; Childers, "National Socialism and the New Middle Class"; and finally, Richard F. Hamilton, *Who Voted for Hitler?* An excellent critical summary of much of this literature is found in Jürgen W. Falter, "Wer verhalf der NSDAP zum Sieg?"

7. Hackett, for example, deals only with the 1930 election, Wernette with the 1930 and 1932 campaigns. Hamilton's more recent work analyzes only the July

elections of 1932, with cursory descriptions of previous elections. The older literature is equally limited chronologically. See, for example, Pratt, "The Social Bases"; and James K. Pollock, "An Areal Study of the German Electorate, 1930–1933."

8. See Thomas Childers, "Inflation, Stabilization, and Political Realignment in Germany, 1924–1928." See also the works of Larry Eugene Jones, "'The Dying Middle': Weimar Germany and the Fragmentation of Bourgeois Politics"; "Inflation, Revaluation, and the Crisis of Middle-Class Politics: A Study of the Dissolution of the German Party System, 1923–1928"; and "The Dissolution of the Bourgeois Party System in the Weimar Republic."

9. See, for example, Werner Kaltefleiter, *Wirtschaft und Politik in Deutschland* pp. 32–34; and Heinrich Bennecke, *Wirtschaftliche Depression und politischer Radikalismus, 1918–1938,* pp. 42–55.

10. Hamilton's work, for example, is based on a sample of only thirteen of the country's largest cities. And Hackett confines his analysis to Berlin and Bavaria. Hamilton, *Who Voted for Hitler?* pp. 64–219, and Hackett, "The Nazi Party in the Reichstag Election of 1930," pp. 403–31. Pratt's sample is national in scope but limited to cities with over 20,000 inhabitants, thus ignoring the small towns and rural areas where over half the German population lived. Pratt, "The Social Bases," pp. 60–80. The still very useful study of Charles P. Loomis and J. Allan Beegle, "The Spread of German Nazism in Rural Areas," is, on the other hand, limited to the rural areas of Schleswig-Holstein, Hannover, and Bavaria.

11. Among the most noteworthy are William S. Allen, *The Nazi Seizure of Power*; Rudolf Heberle's classic, *Landesbevölkerung und Nationalsozialismus*; Jeremy Noakes, *The Nazi Party in Lower Saxony, 1921–1933*; Herb Kühr, *Parteien und Wahlen in Stadt- und Landkreis Essen in der Zeit der Weimarer Republik*; Günther Plum, *Gesellschaftsstruktur und politisches Bewusstsein in einer katholischen Region, 1928–1933*; and Wilfried Böhnke, *Die NSDAP im Ruhrgebiet, 1920–1933.*

12. See Nils Diederich, *Empirische Wahlforschung*, p. 25.

13. *Statistik des Deutschen Reichs,* 408:112–15.

14. For a useful summary of the occupational categories of the census, see ibid., 102:98–100, 123–91.

15. Although a number of cities reported their returns by borough, census figures for those boroughs were not recorded. Only in the Reich's two largest cities, Berlin and Hamburg, are both sets of figures available. As a result, Hamilton, who attempts to analyze the Nazi vote by neighborhood in several other cities, is compelled to make highly impressionistic assumptions about the social composition of those areas under examination. Hamilton, *Who Voted for Hitler?* pp. 129–219.

16. The literature on "ecological fallacy" is truly mammoth. Among the more useful are: W. S. Robinson, "Ecological Correlations and the Behavior of Individuals"; Leo A. Goodman, "Some Alternatives to Ecological Correlation"; W. P. Shively, "'Ecological' Inference: The Use of Aggregate Data to Study Indi-

viduals"; Mattei Dogan and Stein Rokkan, eds., *Quantitative 'Ecological' Analysis in the Social Sciences*; Allan J. Lichtman, "Correlation, Regression, and the Ecological Fallacy: A Critique" and J. Morgan Kousser, "Ecological Regression and the Analysis of Past Politics."

17. See, for example, Theodor Geiger, *Die soziale Schichtung des deutschen Volkes*, pp. 72–138.

18. See, for example, the treatment of social background found in the 1927 survey of its membership by the liberal white-collar union, the GdA, and in the official measurement of social background used in the university statistics reported regularly in the *Vierteljahreshefte zur Statistik des Deutschen Reichs*. In both instances, the standard measurement was occupation of father. See *Die wirtschaftliche und soziale Lage der Angestellten*.

19. Robert Michels, *Umschichtungen in den herrschenden Klassen nach dem Kriege*, pp. 104–5; on the role of occupation, see Talcott Parsons, "Democracy and Social Structure in Pre-Nazi Germany," p. 112. See also the highly informative discussion of status and occupation in Frank Domurad, "The Politics of Corporatism: Hamburg Handicraft in the Late Weimar Republic, 1927–1933."

20. This emphasis on occupational and demographic categories is clearly reflected in the DDP's *Aufklärungs- und Werbematerial* for the 1928 elections, a typical circular sent to party locals describing campaign leaflets available from party headquarters. Leaflets were entitled: *Employees, Civil Servants, Farmers, Women, Youth, Commercial Middle Class*, and *Pensioners*, BA, ZSg.l, 27/19(6). A similar DVP circular for the 1932 elections lists an almost identical set of leaflets, BA, ZSg.l, 42/8(3). See also the leaflets, pamphlets, and posters in the NSDAP Hauptarchiv for the elections of 1924 and 1932, Reels 14–15.

21. This reliance on the print media is vividly reflected in the formulation of National Socialist electoral strategy in the critical campaigns of 1932. See chapter 4. The analysis of partisan campaign literature is based on a systematic examination of the party press and the leaflet/pamphlet collections of the Bundesarchiv Koblenz, the Geheimes Staatsarchiv (Berlin), the Zentrales Staatsarchiv Potsdamm, the Landesarchiv Berlin, the NSDAP Hauptarchiv, the Hoover Institution Archives, and the Bayerisches Hauptstaatsarchiv Munich.

22. Hamilton, for example, offers a brief description of the 1932 campaigns as reflected in the local press but never actually examines the appeals of the various parties: Hamilton, *Who Voted for Hitler?* pp. 229–419. The only systematic analysis of Nazi appeals to a particular socio-occupational group is Max H. Kele's *Nazis and Workers*.

23. Z. A. B. Zeman's *Nazi Propaganda* contains only one thin chapter on the period before 1933. Dietrich Orlow's *The History of the Nazi Party, 1919–1933*, contains valuable information on the organization of the party's propaganda apparatus but is only tangentially concerned with the content of Nazi campaign appeals. The most effective treatment of the NSDAP's recruitment campaigns during the Weimar Republic is found in Noakes, *The Nazi Party in Lower Saxony*.

24. Abel's analysis of this material is found in Theodore Abel, *Why Hitler*

Came to Power, Englewood Cliffs, 1932. The essays, available at the Hoover Institution Archives, have been subsequently reinterpreted by Peter H. Merkl, *Political Violence under the Swastika*. The analysis in the following chapters is based on an original reading of those biographies.

25. Particularly important are Heinrich August Winkler, *Mittelstand, Demokratie und Nationalsozialismus*; Iris Hamel, *Völkischer Verband und Nationale Gewerkschaft*; Hans Speier, *Die Angestellten vor dem Nationalsozialismus*; Hans Mommsen, "Die Stellung der Beamtenschaft in Reich, Ländern und Gemeinden in der Ära Bruning"; Andreas Kunz, "Stand versus Klasse. Beamtenschaft und Gewerkschaften im Konflikt um den Personalabbau 1923/24"; Martin Schumacher, *Land und Politik*; the works of Hans-Jürgen Puhle, especially *Politische Agrarbewegungen in kapitalistischen Industriegesellschaften*; and Timothy Mason, *Sozialpolitik im Dritten Reich*.

26. See Michael H. Kater, "Sozialer Wandel in der NSDAP im Zuge der Nationalsozialistischen Machtergreifung," pp. 25–67; and Kater's "Methodologische Überlegungen über Möglichkeiten und Grenzen einer Analyse der sozialen Zusammensetzung der NSDAP von 1925 bis 1945," and Jürgen Genuneit, "Methodische Probleme der quantitativen Analyse früher NSDAP-Mitgliederlisten," both in Mann, *Die Nationalsozialisten*. See also Madden, "The Social Composition of the Nazi Party."

Chapter I

1. The relationship between cleavages and the development of modern party systems has been most extensively explored by Seymour Martin Lipset and Stein Rokkan, "Cleavage Structures, Party Systems, and Voter Alignments: An Introduction," in Lipset and Rokkan, eds., *Party Systems and Voter Alignments*, pp. 1–64. See also M. Rainer Lepsius, "Parteiensystem und Sozialstruktur. Zum Problem der Demokratisierung der deutschen Gesellschaft," pp. 56–80.

2. Analyses of electoral constituencies in the imperial period are relatively scarce in the literature on *Wahlsoziologie*. For a promising beginning, however, see Wolfgang Wölk, "Sozialstruktur, Parteienkorrelation und Wahlentscheidung im Kaiserreich am Beispiel der Reichstagswahl von 1907," pp 505–48. Also useful are Alfred Milatz, "Die linksliberalen Parteien und Gruppen in den Reichstagswahlen 1871 bis 1912," pp. 273–92; and Lothar Gall, "Liberalismus und 'bürgerliche Gesellschaft.' Zur Charakter und Entwicklung der liberalen Bewegung in Deutschland," pp. 324–56.

3. See Hans-Jürgen Puhle, "Parlament, Parteien und Interessenverbände 1908–1914," pp. 343–44; and Dirk Stegmann, *Die Erben Bismarcks*, p. 127.

4. For an excellent study of the increasing difficulties encountered by the National Liberals in integrating the various components of their traditional constituency after 1890, see Dan S. White, *The Splintered Party*. See also Thomas Nipperdey, "Die Organisation der bürgerlichen Parteien in Deutschland," pp. 100–119; Nipperdey's more extensive treatment of political organization in his

Die Organisation der deutschen Parteien vor 1918; and James J. Sheehan, *German Liberalism in the Nineteenth Century*, Chicago, 1978, pp. 239–57.

5. See the works of Hans-Jürgen Puhle: *Agrarische Interessenpolitik und preussischer Konservatismus im Wilhelmischen Reich (1893–1914)*; *Von der Agrarkrise zum Präfaschismus*; and *Politische Agrarbewegungen in kapitalistischen Industriegesellschaften*. See also the classic work of Alexander Gerschenkron, *Bread and Democracy in Germany*. Although it was the largest and the most influential of the agricultural interest groups, the BdL was by no means the only important organization representing farmers in imperial Germany. Small holding peasants in the heavily Catholic south and west were organized in a number of regional Christian Peasants' Associations, which by 1906 counted over three hundred thousand members. These organizations were loosely linked to the Catholic Zentrum, whose policies they tried to influence, and played only a marginal role in imperial politics. Other regional peasant organizations were active in the Protestant areas of north-central Germany, but they, too, paled in national significance beside the BdL. See Puhle, *Politische Agrarbewegungen*, pp. 55–63.

6. Winkler, *Mittelstand, Demokratie und Nationalsozialismus*, pp. 44–49.

7. See Schulamit Volkov, *The Rise of Popular Antimodernism in Germany*, pp. 266–96; Robert Gellately, *The Politics of Economic Despair*, pp. 148–96. On the anti-Semitic parties see Peter Pulzer, *The Rise of Political Anti-Semitism in Germany and Austria*, pp. 313–19; and Richard S. Levy, *The Downfall of the Anti-Semitic Parties in Imperial Germany*.

8. The political isolation of the *Mittelstandsbewegung* is treated in Volkov, *Popular Antimodernism*, pp. 266–96; and Winkler, *Mittelstand, Demokratie*, pp. 65–69.

9. *Statistik des Deutschen Reichs*, vols. 2, 211, 408. The classical definition of the "new middle class" as a *Zwischenschicht* between the entrepreneurial *Mittelstand* and the blue-collar proletariat was formulated by Emil Lederer in two works: *Die Privatangestellten in der modernen Wirtschaftsentwicklung*, and his subsequent collaborative analysis with Jakob Marschak, "Der neue Mittelstand." See also Jürgen Kocka, *Unternehmensverwaltung und Angestelltenschaft am Beispiel Siemens 1847–1914*.

10. See Herbert von Borch, *Obrigkeit und Widerstand*; Otto Hintze, "Der Beamtenstand"; and Max Weber's critique of the conservative orientation of the professional civil service in "Beamtenschaft und politisches Führertum," pp. 147ff.

11. Geiger, *Soziale Schichtung*, p. 98.

12. See Heinz Hamm, "Die wirtschaftlichen und sozialen Berfusmerkmale der kaufmännischen Angestellten (im Vergleich mit denjenigen der Arbeiter)," pp. 52–59. The wide range of white-collar social backgrounds was first revealed in a 1908 survey conducted by one of the largest *Angestelltenverbände*, the Deutschnationaler Handlungsgehilfenverband (DHV). Breaking down its membership according to father's occupation, the DHV disclosed that its members sprang from the following backgrounds: 19% blue collar, 12% white collar,

16% civil service, 30% old middle class, 8% agriculture, with the remainder scattered among the free professions.

13. Fritz W. Fischer, "Die Angestellten, ihre Bewegung und ihre Ideologien." See also Otto Süssengut, "Die Angestellten als Stand und Klasse."

14. Fischer, "Angestellten," pp. 41–43. See also Jürgen Kocka, "The First World War and the 'Mittelstand': German Artisans and White Collar Workers," pp. 101–24.

15. Statistisches Jahrbuch für das Deutsche Reich, 46:25.

16. For a summary of these developments see Wolfgang Köllmann, "Politische und soziale Entwicklung der deutschen Arbeiterschaft 1850–1914," pp. 316–30.

17. See Gerhard A. Ritter, Die Arbeiterbewegung im Wilhelminischen Reich; Guenther Roth, The Social Democrats in Imperial Germany; and Vernon L. Lidtke, The Outlawed Party.

18. The classic analysis of this development remains Eckhard Kehr's Schlachtflottenbau und Parteipolitik 1894–1901.

19. Stegmann, Erben Bismarcks, pp. 59–75.

20. The inability of traditional liberalism and conservatism to integrate the radical nationalist and antisocialist movements of the Wilhelmine era into the existing party system is examined by Geoff Eley, Reshaping the German Right.

21. Puhle, "Parlament, Parteien und Interessenverbände 1890–1914," p. 357. See also James C. Hunt, The People's Party in Wurttemberg and Southern Germany, 1890–1914.

22. See Rudolf Lill, "Die deutschen Katholiken und Bismarcks Reichsgründung," pp. 345–65; and Walter Tormin, Geschichte der deutschen Parteien seit 1848, pp. 84–86. On the Zentrum's electoral base see Johannes Schauff, Die deutschen Katholiken und die Zentrumspartei; and C. H. E. Zangerl, "Courting the Catholic Vote: The Center Party in Baden, 1903–1913," pp. 220–40. The interest structure of the Zentrum is examined in David G. Blackbourn, Class, Religion, and Local Politics in Wilhelmine Germany.

23. David G. Blackbourn, "The Political Alignment of the Centre," pp. 821–50.

24. Erich Eyck, Bismarck and the German Empire, pp. 202–10.

25. Johannes Schauff," Das Wahlsystem des Deutschen Reichs und die Zentrumspartei," pp. 299–309.

26. The relationship between German Catholics and the state in the aftermath of the Kulturkampf is treated in Rudolf Morsey, "Die deutschen Katholiken und der Nationalstaat zwischen Kulturkampf und Erstem Weltkrieg," pp. 270–98. The impact of Bismarck's strategy of "negative integration" on German political culture is examined in Hans-Ulrich Wehler, Das Deutsche Kaiserreich 1871–1918, pp. 96–100.

27. The small regional parties of the imperial period have attracted relatively little scholarly attention. For an examination of the Hannoverian Guelf Party and others see Dieter Fricke, ed., Die bürgerlichen Parteien in Deutschland.

28. For an examination of the domestic political scene during the war, see

Klaus Epstein, *Matthias Erzberger and the Dilemma of German Democracy*; Fritz Fischer, *Griff nach der Weltmacht*; and F. Klein, ed., *Politik im Krieg 1914–1918*.

29. See Gerald D. Feldman, *Army, Industry, and Labor in Germany 1914–1918*; Gerald D. Feldman, *Iron and Steel in the German Inflation, 1916–1923*; and G. D. Feldman and Heidrun Homburg, *Industrie und Inflation. Studien und Dokumente zur Politik der deutschen Unternehmer 1916–1923*.

30. Feldman, *Iron and Steel*; and Charles S. Maier, *Recasting Bourgeois Europe*.

31. Jürgen Kocka, *Klassengesellschaft im Krieg*, pp. 85–93; and Feldman, *Army, Industry, and Labor*, pp. 149–90, 464.

32. Winkler, *Mittelstand, Demokratie und Nationalsozialismus*, pp. 49–64; and Kocka, *Klassengesellschaft*, pp. 88–93.

33. Puhle, *Politische Agrarbewegungen*, p. 39.

34. H. Haushofer, *Die deutsche Landwirtschaft im technischen Zeitalter*, p. 222.

35. Martin Schumacher, *Land und Politik*, pp. 33–84.

36. See Robert G. Moeller, "Dimensions of Social Conflict in the Great War: The View from the German Countryside," pp. 142–68; as well as Moeller's dissertation, "Peasants, Politics and Pressure Groups in War and Inflation; A Study of the Rhineland and Westphalia, 1914–1924," pp. 218–75.

37. Schumacher, *Land und Politik*, pp. 60–75; and Feldman, *Army, Industry, and Labor*, pp. 108–16.

38. Kocka, *Klassengesellschaft im Krieg*, pp. 71–85.

39. Ibid., pp. 76–82.

40. Ibid., pp. 75–76.

41. Fischer, "Die Angestellten," pp. 41–42. See also Hans Speier, *Die Angestellten vor dem Nationalsozialismus*, pp. 124–44.

42. Kocka, *Klassengesellschaft*, pp. 82–85.

43. Ibid.

44. See below, chapter 3 text at nn. 139–51.

45. Kocka, *Klassengesellschaft*, pp. 12–21; and Feldman, *Army, Industry, and Labor*, pp. 471–72.

46. Feldman, *Army, Industry, and Labor*, pp. 197–249, 473–77.

47. The standard work on the divisions within Social Democracy during this period remains Carl E. Schorske, *German Social Democracy, 1905–1917*. The relationship between the SPD and the unions is also given the extensive treatment in Ritter, *Die Arbeiterbewegung*. For the impact of revisionist thought on internal Social Democratic politics see Gerhard A. Ritter, "Bernsteins Revisionismus und die Flügelbildung in der Sozialdemokratischen Partei," pp. 342–57.

48. See Schorske, *German Social Democracy*, pp. 285–98; and Suzanne Miller, *Bürgfrieden und Klassenkampf*.

49. Susanne Miller, *Die Bürde der Macht*, pp. 71–114. See also David W. Morgan, *The Socialist Left and the German Revolution*.

50. Miller, *Die Bürde der Macht*, pp. 225–36.

51. "Programm des Spartakusbundes. Was will der Spartakusbund?" in E. Heilfron, ed., *Die Deutsche Nationalversammlung im Jahre 1919*.

52. "Aufruf der Parteileitung der Unabhängigen Sozialdemokratischen Partei Deutschlands. 9. Dezember 1918," ibid., pp. 145–47.

53. *Für Recht-Gegen Gewalt!* MSPD leaflet, 1919, Landesarchiv Berlin, Rep. 240, Acc. 2174, Nr. 2.

54. Miller, *Die Bürde der Macht*, pp. 311–62.

55. Ibid.

56. The conflict between the National Liberals and the Progressives and the foundation of their successor parties are traced in Henry A. Turner, Jr., *Stresemann and the Politics of the Weimar Republic*. See also Lothar Albertin, *Liberalismus und Demokratie am Anfang der Weimarer Republik*; Wolfgang Hartenstein, *Die Anfänge der Deutschen Volkspartei 1918–1920*; and Ernst Portner, "Der Ansatz zur demokratischen Massenpartei im deutschen Linksliberalismus," pp. 150–161.

57. "Aufruf der Deutschen Volkspartei," and "Die Deutsche Volkspartei: die Partei des Mittelstandes," DVP placard, reproduced in Heilfron, *Die Deutsche Nationalversammlung*, pp. 132–34, and Table 15.

58. "Wahlaufruf der Deutschen Demokratischen Partei vom 15. Dezember 1918," in ibid., pp. 140–42. For an examination of the relationship between the DDP and the SPD during the Weimar Republic see Hartmut Schustereit, *Linksliberalismus und Sozialdemokratie in der Weimarer Republic*.

59. See Werner Stephan, *Aufstieg und Verfall des Linksliberalismus 1918–1933*.

60. See Maier, *Recasting Bourgeois Europe*, pp. 158–72; and Albertin, *Liberalismus*. See also Hartenstein, *Die Anfänge*, pp. 59–73. Shifts within the middle-class electorate are treated in the following chapter.

61. Conservative efforts to harness the radical nationalist, antisocialist, and anti-Semitic movements of the Wilhelmian era are insightfully examined in Eley, *Reshaping the German Right*, pp. 316–34.

62. "Wahlaufruf der Deutschnationalen Volkspartei," in Heilfron, *Die Deutsche Nationalversammlung*, pp. 125–28.

63. The demand for a corporatist *Wirtschaftsparlament* is embodied in the party's official platform for the 1920 elections ("Wahlaufruf der DNVP"). See also "Muss das deutsche Bürgertum untergehen?" and "Bürgertum und Proletariat," both in the conservative *Kreuz-Zeitung*, 11 and 25 May 1920.

64. See, for example, "Der Dolchstoss von hinten," *Kreuz-Zeitung*, 27 May, 1920.

65. See the "Grundsätze der Deutschnationalen Volkspartei, 1920," in Wolfgang Treue, *Deutsche Parteiprogramme seit 1861*, pp. 69–70. See also *Die Juden—Deutschland's Vampyre*, and *Landleute lasst Euch nicht beschwindeln!* DNVP leaflets, 1919, Weimarer Republic Collection, Hoover Institution Archives. In the latter leaflet, the Nationalists typically explained to their peasant constituents that "the 'Junkers' are not responsible for the war; the Jews are."

66. See Rudolf Morsey, *Die Deutsche Zentrumspartei 1917–1923*; and Johannes Schauff, *Die deutschen Katholiken.*

67. "Die Leitsätze für die Politik der Zentrumspartei (Christliche Volkspartei)," in Heilfron, *Die Deutsche Nationalversammlung*, pp. 137–39.

68. Beginning in 1919, certain *Wahlkreise* divided their votes by sex. The number of areas involved varied from election to election, and the resulting collection of data hardly constitutes a valid statistical sample. Still, the material is extensive and does provide a very useful tool in examining electoral choice by sex. A summary of those results is found in Herbert Tingsten, *Political Behavior*, pp. 37–65.

69. See Bernhard Vogel, Dieter Nohle, and Rainer-Olaf Schultze, *Wahlen in Deutschland*, pp. 142–45; and Heino Kaack, *Geschichte und Struktur des deutschen Parteiensystems*, pp. 88–89.

70. See below, chapter 4, text at nn. 17–24.

71. See "Die Deutschvölkische Freiheitspartei (DVFP) 1922–1933," in Fricke, *Die Bürgerlichen Parteien*, pp. 765–70; and Uwe Lohalm, *Völkischer Radikalismus.*

72. On the early years of the NSDAP see Georg Franz-Willing, *Die Hitlerbewegung*; Reginald Phelps, "Hitler and the Deutsche Arbeiterpartei," pp. 245–61; Werner Maser, *Der Sturm auf die Republik.*

73. See the "Guidelines of German Workers' Party," in Barbara Miller Lane and Leila J. Rupp, *Nazi Ideology before 1933*, pp. 9–11.

74. Ibid., p. 10.

75. "The Program of the NSDAP," ibid., pp. 41–43.

76. Ibid.

77. Ibid.

78. Karl Dietrich Bracher, *Die Deutsche Diktatur*, pp. 28–48. See also Barbara Miller Lane, "Nazi Ideology: Some Unfinished Business," pp. 3–30; and Martin Broszat, "Die völkische Ideologie und der Nationalsozialismus," pp. 53–68.

79. Dietrich Orlow, *The History of the Nazi Party 1919–1933*, pp. 14–18.

80. Phelps, "Hitler and the Deutsche Arbeiterpartei," pp. 245–61. See also Roland V. Layton, Jr., "The *Völkischer Beobachter*, 1920–1933: The Nazi Party Newspaper in the Weimar Era," pp. 353–82.

81. Orlow, *History of the Nazi Party*, pp. 23–30.

82. Ibid., pp. 36–37.

83. Ibid., pp. 39–45.

84. The social and political impact of the inflation on the different elements of the electorate are treated in chapter 3. See Maier, *Recasting Bourgeois Europe*, pp. 66–70; and Gerald D. Feldman, "Wirtschafts- und sozialpolitische Probleme der Demobilmachung," in Hans Mommsen, Dietmar Petzina, and Bernd Weisbrod, eds., *Industrielles System und politische Entwicklung in der Weimarer Republik.*

85. "Zahlen zur Geldentwertung in Deutschland 1914 bis 1923," *Sonderhefte zu Wirstchaft und Statistik*, Sonderheft 1, v, 15, Berlin, 1925.

86. The recent scholarly literature on the reparations issue and its corrosive impact on international politics in this period is substantial. Among the most useful are Marc Trachtenberg, *Reparation in World Politics*; Walter A. McDougall, *France's Rhineland Diplomacy, 1914–1924*; Jacques Bariety, *Les relations franco-allemandes apres la Premiere Guerre Mondiale*; and Steven A. Schuker, *The End of French Predominance in Europe*.

87. Georg Franz-Willing, *Krisenjahr der Hitlerbewegung, 1923*, pp. 389–92; and the same author's *Putsch und Verbotszeit der Hitler Bewegung, November 1923–Februar 1925*, pp. 66–141; and Harold J. Gordon, Jr., *Hitler and the Beer Hall Putsch*.

Chapter II

1. "Zahlen zur Geldentwertung in Deutschland 1914 bis 1923," *Sonderhefte zu Wirtschaft und Statistik*, Sonderheft 1, v, 15.

2. Constantin Bresciani-Turroni's *The Economics of Inflation. A Study of Currency Depreciation in Post-War Germany 1914–1923*, remains the standard work on the German inflation. A stimulating reexamination of the inflation is also found in Carl-Ludwig Holtfrerich, *Die deutsche Inflation 1914–1923*. Also useful are Karsten Laursen and Jørgen Pedersen, *The German Inflation 1918–1923*; Frank D. Graham, *Exchange, Prices, and Production in Hyper-Inflation*. For a review of more recent literature on the inflation and a prospectus of works currently in progress, see Otto Büsch and Gerald D. Feldman, eds., *Historische Prozesse der deutschen Inflation, 1914–1924*.

3. "Zahlen zur Geldentwertung," pp. 35, 37.

4. See the comparative figures of over two hundred communities between July 1923 and February 1925 in *Vierteljahreshefte zur Statistik des Deutschen Reichs*, vol. 30, no. 1, 66–68; vol. 30, no. 4, 48–50; vol. 34, no. 1, 89–92.

5. Quoted in Fritz K. Ringer, ed., *The German Inflation of 1923*, p. 144.

6. The best synthetic treatment of this period is found in Maier, *Recasting Bourgeois Europe*. See also Günter Arns, "Regierungsbildung und Koalitionspolitik in der Weimarer Republik 1919–1924," pp. 155–74.

7. For details see Karl-Bernhard Netzband and Hans-Peter Widmaier, *Währungs- und Finanzpolitik in der Ära Luther 1923–1925*, pp. 31–32. For a contemporary evaluation of the effects of the reform see *Wirtschaft und Statistik* 3 (1923):769–70.

8. See E. Bischof, *Rheinscher Separatismus 1918–1924*; K.-D. Erdmann, *Adenauer in der Rheinlandpolitik nach dem Ersten Weltkrieg*. See also McDougall, *France's Rhineland Diplomacy*, pp. 305–39.

9. Descriptions of the political environment in Bavaria abound. See Karl Schwend, *Bayern zwischen Monarchie und Diktatur*, pp. 199–260; Werner G. Zimmerman, *Bayern und das Reich*, pp. 134–49; Hans Fenske, *Konservativismus und Rechtsradikalismus in Bayern 1918*, pp. 189–260. Still helpful is Carl Landauer, "The Bavarian Problem in the Weimar Republic, 1918–1923," pp. 93–115 and 205–23.

10. Ossip K. Flechtheim, *Die KPD in der Weimarer Republik*; Hermann Weber, *Die Wandlung des deutschen Kommunismus*, 1:43–52. A more detailed account of the Saxon situation is found in Werner T. Angress, *Stillborn Revolution*, pp. 379–474.

11. Harold J. Gordon, Jr., "Die Reichswehr und Sachsen 1923," pp. 677–92.

12. Arns, "Regierungsbildung und Koalitionspolitik," pp. 171–77.

13. In August, job referral agencies reported almost three applicants for each available position. At the close of the year, that ratio stood at over nine to one. By January 1924, almost half the membership of the leading industrial unions were either unemployed or working on reduced schedules. See *Statistisches Jahrbuch für das Deutsche Reich 1924–1925*, 44:289; and *Wirtschaft und Statistik*, 5 (1925):62.

14. Michael Stürmer, *Koalition und Opposition in der Weimarer Republik 1924–1928*, pp. 37–38. The Social Democrats opposed the revalorization settlement, while the Nationalists sought an even higher rate. See Arns, "Regierungsbildung und Koalitionspolitik," pp. 178–85.

15. Orlow, *The History of the Nazi Party*, 46. See also Georg Franz-Willing, *Putsch und Verbotszeit der Hitlerbewegung, November 1923–Februar 1925*, pp. 191–208.

16. Joseph Nyomarkay, *Charisma and Factionalism in the Nazi Party*, p. 68; and Noakes, *The Nazi Party in Lower Saxony*, p. 41.

17. *Hessischer Beobachter*, 3 May 1924, Nr. 4, quoted in Eberhard Schön, *Die Entstehung des Nationalsozialismus in Hessen*, p. 58.

18. The most extensive treatment of this period is found in Schuker, *The End of French Predominance in Europe*, pp. 171–231.

19. The words were those of Nationalist leader Karl Helferrich, *Helferrichs Reichstagsreden 1922–1924*, ed. J. W. Reichert, pp. 323–32. For the Communist reaction see *Die Rote Fahne*, 22 March 1924.

20. "The Primacy of Foreign Policy," *Germania*, 12 April, 1924.

21. *Berliner Tageblatt*, 16 April 1924.

22. *Berliner Tageblatt*, 23 April 1924.

23. *Denkt am Deutschen Rhein*, Zentrum leaflet, 1924, Landesarchiv Berlin, Rep. 240, Acc. 1962, Nr. 17. "A Nationalist regime, to Poincare's joy, will provoke new sanctions," this typical Zentrum *Flugblatt* declared, "And in the mistaken belief that it can avoid reparations and controls, [a Nationalist government] will lose the occupied territories. That would mean the loss of the Rhineland forever."

24. "Das Ausland und die Deutschen Wahlen," *Der Tag*, 22 March 1924.

25. "Lösung: Wählt National!" *Der Tag*, 3 May 1924.

26. "Wahlreden und Wahldemogogie," *Die Neue Preussische Zeitung* (Kreuz-Zeitung), 30 April 1924.

27. Quoted in Jeremy Noakes, Geoffrey Pridham, *Documents on Nazism, 1919–1945*, pp. 61–63.

28. The Nazi vote exceeded the party's national levels in a number of electoral districts in central and northern Germany, among them Mecklenburg (20.8%), Thuringia (9.9%), Merseburg (8.7%), Hannover East (8.6%), Leipzig

(7.9%), and Schleswig-Holstein (7.4%). *Statistisches Jahrbuch 1924–1925* 44:390–91.

29. Stürmer, *Koalition und Opposition*, pp. 58–73, 74–78.

30. In the three months prior to the May election, unemployment among organized industrial workers, while declining steadily, averaged 17.4%; in the three months of the fall campaign, the average had fallen to 8.7%. Real wages also increased appreciably. The difference between average nominal wages and the cost-of-living index in twenty-five major cities stood at seven in March (100:93), but at twenty-eight in December (135:107). *Statistisches Jahrbuch, 1924–1925*, 44:289; *Wirtschaft und Statistik*, 5 (1925):62.

31. Although the *Völkischen* were the dominant force within the NSFB, the party still represented a very loose *Dachorganisation* for the various regional *völkisch* and National Socialist groups. See Wolfgang Horn, *Führerideologie und Parteiorganisation in der NSDAP (1919–1933)*.

32. Geoffrey Pridham, *Hitler's Rise to Power*, pp. 30–31.

33. Noakes, *The Nazi Party in Lower Saxony*, pp. 49–54.

34. "Los von Heute," *Der Tag*, 23 November 1924. See also "Schluss mit der sogenannten Grossen Koalition," ibid., 14 November 1924; and "An alle Angehörigen des werktätigen Mittelstandes," *Kreuz-Zeitung*, 3 May 1924.

35. "Wahlaufruf der Deutschnationalen Volkspartei," *Reichstags-Handbuch* III, Wahlperiode 1924, Berlin, 1925, p. 131. "We want a *Volksgemeinschaft* which builds on a Christian foundation, spurns class struggle, and liberates the worker from terror. . . . A division of the *Volk* into propertied and nonpropertied is not compatible with the basic concept of this *Volksgemeinschaft*."

36. "Farbe bekennen!" *Der Tag*, 30 November 1924.

37. *Berliner Stimmen. Zeitschrift für Politik, Nachrichtenblatt der DVP im Wahlkreisverband Berlin*, Nr. 13, 18 November, 1924. "It is not a struggle of the bourgeoisie against the workers," the party insisted, "but a struggle against socialism as a *Weltanschauung*."

38. *Mittelstand aufgepasst! Was hat die Wirtschaftspartei versprochen?* DVP leaflet, 1924, Landesarchiv Berlin, Rep. 240, Acc. 1964, Nr. 43.

39. "Wählt für das Reich!" *Berliner Stimmen*, Nr. 19, 1924.

40. Ibid. A reference to Democratic opposition to the entry of DNVP into a new center-right cabinet.

41. "Nicht 'bürgerlich' oder 'sozialistisch' sondern demokratisch," *Berliner Tageblatt*, 14 November 1924.

42. "Deutscher Mittelstand!" ibid., 3 May 1924. "German middle class! . . . For whom will we vote on 4 May? Certainly not the Social Democrats or Communists, who both want to ruin the *Mittelstand*." Indeed, the DDP joined the chorus of center and rightist parties claiming responsibility for frustrating leftist efforts to expropriate the middle class.

43. Ibid., 23 November 1924.

44. Ibid., 5 December 1924.

45. Ibid., 15 November 1924.

46. Excluding the agricultural sector, which accounted for 45% of all self-

employed proprietors, commerce and handicrafts accounted for over 70% of the self-employed in the labor force during the mid-twenties. *Statistik des Deutschen Reichs*, 408 : 124.

47. Quoted in Ringer, *The German Inflation*, p. 100.

48. Quoted in Heinrich August Winkler, *Mittelstand, Demokratie und Nationalsozialismus*, p. 77. See also pp. 78–83. Franz Eulenburg, in his classic analysis of the social impact of the inflation, concludes that because of the severe credit shortage, the loss of savings, and the greater share of government contracts won by large concerns, the situation of the handicrafts had, indeed, become precarious. "The artisan," he argues, "must be viewed as another victim of the inflation." Eulenburg, "Die sozialen Wirkungen der Währungsverhältnisse," p. 773. Laursen and Pedersen, while stressing the "extreme inequalities within the entrepreneurial group," also conclude that the small, marginal shopkeeper and artisan were adversely affected by the inflation. *The German Inflation*, pp. 117–18.

49. *Vierteljahreshefte zur Statistik des Deutschen Reichs*, 35 (1926): 146–49.

50. Quoted in Winkler, *Mittelstand, Demokratie und Nationalsozialismus*, p. 7. See also 78–83.

51. Theodore Abel Collection, Hoover Institution Archives, Stanford University, Biography 102. See also Biography 211.

52. Heinrich August Winkler, "From Social Protectionism to National Socialism: The German Small-Business Movement in Comparative Perspective," pp. 1–18.

53. Hans Meusch, the general secretary of the German Chamber of Handicrafts and commerce, quoted in Winkler, *Mittelstand, Demokratie und Nationalsozialismus*, pp. 112–13.

54. *Die Abrechnung am 4. Mai*, DVFP leaflet, 1924, NSDAP Hauptarchiv, Reel 42, Folder 843. Cited hereafter as HA/Reel/Folder.

55. *Wahlaufruf der DVFP (Völkisch-Sozialer Block)*, and *DVFP-Allgemeine grundsätzliche Richtlinien*, völkisch coalition leaflets, 1924, Geheimes Staatsarchiv Preussischer Kulturbesitz, Berlin, Hauptabteilung XII, IV, Nr. 212. Cited hereafter as GStA, HA.

56. *Handwerk und Gewerbe und die völkische Bewegung*, völkisch coalition leaflet, 1924, Bundesarchiv Koblenz, Zeitgeschichtliche Sammlung 1, 45/13. Cited hereafter as BA, ZSg.

57. *Was will der völkisch-sozialer Block?* völkisch coalition leaflet, 1924, BA, ZSg. 1, 45/13.

58. *Ziele der DVFB*, völkisch coalition leaflet, 1924, GStA, HA III, IV, Nr. 211.

59. See *An die schaffende Bevölkerung zur Aufklärung*, völkisch coalition leaflet, 1924, HA/42/843.

60. *Was will die Deutsche Partei Baden (Völkisch-Sozialer Block)?* völkisch coalition leaflet, 1924, BA, ZSg.1, 45/13.

61. *Zu den Stadtverordnetenwahlen*, Leipzig, völkisch coalition leaflet, 1924, BA, ZSg.1, 45/13.

62. *Halt! Nur einen Augenblick! Die ganze Zukunft liebe Volksgenossen steht auf dem Spiel*, *völkisch* coalition leaflet, 1924, BA, ZSg.1, 45/13.

63. *Lenins Letzte Worte*, *völkisch* coalition leaflet, 1924, BA, ZSg.1, 45/13.

64. *Handwerk und Gewerbe und die völkische Bewegung*, *völkisch* coalition leaflet, 1924, BA, ZSg.1, 45/13.

65. *Nationale Realpolitik zum Schutz des deutschen Mittelstandes*, *völkisch* coalition leaflet, 1924, GStA, HA XII, IV, Nr. 212.

66. *Handwerk und Gewerbe und völkische Bewegung*, *völkisch* coalition leaflet, 1924, BA, ZSg.1, 45/13.

67. *Das Handwerk und die DNVP*, DNVP leaflet, 1924, GStA, HA II, IV, Nr. 187. See also "Die Bedeutung des Handwerks für Staat und Volkswirtschaft," *Kreuz-Zeitung*, 3 April 1924 and "An alle Angehörige des werktätigen Mittelstandes," in the same publication, 2 May 1924.

68. See, for example, "DDP und gewerblicher Mittelstand," *Materialen zur Demokratischen Politik*, Nr. 88, 1924; and *Wahlaufruf*, DDP leaflet, 1924, BA, ZSg.1, 27/19(4). For the DVP see "Mittelstandspolitik der Deutsche Volkspartei," *Flugschriften der Deutschen Volkspartei*, Nr. 55, 1924; *Kaufmännischer und gewerblicher Mittelstand, Handwerker Kaufleute, Gewerbetreibende!*; and *Handwerker und Gewerbetreibende!*, DVP leaflets, 1924, GStA, HA XII, IV, Nr. 165.

69. See appendix 1, on methodology.

70. Werner T. Angress, "The Political Role of the Peasantry in the Weimar Republic," pp. 533–36; See also Puhle, *Politische Agrarwebegungen*, pp. 81–82.

71. See Martin Schumacher, *Land und Politik*, pp. 130–215, 271–73; and Jens Flemming, *Landwirtschaftliche Interessen und Demokratie*, pp. 105–13. Most recently see the dissertation of Robert G. Moeller, "Peasants, Politics and Pressure Groups in War and Inflation: A Study of the Rhineland and Westphalia, 1914–1924."

72. See Eulenburg, "Die soziale Wirkung der Währungsverhältnisse," pp. 763–64; Max Sering, *Die deutsche Landwirtschaft unter Volks- und weltwirtschaftlichen Gesichtspunkten*, p. 40.

73. See Robert G. Moeller, "Winners as Losers in the German Inflation; Peasant Protest over the Controlled Economy, 1920–1923," pp. 255–307.

74. Frieda Wunderlich, *Farm Labor in Germany 1810–1945*, pp. 41–43.

75. John Bradshaw Holt, *German Agricultural Policy, 1918–1934*, pp. 71–80.

76. Ibid., pp. 128–32. See also Robert G. Moeller, "Peasants, Politics and Pressure Groups," pp. 328–413.

77. Quoted in Schumacher, *Land und Politik*, p. 285.

78. The most systematic examination of party agricultural programs in the early Weimar Republic is found in ibid., particularly pp. 432–94.

79. See "Landwirtschaft und Deutschnationale Volkspartei," in *Jahrbuch der DNVP 1920*, Berlin, 1920, pp. 24–28; and "Die Aufgaben der DNVP gegenüber der Landwirtschaft," *Deutschnationale Flugschriften*, Berlin, 1919.

80. Puhle, *Politische Agrarbewegungen*, pp. 83–84.

81. The RLB could not even prevent its affiliates in Württemberg and Thuringia from entering the elections with their own lists, despite the RLB's official political neutrality. See Klaus Müller, "Agrarische Interessenverbände in der Weimarer Republik," p. 388.

82. While regional parties accounted for only 4% of the vote in the urban sample, they made up 8% of the rural vote in 1924.

83. See, in particular, the treatment of rural political movements in Rudolf Heberle, *From Democracy to Nazism*, pp. 32–89; Müller, "Agrarische Interessenverbände," pp. 391–92; and Moeller, "Peasants, Politics and Pressure Groups," pp. 414–64. Symptomatic of the rural views was the liberal DBb's approach to the DNVP's anti-Semitism in 1924. The DBb noted that while the Nationalists railed against the Jews in their campaign literature, prominent conservatives had close financial and business ties with Jews. The DBb found the Nationalists' anti-Semitic campaign in 1924 "dishonest" but by no means dishonorable. *Politisches ABC*, DBb pamphlet, 1924, Weimar Republic Collection, Hoover Institution Archives.

84. See "Deutschnationale Volkspartei und Landwirtschaft im Reichstag und Preussischen Landtag von 1920 bis 1924," *Deutschnationale Flugschriften*, Nr. 149, Berlin, 1924. The quote is from "Reichstagswahl-Preussenwahl, Ein letztes Wort," *Kreuz-Zeitung*, 7 December 1924.

85. See, for example, "Landwirtschaft und Parteipolitik," *Flugschriften der Deutschen Volkspartei*," Nr. 57, Berlin, 1924, and "DDP und Landwirtschaft," *Materialien zur Demokratischen Politik*, Nr. 84, Berlin, 1924.

86. See the DVP's *Nachtrag zum Wahlhandbuch 1924*, pp. 297–98.

87. The results of the 1920 elections are reported by size of community in *Statistik des Deutschen Reichs*, vol. 291. The almost apologetic tone of the DDP's appeals to agriculture is vividly reflected in the party's "DDP and Landwirtschaft."

88. The disintegration of the DDP-DBb alliance is treated most extensively in Jens Flemming, *Landwirtschaftliche Interessen und Demokratie*.

89. Schumacher, *Land und Politik*, pp. 454–66.

90. See the DVP's *Nachtrag zum Wahlhandbuch 1924*, pp. 188–89.

91. Ibid., pp. 292–93.

92. Point three of the program demanded land for colonization to assure "the nourishment of our *Volk* and the settlement of our excess population," and point seventeen called for "an appropriate land reform for our national needs, formulation of a law for the expropriation of land without compensation for the purpose of public use, abolition of ground rents, and the prohibition of land speculation." On the National Socialist romantic views of rural life see Paul Honigsheim, "The Roots of the Nazi Concept of the Ideal German Peasant," *Rural Sociology*, 12 (March 1947): 3–21; and Klaus Bergmann, *Agrarromantik und Grossstadtfeindschaft*.

93. *Deutscher Bauer! Was will Adolf Hitler und der Nationalsozialismus?* NSDAP leaflet, 1922, Weimar Republic Collection, Hoover Institution Archives, Box 9, Folder 129.

94. *Bauer! völkisch* coalition leaflet, 1924, HA/42/869.

95. *Deutsche Bauer! völkisch* coalition leaflet, ibid.

96. *Bauer!* in ibid.

97. *Deutsche Bauer, erwache eh' es zu spät ist! völkisch* coalition leaflet, 1924, HA/42/857.

98. *Bauern! völkisch* coalition leaflet, 1924, Weimar Republic Collection, Hoover Institution Archives, Box 9, Folder 129.

99. Bresciani-Turroni, *The Economics of Inflation*, pp. 315–20; Laursen and Pedersen, *The German Inflation*, pp. 118–20. According to Eulenburg, perhaps as many as half the pensioners rentiers, and others living on fixed incomes may have been forced to seek work as a result of the inflation. Eulenburg, "Die soziale Wirkung der Währungsverhältnisse," pp. 757–58.

100. Theodore Abel Collection, Hoover Institution Archives, Biography 17.

101. See Werner Fritsch, "Sparerbund für das Deutsche Reich (Spb) 1922–1939," 2:648–53.

102. See Claus-Dieter Krohn, *Stabilisierung und ökonomische Interessen*, pp. 23–53; and Netzband and Widmaier, *Währungs- und Finanzpolitik*, pp. 168–223. See also David B. Southern, "The Impact of the Inflation: Inflation, the Courts and Revaluation," in R. Bessel and E. J. Feuchtwanger, *Social Change and Political Development in Weimar Germany*, pp. 55–76.

103. Larry Eugene Jones, "Inflation, Revaluation, and the Crisis of Middle Class Politics: A Study in the Dissolution of the German Party System, 1923–1928," pp. 143–68. See also Michael L. Hughes, "Economic Interest, Social Attitudes, and Creditor Ideology: Popular Responses to Inflation," in Gerald D. Feldman et al., *Die Deutsche Inflation*, pp. 385–408.

104. *Bedrängte, betrogene und beraubte Sparer*, Revalorization and Construction party leaflet, 1924, GStA, HA XII, IV, Nr. 220.

105. *Aufruf der Aufwertungs- und Aufbaupartei*, and *Wahlaufruf und Programm der Aufwertungs- und Wideraufbaupartei*, leaflets, 1924, GStA, HA XII, IV, Nr. 220.

106. *Was wird mit der Aufwertung*, and *Das hat die Welt noch nicht gesehen*, Revalorization and Reconstruction party leaflet, 1924, GStA, HA XII, IV, Nr. 220.

107. *Deutsche Sparer! Deutsche Kleinrentner! Deutsche Hypothengläubiger! Fort mit der 3. Steuerverordnung! völkisch* coalition leaflet, 1924, GStA, HA XII, IV, Nr. 212; and "Wahlaufruf der Nationalsozialistischen Freiheitspartei," *Reichstags-Handbuch*, p. 155.

108. *Deutschvölkische Freiheitspartei (Allgemeine grundsätzliche Richtlinien)*, and *Nationalsozialistische Freiheitsbewegung Grossdeutschlands, völkisch* coalition leaflets, 1924, GStA, HA XII, IV, Nrs. 211 and 212.

109. *Der Dank des Vaterlands ist Euch gewiss, völkisch* coalition leaflet, 1924, HA/42/843.

110. *Beamte! Angestellte! Pensionäre! der Reichs-, Staats- und Kommunalverwaltungen! völkisch* coalition leaflet, 1924, GStA, HA XII, IV, Nr. 212.

111. *Deutsche Sparer, völkisch* coalition leaflet, 1924, GStA, HA XII, IV, Nr. 212.

112. Werner Liebe, *Die Deutschnationale Volkspartei 1918–1924*, p. 180.

113. Quoted in *Kreuz-Zeitung*, 4 April 1924.

114. "Das Ziel der Rechtsparteien. Keine Illusionspolitik! Es gilt die Revolution zu beenden," *Der Tag*, December 2 1924.

115. *Sparer! Rentner!* DNVP leaflet, 1924, BA, ZSg.1, 44/9.

116. *Der Parteitag der DVP für Aufwertung*, DVP leaflet, GStA, HA xii, iv, Nr. 166; Stresemann is quoted in *Neue Tägliche Rundschau*, 1 December 1924. For more on the DVP's approach to this issue see "Fragen der Kleinrentner—DVP und Aufwertung," in *Flugschriften der Deutschen Volkspartei*, Nr. 49, 1924.

117. "Aufwertung!" in *Für Vaterland und Freiheit. Wahlzeitung der DDP*, Nr. 4, 1924, and "Die Demokratie und die Aufwertung," *Materialen zur Demokratischen Politik*, Nr. 112, 1924, both in BA, ZSg.1, 27/1.

118. Jones, "Inflation, Revaluation," pp. 155–66.

119. Maier, *Recasting Bourgeois Europe*, pp. 359–63. While stressing the "unequal destinies" of middle-class groups, Maier argues that the *Mittelstand* was not destroyed by the inflation. He points out, for example, that "the percentage of national income earned by German assets was almost as large by 1929 as in 1914," adding, however, that "the holdings may have become far more concentrated." It is precisely this redistribution of income that could be profoundly unsettling in a social and political sense. Maier's reliance on objective economic criteria to ascertain the inflation's impact on social groups results in a useful corrective to the simplistic view of a homogeneous middle-class impoverished by the inflation. This approach, however, tends to underestimate not only the economic dislocations of the inflation but the psychological ramifications of the crisis emphasized so strongly in contemporary accounts. The analysis of Laursen and Pedersen, *The German Inflation*, suffers from this same orientation, pp. 109–22.

120. *Statistisches Jahrbuch*, 1924–1925, 44:289. See also Josef Nothaas, "Die Stellenlosigkeit der Angestellten," p. 290.

121. See *Wirtschaft und Statistik*, 4 (1924):119, and 5 (1925):60; as well as *Statistisches Jahrbuch*, 1924–1925, 44:285.

122. "Beamtenabbau und Wirtschaft," *Vom Gange deutschen Wirtschaftslebens. Beilage zur Deutsche Handels-Wacht/Zeitschrift des Deutschnationalen, Gehilfen-Verbandes*, Nr. 4, 7 May 1924.

123. "Der Kaufmannsgehilfe im Einzelhandel," *Deutsche Handels-Wacht*, Nr. 17 (754), 18 June 1924.

124. "Wahlaufruf," *Der Angestellte. Monatsschrift des Gewerkschaftsbundes der Angestellten*, 1 December 1924, Nr. 3 (Gaubezirk Mainz), BA, ZSg.1, 192/1.

125. "An alle Angestellten," *Der Freie Angestellte. Zeitschrift des Zentralverbandes der Angestellten*, 26 November 1924, Nr. 22, GStA, HA xii, iv, Nr. 266.

126. See Rudolf Jobst, "Die Deutsche Angestelltenbewegung in ihrer grundsätzlicher Stellung zu Kapitalismus und Klassenkampf," pp. 72–76. See

also the DHV pamphlet *Soziale Reaktion und Afa-Bund Arm in Arm*, GStA, HA xii, iv, Nr. 226.

127. Auch eine Wahl-Bilanz," *Deutsche Handels-Wacht*, Nr. 38 (775), 24 December 1924.

128. The DHV, for example, opposed the introduction of agricultural tariffs and, perhaps more fundamentally, remained opposed to monarchy. Fritz Croner, "Die Angestelltenbewegung nach der Währungsstabilisierung," pp. 128–31.

129. *Handlungsgehilfen-Angestellte, Augen auf!* DNVP leaflet, 1924, GStA, HA xii, iv, Nr. 187.

130. *Privatangestellte!* and *Angestellte, aufgepasst!* DNVP leaflets, 1924, BA, ZSg.1, 44/9.

131. "Der Angestellte wählt rechts," *Der Tag*, 7 December 1924.

132. See, e.g., *Die Partei der Privatangestellten, national und sozial ist die Deutsche Volkspartei*, DVP leaflet, 1924, Landesarchiv Berlin, Rep. 240, Acc. 1964, Nr. 42. See also "Angestelltenfragen im Reichstag," *Flugschriften der Deutschen Volkspartei*, Nr. 51, Berlin, 1924.

133. *Satzung und Bundesprogramm des Gewerkschaftsbundes der Angestellten*, Berlin, 1924, pp. 28–31.

134. See, e.g., *Allgemeine, grundsätzliche Richtlinien*, völkisch coalition leaflet, 1924, GStA, HA xii, iv, Nr. 211; *Der völkische Block. Was will er?* and *Richtlinien der Grossdeutschen Volksgemeinschaft*, völkisch coalition leaflets, 1924, HA/42/857, 869.

135. See, e.g., the leaflets *Beamte! Beamtinnen! Angestellte! Pensionäre!* and *Beamte, Arbeiter, Angestellte*, völkisch coalition leaflets, 1924, both in HA/42/843, 869.

136. *An die deutsche Arbeiterschaft der Stirn und der Faust*, völkisch coalition leaflet, 1924, HA/42/857.

137. See chapter 4, text at nn. 155–60.

138. The National Socialists assumed a strong antiunion stance in 1924 and hence were alienated from the important white-collar organizations. For the Nazi position see *An die schaffende Bevölkerung zur Aufklärung*, völkisch coalition leaflet, 1924, HA/42/843.

139. See Jane Caplan, "The Politics of Administration: The Reich Interior Ministry and the German Civil Service, 1933–1943," pp. 707–31.

140. Theodore Abel Collection, Hoover Institution Archives, Biography 276.

141. Ibid., Biography 112.

142. Andreas Kunz, "Stand versus Klasse. Beamtenschaft und Gewerkschaften im Konflikt um den Personalabbau 1923/24," pp. 55–86.

143. Ibid., pp. 55–70.

144. Quoted in ibid., p. 72.

145. In 1922 the DBB's membership accounted for 56% of all organized civil servants, and the ADB's 25%. By 1928 the DBB's share had soared to 78%, while the ADB's had fallen to just over 10%. The absolute figures are presented in ibid., p. 58.

146. Ibid., pp. 67–69. The problem of civil-service salaries and real income is treated extensively in Andreas Kunz, "Verteilungskampf oder Interessenkonsensus? Einkommensentwicklung und Sozialverhalten von Arbeitnehmergruppen in der Inflationszeit 1914–1924," pp. 347–84.

147. See *Statistisches Jahrbuch, 1924–1925*, 64:286; and Peter Quante, "Beiträge zur Statistik der Beamtengehälter," pp. 1–8. For an impassioned attack on this "leveling process," see Alfred Weber, *Die Not der geistigen Arbeiter*, pp. 16–25, 41–51.

148. Theodore Abel Collection, Hoover Institution Archives, Biography 233.

149. For salary figures see *Statistisches Jahrbuch . . . 1924–1925*, 64:286. The quotations are from Georg Schreiber, *Die Not der deutschen Wissenschaft und der geistigen Arbeiter*, cited in Ringer, *The German Inflation*, pp. 107–108.

150. *Statistisches Jahrbuch . . . 1924–1925*, 64:286.

151. On conflicts within the civil service, see Kunz, "Verteilungskampf oder Interessenkonsensus?" The "persecution" of the civil service is dealt with in *Gewerkschaftsbericht des Deutschen Beamtenbundes für die Zeit von September 1924 bis Oktober 1926*, Berlin, 1926, p. 108.

152. *Wahlaufruf der DVFP*, völkisch coalition leaflet, 1924, GStA, HA XII, IV, Nr. 212.

153. *Beamten! Beamtinnen!* völkisch coalition leaflet, 1924, HA/42/843.

154. *Wahlaufruf der Deutschvölkischen Freiheitspartei*, völkisch coalition leaflet, 1924, GStA, HA XII, IV, Nr. 212.

155. *Beamten! Beamtinnen!* völkisch coalition leaflet, 1924, HA/42/843.

156. *Schwarz-rot-gold oder rot?* völkisch coalition leaflet, 1924, Landesarchiv Berlin, Rep. 240, Acc. 1941, Nr. 18.

157. See "Die Beamten und der 7. Dezember," *Kreuz-Zeitung*, 29 November 1924; *Beamte! Was taten dis Deutschnationalen fur Euch?*; *Die Stellungnahmne der DNVP zu den Goldgehältern und zum Abbau des Berufsbeamtentums*; *Beamte! Die Stunde der Ablösung ist da!*; and *Wer hat das Beamtenelend verschuldet?* DNVP leaflets, 1924, GStA, HA XII, IV, Nrs. 186–188.

158. *Beamte! Die Stunde der Ablösung ist da!* DNVP leaflet, 1924, GStA, HA XII, IV, Nr. 186.

159. *Beamte, Arbeiter, Angestellte*, völkisch coalition leaflet, HA/42/869. 1924.

160. "Beamtentum und Volkskultur," *Der Tag*, 9 March 1924.

161. "Beamtenschaft und Reichstagswahl," *Berliner Stimmen*, Nr. 19, 1924.

162. See the original DVP program in *Die Programme der politischen Parteien Deutschlands*, ed. H. Krey, p. 32.

163. "Beamtenschaft und Reichstagswahl," *Berliner Stimmen*, Nr. 19, 1924; See also "Beamtenpolitik der DVP," in *Flugschriften der Deutschen Volkspartei*," Nr. 58, Berlin, 1924.

164. *Welche Partei wählt der deutsche Beamte? Die Partei, die die Autorität des Staates aufgerichtet hat*, and *Achtung! Beamte!* DVP leaflets, 1924, GStA, HA XII, IV, Nr. 165.

165. *Berliner Tageblatt*, 23 April and 3 May 1924. The DDP position on the *Personalabbau* is spelled out in "Beamtenfragen," *Materialen zur Demokratischen Politik*, Nr. 93, Berlin, 1924.

166. *Der Wähler, Führer zur Reichs- und Landstagswahl am 7. Dezember*, Nr. 3, 1924, DDP pamphlet, Landesarchiv Berlin, Rep. 240, Acc. 1964, Nr. 204.

167. *Statistisches Jahrbuch, 1924–1925*, 64:289.

168. Peter Merkl, *Political Violence under the Swastika*, p. 47.

169. *Wirtschaft und Statistik*, 5 (1925):62.

170. See Peter-Christian Witt, "Finanzpolitik und sozialer Wandel in Kreig und Inflation 1918–1924," pp. 395–426.

171. For the impact of the inflation on the working class and its organizations, see Maier, *Recasting Bourgeois Europe*, pp. 363–64; as well as Hans Hermann Hartwich, *Arbeitsmarkt, Verbände und Staat 1918–1933*, pp. 67, 102.

172. *Wirtschaft und Statistik*, 5 (1925):60.

173. Ibid., pp. 62, 118, and 375. See also *Statistisches Jahrbuch . . . 1924–1925*, 64:289.

174. "Sozialpolitik und Reichstagswahl," *Vorwärts*, 11 November 1924.

175. "Wer Hatte Recht? Sozialdemokraten, Kommunisten und Dawes Plan," *Vorwärts*, 5 December 1924.

176. *Die Rote Fahne*, 29 April 1924.

177. Ibid., 25 March and 29 April 1924.

178. Ibid., 29 March 1924.

179. Ibid., 7 December 1924. Both the Nazis and Nationalists employed a similar slogan.

180. *An die deutsche Arbeiterschaft der Stirn und der Faust*, *völkisch* coalition leaflet, HA/42/857.

181. *Aus dem Schulbuch der Marxisten*, *völkisch* coalition leaflet, 1924, BA, ZSg.1, 45/13.

182. *Deutsche Arbeiter*, *völkisch* coalition leaflet, 1924, BA, ZSg.1, 45/13.

183. *Deutschvölkische Freiheitspartei (Allgemeine grundsätzliche Richtlinien)*, *völkisch* coalition leaflet, 1924, GStA, HA xii, iv, Nr. 212.

184. *Zu den Stadtverordnetenwahl*, Leipzig, *völkisch* coalition leaflet, 1924, BA, ZSg.1, 45/14.

185. *Rechts oder links. Nationalistisch oder sozialistisch*, *völkisch* coalition leaflet, 1924, HA/42/869.

186. *An die deutsche Arbeiterschaft der Stirn und der Faust*, *völkisch* coalition leaflet, 1924, HA/42/857.

187. *Zu den Stadtverordnetenwahl*, *völkisch* coalition leaflet, 1924, BA, ZSg.1, 45/14.

188. See, for example, *Kommunisten und Völkischen*, SPD leaflet, 1924, GStA, HA xii, iv, Nr. 63.

189. *Arbeiter, Angestellte, Beamte! Werktätige in Stadt und Land!* and 'Nieder mit der Judenrepublik,' KPD leaflets, 1924, GStA, HA xii, iv, Nr. 90.

190. Degree of union organization was a significant factor in distinguishing the sources of Social Democratic and Communist electoral support. In forty of the republic's largest cities, which include the major seats of German industry, the SPD vote rose and the KPD vote fell as the percentage of the population organized in the Free Trade Unions increased. In those cities where the proportion of the population belonging to ADGB affiliates reached 18%, the average Social Democratic vote in May was 33%, far exceeding its 20% nationally. In those cities where less than 8% of the inhabitants were organized in the Free Trade Unions, the average margin of Communist ascendance over the SPD reached almost 16%. In each of these cities, mining and/or iron and steel production employed over 20% of the labor force. These calculations are based on membership figures for 1924 provided in the *Jahrbuch des ADGB, 1924,* p. 314. See Thomas Childers, "The Social Bases of Electoral Politics in Urban Germany, 1919–1933: A Sociological Analysis of Voting Behavior in the Weimar Republic," pp. 118–24.

191. For an explanation of the resulting new categories, see methodological appendix.

192. Theodore Abel Collection, Hoover Institution Archives, Biography 19.

193. See, for example, *Wahlaufruf der DVFP,* GStA, HA XII, IV, Nr. 212. See also *Völkisch-Sozialer Block (Wahlkreis Ostsachsen). Was wir wollen und was wir fordern,* and *An die schaffende Bevölkerung zur Aufklärung,* HA/42/843, 871; *Deutsche Arbeiter!* BA, ZSg.1, 45/13; and *National-Sozialistische Freiheitsbewegung Deutschlands. Vereinigte Völkische Liste,* Landesarchiv Berlin, Rep. 240, Acc. 1941, Nr. 17.

194. Quoted in Reginald Phelps, "Dokumente aus der Kampfzeit der NSDAP—1923," p. 1037.

195. The DNVP was particularly concerned about the hostile attitude of the *völkisch* movement toward the monarchy and religion. See, for example, "Das Ziel der Wahl," *Der Tag,* 9 March 1924. Furthermore, the conservative *Nord-westdeutsche Handwerkzeitung* viewed National Socialism in 1924 as "eine reine Arbeitnehmerbewegung," concluding that the Nazis "can never become the representatives of the commercial middle class." Quoted in Winkler, *Mittelstand, Demokratie und Nationalsozialismus,* p. 159. The Social Democrats, on the other hand, argued that the Nazis "are fighting Marxism in order to deprive the workers of their rights" and that the party "represents the interests of management." *Vorwärts,* 27 April 1924. The Communists concurred, maintaining that "in all matters of economic exploitation, the Fascists stand with the other bourgeois parties against the working masses." "Wahlaufruf der KPD," *Reichstags-Handbuch III. Wahlperiode 1924,* p. 143.

196. *Ziele der NSFB, völkisch* coalition leaflet, 1924, GStA, HA XII, IV, Nr. 211.

197. "Der völkische Block," confidential *völkisch* manuscript, 8 February 1924, BA ZSg.1, 45/13.

198. *Ziele der DVFP, völkisch* coalition leaflet, 1924, GStA, HA XII, IV, Nr. 212.

199. *An die Berliner Bevölkerung, völkisch* coalition leaflet, 1924, HA/42/843.

200. Communist strength among Catholics was limited primarily to the coalmining and industrial centers in the Ruhr, representing, in effect, a demographic coincidence.

201. See Johannes Schauff, *Die Deutschen Katholiken und die Zentrumspartei*, p. 129.

202. For a breakdown of the Bavarian results, see Dietrich Thränhardt, *Wahlen und politische Stukturen in Bayern 1848–1953*, pp. 125–80. See also Pridham, *Hitler's Rise*, pp. 146–83.

203. *Katholische Wähler und Wählerinnen*, und *Dem Christlichen Volke*, Zentrum leaflets, 1924, BA, ZSg.1, 108/8. See also "Nach Walhall," *Germania*, 7 April 1924.

204. *Auf der ganzen Linie versagt*, Zentrum leaflet, 1924, BA, ZSg.1, 108/8.

205. See, for example, *Entscheidet Sich für Die Politik der Mitte*, and *Ein Wort zur Wahl*, Zentrum leaflets, 1924, BA, ZSg.1, 108/8; "Die Mittlere Linie," *Germania*, 26 April 1924, and "Stärkt die Mitte," *Germania*, 27 November 1924.

206. Wähler und Wählerinnen, Zentrum leaflet, 1924, Landesarchiv Berlin, Rep. 240, Acc. 1962, Nr. 21.

207. "Katholische Arbeiterschaft und Reichstagswahl," *Germania*, 15 November 1924.

208. *Kulturkampf! völkisch* coalition leaflet, 1924, HA/42/857.

209. Although details were never spelled out, the party did advocate the exclusion of Jews from the educational system. "Jews must not be permitted to be teachers of German children and youths," the *völkisch* platform of 1924 declared. See *DVFP Allgemeine grundsätzliche Richtlinien*, GStA, HA XII, IV, Nr. 212; and *Die völkischen Grundsätze und Forderungen*, HA/42/869.

210. *Evangelische Christen schützt Euer Christentum vor Parteipolitik, völkisch* coalition leaflet, 1924, HA/42/843.

211. Ibid.

212. *Kirche und Politik*, and *Kulturkampf, völkisch* coalition leaflets, 1924, HA/42/869, 857.

213. See *Seid bereit. Überall rüsten christentumsfeindliche Mächte zum Kampf*, and *Hände weg!* DNVP leaflets, 1924, BA, ZSg.1, 44/9.

214. *Evangelische Christen, schützt Euer Christentum vor Parteipolitik, völkisch* coalition leaflet, 1924, HA/42/869.

215. *Die Judenfrage*, and *Die völkischen Grundsätze und Forderungen, völkisch* coalition leaflets, 1924, HA/42/843, 869.

216. "Christliche Frau, erkenne deine Pflicht!" *Germania*, 4 June 1920. See also "An die Frauen," *Germania*, 23 April 1924.

217. "An die deutsche Frau," *Der Tag*, 3 December 1924; and "Christentum und Deutschtum, die Losungsworte unserer Zukunft," *Kreuz-Zeitung*, 26 October 1924. Similar themes were regularly developed in "Kirche, Heimat, Haus," a daily section of the conservative *Der Tag*.

218. *Berliner Stimmen. Zeitschrift für Politik. Nachrichtenblatt der DVP im Wahlkreis Berlin*, 18 November 1924.

219. "Die Wählerin. Hausfrauen und Mütter!" in *Der Wähler, Führer zur Reichs- und Landtagswahl am 7. Dez.*, Nr. 3, 1924.

220. See Brian L. Peterson, "The Politics of Working-Class Women in the Weimar Republic," pp. 87–111. The difficulties encountered by the KPD in developing a female constituency are examined in Silvia Kontos, *Die Partei kämpft wie ein Mann. Die Frauenpolitik der KPD in der Weimarer Republik.*

221. Tingsten, *Political Behavior*, pp. 37–65; and R. Hartwig, "Wie die Frauen im deutschen Reich von ihren politischen Wahlrecht Gebrauch machen," pp. 497–515.

Chapter III

1. The first *Bürgerblock* cabinet, headed by the DVP's Hans Luther, consisted of the DNVP, DVP, and Zentrum and served until 5 December 1925, when the DDP entered the coalition. Democratic participation, however, was terminated a year later, leaving the original coalition partners in a government presided over by the Zentrum's Wilhelm Marx. For details, see Stürmer, *Koalition und Opposition in der Weimarer Republik, 1924–1928*, pp. 84–181.

2. E. D. Graper, "The German Presidential Election," pp. 592–600.

3. The organizational and propagandistic components of the "urban plan" are treated most extensively in Dietrich Orlow, *History of the Nazi Party, 1919–1933*, pp. 76–127.

4. Peter D. Stachura, "Der Kristische Wendepunkt? Die NSDAP und die Reichstagswahlen vom 20. Mai 1928," pp. 66–99.

5. Hitler's *Mein Kampf*, 374, cited in Stachura, "Der kritische Wendepunkt?" pp. 75–76. See also Joseph Nyomarkay, *Charisma and Factionalism in the Nazi Party*, pp. 76–86.

6. Rundschreiben, 20 March 1926, HA/70/1529.

7. Ibid.

8. Joseph Goebbels, "Neue Methoden der Propaganda," *Nationalsozialistische Briefe*, 15 August 1926.

9. Orlow, *History of the Nazi Party*, pp. 114–26.

10. Rundschreiben nos. 76–77, Ruhr Gau, 26 April and 7 May 1928, HA/5/136.

11. Rundschreiben no. 9, Gau Brandenburg, 20 January 1928; and Rundschreiben no. 77, Ruhr Gau, 7 May 1928, HA/5/136. See also the appeals for contributions to the party's national campaign fund in the *Völkischer Beobachter* (hereafter *VB*), 15/18 April 1928.

12. See "Anordnungen der Propagandaleitung" (signed Himmler), *VB*, 8/9 May 1928, concerning the distribution of leaflets.

13. See the running advertisements in the *VB*, for the party's publishing house, the Franz Ehlers Verlag in Munich, from which leaflets, pamphlets, off-

prints from the *VB*, and the speeches of leading Nazis could be ordered. A typical advertisement on 10 May 1928, for example, offered a kilo of election placards for two marks.

14. Memorandum of 7 May 1928, addressed to "alle Gaue und selbständige Ortsgruppen der NSDAP," HA/24A/1758.

15. Oran J. Hale, *The Captive Press in the Third Reich*, pp. 40–41. According to a resolution adopted at the 1928 party congress, editors who failed to follow the guidelines established by the *Reichsleitung* could be expelled from the party; the party's official recognition of the paper would be revoked; and the paper would be boycotted by the party's membership.

16. By 1928 the NSDAP was represented in only seven of the republic's eighteen state legislatures. For provincial election returns, see *Statistisches Jahrbuch, 1928*, pp. 543–44.

17. Walter H. Kaufmann, *Monarchism in the Weimar Republic*, p. 177.

18. Results of the regional elections between 1924 and 1928 are found in the *Statistisches Jahrbuch für das Deutsche Reich*, vols. 43–51.

19. *Deutscher Mittelstand führt erbitterte Klage*, DVP leaflet, 1928, BA, ZSg.1, 42/8(1).

20. *Das Handwerk und die Wahl*, DVP leaflet, GStA., HA XII, IV, Nr. 169. See also *100% Wirtschaftspartei?*; *Wir und die Anderen*; *Deutscher Mittelstand!*; and *Der Bürger erwacht!*; DVP leaflets, 1928, BA, ZSg.1, 42/8(1).

21. *Deutscher Hannovaner!* DDP leaflet, 1928, BA, ZSg.1, 27/19(6).

22. See below, text at nn. 133–43.

23. See *Was bei Splitterparteien herauskommt!* DNVP leaflet, 1928, GStA, HA XII, IV, Nr. 192. See also *Gebrochene Wahlversprechungen der DNVP?* BA, ZSg.1, 44/9(4).

24. See Thomas Childers, "Inflation, Stabilization, and Political Realignment in Germany 1924–1928," pp. 409–31.

25. "Aus der Bewegung," *VB*, 31 May 1928.

26. "Bekanntmachung," *VB*, 1 April 1928. See also Orlow, *History of the Nazi Party*, pp. 117–19, 136–38; and Stachura, "Der kritische Wendepunkt?" pp. 93–95. The local implications of the new National Socialist strategy are effectively treated in Noakes, *Nazi Party in Lower Saxony*, pp. 108–55.

27. "Propaganda-Aktion," 24 December 1928, HA/10/203. For an example of the planning behind a similar Nazi propaganda offensive see the "8-Wochen Werbeplan" of the Gau München-Oberbayern in September-October 1929, in HA/9/190.

28. The Müller government hoped to achieve evacuation of the Rhineland in exchange for German acceptance of the plan. For details of the negotiations see Jon Jacobson, *Locarno Diplomacy*, pp. 124–83.

29. In order for a referendum to be held, petitions containing signatures of one-tenth of the electorate were required. If the Reichstag then rejected the legislation proposed in the petition, the issue was to be placed before the general electorate in a popular referendum.

30. "Wahlaufruf der Nationalsozialistischen Deutschen Arbeiterpartei," *Reichstags-Handbuch. V. Wahlperiode 1930*, Berlin, 1930, p. 161. See also

Gottfried Feder, "Betrachtungen zum Youngplan," *Nationalsozialistische Mon-atshefte*, (*NSMH*), Heft 6, September 1930, 249–56.

31. *Das Dritte Versailles*, leaflet of the Reichausschuss für das Deutsche Volksbegehren, BA, ZSg.1, 83/2. See also *Sklaverei Bedeutet der Pariser Tribut-plan*, BA, ZSg.1, 83/4.

32. Feder, "Bechtrachtungen zum Youngplan," pp. 249–56.

33. Erich Eyck, *A History of the Weimar Republic*, 2:204–25. For a regional breakdown of the results see *Statistisches Jahrbuch, 1929*, 68:566–67.

34. Franz-Josef Heyen, *Nationalsozialismus im Alltag*, pp. 19, 33.

35. Rolf Wagenführ, "Die Industriewirtschaft. Entwicklungstendenzen der deutschen und internationalen Industrieproduktion 1860 bis 1932," p. 62. See also *Statistische Beilage zum Reichsarbeitsblatt 1930*, Nr. 7:1–4.

36. For details on the unemployment insurance debate see Ludwig Preller, *Sozialpolitik in der Weimarer Republik*, pp. 418–42; and Helga Timm, *Die Deutsche Sozialpolitik und der Bruch der grossen Koalition im Marz 1930*, pp. 124–34.

37. Werner Conze, "Die Krise des Parteienstaates in Deutschland 1929/30," p. 65. See also Martin Vogt, "Die Stellung der Koalitionsparteien zur Finanz-politik 1928–1930," pp. 439–62; and Ilse Mauer, *Reichsfinanzen und grosse Koalition*, pp. 80–85.

38. Timm, *Die Deutsche Sozialpolitik*, pp. 178–89.

39. Karl Dietrich Bracher, *Die Auflösung der Weimarer Republik*, pp. 303–9.

40. Ibid., pp. 335–47; Conze, "Die Krise des Parteienstaates," pp. 74–83.

41. The results of the elections are found in *Statistisches Jahrbuch . . . 1930*, 69:564–65, and 50:546–47. For an examination of two of these elections see Ellsworth Faris, "Takeoff Point for the National Socialist Party: The Landtag Election in Baden, 1929," pp. 140–71; and Donald R. Tracey, "The Develop-ment of the National Socialist Party in Thuringia, 1924–1930," pp. 23–50. In November 1929 the NSDAP had also increased its share of the vote in the *Ge-meindetag* elections, more than doubting its vote in each of the fifteen cities holding such campaigns. See Jerzy Holzer, *Parteien und Massen. Die politisches Krise in Deutschland 1928–1930*, pp. 60–61.

42. While the "opposition wing" of the party strongly endorsed the DNVP's withdrawal from the first Luther cabinet in protest of Stresemann's Locarno policy, the Reichslandbund, the Schlesischer Landbund, and other agrarian or-ganizations vigorously opposed the party's decision. The Brandenburgischer Landbund, for example, warned that a DNVP strategy of "absolute opposition" would preclude Nationalist influence in matters of great importance to German agriculture and would, thus, force the Bund to turn to those parties in a posi-tion to offer tangible support. See Manfred Dörr, "Die Deutschnationale Volks-partei 1925 bis 1928," pp. 212–20. In addition, the Arbeitsausschuss Deutsch-nationaler Industrieller cautioned the Nationalist leadership it "could not share the prevalent view that the DNVP would achieve more in opposition than in coalition." Quoted in Attila Chanady, "The Disintegration of the German Na-tional People's Party 1924–1930," pp. 76–77; see also pp. 67–68, 71–73. Similarly, the Vereinigung deutschnationaler höheren Ministerialbeamten com-

plained that the party's civil-service constituents would have to seek representation in other parties if the DNVP could not place its supporters in key administrative positions. Bracher, *Die Auflösung*, p. 311; and Stürmer, *Koalition und Opposition*, pp. 248–54.

43. For the dilemma of the DNVP between 1925 and 1928 see Kaufmann, *Monarchism*, pp. 153–77. Chanady argues convincingly that "the transition from convenient opposition to responsible government work brought to the surface latent structural and ideological cleavages which subsequently became a potent cause of disintegration." Chanady, "The Disintegration," p. 65. See also Dörr, "Die Deutschnationale Volkspartei" pp. 391–465.

44. Iris Hamel, *Völkischer Verband und nationale Gewerkschaft*, pp. 217–28. Also see Larry E. Jones, "The Crisis of White Collar Interest Politics: Deutschnationaler Handlungsgehilfen-Verband and Deutsche Volkspartei in the World Economic Crisis," pp. 813–14.

45. Bracher, *Die Aüflosung*, pp. 318–19.

46. Chanady, "The Disintegration," pp. 84–88.

47. Ibid., pp. 88–91. On the founding of the new conservative splinter parties see Günter Opitz, *Der Christlich-Soziale Volksdienst*, pp. 130–33, 145–50; and Erasmus Jonas, *Die Volkskonservativen 1928–1933*, pp. 47–82. Westarp's own explanation of his break with the DNVP is found in his article "Die Gründe der Trennung von der Deutschnationalen Volkspartei," *Kreuz-Zeitung*, 24 July 1930.

48. Attila Chanady, "The Dissolution of the German Democratic Party in 1930," p. 1442. See also Larry E. Jones, "The Dying Middle: Weimar Democracy and the Failure of Bourgeois Unity, 1924–1930," pp. 470–71.

49. Quoted in Chanady, "The Dissolution," p. 1443.

50. Ibid.

51. For an analysis of "economic democracy" see Timm, *Die Deutsch Sozialpolitik*, p. 52–60.

52. Gustav Stolper, *Die wirtschaftlich-soziale Weltanschauung der Demokratie*, p. 7.

53. Jones, "The Dying Middle," pp. 459–67. Hellpach's goal was the formation of "a large, strong conservative people's party."

54. Erich Matthias and Rudolf Morsey, "Die Deutsche Staatspartei," in *Das Ende der Parteien 1933*, ed. Erich Matthias and Rudolf Morsey, p. 34. See also Werner Schneider, *Die Deutsche Demokratische Partei in der Weimarer Republik 1924–1930*, pp. 253–63.

55. *Was ist die Deutsche Staatspartei?* DSP leaflet, 1930, BA, ZSg.1, 27/20(2).

56. *Sammlung in der Deutschen Staatspartei*, DSP leaflet, 1930, BA, ZSg.1, 27/20(2).

57. *Die Staatspartei kämpft für Deutschlands Zukunft*, DSP leaflet, 1930, BA, ZSg.1, 27/20(2). See also "Weshalb darf ein Staatsbürger nicht Interessenparteien wählen?" *Materialen zur Demokratischen Politik*, Nr. 147, 1930, BA, ZSg.1, 27/1.

58. "Was ist die Deutsche Staatspartei?" BA, ZSg.1, 27/20(2).

59. See Werner Stephan, *Aufstieg und Verfall des Linksliberalismus 1918–1933*.

60. Henry A. Turner, Jr., *Stresemann and the Politics of the Weimar Republic*, p. 241; Lothar Döhn, "Zur Verschränkung der Deutschen Volkspartei mit grosswirtschaftlich-industriellen Interessen im Herrschaftssystem der Weimarer Republik," p. 905.

61. Stresemann quoted in Jones, "The Dying Middle," p. 201.

62. Ibid., 544–59.

63. In the Landtag elections of 12 May 1929, the DVP had captured 13.4% of the vote; a year later only 8.7%. *Statistisches Jahrbuch für den Freistaat Sachsen 1930*, 49:327.

64. Larry Eugene Jones, "Sammlung oder Zersplitterung? Die Bestrebungen zur Bildung einer neuen Mittelpartei in der Endphase der Weimarer Republik 1930–1933," pp. 268–69.

65. Orlow, *History of the Nazi Party*, pp. 139–48.

66. "Geschlossen und zuversichtlich in den Wahlkampf. NS-Führertag in München," *VB*, 9 September 1930.

67. "Achtung! Reichstagswahlen!" ibid., 25 July 1930.

68. See Rundschreiben no. 6 of Gau Gross-Berlin, 5 August 1930, HA/70/1529.

69. Ibid.

70. Ibid.

71. The list of official Reich speakers is found in HA/24A/1758.

72. See "Die Parole des Kampfes: Jagt sie weg, die 'Haufen von Interessenten!'" *VB*, 20/21 July 1930.

73. "Am 18. August beginnt die Lawine," *VB*, 17/18 August 1930.

74. On the role of Nazi violence during the campaign, see Dee Richard Wernette, "Political Violence and German Elections," pp. 101–35.

75. See, for example, James K. Pollock, "The German Reichstag Election of 1930," pp. 989–95; Hans Neisser, "Sozialstatistische Analyse des Wahlergebnisses," pp. 654–59; and Maximilian Meyer, "Der Nichtwähler," pp. 495–525.

76. For a summary of the Reich Statistical Bureau's studies of the 1924 election see *Wirtschaft und Statistik*, 1926, p. 235. The figures for Mainz are found in the same journal, 1926, p. 896. A more extensive presentation of the Reich Statistical Bureau's findings is found in *Statistik des Deutschen Reiches*, 315:35–40. For Nuremberg, see Meyer, "Der Nichtwähler," pp. 495–525.

77. Theodore W. Meckstroth, "Conditions of Partisan Realignments: A Study of Electoral Change," pp. 132–43, 177. Meckstroth's skepticism about the role of new voters in the Nazi breakthrough of 1930 is shared by Lipset, "'Fascism'—Left, Right, and Center," pp. 130–76; W. Phillips Shively, "Party Identification, Party Choice, and Voting Stability: The Weimar Case," pp. 1203–25; and Allan Schnaiberg, "A Critique of Karl O'Lessker's 'Who Voted for Hitler?'" pp. 732–35.

78. For example, O'Lessker, "Who Voted for Hitler?"; Shively, "Party Identification, Party Choice, and Voting Stability," pp. 1203–25.

79. *Statistik des Deutschen Reichs*, 348:211–12; 391:42. See also *Finanzen*

und Steueren im In- und Ausland. Ein Statistisches Handbuch, Statistisches Reichsamt, Berlin, 1930, p. 336.

80. Bernhard Benning and Robert Nieschlag, "Umsatz, Lagehaltung und Kosten im deutschen Einzelhandel 1924 bis 1932," pp. 10, 78.

81. "Das Deutsche Volkseinkommen vor und nach dem Kriege," *Einzelschriften zur Statistik des Deutschen Reichs*, 34:86.

82. Benning and Nieschlag, "Umsatz, Lagehaltung and Kosten," pp. 10,13. Rates of growth for the consumer cooperatives, presented as a percentage of the previous year's turnover, were: 1925 = 50%, 1926 = 17%, and 1928 = 17%.

83. Heinz Grünbaum, "Die Umsatzschwankungen des Einzelhandels als Problem der Betriebspolitik," pp. 5–6; Benning and Nieschlag, "Umsatz, Lagehaltung und Kosten," p. 65.

84. See *Vierteljahreshefte zur Statistik des Deutschen Reichs*, 35, Heft 1 (1926):146–49; and 39, Heft 2 (1931):18.

85. Helmuth Storch, "Einmalige Erhebung über die laufend unterstützten arbeitsfähigen Erwerbslosen in den Städten über 50,000 Einwohnern," pp. 111–12. Only persons from the domestic services sector exceeded the self-employed in longevity of unemployment relief.

86. Theodore Abel Collection, Hoover Institution Archives, Biography 76. For a similar experience see Biography 167.

87. See Benning and Nieschlag, "Umsatz' Lagehaltung und Kosten," p. 13; and "Mittelständische Wirtschaft," p. 204.

88. Based on figures provided in *Statistik des Deutschen Reichs*, 191:97; 430:115.

89. *Vierteljahreshefte zur Statistik des Deutschen Reichs*, 40, Heft 2 (1932): 18–19. See also *Vierteljahrshefte zur Konjunkturforschung* (1933):Teil B, 258.

90. Benning and Nieschlag, "Umsatz' Lagehaltung und Kosten," pp. 10, 65.

91. John Bradshaw Holt, *German Agricultural Policy, 1918–1934*, pp. 129–36. See also the reports of the Enquete-Ausschuss on agriculture, *Die Verschuldungs- und Kreditlage der deutschen Landwirtschaft*, pp. 33–41; and *Die Förderung der Landwirtschaft durch öffentliche Mittel*, pp. 4–16.

92. Georges Castellan, "Zur sozialen Bilanz der Prosperität 1924–1929," p. 106.

93. David Abraham, *The Collapse of the Weimar Republic*, pp. 70–71.

94. Ibid., p. 84.

95. Castellan, "Zur sozialen Bilanz," p. 105. This represented a considerable deterioration of agriculture's position since 1913, when average per capita farm income had stood 22% below the national average.

96. Walter G. Hoffmann, *Das Wachstum der deutschen Wirtschaft*, p. 562.

97. Ibid., p. 542.

98. Abraham, *The Collapse of the Weimar Republic*, pp. 91–92, 94.

99. Alexander Gerschenkron, *Bread and Democracy in Germany*, pp. 149–51.

100. A summary of the figures on foreclosures is found in Abraham *The Collapse of the Weimar Republic*, p. 86; figures on indebtedness are located in *Vierteljahrshefte zur Konjunkturforschung*, Sonderheft 22 (1931):37, 111.

101. Gerschenkron, *Bread and Democracy in Germany*, p. 134.

102. Hoffmann, *Das Wachstum der deutschen Wirtschaft*, p. 542. See also Holt, *German Agricultural Policy*, pp. 104–10.

103. Abraham, *The Collapse of the Weimar Republic*, pp. 91–92.

104. See Gerhard Stoltenberg, *Politische Strömungen im schleswig-holsteinischen Landvolk 1918–1933*, pp. 107–15; and Rudolf Heberle, *From Democracy to Nazism*, pp. 62–89.

105. Hans-Jürgen Puhle, *Politische Agrarbewegungen in kapitalistischen Industriegesellschaften*, p. 90; and Jones, "Dying Middle," p. 37. On the spread of rural unrest into the surrounding provinces and the inability of the DNVP to direct it, see Noakes, *The Nazi Party in Lower Saxony*, pp. 118–20. An alternate view is found in Werner Methfessel, "Christliche-Nationale Bauern- und Landvolkspartei (CNLB), 1928–1933," pp. 241–44.

106. In Württemberg the Nationalist vote fell from 10.9 percent in December 1924 to 6.2 percent in 1928. In the predominantly Protestant, rural communities of the Württemberg sample, the DNVP slipped from 12 percent to 6 percent.

107. See Puhle, *Politische Agrarbewegungen*, 90–91.

108. Although Hugenberg was hardly a stranger to agricultural affairs, his determination to pursue a radical rejectionist policy toward the Weimar state and his prominent association with industry quickly led to difficulties with important elements within the RLB and the Green Front. See Dieter Gessner, *Agrarverbände in der Weimarer Republik*, pp. 219–34.

109. See Werner Angress, "The Political Role of the Peasantry in the Weimar Republic," pp. 543–45; and Puhle, *Politische Agrarbewegungen*, p. 91.

110. There is remarkably little in the literature on National Socialist agrarian policy before 1928. The most systematic treatment is found in Edmund N. Todd, "National Socialist Agrarian Policies: 1919–1928," especially pp. 37–106. Todd's analysis of Nazi literature on agriculture clearly demonstrates that while the party heightened its emphasis on the rural voter after 1928, the NSDAP did not "discover" the farmer in that year but rather built upon an already well-established set of policies and appeals. A cursory discussion of these pre-1928 policies is also found in John Farquaharson, *The Plough and the Swastika*.

111. "An den deutschen Bauern!" *Der Angriff* (hereafter *DA*), 7 May 1928. See also Wilhelm Frick, "Die Nationalsozialisten im Reichstag, 1924–1928," *NSMH*, Heft 4 (1928): 39–40. *Bauern!*, NSDAP leaflet, BHStA, Abt. V, F 9.

112. Horst Gies, "The NSDAP and the Agrarian Organizations in the Final Phase of the Weimar Republic," p. 46.

113. The entire proclamation is translated in Barbara Miller Lane and Leila J. Rupp, *Nazi Ideology before 1933*, pp. 118–23. See also Hermann Schneider, "Unser täglich Brot; Lebensfragen der deutschen Landwirtschaft," *Nationalsozialistische Bibliothek* (hereafter *NSB*) (1930): 26–32.

114. Gies, "The NSDAP and the Agrarian Organizations," pp. 48–51.

115. Hans Buchner, "Die sozialkapitalistischen Konsumvereine," *NSB* (1929): 41–59.

116. "Wer schützt Dich, Mittelstand," *DA*, 30 April 1928.

117. "Das Gericht vom 14. September," *VB*, 10 September 1930.

118. Graf E. Raventlow, "Nemesis über dem Burgertum," *NSMH*, Heft 1, (1930):9.

119. "Gewerbetreibende, Handwerker!" *Der Angriff*, 7 May 1928.

120. Quoted in Heinrich August Winkler, *Mittelstand, Demokratie und Nationalsozialismus*, p. 168.

121. *Hitlers Kern: Sowjetstern*, DDP leaflet, 1930, BA, ZSg.1, 27/20 (2).

122. See "Der Einzelhandel am 14. September," and "Sozialdemokratie gegen selbstständige Gewerbetreibende," in the DVP's *Berliner Stimmen*, 7 September 1930; and *Deutsche Allgemeine Zeitung*, 10 September 1930.

123. *Herunter der Maske!* DVP leaflet, 1930, BA, ZSg.1, 42/8 (2).

124. *Rettet Deutschland!* DVP leaflet, 1930, BA, ZSg.1, 42/8 (2).

125. *Staatsbürger!* BA, ZSg.1, 27/20(2); and "Das wirtschafts und sozialpolitische Manifest der Deutschen Staatspartei," GStA, HA xii, iv, Nr. 145. See also *Wahlzeitung für die Deutsche Staatspartei*, September 1930, Nr. 1; and *Frankfurter Zeitung*, 6 September 1930.

126. *An alle Handwerker und Kaufleute*, DSP leaflet, GStA, HA xii, iv, Nr. 145.

127. "Staatspartei verhindert Verfall der Mitte," *Wahlzeitung für die DSP*, September 1930, Nr. 1.

128. "Die Klassenkampftheorie und ihre Widerlegung," *VB*, 23 July 1930, "Marxismus/Bürgertum, Nationalsozialismus," *VB*, 9 August 1930; and "Nationalsozialismus und Privateigentum," *VB*, 28 August 1930.

129. "Das abgewirtschaftete Young-Bürgertum ruft zum Sammeln," *VB*, 24 July 1930.

130. Joseph Goebbels, "Das patriotische Bürgertum," pp. 223–25.

131. "Die neue Staatspartei," *NSMH*, Heft 5 (1930):239. See also "Die Demokratie ist die Fassade der Schieberplutokratie," *VB*, 13 September 1930; and "Wählt das System tot!" *VB*, 23 July 1930.

132. *Achtung Mittelstandler!* DNVP leaflet, 1930, BA, ZSg.1, 44/9 (5).

133. Larry Eugene Jones, "Inflation, Revaluation, and the Crisis of Middle-Class Politics," pp. 157–60. See also Dörr, "Die Deutschnationale Volkspartei," pp. 325–33.

134. Jones, "Inflation, Revaluation," p. 161. See, e.g., "Die Aufwertungs-Betrug der Deutschnationalen," *Materialen zur Demokratischen Politik*, Nr. 125, 1925.

135. *Ohne Deutschnationale keine Aufwertung*, DNVP leaflet, 1925, GStA, HA xii, iv, Nr. 189.

136. *Aufwertungsfrage und DNVP*, DNVP leaflet, 1925, GStA, HA xii, iv, Nr. 189.

137. *Was will die Volksrecht-Partei?* VRP leaflet, 1928, BA, ZSg.1, 261/1.

138. Jones, "Inflation, Revaluation," pp. 162–63. The positions of the other parties are briefly sketched in Ulrich Schuren, *Der Volksentscheid zur Fürstenenteignung*, 1926, pp. 120–36.

139. "Graf Westarp an den Steuerbund," and "Kleinrentner," DNVP leaflets, GStA, HA XII, IV, Nr. 191.

140. "Opfer der Inflation! Kleinrentner, Sparer, Witwen!" DNVP leaflet, 1927, BA, ZSg.1, 44/9 (1).

141. The election results are found in *Statistisches Jahrbuch, 1931*, 50:546–547.

142. *Gebrochene Wahlversprechungen der DNVP?* See also the DNVP's attacks on the SPD in *Die SPD gegen Aufwertung!* DNVP leaflets, 1928, BA, ZSg.1, 44/9 (4).

143. "Rentner! Ihr seid bestohlen und betrogen worden!" DNVP leaflet, 1928, BA, ZSg.1, 44/9 (4). For the VRP's response see *Der Rhenische Sparer, Volksrecht und Aufwertung,* 5 May 1928, Nr. 15, BA, ZSg.1, 26/1.

144. *Was taten die Deutschnationalen, die Volkspartei, das Zentrum, BVP, Wirtschaftspartei und die Demokraten im letzten Reichstag?* VRP leaflet, 1928, BA, ZSg.1, 261/1.

145. *Volksbegehr. Organ des Verbandes der Interessenten zur Erlangung der Aufwertung z.V.*, Nr. 15, 15 May 1928, BA, ZSg.1, 261/1.

146. *Hilfe für die Kleinrentner muss die Reichstagswahl bringen,* DDP leaflet, 1928, GStA, HA XII, IV, Nr. 192.

147. *Rentner, Rentnerinnen!* DVP leaflet, 1928, BA, ZSg.1, 42/8 (1).

148. Maier, *Recasting Bourgeois Europe*, p. 493.

149. See Frick, "Die Nationalsozialisten im Reichstag, 1924–1928," p. 45.

150. Werner Fritsch, "Reichspartei für Volksrecht und Aufwertung (Volksrechtspartei) 1926–1933," pp. 555–60.

151. *Vierteljahreshefte zur Statistik des Deutschen Reichs,* (1928): 37, Heft 3, 77; 38, Heft 3 (1929): 91.

152. In Saxony, for example, where the *Aufwertungsparteien* had done quite well in both 1926 and 1928, their vote failed to reach even 2 percent of electorate in 1930. Regional results are found in *Statistisches Jahrbuch 1931,* 50:548–49; for 1932, 51:544–45.

153. Preller, *Sozialpolitik in der Weimarer Republik,* pp. 395–99. For the results of the survey see J. Nothaas, "Sozialer Auf- und Abstieg im deutschen Volk," pp. 65–73.

154. See, for example, "Frontkämpfer, Kriegsbeschädigte wählen Liste 9 der Nationalsozialisten," and "Entrechnung der deutschen Kriegsopfer. Die Notverordnung des 'Frontkämpferkabinetts' gegen die Kriegsbeschädigten," *VB,* 3/4 August 1930; see also "Marxistische 'Wohlfahrtsfürsorge,'" and "Was die 'Frontsoldaten-Regierung' den Kriegsopfern zumutet," *VB,* 8 August 1930.

155. Meckstroth, "Conditions of Partisan Realignments," p. 167.

156. Ulf Kadritzke, *Angestellte—die geduldigen Arbeiter,* p. 353.

157. "Die Stellenlosigkeit der Kaufmannsgehilfen," 2. *Schriftenreihe des DHV,* Nr. 7, Hamburg, 1925, pp. 18ff. See also "Die Not der älteren Angestellten—Standesnot," in the DHV's *Deutsche Handels-wacht,* 25 January 1928; and "Einige Worte über Personalpolitik," in the GDA's *Gewerkschaftliche Aufklärungs-Blätter für unsere Mitarbeiter,* January 1928, Nr. 1.

158. Carl Dreyfuss, "Beruf und Ideologie der Angestellten," p. 246.

159. Quoted in ibid., p. 221.

160. Based on figures in *Statistik des Deutschen Reichs*, 406:139–40. See also Renata Bridenthal, "Beyond Kinder, Küche, Kirche: Weimar Women at Work," p. 161. Bridenthal's figures include female civil servants.

161. "Ein Wendepunkt?" *Deutsche Handels-Wacht*, 25 September 1930.

162. "Wo stehen die Angestellten?" *Angestelltenstimme. Blätter zur Reichstagswahl 1928*, Nr. 1, 21 May 1928.

163. Ibid., Nr. 4, Anfang Mai, 1928.

164. *Reichsarbeitsblatt. Amtsblatt des Reichsarbeitsministeriums, des Reichsversicherungsamts, der Reichsanstalt für Arbeitsvermittlung und Arbeitslosenversicherung und der Reichsversicherungsanstalt für Angestellte*, 10, Heft 7 (1930): 2–3; 10, Heft 27 (1930):421. See also *Vierteljahreshefte zur Statistik des Deutschen Reichs*, 39, Heft 4 (1930):61.

165. *Statistisches Jahrbuch, 1928*, 47:373–74; for 1930, 49:310–11.

166. Dreyfuss, "Beruf und Ideologie der Angestellten," pp. 245–53.

167. Hans Mommsen, "Die Stellung der Beamtenschaft in Reich, Ländern und Gemeinden in der Ära Brüning," pp. 151–65.

168. Among the most useful studies of the civil service are Wolfgang Runge, *Politik und Beamtentum im Parteienstaat*; Rudolf Morsey, "Zur Beamtenpolitik des Deutschen Reichs von Bismarck bis Brüning," and Hans Fenske, "Monarchisches Beamtentum und demokratischer Staat: Zum Problem der Bürokratie in der Weimarer Republik," both in *Demokratie und Verwaltung*. Although focusing on a later period, Jane Caplan's "The Politics of Administration: The Reich Interior Ministry and the German Civil Service, 1933–1943," pp. 707–36, and Hans Mommsen's *Beamtentum im Dritten Reich*, also provide important insights into the problems of the civil service in the last years of the Weimar Republic.

169. Leonhard Achner, "Der Arbeitsmarkt der geistigen Berufe," pp. 481–95.

170. Winkler, for example, states categorically that "the white-collar workers were the group which was most afraid of proletarianization." Similarly, Franz Neumann maintains that the "salaried and professional employee did not want to 'be reduced to the level of the masses.' He fought to retain his tenuous middle-class status." See Heinrich August Winkler, "From Social Protectionism," p. 10; and Franz Neumann, *Behemoth*, p. 411.

171. F. W. Fischer, "Die Angestellten, ihre Bewegung und ihre Ideologie," pp. 95–106; and Rudolf Jobst, "Die deutsche Angestelltenbewegung in ihrer grundsätzlicher Stellung zu Kapitalismus und Klassenkampf," pp. 72–76. See also Jürgen Kocka, "Zur Problematik der deutschen Angestellten 1914–1933," pp. 807–8.

172. Figures on union membership are found in Kocka, ibid., p. 799.

173. See the DHV's anti-Hugenberg positions in "Kampf um den Staat," *Deutsche Handels-Wacht*, 25 July 1930; and "Parteiwandlung," ibid., 10 August 1930.

174. Larry Eugene Jones, "Between the Fronts: The German National Union of Commercial Employees from 1928 to 1933," p. 473.

175. Fischer, "Die Angestellten," pp. 95–106.

176. *Statistik des Deutschen Reichs*, 402:139, 173. During the Weimar years, 66% of the ZdA members lived in *Grossstädten*, followed by the GDA with 55.6% and the DHV with 41.2%. Heinz Hamm, "Die wirtschaftlichen und sozialen Berufsmerkmale der kaufmännischen Angestellten," p. 42.

177. Rudolf Heberle, *From Democracy to Nazism*, p. 89; Pratt, "The Social Bases of Nazism and Communism in Urban Germany," pp. 261–66; Alexander Weber, "Soziale Merkmale der NSDAP-Wähler," pp. 217–18.

178. "Die Not der älteren Angestellten," *VB*, 31 March 1928. See also Hans Bechly, "Ein Wendepunkt?" *Deutsche Handels-Wacht*, 25 September 1930; and Claudia Koonz, "Nazi Women before 1933: Rebels against Emancipation," pp. 553–63.

179. Herbert Tingsten, *Political Behavior*, pp. 37–65.

180. Leaving aside the socialist-oriented white-collar unions, 25% of the liberal GdA's membership and 19% of the DHV's came from working-class families. For the GdA see *Die wirtschaftliche und soziale Lage der Angestellten*, p. 47. The figures for the DHV are found in Speier, *Die Angestellten vor dem Nationalsozialismus*, p. 45.

181. Nazi appeals explicitly to white-collar employees were quite rare. A systematic examination of the extensive leaflet collections of the Bundesarchiv, the Geheime Staatsarchiv, the NSDAP Hauptarchiv, the Landesarchiv Berlin, and in the pages of the *VB* and *DA* reveals that such appeals were far surpassed by political literature addressed to farmers, civil servants, artisans, pensioners, and even workers.

182. Ralf Dahrendorf, *Class and Class Conflict in Industrial Society*, pp. 51–57.

183. Kocka, "Problematik," p. 792.

184. Theodor Geiger, *Die Soziale Schichtung des deutschen Volkes*, p. 98. Referring to the social position and ethos of German civil servants, Geiger observed that "they are not a class and hardly an estate [*Stand*]. They are, instead, . . . almost a caste." See also Bracher, *Die Auflösung*, pp. 158–70.

185. Mommsen, "Die Stellung der Beamtenschaft," pp. 151–63; and Jane Caplan, "The Politics of Administration," pp. 709–11.

186. Mommsen, "Die Stellung der Beamtenschaft," pp. 151–63.

187. Mommsen, *Beamtentum in Dritten Reich*, p. 26.

188. "Beamte, erinnert Ihr Euch nach?" *DA*, 17 August 1930.

189. Ibid.

190. *Erhaltet das Berufsbeamtentum!* DVP leaflet, 1930, GStA, HA XII, IV, Nr. 170, and the DVP leaflet *Die 5. Reichstagswahl ist Schicksalswahl*, BA, ZSg.1, 42/8 (2).

191. "Beamtenschaft im Wahlkampf," *Sondermaterial für den Wahlkampf 1930*, DVP pamphlet, 1930, BA, ZSg.1, 42/4 (8).

192. *An die deutsche Beamtenschaft*, DSP leaflet, 1930, GStA, HA XII, IV,

Nr. 145; and "Beamte, Beamtinnen!" *Wahlzeitung für die Deutsche Staatspartei*, September 1930, BA, ZSg.1, 27/20 (2).

193. Hans Gretz, "Der Kampf um die Arbeiterjugend," *NSMH*, Heft 2, (1930):74–76.

194. Joseph Goebbels, "Das patriotische Bürgertum," p. 228.

195. "An die deutschen Arbeiter!" *DA*, 24 August 1930.

196. "Der Youngverrat der Marxisten," *DA*, 31 July 1930.

197. "Deutsche Arbeiter! Wo stehst du?" *DA*, 24 July 1930.

198. "Ein Wort an die KPD-Proleten!" *DA*, 24 August 1930.

199. "Bürger und Proletarier," *DA*, 21 July 1930.

200. "Wo steht der Arbeiterjugend?" *DA*, 31 July 1930.

201. See Tables 2.6 and 3.7.

202. *Vierteljahreshefte zur Statistik des Deutschen Reichs*, 36, Heft 4, (1928):144–45; 37, Heft 4 (1929):66–67; 39, Heft 4 (1930):56–57.

203. *Statistisches Jahrbuch*, 1931, 50:301.

204. The figures are presented in Jürgen Kuczynski, *Darstellung der Lage der Arbeiter in Deutschland von 1917/18 bis 1932/33*, pp. 209–14. See also Gerhard Bry, *Wages in Germany 1871–1945*, pp. 187–90.

205. *Gegen Geldsack und Hakenkreuz um Demokratie und Lohn*, SPD leaflet, 1930, BA, ZSg.1, 90/41; *Adolf Hitlers politischer Bankrott*, KPD leaflet, 1930, GStA, HA xii, iv, Nr. 102.

206. "Was ist die KPD?" *Volksgericht, Blätter zur Reichstagswahl 1930*, and *Der Faschismus*, SPD leaflets, 1930, both in BA, ZSg.1, 90/41.

207. *Wo ist der Ausweg aus der Krise?* KPD leaflet, 1930, Landesarchiv Berlin, Rep. 240, Acc. 2088, Nr. 84.

208. Ossip K. Flechtheim, *Die KPD in der Weimarer Republik*, pp. 257–60. See also *Die Rote Fahne*, 7 September 1930.

209. "Aufruf der Kommunistischen Partei Deutschlands," *Reichstags-Handbuch*, 1930, p. 173.

210. "Programmerklärung zur nationalen und sozialen Befreiung Deutschlands," *Die Rote Fahne*, 24 August and 1 September 1930.

211. Ibid.

212. *Vorwärts*, 14 August 1930.

213. *Die Rote Fahne*, 7 September 1930.

214. "Letzter Appell an alle Werktätigen," *Die Rote Fahne*, 12 September 1930.

215. Petrich, quoted in Timm, *Die Deutsche Sozialpolitik*, p. 186.

216. *Sozialdemokratischer Parteitag 1929*, p. 71.

217. Richard N. Hunt, *German Social Democracy 1918–1933*, pp. 186–87.

218. *Vorwärts*, 16 August 1930.

219. Ibid., 13, 14, and 7 September 1930.

220. The unemployed from white-collar occupations, domestic services, agriculture, artistic endeavors, and the hotel and restaurant business comprised approximately 15% of the total jobless population in 1930. Blue-collar workers from the industrial, mining, and manufacturing sectors, therefore, made up,

allowing for some error, over 80% of the unemployed. *Statistisches Jahrbuch,*
1930, 50:301.

221. See "Die Nationalsozialisten," *Deutsch-Nationales Rüstzeug,* 1930, Nr.
11; and *Die Nationalsozialisten und wir,* DNVP leaflet, 1930, both in BA,
ZSg.1, 44/10. For the DDP/DSP appraisal of Nazi anti-Semitism see "Die Nationalsozialisten," *Materialien zur Demokratischen Politik,* 1928, Nr. 140; and
"Spiegel der Parteien," *Materialien zur Demokratischen Politik,* 1930, Nr. 151.

222. Tingsten, *Political Behavior,* pp. 37–65. See also R. Hartwig, "Das
Frauenwahlrecht in der Statistik," pp. 167–79.

223. Koonz, "Nazi Women before 1933," pp. 553–63.

224. See Günther Plum, *Gesellschaftsstruktur und politisches Bewusstsein in
einer katholischen Region 1928–1933;* and Burnham, "Political Immunization
and Political Confessionalism: The United States and Weimar Germany," pp.
1–30.

225. *Die Nationalsozialisten sind Todfeinde des Christentums,* Zentrum leaflet, 1930, GStA, HA xii, iv, Nr. 119.

226. Quoted in Rudolf Morsey, "The Center Party between the Fronts,"
p. 71.

227. "Mittelstand und Zentrum," *Germania,* 13 August 1930; and "Wähler
und Wählerinnen der Deutschen Zentrumspartei," ibid., 19 July 1930.

228. "Wen wählst du?" *Germania,* 9 September 1930.

229. *Wähler und Wählerinnen!* Landesarchiv Berlin, Rep. 240, Acc. 2088, Nr.
81.

Chapter IV

1. Karl Dietrich Bracher, *Auflösung der Weimarer Republik,* pp. 335–347,
370–377. See also Helmut Heiber, *Die Republik von Weimar,* p. 230.

2. "Das Deutsche Volkseinkommen," p. 84. Statistics for industrial production are found in Rolf Wagenführ, "Die Industriewirtschaft," p. 62. For figures
on bankruptcies and savings, see below, text at nn. 77–78.

3. Bracher, *Die Auflösung der Weimarer Republik,* pp. 398–406.

4. For details on the numerous decrees and their relationship to existing social and economic legislation see Ludwig Preller *Die Sozialpolitik in der
Weimarer Republik,* pp. 391–495.

5. The term was coined by William S. Allen, *The Nazi Seizure of Power.* His
case study of Thalburg (Northeim) remains the best single examination of this
strategy in action.

6. Wolfgang Schäfer, *NSDAP,* p. 17.

7. In December 1931, for example, the NSDAP, according to secret party reports, held over thirteen thousand "rallies, demonstrations, and other public
meetings" throughout the Reich, while its opponents together held fewer than
five hundred. See "Monatsbericht der Reichspropagandaleitung. Information
über den Gegnern, Dezember 1931," in HA/15/285.

8. Z. A. B. Zeman, *Nazi Propaganda* pp. 20, 28–29.

9. Dietrich Orlow, *History of the Nazi Party*, p. 205.

10. See the instructions of the RPL to the Gauleitungen, 23 March 1932, HA/16/290.

11. In Oldenburg the NSDAP won 48.4% of the vote, in Hamburg 31.2%, in Hessen, 44.0%, and in Anhalt 40.9%. See *Statistisches Jahrbuch 1932*, 51:544.

12. Bracher, *Die Auflösung der Weimarer Republik*, pp. 341–42.

13. Ibid., pp. 360–67.

14. On the issue of business support for the NSDAP see Henry A. Turner, Jr., "Big Business and the Rise of Hitler," pp. 56–70; Eberhard Czichon, *Wer verhalf Hitler zur Macht?*; and Dirk Stegmann, "Kapitalismus und Faschismus, 1929–1934; Thesen und Materialien."

15. Bracher, *Die Auflösung der Weimarer Republik*, pp. 397–404.

16. Zeman, *Nazi Propaganda*, p. 30.

17. "Wer Hindenburg wählt, wählt Brüning," NSDAP leaflet, 1932, HA/15/287. See also the instructions of the RPL from 16 March 1932 addressed to regional leaders: "Above all it is important to make clear [to the electorate] that if Hindenburg is reelected, pensions will not only be cut but eliminated entirely, that the emergency decrees will further reduce the standard of living for the middle class, and that additional taxes will be the inevitable result." HA/16/290.

18. Zeman, *Nazi Propaganda*, p. 31.

19. The position papers for the four national elections of 1932 are found in HA/15/286 (first ballot of the presidential elections); HA/16/290 (second ballot of the presidential elections); HA/15/289 (July Reichstag election); and HA/14/263 (November Reichstag election).

20. RPL Sonderschreiben an alle Gaue und Gaupropagandaleitungen, 20 February 1932.

21. See, for example, the RPL communiqué for the fall Reichstag campaign, HA/14/263, and the RPL circulars of 1 March 1932, HA/15/287; 4 July 1932, HA/15/288; and 16 June 1932, HA/15/289.

22. RPL circular, 23 March 1932, HA/16/290.

23. See the RPL circular to the Prussian *Gauleitungen* of 2 April 1932, HA/15/286.

24. See the circular of the *Wahlpropagandaleitung* Bayern, April 1932, HA/30/576.

25. The RPL circular of 4 July 1932, concluded with the plea: "We once again most urgently request that the guidelines given here be adhered to exactly so that the whole operation is conducted with tremendous force and energy. [If executed according to plan] it cannot fail to have an impact on the enemy." HA/15/289.

26. RPL circular of 26 October 1932, HA/14/263.

27. See, for example, the lists of draft leaflets in HA/15/286, 287, 288.

28. RPL circular of 23 March 1932, HA/15/288.

29. RPL circular of 2 April 1932, HA/15/286.

30. RPL circular of 23 March 1932, HA/15/288.

31. See, for example, the RPL's circular of 20 October 1932, HA/14/263, which pointedly reminds the *Gauleitungen* that "it is expected that our propaganda will be conducted more than ever before according to the RPL guidelines. The guidelines are not written for fun; their purpose is to achieve a uniform line in the campaign."

32. The election results are found in *Statistisches Jahrbuch . . . 1932*, 51:544–45.

33. Bracher, *Die Auflösung der Weimarer Republik*, pp. 424–62.

34. Ibid., 465–71.

35. Preller, *Die Sozialpolitik*, pp. 397–99.

36. Bracher, *Die Auflösung der Weimarer Republik*, pp. 491–526.

37. Confidential RPL memorandum to all regional offices, 4 June 1932, HA/15/289.

38. "Denkschrift der RPL zur Reichstagswahl 1932," 18 June 1932, ibid.

39. Quoted in Erich Matthias and Rudolf Morsey, eds., *Das Ende der Parteien 1933*, p. 54.

40. *Statistisches Jahrbuch, 1933*, 52:544–45.

41. Quoted in Matthias and Morsey, *Das Ende der Parteien 1933*, p. 61. The negotiations between the various bourgeois parties in early 1932 are treated in Larry Eugene Jones, "Sammlung oder Zersplitterung? Die Bestrebungen zur Bildung einer neuen Mittelpartei in der Endphase der Weimarer Republik 1930–1933," pp. 265–304.

42. *Volk gegen Junker!* DSP leaflet, 1932, BA ZSg.1, 27/20.

43. *Bürgertum erwache!* ibid.

44. *Keine Stimme geht verloren* and *Schwindler und Miesmacher trieben ihr Unwesen*, ibid.

45. Although both papers generally expressed the views of the DDP/DSP, neither was an official organ of the party. Indeed, throughout the Weimar Republic the DDP/DSP never possessed an official national press. See Modris Eksteins, *The Limits of Reason*, pp. 30–69. See also Michael Bosch, *Liberale Presse in der Krise*.

46. Hans Booms, "Die Deutsche Volkspartei," in Matthias and Morsey, *Das Ende der Parteien 1933*, p. 528.

47. Lothar Döhn, *Politik und Interesse*, pp. 200–208.

48. Bracher, *Die Auflösung der Weimarer Republik*, 385–86, and Booms, "Die Deutsche Volkspartei," p. 530. Dingeldey was convinced that the appeal of National Socialism would be substantially reduced if the Nazis could be induced to accept government responsibility.

49. See Jones, "Sammlung oder Zersplitterung," pp. 281–92; and Booms, "Die Deutsche Volkspartei," pp. 530–31.

50. *Wissen die Parteien, was sie wollen?* DVP leaflet, 1932, BA, ZSg.1, 42/8 (3).

51. *Was wir wollen, was wir fordern*, ibid.

52. E. Dingeldey quoted in *Deutsche Allgemeine Zeitung*, 30 July 1932.

53. "Die Demokraten in Deutschland," *Deutsche Allegemeine Zeitung*, 27 July 1932; and "Die Zentralvorstandssitzung der DVP," ibid., 11 October 1932.

54. In March, for example, the party collected 31% of the vote in heavily agrarian Mecklenburg-Strelitz. *Statistisches Jahrbuch, 1933*, 52:544–45.

55. Friedrich Frhr. Hiller von Gaertringen, "Die Deutschnationale Volkspartei," in Mathias and Morsey, *Das Ende der Parteien 1933*, p. 555.

56. The two parties had, for example, withdrawn from the Reichstag in early 1931 as a protest against the Brüning government and issued a joint communiqué in July proclaiming the start of "the decisive battle for the destruction of the present system." Ibid.

57. "Nicht vergessen! Warum muss sich die DNVP gegen die National-sozialisten zur Wehr setzen?" *Der Anti-Sozialist. Wahlzeitung der DNVP im Wahlkreis 12 (Thüringen)*, 23 October 1932, BA, ZSg.1, 44/9 (5).

58. *Deutsche Frauen*, DNVP leaflet, 1932, BA, ZSg.1, 44/9.

59. *Mittelstand! Wohin?* ibid.

60. *Kommunisten und Nationalsozialisten Arm in Arm*, ibid.

61. "Hugenbergs Mahnung," *Unsere Partei*, Nr. 14, 14 July 1932.

62. See the RPL communiqués of 18 June, 7, 26, and 28 July. HA/15/289.

63. RPL communiqué of 1 July 1932, HA/15/289.

64. See, for example, the leaflets and placards attached to the communiqués cited above.

65. RPL communiqué, 26 July 1932, HA/15/289.

66. Together the Zentrum and NSDAP would have commanded a majority in the Reichstag. For details on the negotiations see Detlef Junker, *Die Deutsche Zentrumspartei und Hitler 1932/33*, pp. 73–108. See also Rudolf Morsey, "The Center Party between the Fronts," pp. 74–76. Morsey contends that "the Center hoped that parliamentary collaboration with the NSDAP would both calm and stabilize the political situation and prevent the Nazi movement from growing larger."

67. Bracher, *Die Auflösung der Weimarer Republik*, pp. 627–34.

68. RPL communiqué, 27 October 1932, HA/14/263.

69. DNVP party circular, 26 September 1932, BA, ZSg.1, 44/9.

70. *Vorwärts! Kampf ums Aufbau-Programm!* DNVP pamphlet, 1932, Landesarchiv Berlin, Rep. 240, Acc. 2088. See also *Auf zum Endkampf*, DNVP leaflet, 1932, BA, ZSg.1, 44/9.

71. *Nicht vergessen! Warum muss sich die DNVP gegen die Nationalso-zialisten zur Wehr setzen?* DNVP leaflet, 1932, BA Zsg.1, 44.9. See also "Die Nationalsozialisten vor Tisch und nach Tisch," *Unsere Partei*, Nr. 21, 1 November 1932.

72. *Eine unsoziale Regierung?* DNVP leaflet, 1932, BA, ZSg.1, 44/9 (5).

73. "Wahlmüdigkeit," *Deutsche Allgemeine Zeitung*, 16 October 1932. See also "Gegen Hitler?" ibid., 19 October 1932.

74. RPL communiqué, 20 October 1932, HA/14/263.

75. Bernhard Benning and Robert Nieschlag, "Umsatz, Lagehaltung und Kosten im deutschen Einzelhandel 1924 bis 1932," pp. 78, 80.

76. Ibid., p. 10.

77. *Vierteljahreshefte zur Statistik des Deutschen Reichs*, 42, Heft 2 (1932): 125–27.

78. *Statistik des Deutschen Reichs*, 430: 54–55, 86; 482: 62, 229.

79. Theodore Abel Collection, Hoover Institution Archives, Biography 442. See also Biography 454.

80. Heinrich August Winkler, *Mittelstand, Demokratie und Nationalsozialismus*, pp. 140–51.

81. Ibid., 151–56.

82. "Mittelständler, herhören! Wählt Liste 2!" *VB* 31 July 1932. See also "Die grosse Not ist da," NSDAP leaflet, 1932, HA/15/289.

83. "So sehen sie aus, die Errungenschaften des Novembersystems!" *VB*, 3 November 1932.

84. "Der Deutsche Mittelstand wählt Liste 1," *VB*, 28 October 1932. See also Hans Buchner, "Warenhauspolitik und Nationalsozialismus," *NSB* Heft 13 (1931): 44; and "Handwerker, Gewerbetreibende, Einzelhändler. Für Mittelstandspolitik. Gegen Trusts and Warenhäuser," *DA*, 5 November 1932; and "Warenautomat" *DA*, 5 November 1932; and "Warenautomat gegen Ladegeschäft," *DA*, 28 October 1932.

85. "Will Hitler enteignen? Die Wahrheit über den Punkt 17 des Programms der NSDAP," *DA* 1 April 1932. See also "Wollen die Nationalsozialisten enteignen?" NSDAP leaflet, HA/15/287.

86. Hans Buchner, "Warenhauspolitik und Nationalsozialismus," pp. 351–56; and "Mittelständler, herhören!" NSDAP leaflet, 1932, HA/14/289, and "Das Handwerk kann von Papen nichts erwarten," *VB*, 5 November 1932.

87. See Jeremy Noakes, *The Nazi Party in Lower Saxony*, pp. 171–72. For an examination of Nazi infiltration of artisan organizations in Schleswig-Holstein, see Peter Wulf, *Die Politische Haltung des schleswig-holsteinischen Handwerks 1928 bis 1932*, pp. 127–35.

88. Horst Gies, "The NSDAP and Agrarian Organizations in the Final Phase of the Weimar Republik," p. 51.

89. Quoted in ibid.

90. Ibid., pp. 52–53.

91. Ibid., pp. 54–55; and Orlow, *History of the Nazi Party*, p. 194.

92. Gies, "The NSDAP and Agrarian Organizations" pp. 61–66.

93. In East Prussia, Brandenburg, Saxony, Hannover, and Lower Silesia, the NSDAP had won approximately three-quarters of seats. See Dieter Gessner, *Agrarverbände in der Weimarer Republik*, pp. 248–52.

94. Dieter Gessner, "The Dilemma of German Agriculture during the Weimar Republic," in Bessel and Feutwanger, *Social Change and Political Development*, p. 151.

95. Alexander Gerschenkron, *Bread and Democracy in Germany*, pp. 133–45.

96. David Abraham, *The Collapse of the Weimar Republic*, p. 105.

97. Klaus Müller, "Agrarische Interessenverbande," pp. 402–405. See also Gessner, *Agrarverbände in der Weimarer Republik*, pp. 251–58.

98. For details see Bracher, *Auflösung der Weimarer Republik*, pp. 449–55.

99. Abraham, *Collapse of the Weimar Republic*, p. 109.

100. See, for example, the Nazi agricultural objectives as spelled out in *Wer hilft den Bauern?* NSDAP leaflet, 1932, HA/15/288.

101. Gies, "The NSDAP and Agrarian Organizations," pp. 54–56.

102. *Preussisches Landvolk*, NSDAP leaflet, 1932, HA/15/286.

103. *Preussische Landfrau*. The same themes are developed in virtually all Nazi appeals to farmers. See, for example, *Das schwartz-rote System hat die Landwirtschaft verelenden lassen*; *Deutsches Landvolk, der Tag der Abrechnung ist da!*; *Wollen die Nationalsozialisten enteignen?*; *Bauern, auf zur Wahl*; and *Landbündler herhören!* NSDAP leaflets, 1932, HA/15/286–288.

104. *Deutscher Bauer, Du gehörst zu Hitler*, NSDAP leaflet, 1932, HA/15/286.

105. See the Nazi attack on agricultural rationalism in *Bauer und Nationalsozialismus*, NSDAP leaflet, 1932, HA/15/288.

106. *Handwerk und Mittelständler*, DVP leaflet, 1932, BA ZSg.1, 42/8 (3).

107. *Wahlaufruf der DVP*, DVP leaflet, 1932, Landesarchiv Berlin, Rep. 240, Acc. 2088, Nr. 151. See also the attack on Strasser and his alleged plans for the nationalization of industry in *Deutsche Allgemeine Zeitung* (hereafter *DAZ*) 23 October 1932. For an example of the DVP's approach to the rural electorate see "Landwirte!" DVP leaflet, 1932, Weimar Republic Collection, Hoover Institution Archives.

108. Quoted in *DAZ*, 11 November 1932.

109. Papen's speech reported in *DAZ* 21 July 1932.

110. *So steht es um Deutschland/so müsste es Deutschlands Wille sein!* See also *Mittelstand, merkst Du was?* and *Entscheidung! über unsere Staatsgrundlage*, DSP leaflets, 1932, BA, ZSg.1, 27/20 (4).

111. *Frankfurter Zeitung*, 5 July 1932.

112. Winkler, *Mittelstand, Demokratie und Nationalsozialismus*, p. 143.

113. *Mittelstand, merkst Du was?* and *Die Staatspartei ist eine Mittelstandspartei*, DSP leaflets, 1932, BA, ZSg.1, 27/20(3–4). See also "Bürger habt acht, wahlt Liste 8," *Deutscher Aufstieg. Wochenblatt der DSP*, Sondernummer, Berlin, November 1932, in GStA, HA XII, IV, Nr. 146.

114. See *Mittelstand! Wohin?* DNVP leaflet, 1932, BA, ZSg.1, 42/9; and *Deutsche Bauer erwache*, and *Hugenberg oder Hitler?* DNVP leaflets, 1932, Weimar Republic Collection, Hoover Institution Archives.

115. "Für die Rettung der mittelständischen Privatwirtschaft," *Unsere Partei*, Nr. 21, 1 November 1932.

116. See, for example, *Dr. Hugenberg fordert, v. Papen sagt zu. Beseitigung der Notverordnungshärten*, DNVP leaflet, 1932, BA, ZSg.1 44/9; and *Wer allein hilft der deutschen Landwirtschaft?* DNVP leaflet, 1932, Weimar Republic Collection, Hoover Institution Archives.

117. Leaflets addressed to the agrarian population far outnumber appeals to the other occupational and social groups in the DNVP's 1932 campaign literature. See, for example, *Deutsches Landvolk, Rettet die Landwirtschaft*, and *Deutsches Landvolk aufgepasst!* BA, ZSg.1, 44/9; *Bauernnot ist Volksnot*, and

Auch der Bauer muss verdienen! Weimar Republic Collection, Hoover Institution Archives. For the Nazi assessment of Nationalist strength in the countryside see RWL communiqué to the *Gauleitungen*, 2 April 1932, HA/15/286.

118. See Charles P. Loomis and J. Allan Beegle, "The Spread of German Nazism in Rural Areas," pp. 729–30; and Rudolf Heberle, *From Democracy to Nazism*, pp. 113–14, both of whom find the Nazi vote highly correlated with small farming areas.

119. Data on taxable earnings from investments, etc., are found in *Statistik des Deutschen Reichs*, 430:54–55; 482:62. Observations on savings are based on data from municipal banks in approximately ninety cities. In those cities, savings in individual accounts averaged 669 RM in 1930. Two years later the average had fallen to 518 RM, a decline of 23%. *Statistisches Jahrbuch Deutscher Städte 1933*, 28:140.

120. For details concerning the reductions in pension imposed by emergency decree see Preller, *Die Sozialpolitik*, pp. 459–73.

121. RPL communiqué to the Gauleiter, 23 March 1932, HA/16/290.

122. *Rentenempfänger!*; *Die Maske herunter den Lügnern und Verleumdern! Kriegsopfer! Sozialrentner!*; *Sozialrentner*; *Rente, Rente, Rente*; and *Fort mit den Notverordnungspolitik*, NSDAP leaflets, 1932, HA/15/2–6 and 289.

123. "Wie wählen die Kriegsopfer?" *VB*, 23 July 1932.

124. *"Die Nationalsozialisten wollen die Beamten entrechnen. Sie wollen den kleinen Pensionären ihre Rente nehmen."* See also *Soldaten des Weltkrieges! Kriegsbeschädigte! Frontkämpfer!*; *Frontsoldaten! Kriegsopfer! Kriegshinterbliebene!*; *Kriegsopfer, Kriegsbeschädigte!*; and *Kriegsopfer! Habt Ihr Euch schon überlegt, was die Notverordnungen für Euch bedeuten?* all NSDAP leaflets, 1932, HA/15/288.

125. "Sparer, die Augen auf," *Erneuerung. Zeitung für die deutsche Politik, Wirtschaft und Kultur*, Berlin, October 1932, BA, ZSg.1, 42/8 (3).

126. See Hugenberg's public letter to Papen, published in the *Kreuz-Zeitung* 27 July 1932. Criticism of National Socialism economic plans are found in *Angriff oder Rückzug*, and *Vorwärts. Kampf ums Aufbau-Programm!* DNVP pamphlets, 1932, Landesarchiv Berlin, Rep. 240, Acc. 2088, Nrs. 187, 188.

127. *Die Nationalsozialisten bringen Chaos, Bürgerkrieg und Inflation*; and *Inflation! Inflation!* NSDAP leaflets, 1932, HA/15/288.

128. The most extensive attack on the DNVP is found in Hans Weberstadt, "Die politischen Parteien und ihre Sünden," *NSB*, Heft 19 (1932):8.

129. "Herr Reichskanzler von Papen," *DA*, 22 October 1932.

130. *Kommt eine neue Inflation?* and *Hitler zerschlägt die Sozialversicherung*, NSDAP leaflets, HA/15/286.

131. See Hans Mommsen, "Die Stellung der Beamtenschaft in Reich, Ländern und Gemeinden in der Ära Brüning," pp. 151–65. On salaries see Preller, *Die Sozialpolitik*, pp. 396–98, 409–10.

132. Waldemar Besson, *Württemberg und die deutsche Staatskrise 1928–1933*, pp. 241–50.

133. Franz-Josef Heyen, *Nationalsozialismus im Alltag*, p. 67.

134. Orlow, *History of the Nazi Party*, p. 195.

135. Besson, *Württemberg und die deutsche Staatskrise*, p. 243.

136. *Beamte! Auf die Schanzen*, NSDAP leaflet, 1932, Landesarchiv Berlin, Rep. 240, Acc. 2088, Nr. 162. See also Heinrich Müller, "Beamtentum und Nationalsozialismus," pp. 26–59.

137. Noakes, *Nazi Party in Lower Saxony*, pp. 173–74. Nor were such rallies confined to large cities. William S. Allen notes that in "Thalburg," a town of ten thousand inhabitants, an evening meeting on "The Civil Service and National Socialism" drew an audience of over fifteen hundred. Allen, *The Nazi Seizure of Power*, pp. 44–45.

138. See *Die Nationalsozialisten wollen die Beamten entrechnen! Die Auflösung des Berufsbeamtentums*, and *Beamte! Augen auf!* NSDAP leaflets, 1932, HA/15/286, 288.

139. "An die Beamtenschaft," *VB*, 26 October 1932.

140. *Der Beamte als Kämpfer in der Front der NSDAP*, NSDAP leaflet, 1932, HA/15/286.

141. *Die Auflösung des Berufsbeamtentums*, and *Beamter! Beamtenanwarter!* ibid.

142. *Kollegen!* ibid.

143. *Achtung Beamte!* ibid.

144. *Der deutsche Berufsbeamte soll in die Irre geführt werden!* and *Nationalsozialisten und aktuelle Beamtenfragen*, ibid.

145. "Armee und Beamtentum, zwei Säulen des kommenden Staates," *Völkischer Beobachter*, 15 June 1932.

146. See, for example, "Hugenberg fordert. Die Säuberung des Beamtentums in Preussen," *Der Rechte Flügel. Kampfblatt der DNVP. Bezirksverband Emschen-Lippe*, July 1932, 2. Wahlnummer, and "Beamte!" *Attacke*, Nr. 1, June 1932, Stettin, BA ZSg.1, 44/9 (5).

147. *Beamte!* DNVP leaflet, 1932, Landesarchiv Berlin, Rep. 240. Acc. 2088, Nr. 149. See also *Wer rettet Deutschland? Hugenberg oder Hitler?* BA ZSg.1, 44/9 (5).

148. *Beamte aller Kategorien!* DVP leaflet, 1932, BA, ZSg.1, 42/8 (3).

149. *An die Beamten und Angestellten Gross-Hamburgs*, DSP leaflet, 1932, BA, ZSg.1, 27/20 (3).

150. *Beamte-erwacht!* DSP leaflet, 1932, GStA, HA XII, IV, Nr. 146.

151. Although explicit appeals to white-collar employees were rarest in National Socialist campaign literature, they were also underrepresented in the electoral appeals of all the major parties. See the relevant collections of campaign literature in the BA, GStA, and BHStA.

152. This is a rough estimate based on averages of salaries for male employees in Berlin, Breslau, Cologne, Frankfurt a.M., Hamburg, Königsberg, Stuttgart, and Würzburg, *Statistisches Jahrbuch*, 1931, 50:297. For figures on unemployment, see *Statistisches Jahrbuch*, 1932, 51:291; and *Statistische Beilage zur Reichsarbeitsblatt*, Nr. 10, 1932, pp. 2–3.

153. See Carl Dreyfuss, "Beruf und Ideologie der Angestellten," pp. 126–28.

154. *Statistisches Jahrbuch . . . 1932*, 51:287.

155. *Angestellte!* ZdA leaflet, 1932, BA, ZSg.1, 134/1.

156. *Angestellte in Front*, GdA leaflet, 1932, BA, ZSg.1, 192/1.

157. "Haltung und Leistung des Verbandes 1931," *Deutsche Handels-Wacht*, 25 January 1932.

158. "So kann es nicht bleiben," ibid., 28 June 1932; and "Gegen unsoziale Diktatur," ibid., 18 September 1932.

159. "Hugenberg's Rattenfanger-Melodie," ibid., 25 July 1932.

160. "Unser Stand in der Zange," ibid., 15 May 1932.

161. Alfred Krebs, Tendenzen und Gestalten der NSDAP, pp. 17–18; see also Larry Eugene Jones, "Between the Fronts," pp. 471–77; and Iris Hamel, *Völkischer Verband und nationale Gewerkschaft*, pp. 242–43.

162. Jones, "Between the Fronts," pp. 477–79.

163. "Am Rande des Bürgerkrieges," *Deutsche Handels-Wacht*, 29 February 1932; see also "Verbandspolitik oder Parteipolitik," and "Aus unserer Bewegung," ibid., 25 March 1932; and Jones, "Between the Fronts," pp. 479–81.

164. "23. Verbandstag des DHV am 5. Juni 1932 in Hamburg—Unsere politische Haltung. Eröffnungsrede des Verbandsvorstehers Hans Bechly," *Deutsche Handels-Wacht*, 16 June 1932.

165. Hamel, *Völkischer Verband*, pp. 243–61.

166. "Gegen Radikalismus—für eine arbeitsfähige Volksvertretung," GdA. *Zeitschrift des Gewerkschaftsbundes der Angestellten*, 1 November 1932.

167. *Angestellte!* ZdA leaflet, 1932, BA, ZSg.1, 134/1.

168. "Gegen den Faschismus, Nr. 2. Das Wirtschaftsprogramm der Nationalsozialisten," in *Material fur die Funktionäre der freien Angestellten-Verbande*, BA, ZSg. 1, 134/1.

169. "An die Angestellten!" *Vorwärts*, 16 July 1932; and "Angestellte" ibid., 5 November 1932.

170. *Angestellte, Arbeiter!* DVP leaflet, 1932, BA, ZSg.1, 42/8 (3).

171. *An die Beamten und Angestellten Gross-Hamburgs!* DSP leaflet, 1932, BA, ZSg.1, 27/20 (3).

172. See the DNVP's *Deutsche Angestellten-Zeitung. Blätter zur Reichstagswahl 1932*, July 1932, especially "Angestellten-Wahlparole: Schluss mit Marxismus und Volksbetrug!"; and *Was uns allein weiterbringen kann, Unsere Angestellten-Forderungen*, BA, ZSg.1, 44/9.

173. *Angestellte, es geht Euch an!* and *Deutsche Arbeitnehmer*, NSDAP leaflets, 1932, HA/15/289. See also the National Socialist leaflet *Die Sozialisierung ist da!* Landesarchiv Berlin, Rep. 240, Acc. 2088, Nr. 163.

174. See the lists of RPL leaflets distributed to local party organizations for the elections of 1932. HA/14–16/286–288. Typically, in the party's official list of Reich speakers, those with expertise in civil service questions outnumbered those specializing in white-collar themes by four to one. See HA/24A/1758.

175. *Frauen im Beruf*, DVP leaflet, 1932, BA, ZSg.1, 42/8 (3). See also the SPD's leaflet, *Frauen und Mutter*, Landesarchiv Berlin, Rep. 240, Acc. 2088, Nr. 177.

176. *Frauen im Dritten Reich*, NSDAP leaflet, 1932, HA/15/288.

177. See *Adolf Hitler soll die Frauen aus Beruf und Stellung* and *Die National Sozialisten wollen die Frauen aus Beruf und Brot verjagen um damit den Erwerbslosen Männern Platz zu machen*, NSDAP leaflets, HA/15/286, 288.

178. *Frauen der Arbeit* and *Frauen im Dritten Reich*, NSDAP leaflets, 1932, HA/15/289, 288.

179. Krebs, *Tendenzen und Gestalten der NSDAP*, p. 19. On the founding of the NSBO and its performance in the first shop council elections, see Reinhold Muchow, "Die erst Durchbruchsschlacht der NSBO," HA/15/283.

180. Among blue-collar workers the NSBO won only 12 percent of the vote. See the NSBO's publication *Arbeitertum*, HA/15/283.

181. Michael H. Kater, "Sozialer Wandel in der NSDAP im Zuge der nationalsozialistischen Machtergreifung," pp. 34–35.

182. Kele notes that the terms "Arbeiter der Faust und der Stirn" and "workers of the hand and brain" were used with increasing frequency after 1928. It is also significant that, as Kele correctly observes, "the Nazis had difficulty determining which Germans should be classified as 'workers of the Stirn.'" Max H. Kele, *Nazis and Workers*, pp. 10, 143–44.

183. See, for example, the SPD leaflets: *Frauen, merkt es Euch!*; *Wie das Nazigesindel deutsche Frauen Beschimpft!*; and *Frauen, so geht's euch im 'Dritten Reich'!* BA, ZSg.1, 90/41; and "Her zur Eisenern Front," *Vorwärts*, 14 July 1932.

184. Samuel A. Pratt, "The Social Bases of Nazism and Communism in Urban Germany," pp. 177–78.

185. The figures for unemployment by sector are found in *Wirtschaft und Statistik* 12 (1932): 148, 472, 542, and 741. See also *Statistische Beilage zum Reichsarbeitsblatt*, Nr. 34, 1932, pp. 2–3.

186. See *Statistisches Jahrbuch, 1933*, 52: 273. For an interpretation of wages and prices during 1932, see Jürgen Kuczynski, *Die Geschichte der Lage der Arbeiter unter dem Kapitalismus*, p. 218; and Gerhard Bry, *Wages in Germany*, pp. 187–90.

187. Hans-Gerd Schumann, *Nationalsozialismus und Gewerkschaftsbewegung. Die Vernichtung der deutschen Gewerkschaften und der Aufbau der "Deutschen Arbeitsfront,"* pp. 30–38. See also Timothy W. Mason, *Sozialpolitik im Dritten Reich*, p. 69.

188. "Organisation der Nationalsozialistischen Betriebszellen von Reinhold Muchow," 1 January 1931, HA/15/283. See also Max Kele, *Nazis and Workers*, pp. 169–71.

189. For results of the Betriebsräte elections in the Ruhr, see Wilfried Böhnke, *Die NSDAP im Ruhrgebiet 1920–1933*, p. 170.

190. Karl Dietrich Bracher, *Die Deutsche Diktatur*, p. 172.

191. RPL memorandum, 2 April 1932, HA/15/186.

192. Gregor Strasser, "Anti-Kapitalismus," *NSMH*, Heft 28 (1932): 289.

193. Bernhard Köhler, "Arbeitsbeschaffung, Kein Problem, sondern eine Aufgabe," *NSMH*, Heft 23 (1932): 56–59. See also *Wer schafft nun endlich Arbeit?* NSDAP leaflet, 1932, HA/15/286.

194. *Was wir wollen. An alle Arbeiter und Arbeiterinnen!* NSDAP leaflet, 1932, HA/15/286.

195. Hans Buchner, "Deflation und Arbeitslosigkeit," *NSMH*, Heft 10, (1932):318–27.

196. Bernard Köhler, "Arbeitsbeschaffung in Politik und Propaganda," *Unsere Wille und Weg*, Heft 10 (1932):303.

197. Ibid.

198. Bernard Köhler, "Das Recht auf Arbeit," *NSMH*, Heft 28 (1932):292, 295, 297.

199. *Nieder mit den Ausbeutern! Enteignet den Besitzenden!* NSDAP leaflet, 1932, HA/15/286.

200. *Adolf Hitler und der Arbeiter*, NSDAP leaflet, 1932, Landesarchiv Berlin, Rep. 240, Acc. 2088, Nr. 164. See also *Deutsche Arbeiter* and *Arbeiter, Ihr habt nicht zu verlieren als Eure Ketten*, NSDAP leaflets, 1932, HA/15/286.

201. *Unterdrückung, Terror, Verbote, Überfalle auf Andersgesinnte, Hunger und Elend*, NSDAP leaflet, 1932, Landesarchiv Berlin, Rep. 240, Acc. 2088, Nr. 163.

202. See *Die Nationalsozialisten sind Einpeitscher der Reaktion, Die Nazis verraten die Arbeiterschaft*, and *Geld in Massen*, NSDAP leaflets, HA/15/286.

203. *Die soziale Reaktion marschiert!* NSDAP leaflet, 1932, HA/15/289.

204. *Adolf Hitler und die Arbeiter*, NSDAP leaflet, 1932, Landesarchiv Berlin, Rep. 240, Acc. 2088, Nr. 164.

205. Siegfried Bahne, "Die Kommunistische Partei Deutschlands," in Matthias and Morsey, *Das Ende der Parteien 1933*, pp. 656–82.

206. Ibid., p. 673.

207. *Die Rote Fahne*, 7 July 1932.

208. Ibid.

209. Ibid., 1 July 1932.

210. "Manifest der anti-faschistischen Aktion," ibid., 12 July 1932.

211. "Nationalsozialismus. Todfeind der Arbeiterklasse," ibid., 8 July 1932.

212. Ibid., 23 June 1932.

213. The series carried the title: "NSDAP eine Arbeiterpartei?" ibid., 13–15 July 1932.

214. Ibid., 23 June 1932.

215. Ibid., 1, 2 November 1932.

216. Otto Braun, the Social Democratic minister president of Prussia, had, in fact, suggested the formation of a "great coalition of all reasonable elements" in 1930. See Erich Matthias, "Die Sozialdemokratische Partei Deutschlands," in Matthias and Morsey, *Das Ende der Parteien 1933*, pp. 115–18. See also the same author's "The Social Democratic Party and Government Power," pp. 55–57.

217. See Richard Breitman, *German Socialism and Weimar Democracy*, pp. 174–88.

218. See Robert A. Gates, "Von der Sozialpolitik zur Wirtschaftspolitik? Das Dilemma der deutschen Sozialdemokratie in der Krise 1929–1933," pp. 206–25. The union program is analyzed in Michael Schneider, "Konjunktur-

politische Vorstellungen der Gewerkschaften in den letzten Jahren der Weimarer Republik. Zur Entwicklung des Arbeitsbeschaftungsplans des ADGB," in the same volume, pp. 226–36.

219. "Eiserne Front für Einheitsfront," *Vorwärts*, 19 June 1932.

220. See "An das deutsche Volk" and "Einheitsfront. Phantasie und Wirklichkeit," *Vorwärts*, 14 October 1932. See also *Kommunisten wisst Ihr schon?* SPD leaflet, BA, ZSg.1, 90/41.

221. See, for example, *Sozialdemokratie gegen Notverordnungen!* and *Millionen für die Junker! Grosschen fur die Bauern!* BA, ZSg.1, 90/41.

222. Matthias, "The Social Democratic Party and Government Power," pp. 60–65.

223. "KPD entlarvt," *Vorwärts*, 27 October 1932; and "Beschluss der Sozialdemokratie," ibid., 21 July 1932.

224. "KPD entlarvt," ibid., 21 July 1932.

225. "Deutsches Volk. Wählerinnen und Wähler!" ibid., 28 July 1932.

226. "Arbeiterpartei?" ibid., 19 July 1932; *Sind die Nazis Sozialisten? Nein!* SPD leaflet, 1932, BA, ZSg.1, 90/41; and "Hitlerstaat Elendsanstalt," *Vorwärts*, 15 June 1932.

227. "Unser Ziel," *Vorwärts*, 29 October 1932.

228. Detlef Mühlberger, "The Sociology of the NSDAP: The Question of Working Class Membership," pp. 493–511.

229. See, for example, L. D. Stokes, "The Social Composition of the Nazi Party in Eutin, 1925–1932," pp. 1–32; R. Mann, "Entstehung und Entwicklung der NSDAP in Marburg bis 1933," p. 297.

230. Mason, *Sozialpolitik im Dritten Reich*, p. 70.

231. See, for example, Biographies 5, 59, 343, 393, 410, 436, 443, 446, 466, 520, and 566, Theodore Abel Collection, Hoover Institution Archives.

232. See, for example, ibid., Biographies 23, 81, 343, and 366. Support for the NSDAP among municipal workers has drawn frequent comment. See Mason, *Sozialpolitik im Dritten Reich*, pp. 67–68; and Noakes, *The Nazi Party in Lower Saxony*, p. 175.

233. See, for example, Theodore Abel Collection, Hoover Institution Archives, Biographies 19, 40, 246, 257, 369, 433, and 434.

234. See ibid., Biographies 1, 23, 49, and 53. The quotation is from Biography 172.

235. Ibid., Biography 81.

236. Ibid., Biography 23.

237. Ibid., Biography 53. Biography 443, that of a machine worker, similarly reported: "In the plant 95% of the workers were organized by the Communists." A foreman in a furniture factory, Biography 561, also complained that he surpervised "an *Arbeiterschaft* made up exclusively of Marxists and Communists."

238. See Mason, *Sozialpolitik im Dritten Reich*, 69–73, and Böhnke, *NSDAP in Ruhrgebiet*, pp. 169–76.

239. See, for example, Theodore Abel Collection, Biographies 13 and 440.

240. RPL communiqué "an alle Pruessische Gauleitungen," 4 April 1932, HA/15/286.

241. *Sage mir mit wem Du umgehst, und ich sage Dir, wer Du bist,* NSDAP leaflet, 1932, HA/15/286.

242. *Wotans-Anbeter,* ibid.

243. *Deutsche Katholiken hört!* and *An die Evangelische Christenheit,* NSDAP leaflets, 1932, HA/15/289, 286.

244. *Die Nationalsozialisten sind romhörig, Die Nationalsozialisten sind Katholikenfresser und Christenfeinde,* NSDAP leaflets, 1932, HA/15/286.

245. Herbert Tingsten, *Political Behavior,* pp. 37–65. See also Gabriele Bremme, *Die politische Rolle der Frau in Deutschland,* pp. 74–77, 111, 243–52.

246. Jill Stephenson, *The Nazi Organization of Women,* pp. 23–96.

247. Tingsten, *Political Behavior,* pp. 37–65.

248. Ibid.

249. *Germania,* 28 July and 9 June 1932.

250. Ibid., 30 July and 6 November 1932.

Conclusion

1. See Thomas Childers, "Inflation, Stabilization, and Political Realignment in Germany 1924–1928," pp. 409–31.

2. The extensive support for National Socialism among upper middle-class students is examined in Michael H. Kater, *Studentenschaft und Rechtsradikalismus in Deutschland 1918–1933,* pp. 125–44; The Nazi following among middle and high-ranking civil servants grew steadily after 1929 and is treated in Michael Kater, "Sozialer Wandel in der NSDAP im Zuge der nationalsozialistischen Machtergreifung," pp. 34–35; for an analysis of Nazi support in affluent neighborhoods, see Richard F. Hamilton, *Who Voted for Hitler?*

3. Burnham, "Political Immunization and Political Confessionalism: The United States and Weimar Germany," pp. 1–30.

4. See "Die Nationalsozialisten," in *Materialien zur Demokratischen Politik,* Nr. 140, 1928; and "Spiegel der Parteien," in the same DDP publication, Nr. 151, 1930, BA, ZSg.1, 27/1. For an analysis of the Social Democratic approach to anti-Semitism see Donald L. Niewyk, *Socialist, Anti-Semite, and Jew.*

5. The substantial discrepancies between the social promises of the NSDAP before 1933 and social reality in the Third Reich are examined in David Schoenbaum, *Hitler's Social Revolution.* Schoenbaum, for example, notes that "objective social reality" in Nazi Germany "was the very opposite of what Hitler had presumably promised," indicating that "in 1939 the cities were larger, not smaller; the concentration of capital greater than before; the rural population reduced, not increased; women not at the fireside but in the office and the factory; the inequality of income and property distribution more, not less conspicuous; industry's share of the gross national product up and agricul-

ture's down, while industrial labor had it relatively good and small business increasingly bad" p. 285. See also Dahrendorf, *Society and Democracy in Germany*, 365–396.

6. Joseph Goebbels, *Von Kaiserhof zum Reichskanzlei*, p. 87. The entry in Goebbels's diary is dated 23 April 1932.

Methodological Appendix

1. See, in particular, Allan J. Lichtman, "Correlation, Regression, and the Ecological Fallacy: A Critique," pp. 417–43; and J. Morgan Kousser, "Ecological Regression and the Analysis of Past Politics," pp. 237–62.

2. See, for example, the optical comparisons in Alfred Milatz, *Wähler und Wahlen in der Weimarer Republik*, and Richard Hamilton, *Who Voted for Hitler?* pp. 64–220.

3. *Statistik des Deutschen Reichs*, 408:110.

4. Ibid., pp. 114–15.

5. See, for example, ibid., p. 208; Theodor Geiger, *Die soziale Schichtung des deutschen Volkes*, p. 36; and Jürgen Kocka, *Klassengesellschaft im Krieg*, p. 7.

6. *Statistik des Deutschen Reichs*, 408:123–30.

7. Ibid., pp. 132–35.

8. Ibid., p. 150.

9. Ibid., p. 159.

10. Ibid., p. 110.

11. Ibid., 402:98–99.

12. Ibid., 408:186.

13. Ibid., 402:98–99.

Bibliography

Primary Sources

Archival Materials

Bundesarchiv Koblenz (BA)
  Zeitgeschichtliche Sammlung (ZSg) 1, leaflets and pamphlets of various
    parties and interest groups
  8, BVP
  27, DDP/DSP
  42, DVP
  45, DVFP
  65, KPD
  83, Reichsausschuss für das Deutsche Volksbegehren (Youngplan)
  90, SPD
  108, Zentrum
  134, AfA/ZdA
  176, Wirtschaftspartei
  192, GdA
  228, DHV
  261, VRP
  279, CVD
  Zeitgeschichtliche Sammlung (ZSg) 3, leaflets and pamphlets of the NSDAP
  3334, NSDAP
Landesarchiv Berlin
  Repatorien 240 Wahlangelegenheiten
  Acc. 1941
  Acc. 1962
  Acc. 1964
  Acc. 2088
Geheimes Staatsarchiv Preussischer Kulturbesitz (GStA) (Berlin)
  Hauptabeilung (HA) XII, IV Plakate und Flugblätter seit 1878
  44–79, SPD
  80–81, USPD
  82–103, KPD
  104–20, Zentrum
  121–47, DDP/DSP

156–70, DVP
175–95, DNVP
200–216, *Völkisch*
210–16, NSDAP
217–20, Splitterparteien
Zentrales Staatsarchiv Potsdam (ZSt.A)
  Reichswirtschaftsministerium Nr. 6033–36
  Reichstag, Nr. 3399
  Reichsinnenministerium, Nr. 25189, Nr. 25181
Hoover Institution Archives (Stanford)
  Theodore Abel Collection
  Weimar Republic Collection
NSDAP Hauptarchiv (Microfilm)
  Reels 14–15, Rundschreiben der RPL
  Reels 29–30, Rundschreiben der RPL
  Reels 41, 42, Andere Parteien und Verbände
  Reel 58, Propaganda 1932
Bayerisches Hauptstaatsarchiv Munich (BHStA)
  Abteilung V, Flugblattsammlung, leaflets of the NSDAP
  5–13, NSDAP

Statistical Series and Publications

Die Angestellten in der Wirtschaft. Ein Auswertung der amtlichen Berufszählung von 1925. Edited by the Allgemeinen Freien Angestelltenbund. Berlin, 1930.

Das deutsche Handwerk (Generalbericht). Verhandlungen und Berichte des Unterausschusses für Gewerbe, Industrie, Handel und Handwerk (III. Unterausschuss), 8. Arbeitsgruppe (Handwerk). I. Ausschuss zur Untersuchung der Erzeugungs- und Absatzbedingungen der deutschen Wirtschaft. Berlin, 1930.

"Das Deutsche Volkseinkommen vor und nach dem Kriege." *Einzelschriften zur Statistik des Deutschen Reichs.* Vol. 34. Berlin, 1932.

Finanzen und Steueren im In- und Ausland. Ein Statistisches Handbuch. Berlin, 1930.

Handbuch der Arbeit. Die deutsche Arbeiterklasse in Wirtschaft und Gesellschaft. III. Abteilung. Die Koalitionen. Jena, 1931.

Jahrbuch des Allgemeinen Deutschen Gewerkschaftsbundes 1924. Berlin, 1925.

Reichsarbeitsblatt. Amtsblatt des Reichsarbeitsministeriums, des Reichsversicherungsamts, der Reichsanstalt für Arbeitsvermittlung und Arbeitslosenversicherung und der Reichsversicherungsanstalt für Angestellte. Vols. 1–12. (1920–32).

Statistische Beilage zum Reichsarbeitsblatt, Nr. 13 (1931), and Nrs. 19, 22 (1932).

Statistik des Deutschen Reichs. Vols. 2 (1882), 211 (1907), 357–482 (1924–36).

Statistisches Jahrbuch Deutscher Städte. Amtliche Veröffentlichung des Deutschen Städtetages. Vols. 15–27 (1920–32).

Statistisches Jahrbuch für das Deutsche Reich. Vols. 43–51 (1920–32).

Statistisches Jahrbuch für den Freistaat Sachsen 1930. Leipzig, 1931.

Storch, Helmuth. "Einmalige Erhebung über die laufend unterstüzten arbeitsfähigen Erwerbslosen in den Städten über 50,000 Einwohnern." *Statistische Vierteljahresberichte des Deutschen Städtetages. Beilage zur Zeitschrift "Der Städtetag."* Vol. 2 (1929).

Vierteljahreshefte zur Statistik des Deutschen Reichs. Vols. 26–42 (1920–33).

Wirtschaft und Statistik. Vols. 1–13 (1920–33).

Die wirtschaftliche und soziale Lage der Angestellten. Ergebnisse und Erkenntnisse aus der grossen sozialen Erhebung des GDA. Berlin, 1931.

"Zahlen zur Geldentwertung in Deutschland 1914 bis 1923." *Sonderhefte zu Wirtschaft und Statistik.* Sonderheft 1, v, 15. Berlin, 1925.

Newspapers and Party/Interest Group Publications

Der Angriff
Berliner Stimmen
Das Berliner Tageblatt
Die Deutsche Allgemeine Zeitung
Die Deutsche Handels-Wacht
Deutschnationale Flugschriften
DVP Wahlhandbuch 1924, Berlin, 1924.
Flugschriften der Deutschen Volkspartei
Die Frankfurter Zeitung
GDA. Zeitschrift des Gewerkschaftsbundes der Angestellten
Germania
Gewerkschaftsbericht des Deutschen Beamtenbundes für die Zeit von September 1924 bis Oktober 1926. Berlin, 1926.
Jahrbuch der DNVP 1920. Berlin, 1920.
Die Kreuz-Zeitung
Materialien zur Demokratischen Politik
Nachtrag zum Wahlhandbuch der DVP. Berlin, 1924.
Nationalsozialistische Bibliothek
Nationalsozialistische Briefe
Nationalsozialistische Monatshefte
Die Rote Fahne
Der Tag
Unser Wille und Weg
Völkischer Beobachter
Vorwärts
Der Wähler. Führer zur Reichs- und Lantagswahl am 7. Dezember, 1924

Contemporary Works

Achner, Leonhard. "Der Arbeitsmarkt der geistigen Berufe." *Allgemeines Statistisches Archiv*, 20 (1931): 481–95.

Alther, Andreas. "Die örtliche Verteilung der Wähler grosser Parteien in Städtekomplex Hamburg auf Grund der Reichstagswahien vom 14. September 1930." *Hamburgs Verwaltungs- und Wirtschafts-Monatschrift des Statistischen Landesamtes*, 8, 6 (1931).

Assemacher, Paul. "Abrenzung von Handwerksbetrieben gegen Fabrikbetriebe unter besonderer Berucksichtigung des Tischlergewerbes. Ein Beitrag zur Frage des Zuständig keitsbereichs der Handels- und Handwerks-Kammern." Dissertation, Jena, 1929.

Aufhäuser, Siegfried. *Ideologie und Taktik der Angestelltenbewegung.* Berlin, 1931.

Aufmolk, Emmy. "Die gewerbliche Mittelstandspolitik des Reiches (unter besonderer Berucksichtigung der Nachkriegszeit)." Dissertation, Münster, 1930.

Benning, Bernhard; and Nieschlag, Robert. "Umsatz, Lagehaltung und Kosten im deutschen Einzelhandel 1924 bis 1932." *Vierteljahrshefte zur Konjunkturforschung.* Sonderheft 32. Berlin, 1933.

Buchner, Hans. "Die Warenhauspolitik und Nationalsozialismus." *Nationalsozialistische Bibliothek*, Heft 13 (1931): 351–56.

Croner, Fritz. "Die Angestelltenbewegung nach der Währungsstabilisierung." In *Archiv für Sozialwissenschaft und Sozialpolitik* 60 (1928): 103–46.

Dreyfuss, Carl. "Beruf und Ideologie der Angestellten." Dissertation, Munich, 1933. Translated by WPA—Dept. of Social Science, Columbia University, 1938.

Eulenburg, Franz. "Die sozialen Wirkungen der Währungsverhältnisse." *Jahrbücher für Nationalökonomie und Statistik*, 122 (1924): 714–78.

Feder, Gottfried. "Betrachtungen zum Youngplan." *Nationalsozialistische Monatshefte*, Heft 6 (October 1930): 249–56.

Fischer, Fritz W. "Die Angestellten, ihre Bewegung und ihre Ideologien." Dissertation, Heidelberg, 1931.

Freytagh-Loringhoven, Axel von. *Die Deutsch-nationale Volkspartei.* Berlin, 1931.

Frick, Wilhelm. "Die Nationalsozialisten im Reichstag, 1924–1928." *Nationalsozialistische Bibliothek*, Heft 4 (1928): 1–66.

Gaebel, Käthe. "Die Entwicklungstendenzen des gewerblichen Klein- und Mittelbetriebes." *Soziale Praxis*, 43 (1934): 282–89.

Geiger, Theodor. "Panik im Mittelstand." *Die Arbeit*, 7 (1930): 637–59.

———. *Die soziale Schichtung des deutschen Volkes. Soziographischer Versuch auf statistischer Grundlage.* Stuttgart, 1932.

Goebbels, Joseph. "Neue Methoden der Propaganda." *Nationalsozialistische Briefe*, 15 August 1926.

———. "Das patriotische Bürgertum." *Nationalsozialistische Monatshefte*, Heft 5 (1930): 221–29.

———. *Vom Kaiserhof zum Reichskanzlei*. Berlin, 1934.

Grünbaum, Heinz. "Die Umsatzschwankungen des Einzelhandels als Problem der Betriebspolitik." *Vierteljahrshefte zur Konjunkturforschung*, Sonderheft 10 (1928): 1–36.

Hamm, Heinz. "Die wirtschaftlichen und sozialen Berufsmerkmale der kaufmännischen Angestellten (im Vergleich mit denjenigen der Arbeiter)." Dissertation, Jena, 1931.

———. "Das Frauenwahlrecht in der Statistik." *Allgemeines Statistisches Archiv*, 21 (1932): 167–82.

Hartwig, R. "Wie die Frauen im deutschen Reich von ihrem politischen Wahlrecht Gebrauch machen." *Allgemeines Statistisches Archiv*, 17 (1928): 497–515.

Jobst, Rudolf. "Die Deutsche Angestelltenbewegung in ihrer grundsätzlicher Stellung zu Kapitalismus und Klassenkampf." Dissertation, Jena, 1930.

Koslowski, Herbert. "Die Gegenwärtige Lage des ostpreussischen Handwerks verglichen mit der Vorkriegszeit." Dissertation, Königsberg, 1933.

Kracauer, Siegfried. *Die Angestellten. Aus dem neusten Deutschland*. Frankfurt, 1930.

Krebs, Albert. *Tendenzen und Gestalten der NSDAP. Erinnerungen an die Frühzeit der Partei*. Stuttgart, 1959.

Krey, Hermann, ed. *Die Programme der politischen Parteien Deutschlands*. Leipzig, 1932.

Kuczynski, Jürgen. *Löhne und konjunktur in Deutschland 1887 bis 1932*. Berlin, 1933.

Küstermeier, Rudolf. *Die Mittelschichten und ihr politischer Weg*. Potsdam, 1933.

Lederer, Emil. *Die Privatangestellten in der modernen Wirtschaftsentwicklung*. Tübingen, 1912.

———, and Marschak, Jakob. "Der neue Mittelstand." *Grundriss der Sozialökonomie*. Vol. 9, Heft 1. Tübingen, 1926.

Lind, Erwin. "Die Wähler der NSDAP (Eine statistische Untersuchung der Wahlergebnisse in Hessen." *Frankfurter Zeitung*, nos. 895–900, December, 1930.

Meyer, Maximilian. "Der Nichtwähler." *Allgemeines Statistisches Archiv*, 21 (1931): 495–525.

Michels, Robert. *Umsichtungen in den herrschenden Klassen nach dem Kriege*. Stuttgart, 1934.

"Mittelständische Wirtschaft." *Vierteljahrshefte zur Konjunkturforschung*, Sonderheft 7 (1933), Teil 1.

Müller, Heinrich. "Beamtentum und Nationalsozialismus." *Nationalsozialistische Bibliothek*, Heft 30 (1931): 1–59.

Neisser, Hans. "Sozialstatistische Analyse des Wahlergebnisse." *Die Arbeit*, 7 (1930): 654–59.

Nothaas, Josef. "Sozialer Auf- und Abstieg im deutschen Volke." *Kölner Vierteljahreshefte für Soziologie*, 9 (1930): 61–81.

————. "Die Stellenlosigkeit der Angestellten." *Allgemeines Statistisches Archiv*, 16 (1927): 271–322.

Pollock, James K. "The German Reichstag Election of 1930." *American Political Science Review*, 24 (1930): 989–95.

Quante, Peter. "Beiträge zur Statistik der Beamtengehälter." *Zeitschrift des Preussischen Statistischen Landesamtes*, 64 (1924): 1–8.

Raventlow, E. "Nemesis über dem Bürgertum." *Nationalsozialistische Monatshefte*, Heft 1 (1930): 5–11.

Reichert, J. W., ed. *Helferrichs Reichstagsreden 1922–1924*. Berlin, 1925.

Reichstagshandbuch 1924 III. Wahlperiode. Berlin, 1925.

Schauff, Johannes. *Die deutschen Katholiken und die Zentrumspartei. Eine politisch-statistische Untersuchung der Reichstagswahlen seit 1871*. Cologne, 1928.

————. *Neues Wahlrecht. Beiträge zur Wahlreform*. Berlin, 1929.

Schmahl, Eugen. *Entwicklung der völkischen Bewegung*. Giessen, 1933.

Schreiber, Georg. *Die Not der deutschen Wissenschaft und der geistigen Arbeiter*. Leipzig, 1923.

Sering, Max. *Die deutsche Landwirtschaft unter Volks- und weltwirtschaftlichen Gesichtspunkten*. Berlin, 1932.

Speier, Hans. *Die Angestellten vor dem Nationalsozialismus. Ein Beitrag zum Verständnis der deutschen Sozialstruktur 1918–1933*. Göttingen, 1977.

Stephan, Werner. "Zur Soziologie der N.S.D.A.P." *Zeitschrift für Politik*, 20 (1931): 793–800.

Stolper, Gustav. *Die wirtschaftlich-soziale Waltanschauung der Demokratie*. Berlin, 1929.

Sträter, Emma. "Die soziale Stellung der Angestellten." Dissertation, Bonn, 1933.

Suhr, Otto, ed. *Die Lebenshaltung der Angestellten*, Berlin, 1928.

Sussengut, Otto. "Die Angestellten als Stand und Klasse. Ein Beitrag zur Soziologie des wirtschaftlich-sozialen Kampfes in Deutschland." Dissertation, Halle-Wittenberg, 1927/29.

Tiburtisu, Joachim. "Der deutsche Einzelhandel im Wirtschaftsverlauf und in der Wirtschaftspolitik von 1925 bis 1935." *Jahrbücher für Nationalökonomie und Statistik*, 142 (1935): 562–96; 693–719.

Tobis, Franz. *Das Mittelstandsproblem der Nachkriegszeit und seine statistische Erfassung*. Grimmen/Pommern, 1930.

Wagemann, Ernst (Leiter). "Stand und Ursachen der Arbeitslosigkeit in Deutschland." *Vierteljahrshefte zur Konjunkturforschung*. Sonderheft 32. Berlin, 1933.

————. "Umsatz, Lagerhaltung und Kosten im deutschen Einzelhandel 1924 bis 1932." *Vierteljahrshefte zur Konjunkturforschung*. Sonderheft 32. Berlin, 1933.

————. "Die Umsatzschwankungen des Einzelhandels als Problem der Betriebspolitik." *Vierteljahrshefte zur Konjunkturforschung*. Sonderheft 10. Berlin, 1928.

————. "Umsatz und Lagerhaltung im deutschen Einzelhandel seit 1924." *Vier-

teljahrshefte zur Konjunkturforschung. Sonderheft 14. Berlin, 1930.
Wagenführ, Rolf. "Die Industriewirtschaft. Entwicklungstendenzen der deutschen und internationalen Industrieproduktion 1860 bis 1932." *Vierteljahrshefte zur Konjunkturforschung.* Sonderheft 31. Berlin, 1933.
Weber, Alfred. *Die Not der geistigen Arbeiter.* Munich, 1923.
Weber, Max. "Beamtenschaft und politisches Führertum." In Max Weber, *Gesammelte politische Schriften.* Munich, 1921.
Weberstedt, Hans. "Die politischen Parteien und ihre Sünden." *Nationalsozialistische Bibliothek,* Heft 19 (1932): 1–77.
Woytinski, W. *Der deutsche Arbeitsmarkt.* Berlin, 1930.

Secondary Sources

Abraham, David. *The Collapse of the Weimar Republic: Political Economy and Crisis.* Princeton, 1981.
Albertin, Lothar. *Liberalismus und Demokratie am Anfang der Weimarer Republik: Eine vergleichende Analyse der Deutschen Demokratischen Partei und der Deutschen Volkspartei.* Düsseldorf, 1972.
Allen, William S. *The Nazi Seizure of Power: The Experience of a Single German Town, 1930–1935,* Chicago, 1965.
Angress, Werner T. "The Political Role of the Peasantry in the Weimar Republic." *Review of Politics* 21 (1959): 530–50.
———. *Stillborn Revolution: The Communist Bid for Power in Germany, 1921–1933.* Princeton, 1963.
Arns, Günter. "Regierungsbildung und Koalitionspolitik in der Weimarer Republic, 1919–1924" Ph.D. dissertation, Tübingen, 1971.
Bariety, Jacques. *Les relations franco-allemandes apres la Premiere Guerre Mondiale.* Paris, 1977.
Becker, Josef. "Josef Wirth und die Krise des Zentrums während des IV. Kabinetts Marx (1927–1928)." *Zeitschrift für die Geschichte des Oberrheins* 109 (1961): 361–482.
Bennecke, Heinrich. *Wirtschaftliche Depression und politischer Radikalismus, 1918–1938.* Munich, 1970.
Berghahn, Volker R. "Die Harzburger Front und die Kandidatur Hindenburgs für die Präsidentschaftswahlen 1932." *Vierteljahrshefte für Zeitgeschichte* 13 (1965): 64–82.
———. *Der Stahlhelm: Bund der Frontsoldaten, 1918–1935.* Düsseldorf, 1966.
Bergmann, Klaus. *Agrarromantik und Grossstadtfeindschaft.* Meisenheim am Glan, 1970.
Bessel, Richard, "Eastern Germany as a Structural Problem in the Weimar Republic." *Social History* 3 (1978): 199–218.
———; and Feuchtwanger, E. K., eds. *Social Change and Political Development in Weimar Germany.* London, 1981.

Besson, Waldemar. *Württemberg und die deutsche Staatskrise, 1928–1933.* Stuttgart, 1959.

Bischof, E. *Rheinischer Separatismus 1918–1924: Hans-Adam Dortens Rheinstaatsbewegung.* Bern, 1969.

Blackbourn, David G. "Class and Politics in Wilhelmine Germany." *Central European History,* 9 (1976): 220–49.

———. *Class, Religion, and Local Politics in Wilhelmine Germany: The Catholic Centre Party in Wurttemberg before 1914.* New Haven, 1980.

———. "The *Mittelstand* in German Society and Politics 1871–1914." *Social History,* 4 (1977): 409–33.

———. "The Political Alignment of the Centre." *Historical Journal* 18 (1975): 821–50.

Blalock, Hubert M., Jr. *Causal Inferences in Nonexperimental Research.* New York, 1967.

———. "Correlated Independent Variables; The Problem of Multicollinearity." In Edward R. Tufte, ed., *The Quantitative Analysis of Social Problems.* Reading, Mass.

Böhnke, Wilfried. *Die NSDAP im Ruhrgebiet 1920–1933.* Bonn, 1974.

Bolte, Karl Marin. "Ein Beitrag zur Problematik der sozialen Mobilität." *Kölner Zeitschrift für Soziologie und Sozialpsychologie,* 8 (1956): 26–45.

———. "Some Aspects of Social Mobility in Western Germany." In *Transactions of the Third World Congress of Sociology,* Vol. 3. London, 1956.

———. *Sozialer Aufstieg und Abstieg: Eine Untersuchung über Berufsprestige und Berufsmobilität.* Stuttgart, 1959.

———; Aschenbreener, Katrin; Krechkel, Reinhard; and Schultz-Wild, Rainer. *Beruf und Gesellschaft in Deutschland: Berufsstruktur und Berufsprobleme.* Opladen, 1970.

Borch, Herbt von. *Obrigkeit und Widerstand: Zur politischen Soziologie des Beamtentums.* Tübingen, 1954.

Born, Karl-Erich. *Die deutsche Bankenkrise 1931: Finanzen und Politik.* Munich, 1967.

Bosch, Michael. *Liberale Presse in der Krise: Die Innenpolitik der Jahre 1930 bis 1933 im Spiegel des "Berliner Tageblatts," der "Frankfurter Zeitung" und der "Vossische Zeitung."* Frankfurt, 1976.

Bracher, Karl Dietrich. *Die Auflösung der Weimarer Republik: Eine Studie zum Problem des Machtverfalls in der Demokratie.* 4th ed. Villingen, 1964.

———. *Die Deutsche Diktatur: Entstehung, Struktur, Folgen des Nationalsozialismus.* Cologne, 1969.

Bramstedt, Ernest K. *Goebbels and National Socialist Propaganda, 1925–1945.* East Lansing, 1965.

Breitman, Richard. *German Socialism and Weimar Democracy.* Chapel Hill, 1981.

Bremme, Gabriele. *Die politische Rolle der Frau in Deutschland.* Göttingen, 1956.

Bresciani-Turroni, Constantin. *The Economics of Inflation: A Study of Currency Depreciation in Post-War Germany, 1914–1923.* London, 1953.

Bridenthal, Renata. "Beyond Kinder, Küche, Kirche: Weimar Women at Work." *Central European History*, 16 (1973): 148–66.

Bry, Gerhard. *Wages in Germany, 1871–1945.* Princeton, 1960.

Broszat, Martin. "Die Anfänge der Berliner NSDAP 1926–27." *Vierteljahrshefte für Zeitgeschichte*, 8 (1960): 85–118.

————. "Die völkische Ideologie und der Nationalsozialismus." *Deutsche Rundschau* 84 (1958): 53–68.

Burnham, Walter Dean. "Political Immunization and Political Confessionalism: The United States and Weimar Germany." *Journal of Interdisciplinary History*, 3 (1972): 1–30.

Büsch, Otto; and Feldman, Gerald D., eds. *Historische Prozesse der deutschen Inflation, 1914–1924.* Berlin, 1978.

Caplan, Jane. "Civil Service Support for National Socialism: An Evaluation." In Gerhard Hirschfeld, ed., *Der "Führerstaat": Mythos und Realität. Studien zur Struktur und Politik des Deutschen Reiches.* Stuttgart, 1981.

————. "The Imaginary Universality of Particular Interests: 'The Tradition' of the Civil Service in German History." *Social History*, 4 (1979): 299–317.

————. "The Politics of Administration: The Reich Interior Ministry and the German Civil Service, 1933–1943." *Historical Journal*, 20 (1977): 707–36.

Castellan, Georges." Zur sozialen Bilanz der Prosperität 1924–1929." In Hans Mommsen, Dietmar Petzina, Bernd Weisbrod, eds., *Industrielles System und politische Entwicklung in der Weimarer Republik.* Düsseldorf, 1974.

Chanady, Attila. "The Disintegration of the German National People's Party 1924–1930." *Journal of Modern History*, 39 (1967): 65–91.

————. "The Dissolution of the German Democratic Party in 1930." *American Historical Review*, 73 (1968): 1433–53.

Childers, Thomas. "Inflation and Electoral Politics in Germany 1919–1929." In Nathan Schumkler and Edward Marcus, eds., *Inflation Through the Ages: Economic, Social, Psychological, and Historical Aspects.* New York, 1982.

————. "Inflation, Stabilization, and Political Realignment in Germany 1924–1928." In Gerald D. Feldman, Carl Ludwig Holtfrerich, Gerhard A. Ritter, Peter-Christian Witt, eds., *Die Deutsche Inflation: Eine Zwischenbilanz.* Berlin, 1982, pp. 409–31.

————. "National Socialism and the New Middle Class." In Reinhard Mann, ed., *Die Nationalsozialisten: Analysen faschistischer Bewegungen.* Stuttgart, 1980.

————. "The Social Bases of Electoral Politics in Urban Germany, 1919–1933: A Sociological Analysis of Voting Behavior in the Weimar Republic." Ph.D. dissertation, Harvard University, 1976.

————. "The Social Bases of the National Socialist Vote." *Journal of Contemporary History*, 11 (1976): 17–42.

Clemenz, Manfred. *Gesellschaftliche Ursprünge des Faschismus.* Frankfurt, 1972.

Conze, Werner. "Die Krise des Parteienstaates in Deutschland, 1929/1930." *Historische Zeitschrift*, 178 (1954): 47–83.

Coyner, Sandra J. "Class Consciousness and Consumption: The New Middle

Class during the Weimar Republic." *Journal of Social History*, 10 (March 1977): 310–31.

Creekmore, Marion Virgil. "The German Reichstag Election of 1928." Ph.D. dissertation, Tulane University, 1968.

Czichon, Eberhard. *Wer verhalf Hitler zur Macht?* Cologne, 1967.

Dahrendorf, Ralf. *Class and Class Conflict in Industrial Society.* Stanford, 1959.

———. *Society and Democracy in Germany.* Garden City, 1967.

Desai, Ashok V. *Real Wages in Germany, 1871–1913.* Oxford, 1968.

Diederich, Nils. *Empirische Wahlforschung. Konzeptionen und Methoden im Internationalen Vergleich.* Cologne, 1965.

Dogan, Mattei; and Rokkan, Stein, eds. *Quantitative Ecological Analysis in the Social Sciences.* Cambridge, Mass., 1969.

Döhn, Lothar, *Politik und Interesse: Die Interessenstruktur der Deutschen Volkspartei.* Meisenheim am Glan, 1970.

———. "Zur Verschränkung der Deutschen Volkspartei mit grosswirtschaftlich-industriellen Interessen im Herrschaftssystem der Weimarer Republik." In Hans Mommsen, Dietmar Petzina, Bernd Weisbrod, eds., *Industrielles System und politische Entwicklung in der Weimarer Republik.* Düsseldorf, 1974.

Domurad, Frank. "The Politics of Corporatism: Hamburg Handicraft in the Late Weimar Republic, 1927–1933." In Richard Bessell and E. K. Feuchtwanger, eds., *Social Change and Political Development in the Weimar Republic.* London, 1982.

Dörr, Manfred. "Die Deutschnationale Volkspartei 1925 bis 1928." Ph.D. dissertation, Marburg, 1964.

Eksteins, Morris. *The Limits of Reason: The German Democratic Press and the Collapse of Weimar Democracy.* London, 1975.

Eley, Geoff. *Reshaping the German Right: Radical Nationalism and Political Change after Bismarck.* New Haven, 1980.

Epstein, Klaus. *Matthias Erzberger and the Dilemma of German Democracy.* Princeton, 1959.

Erdmann, K.-D. *Adenauer in der Rheinlandpolitik nach dem Ersten Weltkrieg.* Stuttgart, 1966.

Evans, Richard J. *The Feminist Movement in Germany, 1894–1933.* London, 1976.

———. "German Women and the Triumph of Hitler." *Journal of Modern History.* Demand Publication. Abstract printed in vol. 48, no. 1, March 1976.

———, ed. *Society and Politics in Wilhelmine Germany.* London, 1978.

Eyck, Erich. *Bismarck and the German Empire.* New York, 1966.

———. *A History of the Weimar Republic.* 2 vols., Cambridge, Mass., 1966.

Falter, Jürgen W. "Wer verhalf der NSDAP zum Sieg?" *Aus Politik und Zeitgeschichte*, B28–29 (14 July 1979): 3–21.

Faris, Ellsworth. "Takeoff Point for the National Socialist Party: The Landtag Election in Baden, 1929." *Central European History*, 8 (1975): 140–71.

Farquaharson, John. "The NSDAP in Hanover and Lower Saxony." *Journal of Contemporary History* 8 (1973): 103–20.

————. *The Plough and the Swastika: National Socialist Farm Policy 1928–1933.* London, 1979.

Faust, Anselm. *Der Nationalsozialistische Studentenbund: Studenten und Nationalsozialismus in der Weimarer Republik.* 2 vols. Düsseldorf, 1973.

Feldman, Gerald D. *Army, Industry, and Labor in Germany 1914–1918.* Princeton, 1966.

————. *Iron and Steel in the German Inflation, 1916–1923.* Princeton, 1977.

————; Holtfrerich, Carl Ludwig; Ritter, Gerhard A.; and Witt, Peter-Christian, eds. *Die Deutsche Inflation: Eine Zwischenbilanz.* Berlin, 1982.

————; and Homburg, Heidrun, eds. *Industrie und Inflation. Studien und Dokumente zur Politik der deutschen Unternehmer 1916–1923.* Hamburg, 1977.

————.; and Nocken, Ulrich. "Trade Associations and Economic Power: Interest Group Development in the German Iron and Steel and Machine Building Industries, 1900–1913." *Business History Review* 49 (Winter 1975): 413–45.

Fenske, Hans. *Konservativismus und Rechtsradikalismus in Bayern nach 1918.* Bad Homburg, 1969.

————. "Monarchisches Beamtentum und demokratischer Staat: Zum Problem der Bürokratie in der Weimarer Republik." In *Demokratie und Verwaltung (25 Jahre Hochschule für Verwaltungswissenschaften Speyer).* Berlin, 1972.

Figge, Reinhard. "Die Opposition der NSDAP im Reichstag," Ph.D. dissertation, Cologne, 1963.

Fischer, Fritz. *Griff nach der Weltmacht: Die Kriegszielpolitik des Kaiserlichen Deutschland 1914–1918.* Düsseldorf, 1961.

Flechtheim, Ossip K. *Die KPD in der Weimarer Republik.* Frankfurt, 1969.

Flemming, Jens. *Landwirtschaftliche Interessen und Demokratie. Ländliche Gesellschaft, Agrarverbände und Staat 1890–1925.* Bonn, 1978.

Franz, Günther. *Die politischen Wahlen in Niedersachsen, 1867 bis 1949.* Bremen-Horn, 1957.

Franz-Willing, Georg. *Die Hitlerbewegung: Der Ursprung 1919–1922.* Hamburg, 1962.

————. *Krisenjahr der Hitlerbewegung, 1923.* Preussisch-Oldendorf, 1975.

————. "Munich: Birthplace and Center of the National Socialist German Workers' Party." *Journal of Modern History* 29 (1957): 319–34.

————. *Putsch und Verbotszeit der Hitlerbewegung, November 1923–Februar 1925.* Preussisch Oldendorf, 1977.

Fricke, Dieter, ed. *Die Bürgerlichen Parteien in Deutschland. Handbuch der Geschichte der bürgerlichen Parteien und anderer bürgerlicher Interessenorganisationen vom Vormärz bis zum Jahre 1945.* 2 vols. Leipzig, 1968, 1971.

Fritsch, Werner. "Reichspartei für Volksrecht und Aufwertung (Volksrechtspartei) 1926–1933." In Dieter Fricke, ed., *Die Bürgerlichen Parteien.* Leipzig, 1968.

————. "Sparerbund für das Deutsche Reich (Spb) 1922–1939." In Dieter Fricke, ed., *Die Bürgerlichen Parteien in Deutschland.* Leipzig, 1968.

Gall, Lothar. "Liberalismus und 'bürgerliche Gesellschaft.' Zur Charakter und

Entwicklung der liberalen Bewegung in Deutschland." *Historische Zeitschrift* 220 (1975): 324–56.

Gates, Robert A. "Von der Sozialpolitik zur Wirtschaftspolitik: Das Dilemma der deutschen Sozialdemokratie in der Krise 1929–1933." In Hans Mommsen, Dietmar Petzina, Bernd Weisbrod, eds., *Industrielles System und politische Entwicklung in der Weimarer Republik*. Düsseldorf, 1974.

Gellately, Robert. *The Politics of Economic Despair. Shopkeepers and German Politics 1890–1914*. London, 1974.

Gemein, Gisbert Jörg. *Die DNVP in Düsseldorf, 1918–1933*. Ph.D. dissertation, Cologne, 1969.

Gerschenkron, Alexander. *Bread and Democracy in Germany*. New York, 1966.

Gerth, Hans. "The Nazi Party: Its Leadership and Composition." *American Journal of Sociology*, 45 (1940): 517–41.

Gessner, Dieter. *Agrardepression und Präsidialregierungen in Deutschland 1930 bis 1933. Probleme des Agrarprotektionismus am Ende der Weimarer Republik*. Düsseldorf, 1977.

———. *Agrarverbände in der Weimarer Republik. Wirtschaftliche und soziale Voraussetzungen agrarkonservativer Politik vor 1933*. Düsseldorf, 1976.

———. "The Dilemma of Agriculture during the Weimar Republic." In Bessell and Feuchtwanger, *Social Change and Political Development*, pp. 134–51.

Gies, Horst. "The NSDAP and the Agrarian Organizations in the Final Phase of the Weimar Republic." In Henry A. Turner, ed., *Nazism and the Third Reich*. New York, 1972.

Goodman, Leo A. "Some Alternatives to Ecological Correlation." *American Journal of Sociology* 64 (1959): 610–25.

Gordon, Harold J., Jr. *Hitler and the Beer Hall Putsch*. Princeton, 1972.

———. "Die Reichswehr und Sachsen 1923." *Wehrwissenschaftliche Rundschau*, 11 (1961): 677–92.

Gordon, Robert A. "Issues in Multiple Regression." *American Journal of Sociology* 73 (1968): 592–616.

Graham, Frank D. *Exchange, Prices, and Production in Hyper-Inflation: Germany, 1920–1923*. Princeton, 1930.

Graper, E. D. "The German Presidential Elections." *American Political Science Review*, 19 (1925): 592–600.

Grünthal, Günther. *Reichsschulgesetz und Zentrumspartei in der Weimarer Republik*. Düsseldorf, 1968.

Hackett, David A. "The Nazi Party in the Reichstag Election of 1930." Ph.D. dissertation, University of Wisconsin, 1971.

Hamel, Iris. *Völkischer Verband und nationale Gewerkschaft: Der Deutschnationale Handlungsgehilfen-Verband, 1893–1933*. Frankfurt, 1967.

Hamilton, Richard F. *Who Voted for Hitler?* Princeton, 1982.

Hartenstein, Wolfgang. *Die Anfänge der Deutschen Volkspartei, 1918–1920*. Düsseldorf, 1962.

Hartfield, G. *Angestellte und Angestelltengewerkschaften in Deutschland: Entwicklung und Situation von beruflicher Tätigkeit, sozialer Stellung Verbandswesen der Angestellten in der gewerblichen Wirtschaft*. Berlin, 1961.

Hartwich, Hans Hermann. *Arbeitsmarkt, Verbände und Staat 1918–1933.* Berlin, 1967.

Haushofer, Heinz. *Die deutsche Landwirtschaft im technischen Zeitalter.* Stuttgart, 1963.

Heberle, Rudolf. *From Democracy to Nazism.* Baton Rouge, 1945.

Heiber, Helmut. *Die Republik von Weimar.* 4th ed. Munich, 1969.

Heilfron, E., ed. *Die Deutsche Nationalversammlung im Jahre 1919.* Berlin, 1947.

Helbich, W. J. *Die Reparationen in der Ära Brüning: Zur Bedeutung des Young-Plans für die deutsche Politik, 1930–1932.* Berlin, 1962.

Hertzmann, Lewis. *DNVP: Right-Wing Opposition in the Weimar Republic, 1918–1924.* Lincoln, Neb. 1963.

Heyen, Franz-Josef. *Nationalsozialismus im Alltag: Quellen zur Geschichte des Nationalsozialismus vornehmlich im Raum Mainz-Koblenz-Trier.* Boppard am Rhein, 1967.

Hintze, Otto. "Der Beamtenstand." In *Soziologie und Geschichte.* 2nd ed. Göttingen, 1966.

Hoffman, Walter G. *Das Wachstum der deutschen Wirtschaft.* Berlin, 1965.

———; and Müller, J. H. *Das Deutsche Volkseinkommen, 1851–1957.* Tübingen, 1959.

Holt, John Bradshaw. *German Agricultural Policy, 1918–1934. The Development of a National Philosophy toward Agriculture in Postwar Germany.* Chapel Hill, 1936.

Holtfrerich, Carl Ludwig. *Die Deutschen Inflation 1914–1933: Ursachen und Folgen in internationaler Perspektive.* Berlin, 1980.

Holzer, Jerzy. *Parteien und Massen: Die politische Krise in Deutschland, 1928–1930.* Wiesbaden, 1975.

Horn, Daniel. "The National Socialist Schülerbund and the Hitler Youth, 1929–1933." *Central European History* 11 (1978): 355–75.

Horn, Wolfgang. *Führerideologie und Parteiorganisation in der NSDAP (1919–1933).* Düsseldorf, 1972.

Hornung, Klaus. *Der Jungdeutsche Orden.* Düsseldorf, 1958.

Hunt, James C. *The People's Party in Wurttemberg and Southern Germany, 1890–1914: The Possibilities of Democratic Politics.* Stuttgart, 1975.

Hunt, Richard N. *German Social Democracy 1918–1933.* Chicago, 1970.

Jacobson, Jon. *Locarno Diplomacy: Germany and the West, 1925–1929.* Princeton, 1972.

Jochmann, Werner. *Nationalsozialismus und Revolution: Ursprung und Geschichte der NSDAP in Hamburg, 1922–1933. Dokumente.* Frankfurt, 1963.

Jonas, Erasmus. *Die Volkskonservativen 1928–1933.* Düsseldorf, 1965.

Jones, E. Terrence. "Ecological Inference and Electoral Analysis." *Journal of Interdisciplinary History* 2 (1972): 249–62.

Jones, Larry Eugene. "Between the Fronts: The German National Union of Commercial Employees from 1928 to 1933." *Journal of Modern History,* 48 (September 1976): 462–82.

———. "The Crisis of White Collar Interest Politics: Deutschnationaler Handlungsgehilfen-Verband and Deutsche Volkspartei in the World Economic Crisis." In Mommsen et al., *Industrielles System und politische Entwicklung in der Weimarer Republik*, pp. 811–23.

———. "The Dying Middle: Weimar Germany and the Failure of Bourgeois Unity, 1924–1930." Ph.D. dissertation, University of Wisconsin, 1970.

———. " 'The Dying Middle': Weimar Germany and the Fragmentation of Bourgeois Politics." *Central European History* 5 (1972): 23–54.

———. "Inflation, Revaluation, and the Crisis of Middle-Class Politics: A Study in the Dissolution of the German Party System, 1923–28." *Central European History* 12 (1979): 143–68.

———. "Sammlung oder Zersplitterung? Die Bestrebungen zur Bildung einer neuen Mittelpartei in der Endphase der Weimarer Republik 1930–1933." *Vierteljahrshefte für Zeitgeschichte* 25 (1977): 265–304.

Junker, Detlef. *Die Deutsche Zentrumspartei und Hitler 1932/33: Ein Beitrag zur Problematik des politischen Katholizimus in Deutschland.* Stuttgart, 1969.

Kaack, Heino. *Geschichte und Struktur des deutschen Parteiensystems.* Opladen, 1971.

Kadritzke, Ulf. *Angestellte—Die geduldigen Arbeiter: Zur Soziologie und sozialen Bewegung der Angestellten.* Frankfurt, 1975.

Kaelble, Hartmut. "Social Stratification in Germany in the 19th and 20th Centuries: A Survey of Research since 1945." *Journal of Social History* 10 (1976): 144–65.

Kaltefleiter, Werner. *Wirtschaft und Politik in Deutschland: Konjunktur als Bestimmungsfaktor des Parteiensystems.* Cologne, 1968.

Kater, Michael H. "Der Nationalsozialistische Studentenbund von 1926 bis 1928: Randgruppe zwischen Hitler und Strasser." *Vierteljahrshefte für Zeitgeschichte* 22 (1974): 148–90.

———. "Sozialer Wandel in der NSDAP im Zuge der nationalsozialistischen Machtergreifung." In Wolfgang Schieder, ed., *Faschismus als soziale Bewegung: Deutschland und Italien im Vergleich.* Hamburg, 1976.

———. *Studentenschaft und Rechtsradikalismus in Deutschland, 1918–1933.* Hamburg, 1975.

———. "Zur Soziolographie der frühen NSDAP." *Vierteljahrshefte für Zeitgeschichte* 20 (1971): 124–59.

Kaufmann, Walter H. *Monarchism in the Weimar Republic.* New York, 1953.

Kehr, Eckard. *Schlachtflottenbau und Parteipolitik 1894–1901.* Berlin, 1930.

Kele, Max H. *Nazis and Workers: National Socialist Appeals to German Labor, 1919–1933.* Chapel Hill, 1972.

Klein, F., ed. *Politik im Krieg 1914–1918.* Berlin, 1964.

Kocka, Jürgen. *Angestellte zwischen Faschismus und Demokratie. Zur politischen Sozialgeschichte der Angestellten: USA 1890–1940 im Internationalen Vergleich.* Göttingen, 1977.

———. "The First World War and the '*Mittelstand*': German Artisans and White Collar Workers." *Journal of Contemporary History* 8 (1973): 101–24.

————. *Klassengesellschaft im Krieg: Deutsche Sozialgeschichte 1914–1918.* *Kritische Studien zur Geschichtswissenschaften.* Göttingen, 1973.

————. *Unternehmensverwaltung und Angestelltenschaft am Beispiel Siemens, 1847–1914.* Stuttgart, 1969.

————. "Vorindustrielle Faktoren in der deutschen Industrialisierung: Industriebürokratie und 'neuer Mittelstand.'" In Michael Stürmer, ed., *Das Kaiserliche Deutschland: Politik und Gesellschaft, 1870–1918.* Düsseldorf, 1970.

————. "Zur Problematik der deutschen Angestellten 1914–1933." In Hans Mommsen, Dietmar Petzina, Bernd Weisbrod, eds., *Industrielles System und politische Entwicklung in der Weimarer Republik.* Düsseldorf, 1974.

Köllmann, Wolfgang. "Politische und soziale Entwicklung der deutschen Arbeiterschaft 1850–1914." In Gerhard A. Ritter, ed., *Die Deutschen Parteien vor 1918.* Cologne, (1973).

Kontos, Silvia. *Die Partei Kämpft wie ein Mann: Die Frauenpolitik der KPD in der Weimarer Republik.* Stroemfeld, 1979.

Koonz, Claudia. "Nazi Women before 1933: Rebels against Emancipation." *Social Science Quarterly*, March 1976, pp. 553–63.

Kornhauser, William. *The Politics of Mass Society.* London, 1960.

Kousser, J. Morgan. "Ecological Regression and the Analysis of Past Politics." *Journal of Interdisciplinary History* 4 (1973): 237–62.

Krause, Hartfried, USPD. *Zur Geschichte der Unabhängigen Sozialdemokratischen Partei Deutschlands.* Frankfurt, 1975.

Krohn, Claus-Dieter. *Stabilisierung und ökonomische Interessen. Die Finanzpolitik des Deutschen Reiches 1923–1927.* Düsseldorf, 1974.

Kuczynski, Jürgen. *Lage der Arbeiter unter dem Kapitalismus.* Teil 1, Vol. 5, *Darstellung der Lage der Arbeiter in Deutschland von 1917/18 bis 1932/33.* East Berlin, (1966).

Kühnl, Reinhard, *Die nationalsozialistische Linke, 1925–1930.* Meisenheim am Glan, 1966.

————. "Zur Programmatik der nationalsozialistischen Linken: Das Strasser-Programm von 1925/26." *Vierteljahrshefte für Zeitgeschicht*, 14 (1966): 317–33.

Kühr, Herbert. *Parteien und Wahlen im Stadt- und Landkreis Essen in der Zeit der Weimarer Republik unter besonderer Berücksichtigung des Verhältnisses von Sozialstruktur und politischen Wahlen.* Düsseldorf, 1973.

Kunz, Andreas. "Stand versus Klasse: Beamtenschaft und Gewerkschaften im Konflikt um den Personalabbau 1923/24." *Geschichte und Gesellschaft*, 8 (1982): 55–86.

————. "Verteilungskampf oder Interessenkonsensus? Einkommensentwicklung und Sozialverhalten von Arbeitnehmergruppen in der Inflationszeit 1914–1924." In Gerald D. Feldman, Carl Ludwig Holtfrerich, Gerhard A. Ritter, Peter-Christian Witt, eds., *Die Deutsche Inflation: Eine Zwischenbilanz.* Berlin, 1982.

Landauer, Carl. "The Bavarian Problem in the Weimar Republic, 1918–1923." *Journal of Modern History* 16 (1944): 93–115, 205–23.

Lane, Barbara Miller. "Nazi Ideology: Some Unfinished Business." *Central European History*, 7 (1974): 3–30.

———; and Rupp, Leila J. *Nazi Ideology before 1933: A Documentation*. Austin, 1978.

Lasswell, Harold D. "The Psychology of Hitlerism." *Political Quarterly*, 4 (1933): 373–84.

Laursen, Karsten; and Pedersen, Jørgen. *The German Inflation, 1918–1923*. Amsterdam, 1964.

Layton, Roland V., Jr. "The *Völkischer Beobachter*, 1920–1933: The Nazi Party Newspaper in the Weimar Era." *Central European History*, 3 (1970): 353–82.

Lebovics, Herman. *Social Conservatism and the Middle Classes in Germany, 1914–1933*. Princeton, 1969.

Lepsius, M. Rainer, *Extremer Nationalismus: Strukturbedingungen von der Nationalsozialistischen Machtergreifung*, Stuttgart, 1966.

———. "Parteiensystem und Sozialstruktur: Zum Problem der Demokratisierung der deutschen Gesellschaft." In Gerhard A. Ritter, ed., *Deutsche Parteien vor 1918*. Cologne, 1973.

Levy, Richard S. *The Downfall of the Anti-Semitic Parties in Imperial Germany*. New Haven, 1975.

Lichtman, Allan J. "Correlation, Regression, and the Ecological Fallacy: A Critique." *Journal of Interdisciplinary History*, 4 (1974): 417–34.

Lidtke, Vernon L. *The Outlawed Party: Social Democracy in Germany, 1878–1890*. Princeton, 1966.

Liebe, Werner. *Die Deutschnationale Volkspartei, 1918–1924*. Düsseldorf, 1956.

Lill, Rudolf. "Die deutschen Katholiken und Bismarcks Reichsgründung." In Theodor Schieder and Ernst Deuerlein, eds., *Reichsgründung 1870–1871: Tatsachen, Kontroversen, Interpretationen*. Stuttgart, 1970.

Lipset, Seymour Martin. "'Fascism'—Left, Right, and Center." In Lipset, *Political Man: The Social Bases of Politics*. New York, 1960.

———, and Rokkan, Stein, eds. *Party Systems and Voter Alignments: Cross-National Perspectives*. New York, 1967.

Loewenberg, Peter. "The Psycho-Historical Origins of the Nazi Youth Cohort." *American Historical Review*, 76 (1971): 1457–1502.

Lohalm, Uwe. *Völkischer Radikalismus: Die Geschichte des Deutschvölkischen Schutz- und Trutzbundes 1919–1933*. Hamburg, 1970.

Loomis, Charles P.; and Beegle, J. Allan. "The Spread of German Nazism in Rural Areas." *American Sociological Review*, 11 (1946): 724–34.

Madden, James P. "The Social Composition of the Nazi Party, 1919–1930." Ph.D. dissertation, University of Oklahoma, 1976.

Maier, Charles S. *Recasting Bourgeois Europe: Stabilization in France, Germany, and Italy in the Decade after World War I*. Princeton, 1975.

Mann, Rosemarie. "Entstehung und Entwicklung der NSDAP in Marburg bis 1933." *Hessisches Jahrbuch für Landesgeschichte*, 22 (1972): 254–342.

Maser, Werner. *Der Sturm auf die Republik: Frühgeschichte der NSDAP.* Revised edition, Stuttgart, 1963.

Mason, Timothy W. *Sozialpolitik im Dritten Reich. Arbeiterklasse und Volksgemeinschaft.* Wiesbaden, 1977.

———. "Women in Nazi Germany." *History Workshop* (Spring 1976): 74–113.

Matthias, Erich. "The Social Democratic Party and Government Power." In *The Path to Dictatorship 1918–1933.* New York, 1966.

———. "Die Sozialdemokratische Partei Deutschlands." In Matthias and Morsey, *Das Ende der Parteien 1933.* Düsseldorf, 1960.

———; and Morsey, Rudolf, eds. *Das Ende der Parteien 1933.* Düsseldorf, 1960.

Mauer, Ilse. *Reichsfinanzen und grosse Koalition. Zur Geschichte des Reichskabinetts Müller 1928–1930.* Bern, 1973.

McDougall, Walter A. *France's Rhineland Diplomacy, 1914–1924: The Last Bid for a Balance of Power in Europe.* Princeton, 1978.

McIntyre, Jill. "Women and the Professions in Germany, 1930–40." In Anthony Nicholls and Erich Matthias, eds., *German Democracy and the Triumph of Hitler.* London, 1971.

McKibbon, R. I. "The Myth of the Unemployed: Who Did Vote for the Nazis?" *Australian Journal of Politics and History,* 25 (1969): 25–40.

Meckstroth, Theodore W. "Conditions of Partisan Realignments: A Study of Electoral Change." Ph.D. dissertation, University of Minnesota, 1972.

Merkl, Peter H. *Political Violence under the Swastika: 581 Early Nazis.* Princeton, 1975.

Methfessel, Werner. "Christliche-Nationale Bauern- und Landvolkspartei (CNLB), 1928–1933." In *Die bürgerlichen Parteien Deutschlands,* pp. 241–44.

Middleton, Lucy, ed. *Women in the Labor Movement.* London, 1977.

Mielke, Siegfried. *Der Hansa- Bund für Gewerbe, Handel und Industrie 1900– 1914: Der gescheiterte Versuch einer antifeudalen Sammlungspolitik.* Göttingen, 1974.

Milatz, Alfred. "Die linksliberalen Parteien und Gruppen in den Reichstagswahlen bis 1912." *Archiv für Sozialgeschichte,* 12 (1972): 273–92.

———. *Wähler und Wahlen in der Weimarer Republik.* 2nd ed. Bonn, 1968.

Miller, Susanne. *Die Bürde der Macht: Die deutsche Sozialdemokratie 1918– 1920.* Düsseldorf, 1978.

———. *Bürgfrieden und Klassenkampf: Die deutsche Sozialdemokratie im Ersten Weltkrieg.* Düsseldorf, 1974.

Moeller, Robert G. "Dimensions of Social Conflict in the Great War: The View from the German Countryside." *Central European History,* 14 (1981): 142–68.

———. "Peasants, Politics and Pressure Groups in War and Inflation: A Study of the Rhineland and Westphalia, 1914–1924." Ph.D. dissertation, University of California, Berkeley, 1980.

————. "Winners as Losers in the German Inflation: Peasant Protest over the Controlled Economy 1920–1923." In Gerald D. Feldman et al., *Die Deutsche Inflation*, pp. 255–88.

Mommsen, Hans. *Beamtentum im Dritten Reich*. Stuttgart, 1966.

————. "Die Stellung der Beamtenschaft in Reich, Ländern und Gemeinden in der Ära Brüning." *Vierteljahrshefte für Zeitgeschichte*, 21 (1973): 151–73.

————, ed. *Sozialdemokratie zwischen Klassenbewegung und Volkspartei.* Frankfurt, 1974.

————; Petzina, Dietmar; Weisbrod, Bernd, eds. *Industrielles System und politische Entwicklung in der Weimarer Republik*. Düsseldorf, 1974.

Morgan, David W. *The Socialist Left and the German Revolution: A History of the German Independent Social Democratic Party, 1917–1922*. Ithaca, 1975.

Morsey, Rudolf. "The Center Party between the Fronts." In *The Path to Dictatorship 1918–1933*. New York, 1966.

————. *Die Deutsche Zentrumspartei, 1917–1923*. Düsseldorf, 1966.

————. "Die deutschen Katholiken und der Nationalstaat zwischen Kulturkampf und Erstem Weltkrieg." In Gerhard A. Ritter, ed., *Deutsche Parteien vor 1918*. Cologne, 1973.

Mühlberger, Detlef. "The Sociology of the NSDAP: The Question of Working Class Membership." *Journal of Contemporary History*, 15 (1980): 493–511.

Müller, Klaus. "Agrarische Interessenverbände in der Weimarer Republik." *Rheinische Vierteljahrsblätter*, 38 (1974): 386–405.

Muncy, Lysbeth W. "The Junkers and the Prussian Administration from 1918 to 1939." *Review of Politics*, 9 (1947): 482–501.

Netzband, Karl-Bernhard; and Widmaier, Hans-Peter. *Währungs- und Finanzpolitik in der Ära Luther 1923–1925*. Tübingen, 1964.

Neumann, Franz. *Behemoth: The Structure and Practice of National Socialism 1933–1944*. New York, 1944.

Neumann, Sigmund. *Die Parteien der Weimarer Republik*. 3rd ed. Stuttgart, 1973.

Niewyk, Donald L. *Socialist, Anti-Semite, and Jew: German Social Democracy Confronts the Problem of Anti-Semitism, 1918–1933*. Baton Rouge, 1971.

Nilson, S. S. "Wahlsoziologische Probleme des Nationalsozialismus." *Zeitschrift für die Gesamte Staatswissenschaft*, 110 (1954): 279–311.

Nipperdey, Thomas. "Die Organisation der bürgerlichen Parteien in Deutschland." In Gerhard A. Ritter, ed., *Deutsche Parteien vor 1918*. Cologne, 1973.

————. *Die Organisation der deutschen Parteien vor 1918*. Düsseldorf, 1961.

————. "Interessenverbände und Parteien in Deutschland vor dem Ersten Weltkrieg." In Hans-Ulrich Wehler, ed., *Moderne Sozialgeschichte*. Cologne, 1966.

Noakes, Jeremy. *The Nazi Party in Lower Saxony 1921–1933*. Oxford, 1971.

————; and Pridham, Geoffry. *Documents on Nazism, 1919–1945*. New York, 1974.

Nyomarkay, Joseph. *Charisma and Factionalism in the Nazi Party*. Minneapolis, 1967.

————. "Factionalism in the National Socialist German Workers' Party, 1925–26: Myth and Reality of the 'Northern Faction.'" In Henry A. Turner, ed., *Nazism and the Third Reich*. New York, 1972.

O'Lessker, Karl. "Who Voted for Hitler? A New Look at the Class Basis of Nazism." *American Journal of Sociology*, 74 (1968): 63–69.

Opitz, Günter. *Der Christlich-Soziale Volksdienst: Versuch einer protestantischen Partei in der Weimarer Republik*. Düsseldorf, 1969.

Opitz, Reinhard. *Der deutsche Sozialliberalismus, 1917–1933*. Cologne, 1973.

Orlow, Dietrich. *The History of the Nazi Party, 1919–1933*. Pittsburgh, 1969.

Parsons, Talcott. "Democracy and Social Structure in Pre-Nazi Germany." In Talcott Parsons, *Essays in Sociological Theory*. Revised ed., New York, 1964.

Peterson, Brian L. "The Social Bases of German Working Class Politics 1924/25. A Computerized Analysis." Ph.D. dissertation, University of Wisconsin, 1976.

————. "The Politics of Working-Class Women in the Weimar Republic." *Central European History*, 10 (1977): 87–111.

Phelps, Reginald, "Dokumente aus der Kampfzeit der NSDAP—1923." *Deutsche Rundschau*, 84 (1958): 459–68, 1034–44.

————. "Hitler and the Deutsche Arbeiterpartei." *American Historical Review*, 68 (1962–63): 974–986.

Pikart, Eberhard. "Preussische Beamtenpolitik 1918–1933." *Vierteljahrshefte für Zeitgeschichte*, 6 (1958): 119–37.

Plum, Günther. *Gesellschaftsstruktur und politisches Bewusstsein in einer katholischen Region 1928–1933: Untersuchung am Beispiel des Regionsbezirks Aachen*. Stuttgart, 1972.

Pollock, James K. "An Areal Study of the German Electorate 1930–1933." *American Political Science Review*, 38 (1944): 89–95.

————. "The German Reichstag Election of 1930." *American Political Science Review*, 24 (1930): 989–95.

Portner, Ernst. "Der Ansatz zur demokratischen Massenpartei im deutschen Linksliberalismus." *Vierteljahrshefte für Zeitgeschichte*, 13 (1965): 150–61.

Pratt, Samuel A. "The Social Bases of Nazism and Communism in Urban Germany: A Correlation Study of the July 31, 1932, Reichstag Election in Germany." M.A. thesis, Michigan State University, 1948.

Preller, Ludwig. *Die Sozialpolitik in der Weimarer Republik*. Stuttgart, 1949.

Pridham, Geoffrey. *Hitler's Rise to Power: The Nazi Movement in Bavaria, 1923–1933*. London, 1973.

Puhle, Hans-Jürgen. *Agrarische Interessenpolitik und preussischer Konservatismus im Wilhelmischen Reich (1893–1914): Ein Beitrag zur Analyse des Nationalismus in Deutschland am Beispiel des Bundes der Landwirte und der Deutsch-Konservativen Partei*. Hannover, 1967.

————. "Parlament, Parteien und Interessenverbände 1890–1914." In Michael Stürmer, ed. *Das Kaiserliche Deutschland. Politik und Gesellschaft, 1870–1918*. Düsseldorf, 1970.

————. *Politische Agrarbewegungen in kapitalistischen Industriegesellschaften: Deutschland, USA und Frankreich im 20. Jahrhundert*. Göttingen, 1975.

————. *Von der Agrarkrise zum Präfaschismus.* Wiesbaden, 1972.

Pulzer, Peter. *The Rise of Political Anti-Semitism in Germany and Austria.* New York, 1964.

Ranulf, Svend. *Moral Indignation and Middle Class Psychology: A Sociological Study.* Copenhagen, 1938.

Ringer, Fritz K., ed. *The German Inflation of 1923.* London, 1969.

Ritter, Gerhard A. "Bernsteins Revisionismus und die Flügelbildung in der Sozialdemokratischen Partei." In Gerhard A. Ritter, *Deutsche Parteien vor 1918.* Cologne, 1973.

————. *Die Arbeiterbewegung im Wilhelminischen Reich: Die Sozialdemokratische Partei und die Freien Gewerkschaften 1890–1900.* Berlin, 1963.

Robinson, W. S. "Ecological Correlations and the Behavior of Individuals." *American Sociological Review,* 15 (1950): 351–57.

Roeske, Hans Rudolf. *Faschismus: Soziale Herkunft und Soziale Funktion. Untersuchungen am Beispiel des Nationalsozialismus.* Berlin, 1974.

Rogowski, Ronald. "The *Gauleiter* and the Social Origins of Fascism." *Comparative Studies in Society and History,* 19 (1977): 399–430.

Roloff, Ernst August. *Braunschweig und der Staat von Weimar: Wirtschaft und Gesellschaft, 1918–1933.* Braunschweig, 1964.

————. "Wer wählte Hitler? Thesen zur Sozial- und Wirtschaftsgeschichte der Weimarer Republik." *Politische Studien,* 15 (1964): 293–300.

Romeyk, Horst. "Die Deutsche Volkspartei in Rheinland und Westfalen, 1918–1933." *Rheinische Vierteljahrsblätter,* 39 (1975): 189–236.

Roth, Gunther. *The Social Democrats in Imperial Germany. A Study in Working-Class Isolation and National Integration.* Totowa, N. J. 1963.

Runge, Wolfgang. *Politik und Beamtentum im Parteienstaat: Die Demokratisierung der politischen Beamten in Preussen zwischen 1918 und 1933.* Stuttgart, 1965.

Schäfer, Wolfgang. *NSDAP: Entwicklung und Struktur der Staatspartei des Dritten Reichs.* Hannover, 1956.

Schauff, Johannes. "Das Wahlsystem des Deutschen Reichs und die Zentrumspartei." In Gerhard A. Ritter, *Deutsche Parteien vor 1918.* Cologne, 1973.

Schelm-Sprangenberg, Ursula. *Die Deutsche Volkspartei im Lande Braunschweig: Gründung, Entwicklung, soziologische Struktur, politische Arbeit.* Braunschweig, 1964.

Scheuch, Erwin K.; and Wildenmann, Rudolf. *Zur Soziologie der Wahl.* Cologne, 1968.

Schieder, Wolfgang, ed. *Faschismus als soziale Bewegung Deutschland und Italien im Vergleich.* Hamburg, 1976.

Schnaiberg, Allan. "A Critique of Karl O'Lessker's 'Who Voted for Hitler?'" *American Journal of Sociology,* 74 (1969): 732–35.

Schneider, Werner. *Die Deutsche Demokratische Partei in der Weimarer Republik, 1924–1930.* Munich, 1978.

Schoenbaum, David. *Hitler's Social Revolution: Class and Status in Nazi Germany 1933–1939.* New York, 1966.

Schoenhoven, Klaus. *Die Bayerische Volkspartei, 1924–1932*. Düsseldorf, 1972.

Scholder, Klaus. *Die Kirchen und das Dritte Reich: Vorgeschichte und Zeit der Illusionen, 1918–1934*. Frankfurt, 1977.

Schön, Eberhard. *Die Entstehung des Nationalsozialismus in Hessen*. Meisenheim am Glan, 1972.

Schorske, Carl E. *German Social Democracy, 1905–1917*. Princeton, 1955.

Schuker, Stephen A. *The End of French Predominance in Europe: The Financial Crisis of 1924 and the Adoption of the Dawes Plan*. Chapel Hill, 1976.

Schumacher, Martin. *Land und Politik: Eine Untersuchung über politische Parteien und agrarische Interessen, 1914–1923*. Düsseldorf, 1978.

———. *Mittelstandsfront und Republik: Die Wirtschaftspartei—Reichspartei des deutschen Mittelstandes, 1919–1933*. Düsseldorf, 1972.

———. "Stabilität und Instabilität: Wahlentwicklung und Parlament in Baden und Braunschweig, 1918–1933." In Gerhard A. Ritter, ed., *Gesellschaft, Parlament und Regierung: Zur Geschichte des Parlamentarismus in Deutschland*. Düsseldorf, 1974.

Schumann, Hans-Gerd. *Nationalsozialismus und Gewerkschaftsbewegung: Die Vernichtung der deutschen Gewerkschaften und der Aufbau der "Deutschen Arbeits-Front."* Hannover, 1958.

Schuren, Ulrich. *Der Volksentschied zur Fürstenenteignung. 1926*. Düsseldorf, 1978.

Schustereit, Hartmut. *Linksliberalismus und Sozialdemokratie in der Weimarer Republik: Eine vergleichende Betrachtung der Politik von DDP und SPD, 1919–1930*. Düsseldorf, 1975.

Schweitzer, Arthur. *Die Nazifizierung des Mittelstandes*. Stuttgart, 1970.

Schwend, Karl. *Bayern zwischen Monarchie und Diktatur*. Munich, 1954.

Sheehan, James J. *German Liberalism in the Nineteenth Century*. Chicago, 1978.

Shively, W. Phillips. "'Ecological' Inference: The Use of Aggregate Data to Study Individuals." *American Political Science Review*, 63 (1969): 1183–96.

———. "Party Identification, Party Choice, and Voting Stability: The Weimar Case." *American Political Science Review*, 66 (1972): 1203–25.

Speier, Hans. *Die Angestellten vor dem Nationalsozialismus: Ein Beitrag zum Verständnis der deutschen Sozialstruktur, 1918–1933*. Göttingen, 1977.

Stachura, Peter D. "Der kritische Wendepunkt? Die NSDAP und die Reichstagswahlen vom 20. Mai 1928." *Vierteljahrshefte für Zeitgeschichte*, 26 (1978): 66–99.

———. *Nazi Youth in the Weimar Republic*. Santa Barbara, 1975.

Stegmann, Dirk. *Die Erben Bismarcks: Parteien und Verbände in der Spätphase des Wilhelminischen Deutschlands. Sammlungspolitik, 1897–1918*. Cologne, 1970.

———. "Kapitalismus und Faschismus, 1929–1934: Thesen und Materialen." In H. G. Backhaus, ed., *Gesellschaft: Beiträge zur Marxschen Theorie*. Vol. 6. Frankfurt, 1976.

―――. "Zwischen Repression und Manipulation: Konservative Machteliten und Arbeiter- und Angestelltenbewegung 1910–1918; Ein Beitrag zur Vorgeschichte der DAP/NSDAP." *Archiv für Sozialgeschichte*, 12 (1972): 351–432.

Steinberg, Michael Stephen. *Sabers and Brown Shirts: The German Students' Path to National Socialism, 1918–1935.* Chicago, 1977.

Stephan, Werner. *Aufstieg und Verfall des Linksliberalismus 1918–1933: Geschichte der Deutschen Demokratischen Partei.* Göttingen, 1973.

Stephenson, Jill. *The Nazi Organization of Women.* London, 1981.

―――. *Women in Nazi Society.* London, 1975.

Stokes, Lawrence D. "The Social Composition of the Nazi Party in Eutin, 1925–1932." *International Review of Social History*, 23 (1978): 1–32.

Stoltenberg, Gerhard. *Politische Strömungen im schleswig-holsteinischen Landvolk, 1918–1933.* Düsseldorf, 1962.

Stoffregen, Albert. "Die Geschichte der politischen Parteien und Wahlen im Gebiet des Kreises Gandersheim und der Stadt Salzgitter von 1867 bis 1963." Ph.D. dissertation, Marburg, 1966.

Stump, Wolfgang. *Geschichte und Organisation der Zentrumspartei in Düsseldorf 1917–1933.* Düsseldorf, 1971.

Stürmer, Michael, ed. *Das Kaiserliche Deutschland: Politik und Gesellschaft, 1890–1918.* Düsseldorf, 1970.

―――. *Koalition und Opposition in der Weimarer Republik, 1924–1928.* Düsseldorf, 1967.

Thimme, Roland. *Stresemann und die deutsche Volkspartei, 1923–1925.* Lübeck, 1961.

Thränhardt, Dietrich. *Wahlen und politische Strukturen in Bayern 1848–1953: Historisch-soziologische Untersuchungen zum Entstehen und zur Neuerrichtung eines Parteiensystems.* Düsseldorf, 1973.

Timm, Helga. *Die Deutsche Sozialpolitik und der Bruch der grossen Koalition im März 1930.* Düsseldorf, 1952.

Tingsten, Herbert. *Political Behavior: Studies in Election Statistics.* Totowa, N. J., 1963.

Todd, Edmund Neville. "National Socialist Agrarian Policies: 1919–1928." M.A. thesis, University of Florida, 1974.

Tormin, Walter. *Geschichte der deutschen Parteien seit 1848.* Stuttgart, 1968.

Tracey, Donald R. "The Development of the National Socialist Party in Thuringia, 1924–1930." *Central European History*, 8 (1975): 23–50.

Tractenberg, Marc. *Reparation in World Politics: France and European Diplomacy, 1916–1923.* New York, 1980.

Treue, Wolfgang. *Deutsche Parteiprogramme seit 1861.* 4th ed. Göttingen, 1968.

Tufte, Edward R. *Data Analysis for Politics and Policy.* Englewood Cliffs, N.J., 1974.

Turner, Henry A., Jr. "Big Business and the Rise of Hitler." *American Historical Review*, 75 (1969): 56–70.

————. "Fascism and Modernization." In Turner, ed., *Reappraisals of Fascism*.

————. *Stresemann and the Politics of the Weimar Republic*. Princeton, 1963.

————, ed. *Nazism and the Third Reich*. New York, 1972.

————, ed. *Reappraisals of Fascism*. New York, 1975.

Uhlig, Heinrich, *Die Warenhäuser im Dritten Reich*. Cologne, 1956.

Vierhaus, Rudolf. "Die politische Mitte in der Weimarer Republik." *Geschichte und Unterricht*, 15 (1964): 133–49.

Vogel, Bernhard; Nohle, Dieter; Schultze, Rainer-Olaf. *Wahlen in Deutschland. Theorie—Geschichte—Dokumente, 1848–1970*. Berlin, 1971.

Vogt, Martin. "Die Stellung der Koalitionsparteien zur Finanzpolitik 1928–1930." In Mommsen et al., *Industrielles System und politisches Entwicklung in der Weimarer Republik*, pp. 919–31.

Volkov, Shulamit. *The Rise of Popular Antimodernism in Germany: The Urban Master Artisans, 1873–1896*. Princeton, 1978.

Waldman, Loren K. "Models of Mass Movements—The Case of the Nazis." Ph.D. dissertation, University of Chicago, 1973.

Weber, Alexander. "Soziale Merkmale der NSDAP-Wähler: Eine Zusammenfassung bisheriger empirischen Untersuchungen und eine Analyse in den Gemeinden der Länder Baden und Hessen." Ph.D. dissertation, Freiburg, 1969.

Weber, Hermann. *Die Wandlung des deutschen Kommunismus: Die Stalinisierung der KPD in der Weimarer Republik*. 2 vols. Bonn, 1969.

Wehler, Hans-Ulrich. *Das Deutsche Kaiserreich, 1871–1918*. Göttingen, 1973.

————, ed. *Moderne Sozialgeschichte*. Cologne, 1966.

Wernet, Wilhelm. *Zur Frage der Abgrenzung von Handwerk und Industrie: Die wirtschaftlichen Zusammenhänge in ihrer Bedeutung für die Beurteilung von Abgrenzungsfragen*. Münster, 1965.

Wernette, Dee Richard. "Political Violence and German Elections: 1930 and July 1932." Ph.D. dissertation, University of Michigan, 1974.

White, Dan S. *The Splintered Party: National Liberals in Hessen and the Reich, 1867–1918*. Cambridge, Mass., 1976.

Winkler, Heinrich August. "Extremismus der Mitte? Sozialgeschichtliche Aspekte der nationalsozialistischen Machtergreifung." *Vierteljahrshefte für Zeitgeschichte*, 20 (1972): 175–91.

————. "From Social Protectionism to National Socialism: The German Small-Business Movement in Comparative Perspective." *Journal of Modern History*, 48 (1976): 1–18.

————. *Mittelstand, Demokratie und Nationalsozialismus: Die politische Entwicklung von Handwerk und Kleinhandel in der Weimarer Republik*. Cologne, 1972.

————. "Mittelstandsbewegung oder Volkspartei? Zur sozialen Basis der NSDAP." In Wolfgang Schieder, ed., *Faschismus als soziale Bewegung*, pp. 25–67.

————. "Unternehmerverbände zwischen Ständeideologie und Nationalsozialismus." *Vierteljahrshefte für Zeitgeschichte*, 17 (1969): 341–71.

Witt, Peter-Christian. "Finanzpolitik und sozialer Wandel in Krieg und Inflation, 1918–1924." In Mommsen, et al., *Industrielles System und politische Entwicklung in der Weimarer Republik*, pp. 395–426.

Wölk, Wolfgang. "Sozialstruktur, Parteienkorrelation und Wahlentscheidung im Kaiserreich am Beispiel der Reichstagswahl von 1907." In Otto Büsch, Monika Völk, and Wolfgang Wölk, eds., *Wählerbewegungen in der deutschen Geschichte: Analysen und Berichte zu den Reichstagswahlen, 1871–1933*. Berlin, 1978.

Wulf, Peter. *Die politische Haltung des schleswig-holsteinischen Handwerks 1928 bis 1932*. Cologne, 1969.

Wunderlich, Frieda. *Farm Labor in Germany 1810–1945: Its Historical Development within the Framework of Agricultural and Social Policy*. Princeton, 1961.

Zangerl, C. H. E. "Courting the Catholic Vote: The Center Party in Baden, 1903–1913." *Central European History*, 10 (1977): 220–40.

Zeman, Z. A. B. *Nazi Propaganda*. Oxford, 1965.

Zimmermann, Werner G. *Bayern und das Reich*. Munich, 1953.

Zorn, Wolfgang. "Student Politics in the Weimar Republic." *Journal of Contemporary History*, 5 (1970): 128–43.

Index